Canadian Families at the Approach of the Year 2000

Carmelina

Canadian Families at the Approach of the Year 2000

Yves Péron

Hélène Desrosiers

Heather Juby

Évelyne Lapierre-Adamcyk

Céline Le Bourdais

Nicole Marcil-Gratton

Jaël Mongeau

Centre interuniversitaire d'études démographiques
Université de Montréal — Institut national de la recherche scientifique

Canadian Cataloguing in Publication Data

Main entry under title:

Canadian families at the approach of the year 2000

Issued also in French under title: Les familles canadiennes
à l'approche de l'an 2000.
ISBN 0-660-17713-7
CS96-321-MPE no. 4

1. Family – Canada – Statistics. 2. Single-parent family –
Canada – Statistics. 3. Households – Canada – Statistics.
4. Dwellings – Canada – Statistics. 5. Canada – Census, 1991.
I. Péron, Yves, 1938- . II. Statistics Canada.

HQ560 C32 1999   306.85'0971'021
C99-988021-7

DEDICATION

Edward Thomas Pryor, 1931–1992

This series of census analytical volumes is dedicated to the memory of Dr. Edward T. Pryor, a respected and internationally acclaimed sociologist, demographer and author. Dr. Pryor served as Director General of the Census and Demographic Statistics Branch of Statistics Canada and was affectionately known as "Mr. Census." His scholarship, vision, leadership and unfailing dedication to his profession served as inspiration and guidance in the conception and development of this series.

CONTENTS

LIST OF FIGURES

LIST OF TABLES

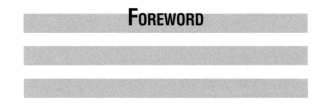

FOREWORD

Canadian Families at the Approach of the Year 2000 is the fourth in a series of monographs produced by Statistics Canada as part of the 1991 Census Analysis Program. The 1991 Census monographs continue a tradition in census analysis that began with the 1931 Census and was repeated in 1961 and 1971. Although several studies were conducted following the 1981 Census, there has not been a formal monograph program associated with the census since 1971. Many of the 1971 series are still used today in university programs and by the general public.

It has always been the purpose of census monographs to provide analysis of topics related to Canadian social and economic life. To this end, the current series deals with some major issues of Canadian life in the 1990s that will continue to have ramifications into the 21st century. These issues concern education, aging of the population, the changing Canadian labour market, families, income distribution, women, and Aboriginal peoples. Using sophisticated analytic techniques, the monographs deal with the selected themes in a comprehensive way and complement the *Focus on Canada* series, which presents more general analyses.

I would like to express my appreciation to all the authors who contributed to this excellent series. I would also like to thank the staff of the Census Analysis Program of Statistics Canada, who so efficiently oversaw the program, as well as the Census Monographs Advisory Committee for their valuable expertise.

I hope the series will help Canadians understand the challenges our country faces as we approach the 21st century, and will contribute to informed discussion of how to deal with them.

DR. IVAN FELLEGI
Chief Statistician, Statistics Canada

FOREWORD

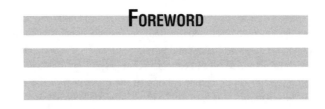

Since the 1960s, Canadian society has undergone significant socio-demographic and economic changes. We have witnessed an increase in the age of first marriage and a noticeable decline in the number of children born to couples. An increased diversity of family types has been fuelled by the growth in common-law unions and lone-parent families. And at the same time, women have increased their participation in the labour market at a substantial rate. *Canadian Families at the Approach of the Year 2000* is a comprehensive analysis of the current state of the family in light of the socio-demographic changes in Canadian society since the 1960s.

Canadian Families at the Approach of the Year 2000 analyses the family from a variety of perspectives. This volume presents a multifaceted analysis that examines over 30 years in the evolution of the structure and composition of families and households from the perspectives of women, men and children. The analysis highlights various socio-economic conditions that affect Canadian families, and it examines the full spectrum of family living arrangements.

As part of the Census Monograph Series, *Canadian Families at the Approach of the Year 2000* joins its companion volumes in providing substantive, in-depth analyses of selected themes, and in demonstrating the power and value of census data on their own and when analytically coupled with other data sources. Topics in the series include aging, income distribution, the family, education, the labour force, and Aboriginal peoples. The monographs are designed to be integrated into a variety of academic programs and to serve as background for formulating and developing public policy.

Planning and overseeing the 1991 Census monograph program was the responsibility of the Census Analysis Division of Statistics Canada. The program manager and those responsible within the division were assisted by the Advisory Committee, whose members reflect the broad interests and professional backgrounds of Canada's socio-economic research community. The committee provided advice on all aspects of the monograph program, including topic suggestions, methodology for competitions, assessment of proposals, and the process for peer review. The Acknowledgements page of this volume lists the Advisory Committee members and Statistics Canada personnel who gave generously of their time and effort to the monograph series.

The invitation to submit research proposals was extended by the Chief Statistician to all members of the Canadian research community, both new scholars and those with proven track records. Proposals were assessed on the basis of their relevance to socio-economic issues facing Canada, the scope of the analytical approach, the suitability of the analytical techniques and methodologies, and the importance of census data to the study. The authors selected represent the full spectrum of Canada's social science research community. They come from universities across Canada, as well as from within Statistics Canada.

By encouraging investigations of the trends and changes in Canadian society, the 1991 Census monograph program continues a valuable tradition in census analysis. As we approach the millennium, many social issues will persist and possibly intensify. Canada, and all Canadians, will benefit from insight provided by the Census Monograph Series. Persons interested in demographic, economic and social issues related to the evolution of the family will find *Canadian Families at the Approach of the Year 2000* an informative analysis.

DR. MONICA BOYD

Chair, Census Monographs Advisory Committee

Authors' Note

What has become of the Canadian family 20 years after the collapse of the birth rate and the beginning of the crisis in marriage? This monograph brings together analyses that attempt to answer this question using data from the 1991 Census and cycle 5 of the 1990 General Social Survey on family and friends. In addition to describing the changes that have occurred in the number, structure and composition of families over time, this study also examines the way in which the conjugal and parental patterns of men and women have diversified, and how changes in adult behaviour have affected the family situation of children. It also provides an in-depth look at the living conditions of families in 1991.

This monograph was prepared by a team of authors from the demography department of the Université de Montréal and from the *Institut national de la recherche scientifique (INRS)— Urbanisation*. Most of the authors are also associated with the new *Centre interuniversitaire d'études démographiques*, which now includes all demographers from both institutions.

The authors would like to thank the members of the Census Analysis Advisory Committee and senior officers of the Census Analysis Division of Statistics Canada. Without their approval of the project and their moral and financial support, this monograph would not have been possible. We especially appreciate our exchanges with Gustave Goldmann and Tom Caplan, directors of the 1991 Census Analysis Program at Statistics Canada.

We are also indebted to everybody who helped in the preparation and implementation of this study. We benefited greatly from the technical support of Julie Archambault, Christiane Desmarais, Paul-Marie Huot, Denis Morissette, Suzanne Péron, Annie Sauriol and Nathalie Vachon. We are also very grateful to Thérèse Labelle-Audy, Francine Provencher and Nicole Wragg for putting the draft document into its final form.

Our thanks go as well to all those who helped turn our draft into a book: first to Francine Dansereau, Yolande Lavoie and the anonymous evaluators chosen by Statistics Canada whose comments and suggestions improved our analysis in several areas; second to editors Julie Bélanger, Janis Camelon, Valérie Catrice, Sherry Galey, Nathalie Turcotte and book designer Danielle Baum of Statistics Canada; and finally to everybody else at Statistics Canada who devoted their time and talent to publishing this book.

THE AUTHORS

With a background in community health, the social sciences, and, more recently, the administration and evaluation of public programs, **Hélène Desrosiers** joined the Quebec Longitudinal Child Development Study at Santé Québec in 1997. Her research and writing focuses on the impact of socio-demographic changes on marital and family trajectories in Canada, as well as on the relations between family organization, living conditions and health.

Heather Juby completed her doctoral studies in demography in the area of household analysis. She further developed her expertise in this area while pursuing post-doctoral studies at the *Institut national de la recherche scientifique (INRS)—Urbanisation* at the Université de Montréal and at Cambridge University, before turning to the analysis of family trajectories of women, men and, finally, children.

Évelyne Lapierre-Adamcyk, a professor in the Department of Demography at the Université de Montréal, has taken part in several studies on fertility and family trends in Quebec and in Canada as a whole. She has participated in such studies as the analysis of the 1971 Quebec Fertility Study and the first Canadian fertility study in 1984. Her work has contributed to the development and improvement of socio-demographic survey data.

Demographer and sociologist **Céline le Bourdais** is professor and researcher at the *Institut national de la recherche scientifique (INRS)—Urbanisation* of the Université du Québec. She has been interested in the study of family change for several years: initially, her work centred on lone-parent families and family restructuring as experienced by women; more recently, she has studied the family trajectories of men and women and has documented the impact of conjugal instability on people's lives.

Nicole Marcil-Gratton, who has been a researcher in the Department of Demography of the Université de Montréal for more than 20 years, first specialized in the study of contraception behaviour, particularly sterilization as a form of contraception. Since the late 1980s, she has been studying the effects of changes in conjugal life on the family environment of children.

Jaël Mongeau has been with *Institut national de la recherche scientifique (INRS)—Urbanisation* since 1970, and currently works as a research officer. After conducting several population surveys, she became interested in residential mobility. More recently, she undertook to describe the socio-economic characteristics and housing conditions of families and households in specific segments of the population such as immigrants and youth under age 30.

Yves Péron was a professor in the Department of Demography at the Université of Montréal between 1968 and 1997. His work has focused on the causes of mortality, public health indicators, and contemporary trends in marriage and the family in Quebec and in Canada as a whole. In this regard, he has developed tables on family and parental life, housing conditions, and access to property by families at various stages in the life cycle.

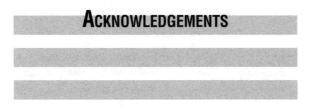

ACKNOWLEDGEMENTS

Statistics Canada wishes to acknowledge the following for their excellent efforts on behalf of the Census Monograph Series:

FOR THE ADVISORY COMMITTEE ON CENSUS MONOGRAPHS

Monica Boyd (Chair)
Florida State University
Visiting Research Fellow,
Statistics Canada

Paddy Fuller
Canada Mortgage and Housing Corporation

Réjean Lachapelle
Statistics Canada

Jacques Légaré
Université de Montréal

Ramona MacDowell
Human Resources Development Canada

Ian Macredie
Statistics Canada

Susan McDaniel
University of Alberta

Allan Maslove
Carleton University

John Myles
Florida State University
Visiting Research Fellow,
Statistics Canada

Elizabeth Ruddick
Citizenship and Immigration Canada

Tom Symons
Trent University

Derrick Thomas
Citizenship and Immigration Canada

James Wetzel
United States Bureau of the Census

Telmet Design Associates
Cover Design

FOR STATISTICS CANADA

Census Analysis Division
Gustave Goldmann (Manager)
Tom Caplan
Nicole Kelly
Patty Paul
Lyse St-Jacques
Andy Siggner
Claudette Trudeau

Official Languages and
Translation Division
Sylvette Cadieux

Library and Information Centre
Brian Drysdale
Glen Gagnon
Mary McCoy
Michele Sura

Communications Division—
Editorial Services
Nathalie Turcotte (Head, French Unit)
Julie Bélanger
Valérie Catrice
Janis Camelon (Head, English Unit)
Sherry Galey

Dissemination Division—Production
Integration
Danielle Baum (Manager)
Production and Interior Design

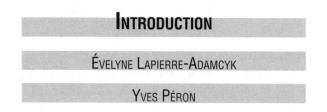

INTRODUCTION

Évelyne Lapierre-Adamcyk

Yves Péron

Like other contemporary western societies, Canadian society relies primarily on the family to ensure its growth and renewal. From a demographic standpoint, the family is central to this reproductive process: it is within the family structure that fertility, the most decisive factor of population dynamics, plays a vital role. The family also influences the migratory component of demographic growth in Canada; in fact, immigration policy accords a special place to family-related criteria when granting immigrant status, whether by welcoming the dependants of independent immigrants, or by furthering family reunification.

The family is the living environment of most individuals, from birth to death. Although in Canadian society the family no longer represents the locus of so-called economic activity, certainly the various phases of life unfold within it, and much of the economic activity of men and women focuses on generating the resources needed to "support their family." As well, although it has diminished in recent decades, the time spent with family is an important part of people's lives, and relatively little time is spent outside the family.

Thus, people are born and raised within a family, which they leave in early adulthood. Next they embark on a period of life outside the family, the duration of which varies depending on the characteristics of the individual. Then comes the time when they form a couple, a relationship that still often constitutes the starting point of a new family, which will take shape as children (generally few) are born into it. When these children have grown, they will leave the parental home. Their parents, now a middle-aged couple, will witness, over a period of increasing duration, the re-creation of their family life cycle by maintaining fairly close ties with their children and grandchildren. Finally comes old age, and then the end of this family cycle and ultimately of life itself. This profile of the family life cycle is straightforward only in appearance; it does not reflect the highly complex life courses that today's men and women, who are less subject to the biological and social constraints of earlier times, follow in pursuit of self-fulfillment.

Since the early 1960s, the end of what might be termed the "golden age of the family," couples have desired fewer children. This appreciably reduced desire to have children is the result of social and economic changes that have also played a part in the de-institutionalization of society: the universality of education; a greater desire for personal autonomy; the emergence of the consumer society and its ability to generate new needs and offer a range of possibilities for meeting most people's aspirations; the growth of the women's liberation movement; women's increased participation in the labour market; and secularization and the waning of religious values. This new social context not only decreases the desire to have children, but technology now also makes highly effective methods of birth control available to couples, enabling them to have only as many children as they want, when they want. And, should birth control fail, the moral and legal barriers that once limited access to abortion are gradually disappearing. Conversely, when the desire to have children cannot be fulfilled naturally, couples can turn to new reproductive techniques, such as artificial insemination, *in vitro* fertilization, or surrogate motherhood, although these methods raise important ethical questions that have not yet been answered.

The transition of fertility from a demographic and social phenomenon, with biological underpinnings, to one now based on the personal freedom of men and women, is the first phase of a fundamental challenge to the institution of marriage, upon which the family is based. The management of fertility has been instrumental in breaking the link that once existed between sexuality, conjugal life, marriage and reproduction. Sexual relations outside of marriage have gradually lost their stigma and no longer seem reprehensible. It is no longer necessary to marry in order to live as husband and wife, and there is virtually no social disapproval of couples who live together. Not only are common-law couples accepted in their community, but they are also deciding, with increasing frequency, to bring children into the world without legalizing their union. Of course, this transformation of the foundation of family life is not occurring everywhere at the same rate, and there are still some significant differences between regions, and between various social groups.

At the same time, unions, whether legalized or not, are becoming increasingly unstable: divorce and separation are more and more common and occur increasingly early on in the union. The dissolution of unions leads to the proliferation of young, lone-parent families that all too often must face considerable economic hardship. In most cases, lone parenthood does not last long: blended families often form, usually around a mother and her children, with a new husband who occasionally brings children of his own into the new family. The traditional nuclear family then gives way to a new family where the unity between spouses, between parents and children, and between siblings, must be reinvented. Clearly the events of the "typical" family life cycle are no longer predictable: it has become so altered and personalized that the term no longer applies. We no longer speak of family life cycles, but of the family life courses of individuals, a term that better underscores the wide range of possible sequences of events and changes in the very nature of family reality, which nevertheless remains an integral part of the lives of men and women.

Women in the workforce also have had a significant impact on family life as, over the last three decades, the working life of women has ceased to be a short-term activity undertaken before marriage and motherhood. Increasingly better educated, better equipped for the labour market, more determined to persevere, and encouraged by the development of occupational fields consistent with their aspirations and skills, women have flooded into the new labour market. Today more and more women are assuming positions and entering fields that not that long ago were the sole preserves of men. They are far from achieving equal opportunity and equality of incomes, but their numbers are such that, without their presence and skills the current economy would be inconceivable.

However, the family and society have not yet fully adapted to this reality: first, household duties and tasks related to the children's education are still unevenly shared, with women carrying a double load. Secondly, there is a definite shortage of child-care services for working parents. Finally, the labour market has not developed the flexibility and adaptability to accommodate the parental obligations of all those who work and have small children.

This very broad description of the evolution of the Canadian family would not have been possible were it not for the many studies done over the years and the availability of the data from such studies. Every one of these in-depth and specialized analyses has helped to elucidate the changes just outlined. These studies have explored fertility and birth control, the declining popularity of marriage and the increase in marital instability, lone parenthood and the blending of families, and other aspects of family life. These studies have been based on selected and longitudinal data; they have used various methodologies, both quantitative and qualitative. Despite this richness and variety, however, no study has profiled the evolution of the Canadian family in its entirety; no study has yet attempted to unveil the subtle features of its new face.

A major data collection such as the 1991 Census and, barely a year earlier, the 1990 General Social Survey, cycle 5: Family and Friends, affords an excellent opportunity to report on the current state of the Canadian family. The present monograph, *Canadian Families at the Approach of the Year 2000,* takes full advantage of this opportunity; its objective is to establish the statistical profile of the family by placing it in the context of the evolution of the Canadian population.

Specifically, this monograph first attempts to describe the structure and composition of households and families in 1991 by comparing them with their counterparts of the early 1960s— that is, before the emergence of new behaviours related to marriage, divorce, and childbearing. Secondly, the monograph approaches the study of changes in the family from the perspective of adults by examining how these changes are reflected in their lives and alter their life courses. Thirdly, the monograph takes a fresh look at family realities by examining them from the perspective of the children who are affected by their parents' decisions—decisions that are constructing a new environment in which today's children are socialized. Finally, the monograph attempts to integrate into the demographic aspects of family life several aspects of the living conditions of families, such as the parents' occupational activity, the financial resources of families, and the housing conditions in which they live.

To achieve these objectives, the complementary data of two main sources—the censuses of Canada (primarily the 1991 Census) and the 1990 General Social Survey (GSS)—were used to piece together the basic evolution of the Canadian family, namely from an institution largely defined by social constraints, to a way of life regulated by sequences of events that are less predictable and more influenced by the pursuit of self-fulfillment. As census definitions are consistently based on traditional criteria, the family statistics taken from successive censuses show the evolution of the number and composition of families. However, census data, being selected, do not reflect all of the events families may go through over time. This inherent limitation of cross-sectional observation is accentuated by the perennial nature of the definitions. The census data provide us with a profile of a very stable Canadian family but, in fact, this stability is illusory.

In contrast, the 1990 GSS includes retrospective data from which it is possible to reconstruct the family path of each family member, and thus show the extent of the changes that have taken place. These data reveal that the apparent stability of family units becomes a varied and shifting landscape when the life courses of the individuals who constitute the family universe are plotted. The collective, selected, cross-sectional data marked by the perennial nature of census definitions are combined with personal, retrospective, hard data that lend themselves to changing definitions. This blending of the two types of data produces results that give us a better understanding of the new conditions of family life.

This monograph consists of seven chapters grouped into three distinct parts. In the first part, households and families are the units of observation and analysis. In the second part, individuals—women, men, and children—are the focus. Finally, in the third part, we turn again to the family to examine living conditions, occasionally focusing on the children.

The first chapter, "Households and Families," briefly establishes the links between the evolution of the population and of households since the 1951 Census. Also, using the concepts of "economic family" and "census family," this chapter discusses the family bonds between household members, and ends with a brief presentation of data on the residential autonomy of families and non-family persons.

The second chapter, "The Evolution of Census Families from 1971 to 1991," begins with a review of the evolution of nuptiality, divorce, and fertility indicators over the last 20 years. It then identifies trends in the incidence of conjugal life, lone parenthood and "non-family" status since 1971. The chapter ends with a general presentation of the evolution of family types; that is, the distribution between married couple families, common-law couple families and lone-parent families. Finally, the factors affecting the increase in the number and diversity of husband–wife and lone-parent families are analysed.

Chapter 3, "Female Family Paths," marks the beginning of part two, where the focus shifts from the family unit to the life course of the individual marked by family events. Here, the realm of censuses is abandoned for that of surveys. The object is to determine the family life courses of women. Three different approaches are used. First, based on the family situations observed at the time of the 1990 GSS and defined according to the concepts used in the census, the marital and family history of women in these situations is described retrospectively. Second, the dynamics, in women's lives, of the formation and dissolution of various forms of family organization are analysed (the intact two-parent, the lone-parent, and the blended family). Finally, an attempt is made to describe the evolution of women's family life courses and estimate the proportion of women who take the various paths followed.

Chapter 4, "Male Family Paths," mirrors Chapter 3, this time reflecting the paths of men whose lives are interspersed with the same family events that mark women's, but at a different rate and intensity. Initially, one might expect a dull repetition of the analysis already conducted of women, but the careful analysis reveals the contrary: it sheds light on original male life courses that differ notably from those of women, particularly in terms of the impact of union dissolution on the subsequent evolution of the individual's life or on the rate at which a new union is formed. This chapter provides interesting results, and further justifies itself in light of the lack of studies on the family lives of men.

The fifth chapter, "Family Status from the Children's Perspective," which completes part two, again adopts and reviews the individual's perspective, this time emphasizing the perspectives of children. The chapter begins with the historic evolution of children's family environment from 1951 to 1991. It delves into certain aspects of this environment in 1991 by showing that the retrospective data of the 1990 GSS illustrate the extent of the changes in family environment when children make the transition from childhood to adolescence. The percentage of children who live in blended families is estimated, and the diversification of the family life courses of children, and the regional variations of this diversification, are also shown.

Chapter 6, "The Living Conditions of Families: Income and Labour Force Activity," begins the third and final part of the monograph by looking once again at families and attempting to better understand their living conditions. The chapter's first section is concerned with family income, showing the make-up of various income quintiles by family type, as well as variations over time and by region. The chapter's second section shows the link between the increased wealth of husband–wife families and the growing proportion of two-income families. This chapter concludes by describing the relationships between income and family environment from the children's perspective.

The final chapter, Chapter 7, "Variations in the Housing Conditions of Canadian Families," examines the links between various family types and the housing conditions that are within the means of each family type. It shows that ownership, which is very strongly linked to financial resources, is one of the main factors distinguishing the various types of families in terms of housing conditions. Variations linked to the life-cycle stage, the influence of income, and the choice of the type of housing, in addition to variations in overcrowding and the financial outlay for housing, are all analysed.

Although connected by the links that exist between the various aspects of family life, the chapters of this monograph can be read and understood independently. The monograph is designed so that the reader can more readily absorb the vast amount of statistical data and more closely examine each aspect of the fundamental changes observed in Canadian families. While this approach inevitably leads to some repetition, we believe that, given the complexity of the data, the methods used and the realities themselves, this repetition may be warranted.

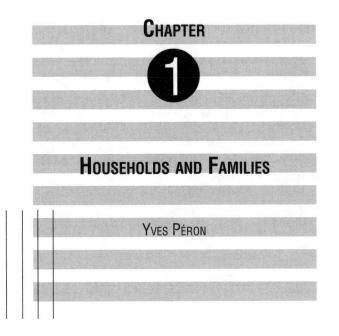

CHAPTER 1

HOUSEHOLDS AND FAMILIES

YVES PÉRON

The terms "household" and "family" have often been used interchangeably; in past Canadian censuses, "family" was the term used for what "household" refers to today. The 1921 Census was the first to distinguish between "household" and "family," the former designating a group of persons living together in the same dwelling, and the latter a group of related persons belonging to the same household. Later, the concepts of "household" and "family" were given more specific meanings, and it became necessary to use two definitions of "family" simultaneously, namely, "economic family" and "census family." But whatever definition is used, "family" is still included in, or confused with, "household." It therefore seemed necessary to devote a chapter to the evolution of households before describing that of families.

The first part of the chapter briefly describes the evolution of the population and of households since the 1951 Census. This census is a good starting point for such a description, as it was the first to cover all of present-day Canada, and the first to define the terms "dwelling" and "household" as they are used today. The description of the evolution of the population focuses on the slowdown in demographic growth from 1951 to 1986 and on the changes in the age pyramid, while that of the evolution of households considers mainly the number and size of private households.

The second part of this chapter is devoted to the family relationships between household members. First, the concept of "economic family" is used to explore the current composition of households. Secondly, the concept of "census family" is used to examine the evolution of household composition. The description of this evolution ends with a brief presentation of data on the residential autonomy of families and of non-family persons.

1.1 POPULATION AND HOUSEHOLDS SINCE 1951

1.1.1 Population: definition and evolution

From 1951 to 1991, a Canadian population census was conducted every five years, or nine times (see Table 1.1). Originally, the term "population" in these censuses always referred to the resident population; the definition of "population" was broadened somewhat in 1991. Until 1991, the population count included, in theory, only those persons who were entitled to reside in Canada permanently and had their usual place of residence within the country's borders. This included diplomats, government officials and military personnel posted abroad, and their family members, as well as seamen housed on board Canadian merchant vessels. In 1991, landed immigrants ("non-permanent residents") were included in the population count along with Canadian citizens (that is, "permanent residents"). "Non-permanent residents" were mainly individuals authorized

TABLE 1.1
POPULATION OF CANADA, BY PROVINCE, 1951 TO 1991

	1951	1956	1961	1966	1971	1976	1981	1986	1991
					Number				
Canada	**14,009,429**	**16,080,791**	**18,238,248**	**20,014,880**	**21,568,310**	**22,992,600**	**24,343,180**	**25,309,330**	**27,296,856**
Newfoundland	361,416	415,074	457,853	493,396	522,105	557,725	567,680	568,350	568,475
Prince Edward Island	98,429	99,285	104,629	108,535	111,640	118,230	122,510	126,645	129,765
Nova Scotia	642,584	694,717	737,007	756,039	788,960	828,570	847,445	873,180	899,945
New Brunswick	515,697	554,616	597,936	616,788	634,560	677,250	696,405	709,445	723,900
Quebec	4,055,681	4,628,378	5,259,211	5,780,845	6,027,765	6,234,445	6,438,400	6,532,460	6,895,960
Ontario	4,597,542	5,404,933	6,236,092	6,960,870	7,703,105	8,264,465	8,625,110	9,101,695	10,084,885
Manitoba	776 541	850,040	921,686	963,066	988,250	1,021,505	1,026,245	1,063,015	1,091,940
Saskatchewan	831,728	880,665	925,181	955,344	926,245	921,325	968,310	1,009,615	988,930
Alberta	939,501	1,123,116	1,331,944	1,463,203	1,627,875	1,838,040	2,237,725	2,365,825	2,545,550
British Columbia	1,165,210	1,398,464	1,629,082	1,873,674	2,184,620	2,466,605	2,744,470	2,883,370	3,282,065
Yukon	9,096	12,190	14,628	14,382	18,390	21,835	23,150	23,505	27,795
Northwest Territories	16,004	19,313	22,998	28,738	34,805	42,610	45,740	52,240	57,650
					%				
Canada[1]	**100.0**	**100.0**	**100.0**	**100.0**	**100.0**	**100.0**	**100.0**	**100.0**	**100.0**
Newfoundland	2.6	2.6	2.5	2.5	2.4	2.4	2.3	2.2	2.1
Prince Edward Island	0.7	0.6	0.6	0.5	0.5	0.5	0.5	0.5	0.5
Nova Scotia	4.6	4.3	4.0	3.8	3.7	3.6	3.5	3.5	3.3
New Brunswick	3.7	3.4	3.3	3.1	2.9	2.9	2.9	2.8	2.7
Quebec	28.9	28.8	28.8	28.9	27.9	27.1	26.4	25.8	25.3
Ontario	32.8	33.6	34.2	34.8	35.7	35.9	35.4	36.0	36.9
Manitoba	5.5	5.3	5.1	4.8	4.6	4.4	4.2	4.2	4.0
Saskatchewan	5.9	5.5	5.1	4.8	4.3	4.0	4.0	4.0	3.6
Alberta	6.7	7.0	7.3	7.3	7.5	8.0	9.2	9.3	9.3
British Columbia	8.3	8.7	8.9	9.4	10.1	10.7	11.3	11.4	12.0
Yukon	0.1	0.1	0.1	0.1	0.1	0.1	0.1	0.1	0.1
Northwest Territories	0.1	0.1	0.1	0.1	0.2	0.2	0.2	0.2	0.2

1. Figures may not add to 100 due to rounding.

Note: The comparison of 1991 Census data with the data of earlier censuses is affected by the change made to the definition of "population" in the 1991 Census. Holders of a Student Authorization, an Employment Authorization, or a Ministerial Permit, and refugee status claimants were counted in the 1991 Census, but not in previous censuses. These persons are non-permanent residents.

Source: Census of Canada, 1951 to 1991.

to reside temporarily in Canada to study, hold temporary employment or await a decision on their refugee claim. Note that foreign nationals on a diplomatic or military posting in Canada, and their family members, were still excluded from the population count. The exact number of "non-permanent residents" included in the 1991 population is not known; however, according to the fifth cycle sample, it is estimated at 223,410 (weighted number) (McKie 1994). Like that of the country as a whole, the population of each province or territory was defined in all censuses as the population of usual residents, and this was always obtained by counting the persons at their usual residence, wherever they might be on Census Day.

In 1991, the population count for the country was 27.3 million, or 27.1 million not including non-permanent residents, nearly twice the 14.0 million counted in 1951 (see Table 1.1). The most populated province was Ontario, whose population had more than doubled in four decades to just over 10 million (36.9% of the total population of Canada). Quebec ranked second, with a population of 6.9 million. This represented just 25.3% of the country's total population, compared with nearly 29% from 1951 to 1966. The westernmost provinces, British Columbia and Alberta, ranked third and fourth, with 3.3 and 2.5 million inhabitants, respectively. These provinces experienced a population increase much higher than the national average, representing 21.3% of Canadians in 1991, compared with just 15.0% in 1951. The remaining six provinces and two territories were decidedly less populated, accounting for just 16.5% of Canada's total population in 1991. Clearly, in recent decades, the fastest population growth has been in the western and central regions of the country.

Table 1.2 shows the factors of Canada's population growth for five-year periods starting June 1. The first five periods are true intercensal periods: all censuses taken between 1951 and 1976 were conducted June 1. The last three periods (those ending in 1981, 1986 and 1991) do not precisely coincide with the corresponding intercensal periods, but deviate quite negligibly as the count was taken on June 2 in 1981, June 3 in 1986 and June 4 in 1991. Consequently, the population on the first day of each of the first six periods is the population count that very day, whereas in the last two cases it is the estimated population one or two days before the census. Total growth for the period was obtained by calculating the difference between the surveyed and estimated populations at five-year intervals; the rate of change for each period was calculated by comparing this total increase to the population at the start of the period. Natural growth was calculated by subtracting registered deaths from registered births. Net migration was calculated by subtracting natural growth from the total increase (see Figure 1.1 for the evolution of natural growth and net migration since 1951).

The dominant features of Canada's population increase since 1951 are the slowdown it experienced until the period 1981 to 1986, and its modest recovery in 1986 to 1991. The greatest increases, in absolute numbers, were over the first two intercensal periods: 2.1 million for the period 1951 to 1956 and 2.2 million for 1956 to 1961. These increases then declined in each subsequent period, to just 1.0 million for the period 1981 to 1986 (see Figure 1.1). This downward trend then reversed itself, and the number of permanent residents rose again by 1.8 million between 1986 and 1991. The slowdown in growth is even more evident if the relative increases are substituted for the absolute increases. The five-year rate of change actually declined steadily, from 14.8% between 1951 and 1956 to 4.2% between 1981 and 1986, before rising again to 6.9% between 1986 and 1991 (see Table 1.2).

TABLE 1.2
NATURAL GROWTH AND NET MIGRATION, BY INTERCENSAL PERIOD, 1951–1956 TO 1986–1991

Period	Total growth	Births	Deaths	Natural growth	Ratio between natural growth and total growth	Immigration
	('000)	('000)	('000)	('000)	%	('000)
1951–1956	2,072	2,106	633	1,473	71.1	783
1956–1961	2,157	2,362	687	1,675	77.7	760
1961–1966	1,777	2,249	731	1,518	85.4	539
1966–1971	1,553	1,856	766	1,090	70.2	890
1971–1976	1,425	1,756	822	934	65.5	841
1976–1981	1,350	1,820	842	978	72.4	588
1981–1986	1,011	1,873	885	988	97.7	500
1986–1991	1,754	1,930	945	985	56.2	874

Period	Emigration	Net migration	Ratio between net migration and total growth	Population at start of intercensal period	Five-year percentage change
	('000)	('000)	%	('000)	%
1951–1956	184	599	28.9	14,009	14.8
1956–1961	278	482	22.3	16,081	13.4
1961–1966	280	259	14.6	18,238	9.7
1966–1971	427	463	29.8	20,015	7.8
1971–1976	350	491	34.5	21,568	6.6
1976–1981	216	372	27.6	22,993	5.9
1981–1986	477	23	2.3	24,343	4.2
1986–1991	105	769	43.9	25,354	6.9

Source: Statistics Canada, 1993a, 119.

FIGURE **1.1**

NATURAL GROWTH AND NET MIGRATION, BY INTERCENSAL PERIOD, **1951–1956** TO **1986–1991**

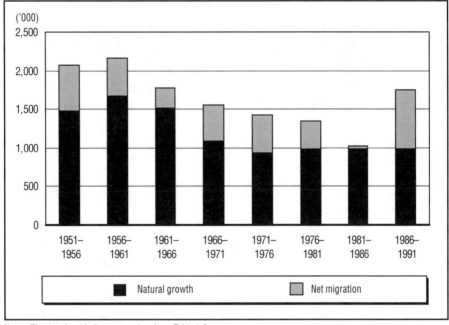

Note: The data for this figure are taken from Table 1.2.
Source: Census of Canada, 1993a, 119.

One reason for this slowing of population growth was the considerable decline in the excess number of births over deaths. The evolution of this natural excess reached two quite distinct levels: 1.5 million or more, and less than 1.0 million (see Figure 1.1). An excess of births over deaths at the first level (1.5 million or more) was reached between 1951 and 1956 and again between 1961 and 1966, that is, during the post-war baby boom. The drop in fertility that began in the mid-1960s immediately resulted in a decline in the number of births and drove natural growth below the threshold of 1.0 million in the period 1971 to 1976. And because fertility continued to be very low during the years that followed, the fact that baby boomers were gradually reaching their childbearing years did not have the anticipated effect on the number of births. Admittedly, the number rose from one period to the next, but so modestly that it was largely offset by the death rate. Thus, from the period 1971 to 1976 through to 1986 to 1991, natural growth had remained below the 1.0 million threshold, making migrations the main source of change in the total population increase.

The data presented for migrations are less reliable than those for births and deaths since net migration can be significantly distorted if the population growth estimate is distorted. This was the case in the period 1981 to 1986. The 1986 Census was less exhaustive than that of 1981, with the result that population growth in 1981 to 1986 was significantly underestimated. In this census, the apparent growth (that is, the difference between population counts) was estimated at 1.0 million, while the real growth (or the difference between corrected populations based on the net undercount) was about 1.3 million (see Table 1.3). For this period, net migration was therefore underestimated by about 300,000, and emigration was overestimated accordingly (since emigration is calculated by subtracting net migration from immigration).

This is not true of the immigration statistics, as they are taken from a continuous recording of new immigrants: only Canadian citizens, former immigrants returning to the country after a lengthy absence, and foreigners settling in Canada without an immigration visa are excluded. These statistics show that Canada has remained open to immigration; throughout the four decades considered, the number of immigrants declined little even in periods of considerable economic hardship. After 1976, the number of immigrants and the population increase varied similarly, both declining in the period 1976 to 1981, and again, slightly, in 1981 to 1986, and both increasing in 1986 to 1991.

TABLE **1.3**

POPULATION COUNT, UNDERCOUNT AND REAL POPULATION, AND APPARENT AND REAL GROWTH, CANADA, **1971** TO **1991**

Year	Population count	Undercount number	%	Real population	Apparent growth number	Real growth
1971	21,568,310	347,813	1.59	21,916,123	1,424,290[1]	1,473,520[1]
1976	22,992,600	397,043	1.70	23,389,643	1,350,580[2]	1,356,938[2]
1981	24,343,180	403,401	1.63	24,746,581	966,150[3]	1,258,786[3]
1986	25,309,330	696,036	2.68	26,005,366	1,764,114[4]	1,859,492[4]
1991	27,073,446	791,412	2.82	27,864,858		

1. Corresponds to the five-year period 1971–1976.
2. Corresponds to the five-year period 1976–1981.
3. Corresponds to the five-year period 1981–1986.
4. Corresponds to the five-year period 1986–1991.

Note: Non-permanent residents, who numbered 223,410, were excluded from the 1991 population count.
Source: Statistics Canada, 1994e, 65.

While the Canadian population grew steadily from 1951 to 1991, its child population did not; the number of children dropped dramatically from 1966 to 1986, and in 1991 remained far below what it had been 25 years earlier (see Table 1.4). This, of course, was the direct outcome of the evolution of births throughout the period, the most striking feature of which was a sharp decline between 1966 and 1971, confirmed in the period 1971 to 1976. (Table 1.2 illustrates this evolution.) During the post-war baby boom, the new generations were always more populous than those leaving the under-15 age group, and the number therefore rose from 4.3 million in 1951 to 6.6 million in 1966. In contrast, beginning in the mid-1960s, the numbers of children under age 15 declined as the generations at the height of the baby boom left this age group and were replaced by the little generations that followed. This decline continued until the period 1986 to 1991 when the little generations were in turn replaced by more recent and more populous generations. After peaking at 6.6 million in 1966, the number of children under age 15 again fell to 5.4 million in 1986, before rising once more to 5.7 million in 1991. As their numbers diminished, children also became less prevalent in a society whose adult population was growing. While in 1961 one-third of Canadians (34.0%) were under age 15, in 1991 the proportion was just one-fifth (20.9%).

TABLE 1.4
POPULATION BY AGE, 1951 TO 1991

Year	Age group			All ages
	Under age 15	Age 15 to 64	Age 65 and older	
	Number			
1951	4,250,717	8,672,439	1,086,273	**14,009,429**
1956	5,225,210	9,611,643	1,243,938	**16,080,791**
1961	6,191,922	10,655,171	1,391,154	**18,238,247**
1966	6,591,757	11,883,575	1,539,548	**20,014,880**
1971	6,380,895	13,443,005	1,744,410	**21,568,310**
1976	5,896,170	15,094,085	2,002,350	**22,992,605**
1981	5,481,110	16,501,100	2,360,975	**24,343,185**
1986	5,391,965	17,219,795	2,697,580	**25,309,340**
1991	5,692,555	18,434,325	3,169,970	**27,296,850**
	Percentage change			
1951–1956	22.9	10.8	14.5	**14.8**
1956–1961	18.5	10.9	11.8	**13.4**
1961–1966	6.5	11.5	10.7	**9.7**
1966–1971	− 3.2	13.1	13.3	**7.8**
1971–1976	− 7.6	12.3	14.8	**6.6**
1976–1981	− 7.0	9.3	17.9	**5.9**
1981–1986	− 1.6	4.4	14.3	**4.0**
1986–1991	5.6	7.1	17.5	**7.9**
	%			
1951	30.3	61.9	7.8	**100.0**
1956	32.5	59.8	7.7	**100.0**
1961	34.0	58.4	7.6	**100.0**
1966	32.9	59.4	7.7	**100.0**
1971	29.6	62.3	8.1	**100.0**
1976	25.6	65.6	8.7	**100.0**[1]
1981	22.5	67.8	9.7	**100.0**
1986	21.3	68.0	10.7	**100.0**
1991	20.9	67.5	11.6	**100.0**

1. Percentages may not add to 100 due to rounding.

Note: Some numbers are the total of undercounts previously rounded off at random. The 1991 population count includes non-permanent residents.

Source: Census of Canada, 1951 to 1991.

The aging of the baby boom generations significantly altered the population age pyramid (see figures 1.2A, 1.2B and 1.2C). Their numbers still small in 1951, the full strength of these generations is reflected in the 1971 pyramid, a sizeable portion (39.7% of the population) of which is accounted for by baby boomers aged 5 to 24. In 1971, the first of the baby boomers would have reached the age at which children generally leave home to form their own household, alone, as part of a couple, or perhaps with one or more other persons. The generations after them would reach this age in the next two decades, and this surge of young adults would stimulate the formation of new households in the midst of slowing population growth. In the 1991 pyramid, baby boomers, now aged 25 to 44, are clearly distinguishable from older and younger generations by their large number. They numbered 9.2 million, constituting one-third (33.8%) of the population, while, in 1971, the same age group represented just one-quarter (25.1%) of the population.

FIGURE 1.2A
AGE PYRAMID, 1951

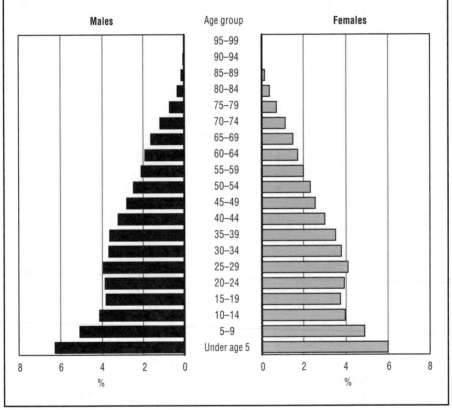

Note: The data for this figure are taken from Table 1A of Appendix 1.
Source: Census of Canada, 1951.

FIGURE 1.2B
AGE PYRAMID, 1971

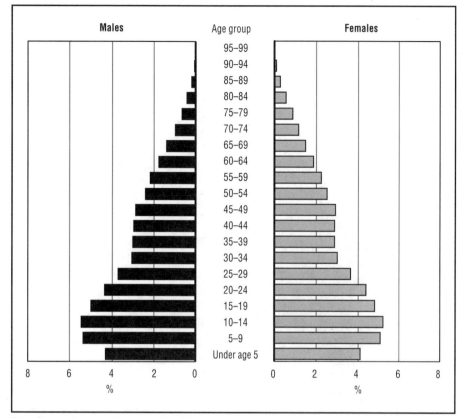

Note: The data for this figure are taken from Table 1B of Appendix 1.
Source: Census of Canada, 1971.

The aging of Canada's population is another notable feature of the population's evolution between 1951 and 1991. The number of elderly tripled in 40 years, from 1.1 to 3.2 million (see Table 1.4). Since the early 1960s, this number has always grown more rapidly than the total population, and the proportion of elderly has risen steadily with each census. The 8% threshold of elderly persons, usually used to demarcate young populations from aging populations, was surpassed just before the 1971 Census. Thereafter, the Canadian population quickly aged owing to the decline in the number of children (aging at the bottom of the pyramid) and the strong increase in the number of elderly (aging at the top of the pyramid). As a result, the proportion of Canadians aged 65 and older grew considerably over 20 years, to 11.6% in 1991. As we know, most of these elderly—notably the oldest among them—were women.

FIGURE 1.2C
AGE PYRAMID, 1991

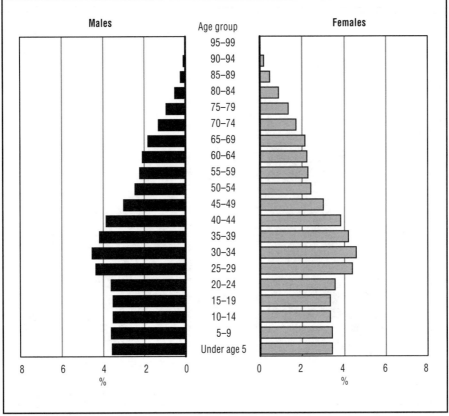

Note: The data for this figure are taken from Table 1c of Appendix 1.

Source: Census of Canada, 1991.

1.1.2 The definition of household

Basically, the population count is done house by house, with a distinction being made between private and collective dwellings. A private dwelling is usually a house or apartment where one person, family or small group of unrelated people resides; specifically, it is "a separate set of living quarters with a private entrance either from outside or from a common hall, lobby, vestibule or stairway inside the building" (Statistics Canada 1992b, p. 160). A collective dwelling is a dwelling of a commercial, institutional or communal nature that has beds to accommodate roomers, boarders or staff members; such dwellings include work camps, military camps, convents, hospitals, hotels, rooming houses, ships, jails, shelters, and so on. Census takers must locate all dwellings situated in the enumeration area assigned to them, in particular occupied dwellings that house the persons to be counted.

For enumeration purposes, the occupants of each dwelling are classified according to their residence, a distinction being drawn between "usual residents," "temporary residents" and "foreign residents." Foreign residents are occupants who reside outside the country and therefore are not part of the Canadian population and are not counted. Temporary residents are occupants who reside in another residence elsewhere in Canada, where they are eventually counted; they are enumerated separately so that it can be later verified that they were indeed counted at their residence as temporarily absent persons.

Usual residents include:

a)   persons residing in the dwelling and present on Census Day

b)   persons residing in the dwelling and temporarily absent on Census Day

c)   persons of no fixed abode and present in the dwelling on Census Day.

These usual residents are enumerated together and, in theory, will be the only ones included in the population count for the census area in which the dwelling is located.

Since the 1951 Census, all usual residents of a given dwelling constitute a domestic group called the "household." If the occupied dwelling is private, the household is called "private" and is typically made up of just a few people, or even just one person. A "private household" is defined as "a person or group of persons other than foreign residents, who occupy a dwelling and do not have a usual place of residence elsewhere in Canada" (Statistics Canada 1992b, p. 140).

In the case of a collective dwelling, the household is called a "collective household," regardless of how many people are in it. It is defined as "a person or group of persons (other than foreign residents), who occupy the same collective dwelling and do not have a usual place of residence elsewhere in Canada" (Statistics Canada 1992b, p.139). Defined thus, the household may be qualified as "household/dwelling"; here occupancy in the same collective dwelling is sufficient to determine membership in the same household.

In censuses prior to 1951, the definition of household was more restrictive; it was not until 1921 that the term was used to designate what had previously been called "family" (Loken 1973). The household was then a household/home, that is, a group of persons occupying the same dwelling and living together while using the same household goods and services. People who lived separately in different areas of the same dwelling did not belong to the same household: in such cases, each housekeeping unit was considered to be a separate household. Thus, with each census before 1951, more households were counted than were occupied dwellings. It should be added, however, that this more restrictive definition of household was associated with a less precise definition of dwelling, which was at times confused with house or building.

Everyone who is enumerated belongs to either a collective household or a private household and must be classified as belonging to one of these two categories. This, however, is never quite the case, as the total population is always a little higher than the total household population (see Table 1.5). The main reason for this anomaly is the inclusion in the total population of persons temporarily away from their residence on Census Day and not enumerated in the households to which they belong. The second, less important, reason is the 1976 decision to no longer count as private those households made up of Canadian nationals on a diplomatic or military posting abroad, and their families (Harrison 1979). From 1961 to 1991, the number of persons not counted in collective or private households remained steady at between 100,000 and 150,000, except in 1976 when the total population included nearly 60,000 people living in dwellings incorrectly classified as unoccupied. The people thus excluded from collective or private households represent only a very small proportion of the population count: in 1991, that figure was 0.4%.

1.1.3 Collective households and private households

Collective households have always been few in number and have traditionally represented a small fraction of the population; nevertheless, their recent evolution is characterized by two very opposite trends (see Table 1.5). Between 1961 and 1976, the number of collective households dropped from nearly 22,500 to less than 16,500, and their population declined from about 484,000 to less than 385,000, or from 2.7% to 1.7% of the total population. In contrast, since 1976 their number and population have risen steadily, to 21,000 and about 447,000, respectively, in 1991. Nevertheless, the proportion of persons living in these households remained virtually unchanged (1.6% in 1991). It seems clear that the recent population increase of these households is attributable to the increase in the number of institutional residents, from 215,000 in 1976 to about 302,000 in 1991. These residents—mostly senior citizens—now account for two-thirds of all members of collective households.

TABLE 1.5
TOTAL POPULATION COUNT, BY TYPE OF HOUSEHOLD AND NUMBER OF PERSONS,[1] 1951 TO 1991

Year	Total population	Private households[3]	Number of persons in private households	Collective households	Number of persons in collective households
1951[2]	14,009,429	3,409,284	13,572,465	11,538	..
1956	16,080,791	3,923,646	15,447,656	24,729	..
1961	18,238,247	4,554,736	17,612,145	22,475	483,718
1966	20,014,880	5,180,473	19,405,615	18,236	463,266
1971	21,568,311	6,041,302	21,033,625	17,585	392,695
1976	22,992,604	7,166,095	22,412,000	16,445	384,530
1981	24,343,181	8,281,531	23,797,378	17,370	405,735
1986	25,309,331	8,991,672	24,773,110	19,800	434,370
1991	27,296,859	10,018,267	26,731,857	21,020	446,885

.. figures not available

1. 100% data.

2. Does not include private and collective households in Yukon and the Northwest Territories.

3. Since 1976, households outside of Canada have not been included.

Source: Census of Canada, various years; Wargon, 1979a.

The interpretation of these results should take into account the fact that collective households represent only a portion of the occupants of collective dwellings on Census Day. Many commercial, institutional or communal dwellings accommodate people for just a few hours, days or weeks, and therefore have very few or no usual residents. Also, the definition of a usual resident of a collective dwelling is fairly narrow, as a resident of an institution is considered a usual resident of a collective dwelling only when he or she no longer has a residence or when the institutional resident has left his or her own residence at least six months prior to the census. Of the 580,000 or so institutional residents counted in 1991, only 302,205 met this condition and qualified as members of a collective household.

It should be noted, moreover, that collective households are difficult to canvass and the data for them are not very detailed. The difficulty in accurately canvassing collective households can be illustrated using an estimate taken from verifications done of the 1991 Census. According to these verifications, the population of these households was underestimated by 47,094 persons, and should have been 494,000, not 447,000 as reported in the census (Statistics Canada 1994a). Not only is it difficult to take an accurate census of the members of collective households, but it is also hard to gather accurate data about the personal characteristics of such members. These difficulties justify, at least in part, two decisions that reduced the available data for these households. The first, taken in 1976, was to no longer reconstitute the families living in these households. The second, in effect in 1981, was to limit the data collected about any institutional resident to sex, age, marital status and mother tongue. In addition to not being very detailed, data on collective households are also not widely distributed; consequently, the statistics on households pertain essentially to private households.

Thanks in part to an abundant housing supply, the number of private households nearly tripled in 40 years from 3.4 million in 1951 to 10.0 million in 1991 (see Table 1.5). Of course, such an increase could not have occurred without a considerable increase in the number of persons old enough to form or maintain their own household. Indeed, the population of those aged 15 and older, which was 9.8 million in 1951, more than doubled in 40 years, to 21.6 million in 1991. And it grew at a faster rate before 1981 than after: from 1951 to 1981, the increase per intercensal period consistently exceeded 10%, while it was just 5.6% for the period 1981 to 1986, and 8.5% for 1986 to 1991. The increase in the household count followed a fairly similar chronology, but at an even faster pace. The increase per intercensal period held at between 13.7% and 18.6% until 1981, then dropped to just 8.6% for the period 1981 to 1986 before rebounding to 11.4% in 1986 to 1991. While these facts illustrate the important part the increase in adult population played in the increase in the number of households, they suggest that the changes that occurred in the composition of this population and in meeting its housing demand also had much to do with this increase.

Evolving at appreciably the same rate as the overall population, the number of persons who belonged to a private household nearly doubled in 40 years, from 13.6 million in 1951 to 26.7 million in 1991. That is to say that the number of household persons clearly grew at a slower rate than that of private households. This is true for all intercensal periods, but particularly from 1966 to 1986: during these two decades, the number of households rose 73.6%, while the number of household persons rose just 27.7%. This discrepancy is attributable to the collapse of the birth rate after the post-war baby boom. The decline in births, beginning in the mid-1960s, stemmed the population growth by reducing the population under age 15 from 6.6 to 5.4 million. During this time, the generations at the height of the baby boom swelled the ranks of those persons aged 15 and older by 48.4%, from 13.4 to 19.9 million, and this resulted in the formation of a very large number of households. Thus, as households became more numerous, they also became smaller: the average number of persons per household dropped from 4.0 in 1951 to 2.7 in 1991.

As for private households and their population, persons counted in these households represented 96.6% of the persons enumerated in 1961, and 97.9% of those enumerated in 1986 and 1991. Their representation in the population count varies, however, by sex and age (see Table 1.6). It is quite high to about age 70, and the slight differences observed before this age may largely be explained by the non-reporting of persons temporarily away from their residence. (It was in fact noted that temporary residents who were male or still young were less likely than others to be enumerated in the households to which they belonged (Statistics Canada 1994a).) After age 70, the proportion of persons counted in private households decreased among women and among both sexes as age increased; this can be attributed to the greater number of persons being institutionalized as they got older. In 1991, of about 211,000 persons aged 75 and older who were no longer living in a private household, 188,320 were residents of an institution. Therefore, the elderly are underrepresented in the population of private households.

TABLE 1.6

POPULATION OF PRIVATE HOUSEHOLDS, TOTAL POPULATION AND PROPORTION OF PERSONS IN PRIVATE HOUSEHOLDS, BY AGE AND SEX,[1] 1991

	Population of private households	Total population	%
Total, female	13,545,215	13,842,280	97.9
Under age 5	926,260	93,0735	99.5
5–9	925,710	929,820	99.6
10–14	910,665	915,085	99.5
15–19	896,985	910,230	98.5
20–24	963,490	976,655	98.7
25–29	1,181,280	1,192,965	99.0
30–34	1,243,000	1,253,360	99.2
35–39	1,142,850	1,150,810	99.3
40–44	1,037,370	1,044,715	99.3
45–49	809,705	816,580	99.2
50–54	655,355	662,175	99.0
55–59	607,230	614,835	98.8
60–64	595,210	604,765	98.4
65–69	566,235	580,665	97.5
70–74	443,025	462,945	95.7
75–79	330,945	362,245	91.4
80–84	193,685	236,660	81.8
85–89	85,080	128,235	66.3
90 and older	31,135	68,790	45.3

TABLE **1.6** (CONCLUDED)

POPULATION OF PRIVATE HOUSEHOLDS, TOTAL POPULATION AND PROPORTION OF PERSONS IN PRIVATE HOUSEHOLDS, BY AGE AND SEX,[1] 1991

	Population of private households	Total population	%
Total, male	**13,186,645**	**13,454,580**	**98.0**
Under age 5	970,785	975,765	99.5
5–9	973,625	978,220	99.5
10–15	957,410	962,925	99.4
15–19	938,265	958,405	97.9
20–24	958,015	985,220	97.2
25–29	1,155,445	1,182,575	97.7
30–34	1,214,455	1,237,685	98.1
35–39	1,116,640	1,133,670	98.5
40–44	1,027,810	1,042,185	98.6
45–49	812,665	824,200	98.6
50–54	653,385	663,285	98.5
55–59	598,085	608,085	98.4
60–64	560,940	571,940	98.1
65–69	479,925	492,505	97.4
70–74	345,955	358,955	96.4
75–79	236,895	252,530	93.8
80–84	123,365	140,135	88.0
85–89	47,385	61,250	77.4
90 and older	15,590	25,050	62.2

1. 100% data.

Source: Census of Canada, 1991, special compilation.

The data on private households are distorted by enumeration errors. Based on the verifications done of the 1991 Census, it is estimated that 272,198 households were not counted and 45,455 were counted twice. The difference between these two figures gives a net undercount of 226,743 households, or 2.21% of the actual count. According to the same verifications, the net undercount of the population of private households can be estimated at 760,160 persons, or 2.77% of the actual count. Verifications done of previous censuses were less thorough in that they overlooked the overcount of some households and their population. Their results suggest that the undercount of households in 1986 and 1991 was greater than for previous censuses.

1.1.4 Size of households

One of the striking features of the recent evolution of Canadian society, like that of other western societies, is undoubtedly the smaller size of households (see Figure 1.3 for the distribution of households by size in 1961, 1976 and 1991). In 1961, Canadian households could be divided into three categories of fairly equal size: small households of one or two people, medium households of three or four people, and large households of five or more people (see Table 1.7). Thirty years later, the proportion of medium households remained unchanged, while the proportion of small households had grown and large households accounted for just one-tenth of the total. Moreover, only large households saw their number decline since 1966—the larger the household, the greater the decline. This erosion is mostly caused by declining fertility, which virtually eliminated the renewal of large families at a time when the children of baby boom-era families were leaving home. The devastating effect of the decline in fertility was doubtless intensified by the desire for greater residential autonomy on the part of both families and any persons who might have lived with them. This search for greater domestic autonomy is also generally cited as the main reason for the impressive increase in the number of people living alone. The decline in large households and the proliferation of small households pushed the average number of persons per household down to 2.7 in 1991 from 3.9 in 1961.

FIGURE 1.3

DISTRIBUTION OF PRIVATE HOUSEHOLDS, BY SIZE, 1961, 1976 AND 1991

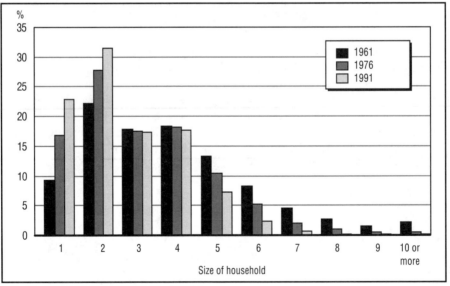

Note: The data for this figure are taken from Table 1.7.

Source: Census of Canada, 1961 to 1991.

TABLE 1.7
PRIVATE HOUSEHOLDS, BY SIZE OF HOUSEHOLD,[1] 1961 TO 1991

Year	Total private households	1	2	3	4	5	6	7	8	9	10 or more	Number of persons in households	Average number of persons per household
							Number						
1961	4,554,736	424,750	1,012,068	809,182	836,912	604,261	372,914	209,247	120,139	69,308	95,955	17,612,145	3.9
1966	5,180,473	589,571	1,197,338	879,391	912,343	665,880	412,480	229,275	128,295	72,393	93,507	19,405,615	3.7
1971	6,034,505	810,397	1,524,410	1,044,946	1,061,287	719,718	418,337	235,798	100,050	54,563	64,999	21,011,820	3.5
1976	7,166,095	1,205,340	1,990,135	1,256,525	1,307,320	750,620	379,520	144,425	67,985	32,080	32,150	22,412,000	3.1
1981	8,281,530	1,681,130	2,397,550	1,450,205	1,544,205	753,065	292,990	92,620	37,800	16,260	15,695	23,797,375	2.9
1986	8,991,675	1,934,705	2,701,175	1,599,325	1,681,590	728,210	239,515	63,235	24,130	10,025	9,760	24,773,110	2.8
1991	10,018,270	2,297,060	3,144,185	1,743,610	1,768,825	731,415	229,525	60,935	23,265	9,990	9,450	26,731,860	2.7
							%						
1961	100.0	9.3	22.2	17.8	18.4	13.3	8.2	4.6	2.6	1.5	2.1		
1966	100.0	11.4	23.1	17.0	17.6	12.9	8.0	4.4	2.5	1.4	1.8		
1971	100.0	13.4	25.3	17.3	17.6	11.9	6.9	3.9	1.7	0.9	1.1		
1976	100.0	16.8	27.8	17.5	18.2	10.5	5.3	2.0	0.9	0.4	0.4		
1981	100.0	20.3	29.0	17.5	18.6	9.1	3.5	1.1	0.5	0.2	0.2		
1986	100.0	21.5	30.0	17.8	18.7	8.1	2.7	0.7	0.3	0.1	0.1		
1991	100.0	22.9	31.4	17.4	17.7	7.3	2.3	0.6	0.2	0.1	0.1		

Size of household

1. 100% data.

Note: Percentages may not add to 100 due to rounding.

Source: Census of Canada, 1961 to 1991.

In 1991, the distribution of private households by size differed considerably from the distribution of the population living in these households (see Figure 1.4). At a disadvantage because of their size, small households had a demographic weight less than their incidence. Thus, people living alone accounted for just 8.6% of the population, while they made up 22.9% of households. However, one- and two-person households together represent nearly one-third (32.1%) of the population and more than half (54.3%) of households. Conversely, the demographic weight of larger-than-average households exceeds their incidence. This is true of three- and four-person households, which make up nearly half (46.1%) of the population, though they represent just slightly more than one-third (35.1%) of all households. This is also true, *a fortiori*, of households of five or more, which account for more than one-fifth (21.8%) of the population, but represent no more than one-tenth (10.6%) of all households. Thus, many subtle distinctions exist and can be made when interpreting the distribution of households. This analysis shows that although they account for the majority of households, small households represent a minority of the population; meanwhile, two-thirds of the population live in households of three or more, that is, in larger-than-average households.

FIGURE 1.4

DISTRIBUTION OF PERSONS LIVING IN PRIVATE HOUSEHOLDS AND HOUSEHOLDS, BY SIZE, 1991

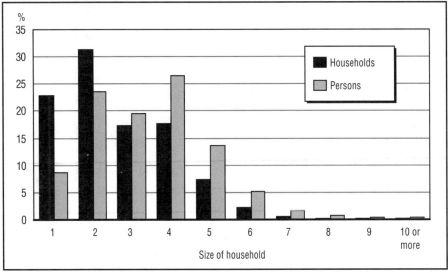

Note: The data for this figure are taken from tables 1.7 and 1.8.
Source: Census of Canada, 1961 to 1991.

As Figure 1.4 shows, for every 100 people who belonged to a private household in 1991, 32 lived alone or with one other person, 46 were living in households of three or four people, and only 22 were living with five or more people. The situation was quite different in 1961, when: 14 lived alone or with one other person; 33 lived in households of three or four people; and 53 lived with five or more people (see Table 1.8). The change in population distribution therefore occurred at the expense of large households, in favour of small or medium households. Primarily because of the near-disappearance of large families, just 3.0% of the population lived in households of seven or more, compared with 23.4% of the population 30 years ago. Furthermore, of the large households, only those with five or six members (18.9% of the population in 1991) retained substantial demographic weight. As small households became more common, the proportion of people living in households of three or four grew, but there was no proportional increase in the number of such households. The opposite was true of small households, whose demographic weight and incidence both increased. Two-person households, often consisting of a couple without children living at home or a lone parent with one child, accounted for only 11.5% of the population in 1961; this figure was about double (23.5%) in 1991. As for the proportion of people living alone, it was still fairly negligible (2.4%) in 1961, but rose to 8.6% in 1991. That is, by 1991, it had become unusual for people to live in a very large household. While such people became "statistically marginal," the reverse was true of people living alone who emerged from the status of "statistically marginal." These were undoubtedly the two most striking features of the evolution of households observed during this 30-year period.

TABLE 1.8

DISTRIBUTION OF PERSONS LIVING IN PRIVATE HOUSEHOLDS, BY SIZE OF HOUSEHOLD,[1] 1961 TO 1991

Year	Number of persons in households	Size of household									
		1	2	3	4	5	6	7	8	9	10 or more
		Number									
1961	17,512,145	424,750	2,024,136	2,427,546	3,347,648	3,021,305	2,237,484	1,464,729	961,112	623,772	1,079,663
1966	19,405,615	589,571	2,394,676	2,638,173	3,649,372	3,329,400	2,474,880	1,604,925	1,026,360	651,537	1,046,721
1971	21,011,820	810,397	3,048,820	3,134,838	4,245,148	3,598,590	2,510,022	1,650,586	800,400	491,067	721,952
1976	22,412,000	1,205,340	3,980,270	3,769,575	5,229,280	3,753,100	2,277,120	1,010,975	543,880	288,720	353,740
1981	23,797,375	1,681,130	4,795,100	4,350,615	6,176,820	3,765,325	1,757,940	648,340	302,400	146,340	173,365
1986	24,773,110	1,934,705	5,402,350	4,797,975	6,726,360	3,641,050	1,437,090	442,645	193,040	90,225	107,670
1991	26,731,860	2,297,060	6,288,370	5,230,830	7,075,300	3,657,075	1,377,150	426,545	186,120	89,910	103,497
		%									
1961	100.0	2.4	11.5	13.8	19.0	17.2	12.7	8.3	5.5	3.5	6.1
1966	100.0	3.0	12.3	13.6	18.8	17.2	12.8	8.3	5.3	3.4	5.4
1971	100.0	3.9	14.5	14.9	20.2	17.1	11.9	7.9	3.8	2.3	3.4
1976	100.0	5.4	17.8	16.8	23.3	16.7	10.2	4.5	2.4	1.3	1.6
1981	100.0	7.1	20.1	18.3	26.0	15.8	7.4	2.7	1.3	0.6	0.7
1986	100.0	7.8	21.8	19.4	27.2	14.7	5.8	1.8	0.8	0.4	0.4
1991	100.0	8.6	23.5	19.6	26.5	13.7	5.2	1.6	0.7	0.3	0.4

1. 100% data.

Note: Percentages may not add to 100 due to rounding.

Source. Census of Canada, 1961 to 1991.

Everyone knows that the number of people with whom one lives varies over a lifetime, that this number is generally larger during one's childhood than in the period after leaving home, and that later, the number is also larger during the years when one's children are living at home compared with the period that follows their departure from the home. The same finding can be made from a census by calculating the average household size by age of a household reference person. The household reference person is defined as the primary household maintainer, that is, the man or woman primarily responsible for paying housing costs such as rent and mortgage (see the 1991 results in Appendix 1, Table 2). Average household size has been divided into two groups by age: average number of persons under age 15, and the average number of persons aged 15 and older. Middle-aged maintainers generally have larger households than younger or older maintainers, mainly because there are more children living at home (see figures 1.5 and 1.6). Also, households of male maintainers are larger than those of their female counterparts, which is hardly surprising as a large proportion of female maintainers live alone or without a spouse. In light of these results, the factors affecting the distribution of households by size include the relatively large number of young and elderly people in the adult population, the relative stability of couples, and fertility. Over the last three decades, these demographic factors have contributed to the evolution toward smaller households.

FIGURE 1.5

AVERAGE NUMBER OF PERSONS PER PRIVATE HOUSEHOLD WHERE HOUSEHOLD MAINTAINER IS FEMALE, BY MAINTAINER'S AGE, 1991

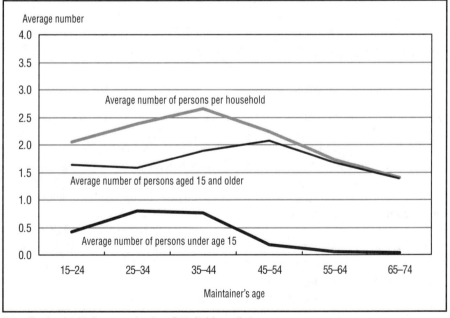

Note: The data for this figure are taken from Table 2 of Appendix 1.
Source: Census of Canada, 1991, special compilation.

FIGURE 1.6

AVERAGE NUMBER OF PERSONS PER PRIVATE HOUSEHOLD WHERE HOUSEHOLD MAINTAINER IS MALE, BY MAINTAINER'S AGE, 1991

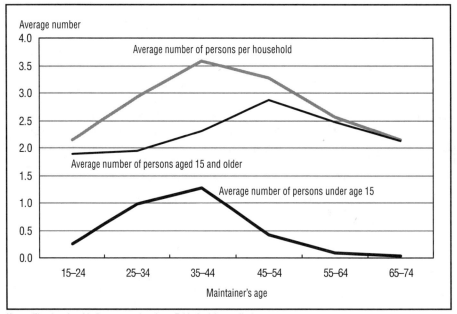

Note: The data for this figure are taken from Table 2 of Appendix 1.

Source: Census of Canada, 1991, special compilation.

1.2   HOUSEHOLDS AND FAMILY RELATIONSHIPS

1.2.1 Households and economic families

During a census, household members are listed in the questionnaire in order, according to their family relationship. Until 1976, the first person listed was called the "head of household," but has since been known simply as "Person 1." Person 1 must be an adult and, if applicable, have a spouse or single children[1] living at home. The other persons must then be listed, beginning with their spouse and children and ending with unrelated persons. Also, the members of a given family unit are to be listed one after the other, beginning with parents or spouses, and then children. The order suggested on the questionnaire or in the instruction booklet is as follows: Person 1, his or her spouse, his or her never-married children, his or her other children and their families, his or her other relatives and their families, and, finally, unrelated persons and their families. These instructions are given to help identify families when the questionnaires are processed.

This vertical listing of household members only becomes significant in light of the responses to the question about the relationship to Person 1. Persons related to Person 1 are reported as having a family relationship, expressed in terms such as husband, wife, son, daughter, father, mother, and so on. For unrelated persons, suggested responses are room-mate, lodger, institutional resident or employee. However, when persons unrelated to Person 1 form a family, the response must include the relationship to the family member first listed. For example, a lodging family must provide responses such as: lodger, lodger's wife, lodger's daughter, lodger's son, and so on. As can be seen, a person need only declare one relationship, that to Person 1 or, if not to Person 1, then to someone unrelated to Person 1.

The reporting of family relationships has posed a number of problems which more recent censuses have attempted to resolve. Until 1976, the terms proposed to respondents were those usually used to designate natural relatives (father, mother, son, daughter, grandson, granddaughter, etc.) and relationships by marriage (husband, wife, son-in-law, daughter-in-law, father-in-law, mother-in-law). Persons living common law were asked to use the same terms in reporting their family relationships. But, in 1976, it became apparent that many people who lived together outside of marriage did not wish to consider themselves married and refused to refer to their partner as their "husband" or "wife"; nor did they welcome the term "cohabitant," but instead preferred such neutral terms as "companion"; "mate" or "friend." As these terms were being used by room-mates or friends occupying the same dwelling, it was difficult to identify, with any certainty, couples and families that were not related by marriage or through a common-law union. As the number of people living common law was expected to increase in the future, there was an urgent need to provide them with a less equivocal, more consistent vocabulary. In 1981, the vocabulary proposed to respondents was therefore expanded to include the expression "common-law partner" (and its combinations with other relationships: "mother of common-law partner," brother of common-law partner," "room-mate's common-law partner," and so on). For the purposes of reconstituting families, the relationships in a common-law union were assumed to be the same as those created by marriage.

From the reporting of family relationships, it is possible to reconstitute, within households, families known as "economic families." According to the definition used in the 1956 Census, an economic family is a group of two or more persons who live in the same dwelling and are related by blood, adoption, marriage or common law. Because an economic family can exist only in households of two or more people, this family group almost always consists of Person 1 and his or her in-laws or other relatives, and only rarely of persons unrelated to Person 1. For the purposes of this analysis, unattached or non-family persons are defined as those persons who live alone or who share a dwelling with one or more unrelated persons.

The data gathered on economic families confirm the familial nature of Canadian households of two or more people. Most members of such households also belong to an economic family. Thus, in 1991, of approximately 24,435,000 people not living alone, only about 1,050,000, or 4.3%, did not live in an economic family. Moreover, almost all economic families—97% in 1991—were the sole occupants of their dwelling and, reciprocally, nearly all households of two or more people—94% in 1991—consisted only of the members of an economic family. In other words, living with others usually means living with relatives or in-laws and no one else.

Non-family persons represent about one-tenth of members of private households, but this proportion varies considerably by age: the proportion of unattached persons is negligible among children, relatively high among young adults, moderate among middle-aged adults, and very high among the elderly (see Figure 1.7 and Appendix 1, Table 3). These age variations show Canadians' preference for a familial household limited to the parents and their never-married children, or limited to the couple if no never-married children are living at home. In fact, given this preference, adults who do not belong to a family unit are considerably less likely to live with related persons. In 1991, just over 80% lived alone or with unrelated persons, and this proportion varied little with age, at least up to age 85. The proportion of non-family adults therefore directly depends on the proportion who have no spouse or dependent children, and is very high among the elderly, especially elderly women, who often are widowed and long separated from their children. It is also quite high among young adults, a fair proportion of whom have left their parents and siblings, but have not yet entered a union or have already dissolved one. Non-family young adults are more likely to live with unrelated persons than alone, whereas the elderly are virtually always the sole occupants of their dwelling.

FIGURE 1.7

AVERAGE NUMBER OF PERSONS PER PRIVATE HOUSEHOLD,
BY AGE AND SEX, 1991

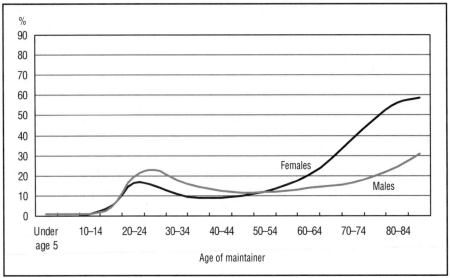

Note: The data for this figure are taken from Table 3 of Appendix 1.
Source: Census of Canada, 1991, special compilation.

1.2.2 Households and census families

The concept of "census family," as defined in the 1936 Census of the Prairie Provinces and used in all national censuses since 1941, is generally preferred to that of "economic family" (Gauthier 1971; Wargon 1979a). The census family is a group of at least two persons living together in a housekeeping unit, who are related and form a family unit. It may consist of a married couple or a couple living common law and their never-married sons and daughters, a lone parent and his or her never-married sons and daughters, or simply a married or common-law couple. Census family members also include:

a) persons whose spouse or partner is also a member of the household

b) lone mothers and fathers with at least one single son or daughter at home

c) single persons who are the son or daughter of another household member.

All other household members, including persons living alone, are known as "non-family persons."

Obviously, the proportion of non-family persons varies according to the stage reached in the life cycle (see Figure 1.8 and Appendix 1, Table 4). The proportion is marginal among children, since they usually live with both, or at least one, of their natural or adoptive parents. It is relatively large among young adults, who are at the age of making the transition from one family unit to another—one consisting of the parents, and the other created by the young person forming his or her own family—a transition that can take some time and may fail several times. At slightly older ages, when couples are having and raising their children, the proportion of non-family persons is smaller, notably among women, who generally retain custody of the children after the dissolution of a union. The proportion of non-family persons is highest among the elderly, who have reached the age where the family unit, which no longer includes children, inevitably dissolves upon the death of a spouse—usually the husband.

FIGURE 1.8
PROPORTION OF NON-FAMILY PERSONS, BY AGE AND SEX, 1991

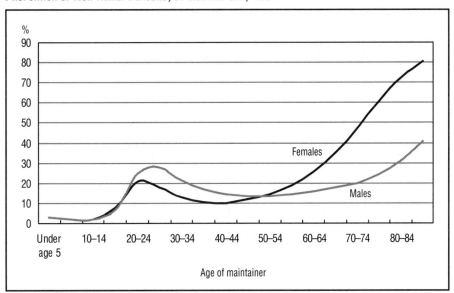

Note: The data for this figure are taken from Table 4 of Appendix 1.

Source: Census of Canada, 1991, special compilation.

Since the 1961 Census, private households have been classified according to whether they consist solely of non-family persons or include at least one family unit. Three main types of household have thus been distinguished: one-family households, multiple-family households and non-family households. A one-family household consists of a single census family, and possibly one or more non-family persons. A multiple-family household consists of at least two census families and perhaps one or more non-family persons. A non-family household does not contain a census family, and is therefore made up of one or more non-family persons. For the 1951 and 1956 censuses, the counts of these main types of household can be found in the tables showing the distribution of households by number of families or number of persons.

The appreciable increase in the number of households since 1951 has been accompanied by a profound change in their distribution by type (see Table 1.9). While the number of family households increased from about 3.0 million in 1951 to about 7.2 million in 1991, the proportion of family households decreased from 88.7% of all households in 1951 to just 72.2% in 1991. However, as a proportion of households of two or more persons—the only category of household that can include a family—family households remained fairly constant, dropping from 95.7% in 1951 to 93.7% in 1991. Since households of two or more persons are still typically family households, the decline in the proportion of family households is almost entirely attributable to the impressive increase in the number of one-person households. Still uncommon in the early 1950s, when they numbered a little over a quarter of a million, their number climbed to about 2.3 million in 1991, accounting for about 23% of all households.

According to the results of the 1991 Census, the propensity to live alone has relatively little to do with the sex of the non-family person, but has much more to do with their age (see Table 1.10). Young people in their twenties are less likely to live alone than their elders, doubtless because of their very modest incomes, but probably also because of the greater number and wider availability of people who are willing to share an apartment. It is only among non-family persons, aged 30 and older, that a majority is found to be living on their own; this majority increases in size with age, at least until the older ages. While living alone is just a temporary state for young singles and newly separated or divorced adults, it is doubtless a more enduring state for people in their fifties, notably women who, after this age, are considerably over-represented in the non-family population and therefore have less chance than men of the same age of living again as part of a couple.

TABLE 1.9

PRIVATE HOUSEHOLDS, BY TYPE,[1] 1951 TO 1991

Type of household		1951[2]	1956	1961	1966	1971	1976	1981	1986	1991
						Number				
Total private households		**3,409,295**	**3,923,646**	**4,554,736**	**5,180,473**	**6,041,302**	**7,166,095**	**8,281,530**	**8,991,675**	**10,018,265**
Family households		3,024,285	3,464,226	3,948,935	4,376,409	4,928,129	5,633,945	6,231,490	6,634,995	7,235,225
One-family households		2,794,860	3,259,499	3,780,992	4,246,753	4,807,011	5,542,295	6,140,335	6,537,880	7,118,655
Multiple-family households		229,425	204,727	167,943	129,656	121,118	91,655	91,155	97,115	116,570
Non-family households		385,010	459,420	605,801	804,064	1,106,376	1,532,150	2,050,045	2,356,675	2,783,035
of one person		252,435	308,613	424,750	589,571	810,397	1,205,340	1,681,130	1,934,710	2,297,060
of two or more persons		132,575	150,807	181,051	214,493	295,979	326,810	368,915	421,965	485,975

		1951[2]	1956	1961	1966	1971	1976	1981	1986	1991
					Distribution of households, by type					
Total private households	Number	**3,409,295**	**3,923,646**	**4,554,736**	**5,180,473**	**6,041,302**	**7,166,095**	**8,281,530**	**8,991,675**	**10,018,265**
	%	100.0	100.0	100.0	100.0	100.0	100.0	100.0	100.0	100.0
Family households	%	88.7	88.3	86.7	84.5	81.6	78.6	75.2	73.8	72.2
One-family households	%	82.0	83.1	83.0	82.0	79.6	77.3	74.1	72.7	71.1
Multiple-family households	%	6.7	5.2	3.7	2.5	2.0	1.3	1.1	1.1	1.2
Non-family households	%	11.3	11.7	13.3	15.5	18.3	21.4	24.8	26.2	27.8
of one person	%	7.4	7.9	9.3	11.4	13.4	16.8	20.3	21.5	22.9
of two or more persons	%	3.9	3.8	4.0	4.1	4.9	4.6	4.5	4.7	4.9

Type of household	1951–1956	1956–1961	1961–1966	1966–1971	1971–1976	1976–1981	1981–1986	1986–1991
				Rate of variation over 5 years (%)				
Total private households	**15.1**	**16.1**	**13.7**	**16.6**	**18.6**	**15.6**	**8.6**	**11.4**
Family households	14.5	14.0	10.8	12.6	14.3	10.6	6.5	9.0
One-family household	16.6	16.0	12.3	13.2	15.3	10.8	6.5	8.9
Multiple-family households	-10.8	-18.0	-22.8	-6.6	-24.3	-0.5	6.5	20.0
Non-family households	19.3	31.9	32.7	37.6	38.5	33.8	15.0	18.1
of one person	22.3	37.6	38.8	37.5	48.7	39.5	15.1	18.7
of two or more persons	13.8	20.1	18.5	38.0	10.4	12.9	14.4	15.2

1. 100% data.
2. The Yukon and Northwest Territories are not included.
Source: Census of Canada, 1951 to 1991.

HOUSEHOLDS AND FAMILIES

TABLE 1.10

NON-FAMILY PERSONS AGED 15 AND OLDER, BY LIVING ARRANGEMENTS, AGE AND SEX,[1] 1991

| Age group | Persons living alone | | Non-family persons | | | | | |
| | | | Living with non-relatives | | Living with relatives | | Total non-family persons | |
	Number	%	Number	%	Number	%	Number	%
Total, female	**1,326,875**	**61.2**	**425,295**	**19.6**	**415,960**	**19.2**	**2,168,150**	**100.0**
15–19	8,315	11.9	38,060	54.4	23,580	33.7	69,960	100.0
20–24	55,820	27.9	103,710	51.9	40,340	20.2	199,865	100.0
25–29	92,100	43.4	84,315	39.7	35,850	16.9	212,265	100.0
30–34	84,990	53.9	48,975	31.1	23,640	15.0	157,615	100.0
35–39	71,420	60.3	30,635	25.9	16,345	13.8	118,405	100.0
40–44	66,750	63.4	23,935	22.7	14,550	13.8	105,230	100.0
45–49	63,760	66.2	18195	18.9	14,400	14.9	96,355	100.0
50–54	65,070	67.8	14570	15.2	16,350	17.0	95,990	100.0
55–59	80,510	70.0	12755	11.1	21,725	18.9	114,995	100.0
60–64	109,920	71.7	12,730	8.3	30,690	20.0	153,345	100.0
65–69	148,955	74.6	11,855	5.9	38,900	19.5	199,710	100.0
70–74	160,550	76.5	9,335	4.5	39,865	19.0	209,750	100.0
75–79	153,055	76.4	7,340	3.7	39,975	20.0	200,370	100.0
80–84	103,870	74.1	4880	3.5	31,460	22.4	140,215	100.0
85–89	47,350	68.9	2685	3.9	18710	27.2	68,745	100.0
90 and older	14,440	57.0	1320	5.2	9580	37.8	25,335	100.0

TABLE 1.10 (CONCLUDED)
NON-FAMILY PERSONS AGED 15 AND OLDER, BY LIVING ARRANGEMENTS, AGE AND SEX,[1] 1991

Age group	Non-family persons						Total non-family persons	
	Persons living alone		Living with non-relatives		Living with relatives			
	Number	%	Number	%	Number	%	Number	%
Total, male	970,180	51.9	573,810	30.7	323,870	17.3	1,867,840	100.0
15–19	6,575	9.9	33,645	50.6	26,260	39.5	66,485	100.0
20–24	59,735	25.2	124,570	52.6	52,415	22.1	236,720	100.0
25–29	128,675	40.2	134,815	42.2	56,350	17.6	319,840	100.0
30–34	133,755	51.9	81,905	31.8	42,120	16.3	257,780	100.0
35–39	112,700	59.1	50,560	26.5	27,360	14.4	190,615	100.0
40–44	92,825	62.9	35,305	23.9	19,440	13.2	147,565	100.0
45–49	69,890	64.6	24,735	22.9	13,550	12.5	108,175	100.0
50–54	57,520	65.4	19,085	21.7	11,280	12.8	87,885	100.0
55–59	57,465	66.9	17,090	19.9	11,385	13.2	85,945	100.0
60–64	61,155	67.6	16,465	18.2	12,790	14.1	90,405	100.0
65–69	58,370	68.5	13,810	16.2	13,010	15.3	85,185	100.0
70–74	47,480	69.5	9,340	13.7	11,460	16.8	68,275	100.0
75–79	40,335	70.4	6,385	11.1	10,600	18.5	57,320	100.0
80–84	26,520	68.9	3,630	9.4	8,360	21.7	38,510	100.0
85–89	12,945	66.7	1,685	8.7	4,775	24.6	19,405	100.0
90 and older	4,235	54.8	785	10.2	2,715	35.1	7,730	100.0

1. 100% data.

Note: Figures may not add to 100 due to rounding.

Source: Census of Canada 1991, special compilation.

If, while growing in number, non-family households have become essentially one-person households, family households have become mainly one-family households, that is, limited to the members of a single family unit. From 1956 to 1976, these households increased from 80% to 90% of the total number of family households, and virtually maintained that level thereafter (see Table 1.11). From 1951 to 1986, the proportion of multiple-family households decreased and, even more significantly, declined in number (see Table 1.9). All of these facts show the desire of families for greater residential autonomy. In fact, the proportion of families living on their own in their dwelling rose from about 74% in 1956 to about 88% in 1976, and has since remained at this level (see Table 1.12).

TABLE 1.11
ONE-FAMILY HOUSEHOLDS WITHOUT OTHER PERSONS,[1] 1956 TO 1991

Year	One-family households without other persons	Total family households	%
1956	2,759,154	3,464,226	79.6
1961	3,262,610	3,948,935	82.6
1966	3,754,530	4,376,409	85.8
1971	4,285,965	4,928,129	87.0
1976	5,025,820	5,633,945	89.2
1981	5,556,385	6,231,490	89.2
1986	5,988,215	6,634,995	90.3
1991	6,505,520	7,235,225	89.9

1. 100% data.

Source: Census of Canada, 1956 to 1991.

TABLE 1.12
CENSUS FAMILIES LIVING ALONE,[1] 1956 TO 1991

Year	One-family households without other persons	Census families	%
1956	2,759,154	3,711,500	74.3
1961	3,262,610	4,147,444	78.7
1966	3,754,530	4,526,266	82.9
1971	4,285,965	5,070,682	84.5
1976	5,025,820	5,727,895	87.7
1981	5,556,385	6,324,976	87.8
1986	5,988,215	6,734,978	88.9
1991	6,505,520	7,356,168	88.4

1. 100% data.

Source: Census of Canada, 1956 to 1991.

1.2.3 The autonomy of minimal household units

The evolution of households by type since 1951 shows that their composition has become more and more simplified. Family households are less complex today than in the past, generally being limited to the members of a family unit. Most non-family households have become one-person households. Thus, in 1991, nearly 9 in 10 households consisted of either one family or one person. In other words, the household is gradually shrinking to a minimal household unit (Ermisch and Overton 1985). "Minimal household unit" means the smallest unit that can form an independent household, of which there are four types:

a)   an adult with no spouse or dependent children

b)   a lone parent and his or her dependent children

c)   a couple with no dependent children

d)   a couple and their dependent children.

These minimal units are not reported as such in the census data, so the following corresponding household and family census categories are used in this analysis:

a)   non-family persons aged 15 and older

b)   lone-parent families

c)   couples without never-married children at home

d)   couples with never-married children at home.

Two indicators are used to assess the autonomy of minimal units: the proportion of units (defined above) living on their own in their dwelling, and the proportion of units acting as the primary household maintainer. (For more information about the autonomy of these new minimal units, see tables 1.13 to 1.18.) The first indicator measures the greatest degree of autonomy, that is, the total residential autonomy. The second indicator measures a slightly lesser degree of autonomy, where the unit maintains control of its dwelling while perhaps agreeing to share use of it with one or more other units, either out of a sense of responsibility or of necessity. The results presented are based only on 1991 Census data, the results for previous censuses having already been presented by Juby (1992).

For non-family adults, both indicators increase with the respondent's age, at least until the older ages. However, age for age, they vary only slightly by sex (see Figure 1.9 and Appendix 1, Table 5). It is therefore the youngest who tend to live alone least often, and who are least often the primary household maintainer. In contrast, the elderly account for a very large proportion of those who live alone and are the household maintainers. All ages combined, of non-family women, 61% live alone and 74% are the primary household maintainer; the corresponding figures for men are 52% and 67%.

FIGURE 1.9

PROPORTION OF NON-FAMILY MALES AND FEMALES, HOUSEHOLD MAINTAINERS
AND LIVING ALONE, 1991

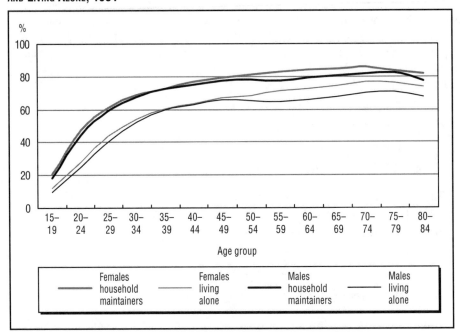

Note: The data for this figure are taken from Table 5 of Appendix 1.

Source: Census of Canada, 1991, special tabulations; 1991 Public Use Microdata File.

The values for the indicators are much higher for couples and depend little on the spouses' age, at least if very young couples are excluded. Thus, the proportion of families forming a one-family household without other persons is about 90% regardless of whether the couple is married or has never-married children at home (see Table 1.13). When the age of the woman or her spouse is taken into account, the differences found between most couples are minimal; only very young couples clearly stand apart from the others with respect to forming a one-family household without other persons. Further, it appears that some of these very young couples do not help pay rent, probably because they are living with their parents (see tables 1.15 and 1.16). Also, 96.9% of two-spouse families are families that include the primary household maintainer.

TABLE 1.13

PROPORTION OF SPOUSES LIVING IN A ONE-FAMILY HOUSEHOLD WITHOUT OTHER PERSONS, BY AGE, SEX AND FAMILY STATUS,[1] 1991

| Age group | Couples without never-married children | | | | Couples with never-married children | | | |
| | Now married | | Living common law | | Now married | | Living common law | |
	Wife	Husband	Female partner	Male partner	Wife	Husband	Female partner	Male partner
				%				
15–19	75.3	84.0[2]	82.7	74.8	72.7[2]	77.8[2]	79.4	76.9[2]
20–24	83.6	83.6	88.6	87.5	84.7	84.0	88.6	84.6
25–29	89.0	87.6	90.9	91.3	90.7	89.5	91.3	89.4
30–34	89.0	88.6	92.6	92.0	91.6	91.2	91.4	91.9
35–39	88.6	88.5	93.8	93.3	91.5	91.5	92.0	91.3
40–44	89.3	88.9	90.7	92.4	90.6	91.3	90.3	91.3
45–49	89.6	89.7	91.4	93.5	89.5	91.0	87.8	90.9
50–54	89.5	89.3	92.2	91.8	88.3	88.1	87.6	90.8
55–59	90.0	89.7	91.8	91.9	87.3	87.3	71.0[2]	86.0
60–64	90.5	90.7	93.3	93.4	85.7	87.3	85.7[2]	83.8[2]
65–69	92.1	91.5	95.2	92.1	88.0	86.1	—	87.9[2]
70–74	93.4	92.9	94.5	96.8	85.7	87.8	—	86.7[2]
75–79	93.1	92.6	91.8[2]	95.4[2]	89.3	83.7	—	—
80–84	92.4	92.6	93.8[2]	97.7[2]	90.5[2]	85.8	—	—
85 and older	92.5	90.6	—	—	85.7[2]	80.9[2]	—	—
All ages	**90.3**	**90.3**	**90.7**	**91.3**	**90.2**	**90.2**	**90.3**	**90.2**

— Percentage omitted (fewer than 10 cases in the sample).

1. The data are from a 3% sample.

2. Percentage calculated from a sample of fewer than 100 cases.

Source: Census of Canada, 1991, Individual Public Use Microdata Files.

TABLE 1.14

PROPORTION OF LONE PARENTS LIVING IN A ONE-FAMILY HOUSEHOLD WITHOUT OTHER PERSONS,
BY AGE,[1] 1991

Age group	Lone mothers	Lone fathers
	%	%
15–19	80	—
20–24	79	26[2]
25–29	78	42
30–34	80	52
35–39	81	66
40–44	83	74
45–49	81	74
50–54	79	73
55–59	78	71
60–64	77	72
65–69	80	69
70–74	79	70
75–79	85	74
80–84	87	77[2]
85 and older	87	75[2]
All ages	**80**	**68**

— Percentage omitted (fewer than 10 cases in the sample).
1. The data are from a 3% sample.
2. Percentage calculated from a sample of fewer than 100 cases.
Source: Census of Canada, 1991, Individual Public Use Microdata Files.

TABLE 1.15

HUSBANDS OR COMMON-LAW PARTNERS, BY TYPE OF CENSUS FAMILY AND AGE,[1] 1991

Age group	Families with primary household maintainer	Families with other household maintainer	Families with no maintainer	Total census families
	Number			
15–24	157,550	2,455	15,240	**175,245**
25–34	1,375,295	9,850	52,760	**1,437,905**
35–44	1,649,255	4,415	30,185	**1,683,855**
45–54	1,183,090	1,850	19,945	**1,204,885**
55–64	926,070	2,395	22,850	**951,315**
65 and older	911,905	3,035	33,310	**948,250**
All ages	**6,203,165**	**24,000**	**174,290**	**6,401,455**
	%			
15–24	89.9	1.4	8.7	**100.0**
25–34	95.6	0.7	3.7	**100.0**
35–44	97.9	0.3	1.8	**100.0**
45–54	98.2	0.2	1.7	**100.0**
55–64	97.3	0.3	2.4	**100.0**
65 and older	96.2	0.3	3.5	**100.0**
All ages	**96.9**	**0.4**	**2.7**	**100.0**

1. 100% data.
Note: Percentages may not add to 100 due to rounding.
Source: Census of Canada, 1991.

TABLE 1.16

WIVES OR COMMON-LAW PARTNERS, BY TYPE OF CENSUS FAMILY AND AGE,[1] 1991

Age group	Families with primary household maintainer	Families with other maintainer	Families without maintainer	Total census families
	Number			
15–24	322,635	4,700	26,400	353,735
25–34	1,625,150	9,370	51,705	1,686,225
35–44	1,649,385	3,380	27,535	1,680,300
45–54	1,099,995	1,920	20,215	1,122,130
55–64	821,020	2,485	23,395	846,900
65 and older	684,975	2,140	25,045	712,160
All ages	**6,203,160**	**24,000**	**174,295**	**6,401,455**
	%			
15–24	91.2	1.3	7.5	100.0
25–34	96.4	0.6	3.1	100.0
35–44	98.2	0.2	1.6	100.0
45–54	98.0	0.2	1.8	100.0
55–64	96.9	0.3	2.8	100.0
65 and older	96.2	0.3	3.5	100.0
All ages	**96.9**	**0.4**	**2.7**	**100.0**

1. 100% data.

Note: Percentages may not add to 100 due to rounding.

Source: Census of Canada, 1991.

Lone-parent families form one-family households with no other persons less often than do other families. Just 68% of male lone-parent families and 80% of female lone-parent families form this type of household (see Table 1.14). While the proportion of lone-parent families living alone depends on the parent's sex, it varies little with the parent's age, at least when families where the parent is very young are excluded. The difference between male and female lone-parent families disappears almost entirely when their degree of autonomy is assessed according to the proportion of maintainers (see tables 1.17 and 1.18). The proportion of primary maintainer families is about 91% among the former and about 93% among the latter. These proportions are closer to those of other families than the differences observed in the proportions of families living alone would seem to suggest.

TABLE 1.17
LONE MOTHERS, BY TYPE OF CENSUS FAMILY AND AGE,[1] 1991

Age group	Families with primary household maintainer	Families with other maintainer	Families without maintainer	Total census families
		Number		
15–24	44,820	1,130	5,040	**50,990**
25–34	173,340	3,730	15,410	**192,480**
35–44	219,370	3,200	11,915	**234,485**
45–54	128,250	1,350	5,645	**135,245**
55–64	75,715	1,050	4,220	**80,985**
65 and older	86,810	930	4,555	**92,295**
All ages	728,305	11,390	46,785	786,480
		%		
15–24	87.9	2.2	9.9	**100.0**
25–34	90.1	1.9	8.0	**100.0**
35–44	93.6	1.4	5.1	**100.0**
45–54	94.8	1.0	4.2	**100.0**
55–64	93.5	1.3	5.2	**100.0**
65 and older	94.1	1.0	4.9	**100.0**
All ages	**92.6**	**1.4**	**5.9**	**100.0**

1. 100% data.
Note: Percentages may not add to 100 due to rounding.
Source: Census of Canada, 1991.

TABLE 1.18
LONE FATHERS, BY TYPE OF CENSUS FAMILY AND AGE,[1] 1991

Age group	Families with primary household maintainer	Families with other maintainer	Families without maintainer	Total census families
		Number		
15–24	1,560	115	785	**2,460**
25–34	17,710	720	3,390	**21,820**
35–44	48,020	775	3,895	**52,690**
45–54	41,815	360	1,935	**44,110**
55–64	22,705	230	1,180	**24,115**
65 and older	21,555	235	1,250	**23,040**
All ages	153,365	2,435	12,435	168,235
		%		
15–24	63.4	4.7	31.9	**100.0**
25–34	81.2	3.3	15.5	**100.0**
35–44	91.1	1.5	7.4	**100.0**
45–54	94.8	0.8	4.4	**100.0**
55–64	94.2	1.0	4.9	**100.0**
65 and older	93.6	1.0	5.4	**100.0**
All ages	**91.2**	**1.4**	**7.4**	**100.0**

1. 100% data.
Note: Percentages may not add to 100 due to rounding.
Source: Census of Canada, 1991.

1.3   CONCLUSION

The evolution of the population since 1951 was marked by a net slowing of demographic growth, at least until 1986. The decline in fertility that began in the mid-1960s led to a reduction in the excess of births over deaths. The generations that peaked in size at the end of the post-war baby boom were succeeded by little generations so that, over time, the base of the age pyramid shrank. The number and proportion of elderly grew, and since 1971 the Canadian population has crossed the aging population threshold. This aging, already well underway, is expected to continue in the coming decades and will peak when the last of the baby boomers reach retirement age.

The number of private households nearly tripled in 40 years, from 3.4 million in 1951 to 10.0 million in 1991. Still rare in the 1950s, the number of one-person households increased with technological progress, rising incomes and, no doubt, a growing desire for residential autonomy. As technology has advanced, living alone has become more feasible; dwellings are no longer units cut off from the outside world, but cells connected to service and communication networks. Housework has become less demanding and is no longer incompatible with activity outside the home. Higher incomes have made living alone more affordable, giving young adults and the elderly the resources to pay for their own housing and related services. In addition, the enhanced value of personal autonomy, the need for privacy, and a wider gap between the lifestyles of different generations have probably all played a role. Households of two or more people have remained familial in nature throughout this period, but have increasingly become strictly one-family households. Families also have more residential autonomy, and there has been a definite decrease in the incidence of multiple-family and one-family households that include non-family persons.

In short, more than ever, family households consist of only the members of the family unit and, since today this unit is quite small, large households have become uncommon. As a result of these many changes, the average number of persons per household has dropped from 4.0 to 2.7 over a period of 40 years.

While censuses show a growing tendency of families and non-family persons to live on their own, they provide no information about the relationships that surround these persons. The interpersonal links revealed by censuses merely reveal the relationships that exist between household members. Of these relationships, marital and filial bonds are the most common, and define these family units. The next chapter examines the recent evolution of these relationships.

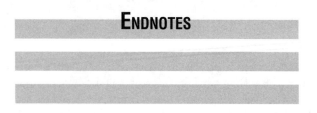

ENDNOTES

1. The terms "never-married" and "single" are used interchangeably in this publication.

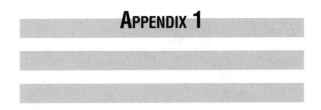

APPENDIX 1

TABLE 1A

POPULATION DISTRIBUTION, BY AGE AND SEX, 1951

Age group	Women	Proportion per 100,000	Men	Proportion per 100,000
Under age 5	843,046	6,018	879,063	6,275
5–9	683,952	4,882	713,873	5,096
10–14	555,661	3,966	575,122	4,105
15–19	525,792	3,753	532,180	3,799
20–24	551,106	3,934	537,535	3,837
25–29	578,403	4,129	552,812	3,946
30–34	530,177	3,784	512,557	3,659
35–39	495,562	3,537	503,571	3,595
40–44	422,767	3,018	445,800	3,182
45–49	356,971	2,548	387,708	2,767
50–54	322,195	2,300	340,461	2,430
55–59	278,126	1,985	292,564	2,088
60–64	241,828	1,726	264,324	1,887
65–69	205,421	1,466	228,076	1,628
70–74	154,674	1,104	160,398	1,145
75–79	94,261	673	94,130	672
80–84	50,828	363	45,963	328
85–89	22,060	157	17,539	125
90–94	5,795	41	4,158	30
95–99	1,932	14	1,039	7
All ages	**6,920,556**		**7,088,873**	

Source: Census of Canada, 1951.

POPULATION DISTRIBUTION, BY AGE AND SEX, 1971

Age group	Women	Proportion per 100,000	Men	Proportion per 100,000
Under age 5	886,555	4,110	929,605	4,310
5–9	1,101,575	5,107	1,152,430	5,343
10–14	1,129,290	5,236	1,181,450	5,478
15–19	1,039,915	4,821	1,074,430	4,982
20–24	947,630	4,394	941,775	4,366
25–29	783,410	3,632	800,710	3,712
30–34	644,550	2,988	660,875	3,064
35–39	618,820	2,869	645,045	2,991
40–44	621,760	2,883	640,765	2,971
45–49	625,630	2,901	613,415	2,844
50–54	533,640	2,474	518,895	2,406
55–59	482,315	2,236	472,415	2,190
60–64	395,320	1,833	381,690	1,770
65–69	323,910	1,502	296,050	1,373
70–74	251,800	1,167	205,575	953
75–79	185,515	860	139,995	649
80–84	118,490	549	85,680	397
85–89	59,385	275	40,625	188
90–94	17,580	82	11,152	52
95–99	5,860	27	2,788	13
All ages	**10,772,945**		**10,795,370**	

Source: Census of Canada, 1971.

TABLE 1C
POPULATION DISTRIBUTION, BY AGE AND SEX, 1991

Age group	Women	Proportion per 100,000	Men	Proportion per 100,000
Under age 5	930,735	3,410	975,765	3,575
5–9	929,820	3,406	978,220	3,584
10–14	915,085	3,352	962,925	3,528
15–19	910,230	3,335	958,405	3,511
20–24	976,655	3,578	985,220	3,609
25–29	1,192,965	4,370	1,182,575	4,332
30–34	1,253,360	4,592	1,237,685	4,534
35–39	1,150,810	4,216	1,133,670	4,153
40–44	1,044,715	3,827	1,042,185	3,818
45–49	816,580	2,991	824,200	3,019
50–54	662,175	2,426	663,285	2,430
55–59	614,835	2,252	608,085	2,228
60–64	604,765	2,216	571,940	2,095
65–69	580,665	2,127	492,505	1,804
70–74	462,945	1,696	358,955	1,315
75–79	362,245	1,327	252,530	925
80–84	236,660	867	140,135	513
85–89	128,235	470	61,250	224
90–94	51,593	189	20,040	73
95–99	17,198	63	5,010	18
All ages	**13,842,280**		**13,454,580**	

Source: Census of Canada, 1991.

TABLE 2

AVERAGE NUMBER OF PERSONS PER PRIVATE HOUSEHOLD, BY AGE AND SEX OF PRIMARY HOUSEHOLD MAINTAINER,[1] 1991

	Age of primary household maintainer							
	15–24	25–34	35–44	45–54	55–64	65–74	Aged 75 and older	All ages
Female primary household maintainers								
Number of persons, of all ages	449,650	1,552,875	1,540,490	862,575	614,870	608,865	492,055	**6,121,395**
Number of persons under age 15	90,105	521,965	438,500	68,200	19,955	12,305	4,480	**1,155,510**
Number of persons aged 15 and older	359,545	1,030,910	1,101,990	794,375	594,915	596,560	487,575	**4,965,870**
Number of households	219,190	650,025	580,790	384,810	355,250	434,025	392,625	**3,016,715**
Average number of persons per household	2.05	2.39	2.65	2.24	1.73	1.40	1.25	**2.03**
Average number of persons under age 15	0.41	0.80	0.76	0.18	0.06	0.03	0.01	**0.38**
Average number of persons aged 15 and older	1.64	1.59	1.90	2.06	1.67	1.37	1.24	**1.65**
Male primary household maintainers								
Number of persons all ages	532,220	4,586,145	6,391,160	4,200,200	2,622,020	1,581,030	697,690	**20,610,465**
Number of persons under age 15	64,670	1,533,595	2,266,650	527,265	85,950	23,435	7,350	**4,508,915**
Number of persons aged 15 and older	467,550	3,052,550	4,124,510	3,672,935	2,536,070	1,557,595	690,340	**16,101,550**
Number of households	247,035	1,569,970	1,782,230	1,281,605	1,024,700	734,230	361,785	**7,001,555**
Average number of persons per household	2.15	2.92	3.59	3.28	2.56	2.15	1.93	**2.94**
Average number of persons under age 15	0.26	0.98	1.27	0.41	0.08	0.03	0.02	**0.64**
Average number of persons aged 15 and older	1.89	1.94	2.31	2.87	2.47	2.12	1.91	**2.30**

1. 100% data.

Source: Census of Canada, 1991, special tabulations.

TABLE 3

UNATTACHED INDIVIDUALS, BY AGE AND SEX,[1] 1991

| | | Unattached individuals | | | | | |
| Age group | Persons in private households | Living alone | | Not living alone | | Total | |
	Number	Number	%	Number	%	Number	%
Total, females	**13,545,215**	**1,326,870**	**9.8**	**449,825**	**3.3**	**1,776,695**	**13.1**
Under age 5	926,260	0	0.0	8,375	0.9	8,375	0.9
5–9	925,710	0	0.0	7,480	0.8	7,480	0.8
10–14	910,665	0	0.0	8,685	1.0	8,685	1.0
15–19	896,985	8,315	0.9	38,060	4.2	46,375	5.2
20–24	963,490	55,820	5.8	103,710	10.8	159,530	16.6
25–29	1,181,280	92,100	7.8	84,315	7.1	176,415	14.9
30–34	1,243,000	84,990	6.8	48,975	3.9	133,965	10.8
35–39	1,142,850	71,420	6.2	30,635	2.7	102,055	8.9
40–44	1,037,370	66,750	6.4	23,935	2.3	90,685	8.7
45–49	809,705	63,760	7.9	18,195	2.2	81,955	10.1
50–54	655,355	65,070	9.9	14,570	2.2	79,640	12.2
55–59	607,230	80,510	13.3	12,755	2.1	93,265	15.4
60–64	595,210	109,920	18.5	12,730	2.1	122,650	20.6
65–69	566,235	148,955	26.3	11,855	2.1	160,810	28.4
70–74	443,025	160,550	36.2	9,335	2.1	169,885	38.3
75–79	330,945	153,055	46.2	7,340	2.2	160,395	48.5
80–84	193,685	103,870	53.6	4,880	2.5	108,750	56.1
85–89	85,080	47,350	55.7	2,685	3.2	50,035	58.8
Aged 90 and older	31,135	14,440	46.4	1,320	4.2	15,760	50.6
Total, males	**13,186,645**	**970,190**	**7.4**	**599,820**	**4.5**	**1,570,010**	**11.9**
Under age 5	970,785	0	0.0	8,770	0.9	8,770	0.9
5–9	973,625	0	0.0	7,975	0.8	7,975	0.8
10–14	957,410	0	0.0	9,265	1.0	9,265	1.0
15–19	938,265	6,575	0.7	33,645	3.6	40,220	4.3
20–24	958,015	59,735	6.2	124,570	13.0	184,305	19.2
25–29	1,155,445	128,675	11.1	134,815	11.7	263,490	22.8
30–34	1,214,455	133,755	11.0	81,905	6.7	215,660	17.8
35–39	1,116,640	112,700	10.1	50,560	4.5	163,260	14.6
40–44	1,027,810	92,825	9.0	35,305	3.4	128,130	12.5
45–49	812,665	69,890	8.6	24,735	3.0	94,625	11.6
50–54	653,385	57,520	8.8	19,085	2.9	76,605	11.7
55–59	598,085	57,465	9.6	17,090	2.9	74,555	12.5
60–64	560,940	61,155	10.9	16,465	2.9	77,620	13.8
65–69	479,925	58,370	12.2	13,810	2.9	72,180	15.0
70–74	345,955	47,480	13.7	9,340	2.7	56,820	16.4
75–79	236,895	40,335	17.0	6,385	2.7	46,720	19.7
80–84	123,365	26,520	21.5	3,630	2.9	30,150	24.4
85–89	47,385	12,945	27.3	1,685	3.6	14,630	30.9
Aged 90 and older	15,590	4,235	27.2	785	5.0	5,020	32.2

1. 100% data.

Source: Census of Canada, 1991, special tabulations.

TABLE 4
NON-FAMILY PERSONS, BY AGE AND SEX, [1] 1991

Age group	Persons in private households	Persons living alone		Non-family persons						
				Living with non-relatives		Living with relatives		Total, non-family persons		
	Number	Number	%	Number	%	Number	%	Number	%
Total, females	**13,545,215**	**1,326,870**	**9.8**	**449,825**	**3.3**	**458,050**	**3.4**	**2,234,750**	**16.5**
Under age 5	926,260	0	0.0	8,375	0.9	20 615	2.2	28 985	3.1
5–9	925,710	0	0.0	7,480	0.8	11,375	1.2	18,850	2.0
10–14	910,665	0	0.0	8,685	1.0	10,080	1.1	18,760	2.1
15–19	896,985	8,315	0.9	38,060	4.2	23,580	2.6	69,960	7.8
20–24	963,490	55,820	5.8	103,710	10.8	40,340	4.2	199,865	20.7
25–29	1,181,280	92,100	7.8	84,315	7.1	35,850	3.0	212,265	18.0
30–34	1,243,000	84,990	6.8	48,975	3.9	23,640	1.9	157,615	12.7
35–39	1,142,850	71,420	6.2	30,635	2.7	16,345	1.4	118,405	10.4
40–44	1,037,370	66,750	6.4	23,935	2.3	14,550	1.4	105,230	10.1
45–49	809,705	63,760	7.9	18,195	2.2	14,400	1.8	96,355	11.9
50–54	655,355	65,070	9.9	14,570	2.2	16,350	2.5	95,990	14.6
55–59	607,230	80,510	13.3	12,755	2.1	21,725	3.6	114,995	18.9
60–64	595,210	109,920	18.5	12,730	2.1	30,690	5.2	153,345	25.8
65–69	566,235	148,955	26.3	11,855	2.1	38,900	6.9	199,710	35.3
70–74	443,025	160,550	36.2	9,335	2.1	39,865	9.0	209,750	47.3
75–79	330,945	153,055	46.2	7,340	2.2	39,975	12.1	200,370	60.5
80–84	193,685	103,870	53.6	4,880	2.5	31,460	16.2	140,215	72.4
85–89	85,080	47,350	55.7	2,685	3.2	18,710	22.0	68,745	80.8
Aged 90 and over	31,135	14,440	46.4	1,320	4.2	9,580	30.8	25,335	81.4

TABLE 4 (CONTINUED)

NON-FAMILY PERSONS, BY AGE AND SEX,[1] 1991

Age group	Persons in private households	Persons living alone		Non-family persons				Total, non-family persons	
				Living with non-relatives		Living with relatives			
	Number	Number	%	Number	%	Number	%	Number	%
Total, males	**13,186,645**	**970,190**	**7.4**	**599,820**	**4.5**	**368,740**	**2.8**	**1,938,745**	**14.7**
Under age 5	970,785	0	0.0	8,770	0.9	21,845	2.3	30,615	3.2
5–9	973,625	0	0.0	7,975	0.8	12,235	1.3	20,215	2.1
10–14	957,410	0	0.0	9,265	1.0	10,800	1.1	20,065	2.1
15–19	938,265	6,575	0.7	33,645	3.6	26,260	2.8	66,485	7.1
20–24	958,015	59,735	6.2	124,570	13.0	52,415	5.5	236,720	24.7
25–29	1,155,445	128,675	11.1	134,815	11.7	56,350	4.9	319,840	27.7
30–34	1,214,455	133,755	11.0	81,905	6.7	42,120	3.5	257,780	21.2
35–39	1,116,640	112,700	10.1	50,560	4.5	27,360	2.5	190,615	17.1
40–44	1,027,810	92,825	9.0	35,305	3.4	19,440	1.9	147,565	14.4
45–49	812,665	69,890	8.6	24,735	3.0	13,550	1.7	108,175	13.3
50–54	653,385	57,520	8.8	19,085	2.9	11,280	1.7	87,885	13.5
55–59	598,085	57,465	9.6	17,090	2.9	11,385	1.9	85,945	14.4
60–64	560,940	61,155	10.9	16,465	2.9	12,790	2.3	90,405	16.1
65–69	479,925	58,370	12.2	13,810	2.9	13,010	2.7	85,185	17.7
70–74	345,955	47,480	13.7	9,340	2.7	11,460	3.3	68,275	19.7
75–79	236,895	40,335	17.0	6,385	2.7	10,600	4.5	57,320	24.2
80–84	123,365	26,520	21.5	3,630	2.9	8,360	6.8	38,510	31.2
85–89	47,385	12,945	27.3	1,685	3.6	4,775	10.1	19,405	41.0
Aged 90 and older	15,590	4,235	27.2	785	5.0	2,715	17.4	7,730	49.6

1. 100% data.

Source: Census of Canada, 1991, special tabulations.

TABLE 5

PROPORTION OF NON-FAMILY MALES, BY AGE, 1991

Age group	Women living alone	Men living alone	Female primary household maintainers	Male primary household maintainers
15–19	12.1	10.0	20.6	18.3
20–24	28.3	24.7	47.5	44.7
25–29	43.6	40.3	61.0	59.2
30–34	54.6	52.3	68.8	67.9
35–39	60.2	59.6	72.7	72.3
40–44	63.7	62.5	77.0	75.1
45–49	67.3	66.1	79.5	77.7
50–54	68.3	65.5	80.8	77.9
55–59	71.1	64.5	82.8	77.4
60–64	72.5	65.9	84.3	79.1
65–69	74.5	67.8	85.0	80.6
70–74	77.1	70.2	85.9	81.9
75–79	76.1	70.9	83.8	82.6
80–84	74.1	67.4	81.5	77.6
Aged 85 and older	63.6	62.6	71.4	72.0

Source: Census of Canada, 1991, Individual Public Use Microdata Files.

CHAPTER

2

THE EVOLUTION OF CENSUS
FAMILIES FROM 1971 TO 1991

YVES PÉRON

This chapter is devoted to the evolution of the number, size and type of census families from 1971 to 1991. Recall that a census family is a group of two or more persons who live in the same dwelling and form a family unit or "nuclear family." Most families fall into the standard concept of family, consisting of a husband and wife, who are either married or living common law, and their never-married (single) children who live with them. Next in number come married or common-law couples with no never-married children at home, either because neither spouse has ever had children or because the children have married or left home. Finally, least common are families that consist of one parent with no spouse and with never-married children living at home.

In this chapter, a family that consists of a couple is termed a "husband–wife family," regardless of the nature of the bond uniting them; a family consisting of just one parent is termed a "lone-parent family," even though, in most cases, the absent parent is still living.

The chapter begins with a review of the evolution of nuptial, divorce and fertility indicators to highlight the changes in family behaviour of Canadian men and women in the 1970s and 1980s. It then looks at trends in conjugal life, lone parenthood and the situation of "non-family" persons since the 1971 Census. The third part of the chapter is a very general discussion of the evolution of family type, that is, of the distribution of families among married-couple families, families of common-law couples, and lone-parent families. The last two sections are devoted to husband–wife families and lone-parent families.

In the study of husband–wife families, the increase in the number of families for each intercensal period is analysed according to the evolution by size and age composition of the population, as well as variations in the incidence of people living together as husband and wife. Changes in the distribution of families by size are then described, taking into account the woman's age and her past fertility or infertility. Finally, families of common-law couples are compared with families of married couples.

The section devoted to lone-parent families first divides these families by the sex of the lone parent, then explores the family characteristics of each gender. The increase in the number of families per intercensal period is analysed according to population development and the incidence of lone parenthood. Changes in family size are also described, taking into account the age of the lone parent. Finally, the diversity of the families enumerated in 1991 is shown by an examination of their distribution by marital status of the lone parent, the number of children they have had, and the age of the oldest child at home.

It should be noted that some family statuses couldn't be determined from the census data gathered. For example, a single person with children who lives with his or her parents cannot be identified as a lone parent unless he or she heads the list of household members. Similarly, a person with no spouse who occasionally has custody of his or her children cannot be considered a lone parent if the children are enumerated as residing with the other parent. Finally, a blended family cannot be distinguished from a husband–wife family unless the children's parentage has been clearly indicated. Chapters 3, 4 and 5 provide more information on the incidence of these situations.

2.1   BEHAVIOURAL CHANGES

2.1.1 The marriage crisis

About 30 years ago, marriage was very popular; most couples married to start a family of their own. Society disapproved so strongly of divorce that most children were born to, and grew up with, married parents. Thus, most nuclear families consisted of a married couple, or a married couple and their children. In less than three decades, that has all changed. A great many couples now live common-law before marrying or have no intention of ever marrying. Many children are born outside of marriage; many others, still quite young, see their parents divorce. This section presents some indicators of this current "marriage crisis."

One of the first indicators is the drop in the yearly incidence of first marriages, which is readily apparent from the evolution of the total marriage rates of singles (see Table 2.1 and Figure 2.1). Established using the total fertility rates model, these marriage rates offset the effects of changes in size and age composition of the population. They do this by providing the number of marriages by adding the marriage rates of the those aged 15 to 49 (for 1,000 men or 1,000 women). In the 1950s, there was an overabundance of marriages, because singles tended to marry at an increasingly early age, such that the yearly rates nearly always exceeded the maximum amount observable within a generation, that is, 1,000. When the age at the time of marriage stabilized in the 1960s, the female rates came closer to the generational marriage rate, that is, between 900 and 950 first marriages per 1,000 before age 50. In contrast, the male rates exceeded 1,000 in the latter half of the decade, probably because the first generations of female baby boomers had just arrived on the marriage market.[1] In 1973, marriages began to decline, and did so very quickly; within five years, the rates had already fallen below 700 marriages per 1,000 men or 1,000 women. This sharp decline can be attributed to the many singles who had decided to live common law and therefore delay marriage for several months, years or forever. And, thereafter, common-law unions continued to gain ground among singles, as either a prelude to, or substitute for, marriage. As people entered their first marriage ever later and with declining frequency, the annual marriage rates remained exceptionally low, despite a slight recovery between 1986 and 1990.

TABLE 2.1
TOTAL MARRIAGE RATE (TMR) OF SINGLE PERSONS, 1951 TO 1993

Year	Total marriage rate per 1,000 women	Total marriage rate per 1,000 men
1951	1,080	1,088
1952	1,067	1,060
1953	1,085	1,069
1954	1,040	1,018
1955	999	977
1956	1,065	1,042
1957	1,045	1,022
1958	1,007	997
1959	999	998
1960	965	980
1961	932	965
1962	912	961
1963	890	951
1964	903	969
1965	910	993
1966	928	1,016
1967	941	1,024
1968	931	1,005
1969	929	993
1970	921	977
1971	912	954
1972	929	968
1973	889	925
1974	844	871
1975	812	835
1976	712	716
1977	698	700
1978	675	675
1979	670	668
1980	666	661
1981	647	640
1982	635	620
1983	614	595
1984	615	588
1985	614	581
1986	585	552
1987	594	554
1988	620	574
1989	630	585
1990	631	582
1991	588	543
1992	561	518
1993	544	504

Source: Statistics Canada, Demography Division. Special compilation.

FIGURE 2.1

TOTAL MARRIAGE RATE (TMR) OF SINGLES, 1951 TO 1993

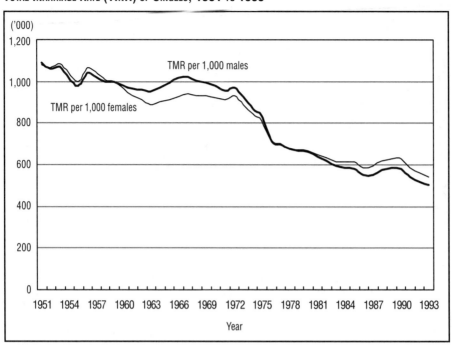

Note: The data for this figure are taken from Table 2.1.

Source: Statistics Canada, Demography Division. Special compilation.

When we look at how the incidence of single status has evolved among young people, we see that recent generations are marrying later (see Table 2.2). Between the 1951 and 1961 censuses, the proportion of singles under age 35 declined appreciably to far lower levels than had been previously reported. Yet, the late 1950s mark the end of this shift in nuptiality, which, for some 20 years, had led Canadians born during the war and inter-war years to give up the practice of putting off marriage and instead marry at young ages (Gee 1980; Dumas and Péron 1992). According to the proportions of singles observed in 1966 and 1971, the new marriage rate model was characterized by especially early and frequent marriages, as only about 44% of women aged 20 to 24, 15% of women aged 25 to 29, and 9% of women aged 30 to 34 were single. Men were also marrying earlier; slightly more than 25% of them were single between ages 25 and 29, and 13% between ages 30 and 34 (1971 Census). Early marriage, once common practice among people born in the inter-war or war years, was quickly abandoned by those born after the war. Initially, the increase in age at marriage was greater in large cities than in small towns and rural areas; greater among educated women than among those with little schooling; and, finally, greater among Catholics than among those of other faiths (Rao 1989a). The data published in the 1976, 1981 and 1986 censuses do not reflect the resulting increase in the number of singles, since singles living common law were included in the category of married persons. These data have therefore been replaced in Table 2.2 by estimates for 1981 and 1986. This table shows that the rise of single life was especially rapid and significant at the youngest ages. According to the 1991 Census, 79% of women aged 20 to 24, 42% of those aged 25 to 29, and 23% of those aged 30 to 34 were single. The proportions were even higher among men: 91% of those aged 20 to 24, 59% of those aged 25 to 29, and 33% of those aged 30 to 34.

TABLE 2.2
PROPORTION OF SINGLE PERSONS, BY AGE, 1951 TO 1991

	Male			Female		
Year	20–24	25–29	30–34	20–24	25–29	30–34
	%			%		
1951	74.4	35.1	19.6	48.5	20.7	13.8
1956	72.2	33.9	18.7	44.3	18.2	11.6
1961	69.5	29.6	17.4	40.5	15.4	10.6
1966	70.0	27.4	15.1	44.2	14.9	9.3
1971	67.6	25.6	13.3	43.5	15.4	9.1
1976	67.7	27.0	13.1	45.3	16.3	9.1
1981	78.7	38.1	17.6	59.6	24.5	12.2
1986	86.2	48.8	24.8	70.7	33.5	16.9
1991	90.6	58.6	33.0	78.5	42.0	23.2

Note: The 1981 and 1986 estimates were obtained by adding single persons living common law to the published data.
Source: Stone and Siggner 1974, 43; Census of Canada, 1951 to 1991.

The increase in single status among young people reflects the rise of common-law unions in recent generations. According to Statistics Canada's 1990 General Social Survey, cycle 5: Family and Friends (GSS), people aged 45 to 54 in 1990 were the last generation of Canadians to virtually all be married before living as a couple. As we have seen, these people, born just before or during the Second World War, belong to generations who married young, and in large numbers. The proportion of individuals who began conjugal life in a common-law union did not become significant until the first post-war generations. As did the incidence of single status among the young, the proportion of those living common law then rose rapidly with each subsequent generation: of those aged 30 to 34 at the time of the survey, 36% of women and 40% of men reported their first union had been a common-law union formed before age 30 (Dumas and Péron 1992). The interval between the first union and the first marriage also increased. Again according to the GSS, only 51% of men and 59% of women who had entered their first common-law union in the first half of the 1980s were married when surveyed in 1990.

Another important indication of the marriage crisis is the high divorce rate observed over a 20-year period (see Table 2.3 and Figure 2.2). Until the late 1960s, Canada had escaped the increasing popularity of divorce that had swept the United States. Although the yearly number of divorces more than doubled from 1951 to 1968, it was still below 12,000 at the end of that period. It is true that Canadian laws in effect at the time were especially restrictive, as they allowed divorce only as a sanction when one spouse failed to meet his or her marital obligations, specifically, the obligation of fidelity. And the courts of Quebec and Newfoundland did not yet have the power to grant divorces. It was not until the 1968 *Divorce Act* that divorce became possible in all provinces, and a minimum period of separation of three or five years was accepted as sufficient proof of a marital breakdown. The first to benefit from these new provisions were couples who had already been separated for some years, and they account in large part for the many divorces granted in the first years of the law's application. But couples who, in 1968, had not yet separated could not cite separation as grounds for divorce until after 1971. This time-lag effect of the 1968 law explains the rise in the divorce rate between 1972 and 1976, when the total rate increased from 2,000 to 3,000 divorces per 10,000 marriages. More recently, the 1985 revision of the *Divorce Act* was followed by a further rise in the divorce rate. By greatly simplifying the divorce procedure and reducing to one year the minimum period of separation required for recognition of marital breakdown, the revised legislation led to a significant rise in the number of divorces in the months after it came into force in June 1986. After peaking at nearly 4,800 divorces per 10,000 marriages in 1987, the total rate settled back down to about 3,800 in 1990 and 1991.

TABLE 2.3
NUMBER OF DIVORCES AND TOTAL DIVORCE RATE (TDR), 1969 TO 1991

Year	Number of divorces	Total divorce rate per 10,000 marriages
1969	21,988	1,367
1970	29,239	1,861
1971	29,685	1,881
1972	32,389	2,004
1973	36,704	2,231
1974	45,019	2,670
1975	50,611	2,932
1976	54,209	3,072
1977	55,370	3,063
1978	57,155	3,108
1979	59,474	3,180
1980	62,019	3,276
1981	67,671	3,526
1982	70,436	3,654
1983	68,565	3,519
1984	65,170	3,305
1985	61,976	3,118
1986	78,304	3,908
1987	96,200	4,789
1988	83,507	4,140
1989	80,998	3,996
1990	78,463	3,841
1991	77,020	3,763

Source: Dumas and Bélanger, 1994, 32.

FIGURE 2.2

TOTAL DIVORCE RATE (TDR), 1969 TO 1991

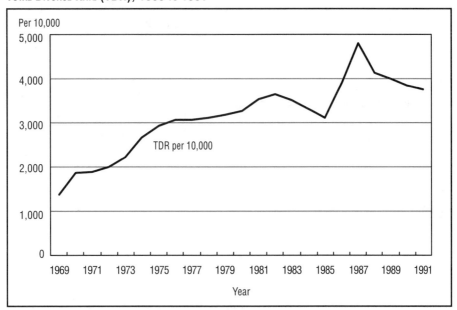

Note: The data for this figure are taken from Table 2.3.
Source: Dumas and Bélanger, 1994, 32.

The values for the total divorce rate since 1976 suggest that between 30% and 40% of couples will divorce before their 26th wedding anniversary. In fact, currently available data show that 29.3% of married couples in the period 1968 to 1969 divorced before completing 25 years of marriage (Dumas and Bélanger 1996). The same proportion (29.0%) of married couples completed 20 years of marriage in the period 1973 to 1974. It can therefore be concluded that more than 30% of these couples will divorce before completing 25 years of marriage. No doubt, the marriages of the most recent cohorts will be even less stable, as their divorce rate already appears to be ahead of most of their predecessors. Thus, of couples married in the period 1983 to 1984, 18.4% were divorced before their tenth anniversary, compared with just 14% of those married in 1973 to 1974 and 11.4% of those married in 1968 to 1969. Given these results, we can estimate that at least one-third of marriages celebrated in the last two decades will end in divorce before their 25th anniversary. As some authors have shown, this average incidence of divorce will be far surpassed by the most vulnerable couples—those who married very young or whose marriage was preceded by a common-law union or a birth outside of marriage (Balakrishnan et al. 1987).

The rate of remarriage among divorced people has evolved quite similarly to the marriage rate among singles (see Table 2.4 and Figure 2.3). In the 1950s and 1960s, the total marriage rate for divorced people almost consistently exceeded 80 remarriages per 100 divorces, among both men and women. The rate even assumed quite paradoxical values in 1969 and 1970, when the 1968 divorce law enabled persons separated for some time to divorce easily, and therefore to remarry, even if this meant simply legalizing an existing common-law union. As they did among single people, marriage rates among divorced people began to decline around 1973 and then drop abruptly. In the 1980s, these rates remained at about 50 remarriages per 100 divorces among women, and at 50 to 58 remarriages per 100 divorces among men. However, as young singles are marrying less than in the past and the number of the newly divorced has risen, divorces now represent a substantial share of newlywed cohorts (19.5% of male newlyweds, and 20.6% of

TABLE 2.4
TOTAL MARRIAGE RATE FOR DIVORCED PERSONS, 1955 TO 1992

Year	Males	Females
	%	
1955	79.9	81.6
1956	84.2	83.3
1957	86.4	84.5
1958	80.1	82.0
1959	84.3	83.8
1960	81.9	81.9
1961	78.8	76.8
1962	80.2	77.6
1963	82.2	81.0
1964	88.9	83.0
1965	89.6	85.9
1966	94.9	87.7
1967	95.2	87.7
1968	91.0	84.3
1969	129.3	120.3
1970	112.8	102.5
1971	95.4	88.2
1972	86.2	78.1
1973	80.6	73.5
1974	77.0	68.9
1975	72.0	64.0
1976	66.7	59.7
1977	63.3	56.9
1978	60.6	54.5
1979	58.6	53.2
1980	57.9	52.2
1981	57.4	52.3
1982	56.2	50.5
1983	55.6	50.6
1984	54.9	49.5
1985	53.1	48.8
1986	49.7	48.4
1987	55.5	53.2
1988	54.3	52.5
1989	51.9	53.1
1990	48.8	46.2
1991	43.0	40.8
1992	41.6	39.6

Note: The total rate was calculated by comparing the number of remarriages in the current year to the average number of divorces in the current year and the five previous years.

Source: Statistics Canada, Demography Division. Special compilation.

FIGURE 2.3

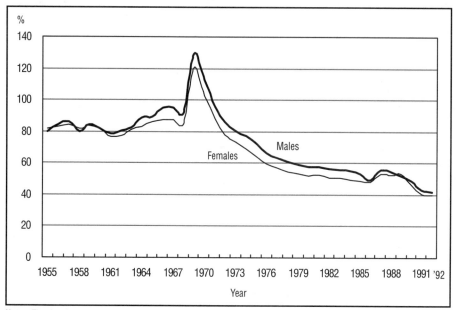

Note: The data for this figure are taken from Table 2.4.

Source: Statistics Canada, Demography Division. Special compilation.

female newlyweds in 1991, compared with about 4% for each in 1961).

Divorced persons are remarrying less often today than they did 20 or 30 years ago because many are living common law. Proportionally, they even outnumber singles living outside the bonds of marriage, regardless of age (see Figure 2.4). According to the 1991 Census, 35% of divorced men and 25% of divorced women were living common law, compared with 13% of single men and 15% of single women (see Table 2.5). But as there are fewer divorced persons than singles, most people (63.6%) living common law are never-married singles.

A final, even more important, indication of the marriage crisis is the very marked increase in recent years in the proportion of births outside of marriage. This proportion, just 11% in 1977, climbed to 27% in 1991, according to the registration statistics. This increase, consisting mainly of children born to single mothers living common law, is a sign that more and more young couples no longer see marriage as a prerequisite for having a family. If this behaviour were to become widespread, it could be the end of marriage. This trend is evident in Quebec, where more than half of first births now occur outside of marriage, and total marriage rates for singles fell in 1993 to 365 marriages per 1,000 women and 324 marriages per 1,000 men.[2]

TABLE 2.5

PROPORTION OF PERSONS LIVING COMMON LAW, BY AGE, SEX AND LEGAL MARITAL STATUS, 1991

Age group	Sex and legal marital status			
	Single men	Single women	Divorced men	Divorced women
			%	
15–19	0.7	2.9	8.6	19.2
20–24	9.8	17.5	27.3	31.9
25–29	21.9	29.0	35.6	37.0
30–34	26.3	29.6	39.7	36.3
35–39	24.2	24.6	40.2	32.7
40–44	19.1	17.6	39.6	28.4
45–49	14.5	13.0	38.4	24.5
50–54	10.9	8.9	34.2	19.0
55–59	8.5	5.8	28.9	12.7
60–64	6.2	3.6	23.0	8.6
65 or older	3.6	1.3	14.6	4.3
All ages	**12.7**	**15.4**	**34.8**	**25.0**

Source: Census of Canada, 1991.

FIGURE 2.4

PROPORTION OF PERSONS LIVING COMMON LAW, BY AGE, SEX AND LEGAL MARITAL STATUS, 1991[1]

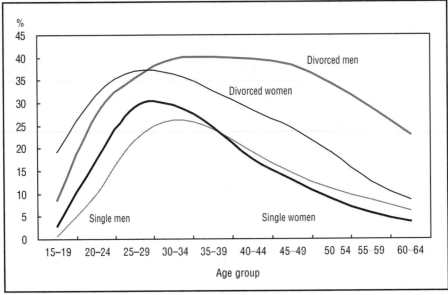

1. 100% data.
Note: The data for this figure are taken from Table 2.5.
Source: Census of Canada, 1991.

2.1.2 The decline in fertility

Another major change in the behaviour of Canadian women and men concerns their fertility. Fertility remained high throughout the 1950s and the first half of the 1960s when the total rate ranged from 3.5 to 3.9 children per woman (see Table 2.6 and Figure 2.5). It then collapsed within a few years, from 3.5 children per woman in 1964 to 2.0 in 1972. This collapse came as more effective methods of birth control became widespread. As early as 1968, 43% of married women in Toronto who reported using birth control had chosen the pill; this figure was 38% for their Quebec counterparts in 1971 (Romaniuc 1984). Couples who had reached, or exceeded, their desired number of children now had more effective means of contraception. This led to a dramatic reduction in the number of children ranking fourth or more in the birth order. Indeed, the number fell from 136,000 in 1964 to 43,000 in 1972, a drop of 93,000 in eight years, compared with a decline of just 11,000 in the number of children ranking first to third in the birth order. Young married couples also adopted modern methods of birth control to delay having children. The interval between marriage and the first birth thus increased from 28.6 months among women married in the period 1961 to 1965, to 36.7 months among women married in 1966 to 1970. For these same women, the interval between the first and second births increased from 35.4 to 43.0 months (Balakrishnan, Lapierre-Adamcyk and Krotki 1993). Thus, a system of managed fertility took root, and held in the 1970s and 1980s when couples who wanted no more children gradually abandoned contraception for a more radical solution, namely, sterilization (Marcil-Gratton and Lapierre-Adamcyk 1989). This management of fertility enables women to limit their offspring to one, two or three children and to avoid early births, which would compromise the completion of their education or their school-to-work transition. Moreover, along with the 20-year decline in fertility, the mother's age on having her first or second child increased significantly (Dumas and Bélanger 1996). In response to women's increasingly older ages at motherhood, the total fertility rate dropped to just 1.6 children per woman until 1987; it recovered marginally to 1.7 children per woman in the early 1990s, still less than half its level during the post-war baby boom.

TABLE 2.6

TOTAL FERTILITY RATE (TFR), 1951 TO 1992

Year	Total fertility rate	Year	Total fertility rate
1951	3.50	1972	2.02
1952	3.64	1973	1.93
1953	3.72	1974	1.88
1954	3.83	1975	1.85
1955	3.83	1976	1.83
1956	3.86	1977	1.81
1957	3.93	1978	1.76
1958	3.88	1979	1.76
1959	3.94	1980	1.75
1960	3.90	1981	1.64
1961	3.84	1982	1.63
1962	3.76	1983	1.62
1963	3.67	1984	1.63
1964	3.50	1985	1.61
1965	3.15	1986	1.59
1966	2.81	1987	1.58
1967	2.60	1988	1.61
1968	2.45	1989	1.66
1969	2.41	1990	1.71
1970	2.33	1991	1.70
1971	2.19	1992	1.71

Source: Dumas and Bélanger, 1994, 39.

FIGURE 2.5

TOTAL FERTILITY RATE, 1951 TO 1992

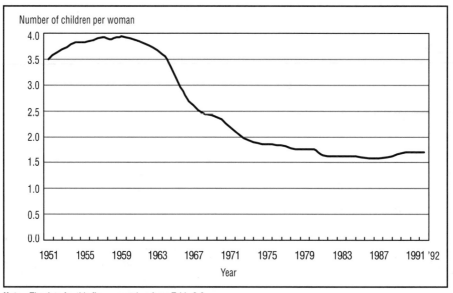

Note: The data for this figure are taken from Table 2.6.

Source: Dumas and Bélanger, 1994, 39.

Table 2.7 and Figure 2.6 show the average number of children born to the women surveyed in 1991. At the time of the 1991 Census, women aged 55 to 69 had had, on average, just over three children, which is hardly surprising considering that most of these women had had their children during the baby boom. Those aged 50 to 54 in 1991 were the first to have had, on average, fewer than three children. Married earlier, and already between the ages of 25 and 29 in 1966, many of these women did not have access to modern forms of birth control until after having one or more children, which explains why their completed fertility[3] was relatively high (2.7 children per woman). In contrast, younger women took advantage of more effective methods of birth control throughout their married lives and had fewer children: on average, 2.2 for women aged 45 to 49 in 1991, and just 2.0 for those aged 40 to 44. A completed fertility of 2.0 children per woman will probably not be reached by the women who were in their thirties when the 1991 Census was taken.

The changes in the average number of children born correspond with equally significant changes in the age of mothers at the birth of their children, according to an analysis of Statistics Canada data gathered during the 1990 GSS. Of the results published by a number of authors, the most interesting concern women's ages at the start and end of their childbearing years (Beaujot et al. 1995). The median age of women at the birth of their first child went from 25.0 in the 1921 to 1930 generations, to 23.9 in the 1931 to 1940 generations, and to 24.2 in the 1941 to 1950 generations. It then rose to 26.4 for women born between 1951 and 1960, and to about 29.1 for women born between 1961 and 1970. As for the median age at the last birth, it dropped from 35.8 among women born between 1921 and 1930, to 31.8 for those born between 1931 and 1940, and to 30.6 for women born between 1941 and 1950. The median age at last birth will likely be 32.2 for women born between 1951 and 1960. These results show us that women in the 1930s and 1940s limited the number of offspring they had, and had these children at earlier ages than their predecessors. Women of more recent generations have adopted a different behaviour, which consists in postponing having their first child until they approach age 30.

TABLE 2.7

AVERAGE NUMBER OF CHILDREN BORN PER WOMAN AGED 15 OR OLDER,[1] BY MARITAL STATUS, 1991

Age group	Never-married women	Ever-married women	All women
15 or older	0.158	2.315	1.815
15–44	0.145	1.628	1.115
15–19	0.027	0.385	0.043
20–24	0.116	0.603	0.288
25–29	0.242	1.087	0.837
30–34	0.348	1.680	1.466
35–39	0.372	1.960	1.793
40–44	0.383	2.102	1.971
45 or older	0.267	3.031	2.861
45–49	0.376	2.356	2.237
50–54	0.376	2.814	2.683
55–59	0.344	3.235	3.084
60–64	0.281	3.386	3.212
65–69	0.230	3.365	3.186
70 or older	0.139	3.181	2.945

1. These data are taken from a 20% sample.
Source: Census of Canada, 1991.

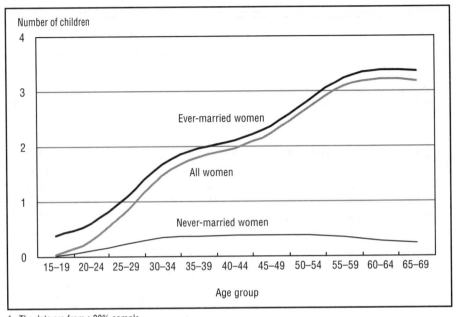

1. The data are from a 20% sample.

Note: The data for this figure are taken from Table 2.7.

Source: Census of Canada, 1991.

One of the consequences of the decline in fertility has been to narrow the differences between sociocultural communities. The 1961 Census records considerable differences in fertility between Catholics and non-Catholics, between francophones and anglophones, between ethnic groups, and so on. Henripin (1972) noted, for example, that Catholic women then aged 50 to 54 had had 4.14 children, while Protestant women in the same age group had had just 2.50 children, and Jewish women had had only 1.87 children. These striking sociocultural differences were still present in the 1971 Census data, but it was already predictable that more personal characteristics, such as education or labour force activity, would have a more decisive impact on the fertility of future generations (Balakrishnan, Ebanks and Grindstaff 1979). The data gathered thereafter have largely borne out this assumption and shown that the differences between sociocultural groups decreased over time. Thus, according to the 1984 Fertility in Canada Survey, Catholics who married between 1966 and 1970 had just 0.16 children more than Protestants (2.31 versus 2.15), while those who married between 1971 and 1975 had had slightly fewer (1.86 versus 1.88). However, as some authors have shown using even more recent data, education continues to play a significant role. According to the 1991 Census, women aged 40 to 44 who had completed elementary school had 2.65 children, those who had completed non-university post-secondary studies had 2.09 children, and those who had completed university had just 1.88 children (Beaujot et al. 1995).

The decline in fertility has been accompanied by a reduction in the size of families. This is clear when we compare the distribution of women by number of children born in several cohorts of completed fertility, that is, cohorts who had reached the end of their childbearing years (see tables 2.8 and 2.9, figures 2.7 and 2.8). In 1991, among women aged 60 to 69, this distribution was still quite dispersed, and the modal size of the family (two children) represented just one-fifth of these women (21.3% of ever-married women, and 20.1% of all women). The distribution is, however, quite clustered among women aged 40 to 49, large families having become uncommon and the modal size of the family (two children) this time corresponding to two-fifths of women (40.9% of ever-married women, and 38.4% of all women). The evolution has therefore been from an aggregate consisting of families of varying sizes to one limited to small families and dominated by the family with two children. The predominance of families with two children is no accident. According to the 1984 Fertility in Canada Survey, half of ever-married 30- to 34-year-old mothers of two children were sterilized, as were two-thirds of their counterparts aged 35 to 39 (Balakrishnan, Lapierre-Adamcyk and Krotki 1993). The family of two children has become the norm for many women of recent generations.

TABLE 2.8

DISTRIBUTION OF WOMEN AGED 40 TO 49, 50 TO 59 AND 60 TO 69, BY NUMBER OF CHILDREN BORN,[1] 1991

	Age group		
	40–49	50–59	60–69
Number of women	1,860,595	1,276,120	1,171,540
Number of children		%	
0	14.9	12.0	14.0
1	13.6	9.3	9.7
2	38.4	24.7	20.1
3	21.4	23.1	18.9
4	7.7	14.6	14.0
5	2.4	7.6	8.7
6 or more	1.7	8.8	14.7
Total	**100.0**	**100.0**	**100.0**

1. These data are taken from a 20% sample.

Note: Percentages may not add to 100 due to rounding.

Source: Census of Canada, 1991.

FIGURE 2.7

DISTRIBUTION OF WOMEN AGED **40** TO **49, 50** TO **59** AND **60** TO **69**, BY NUMBER OF CHILDREN BORN, 1991[1]

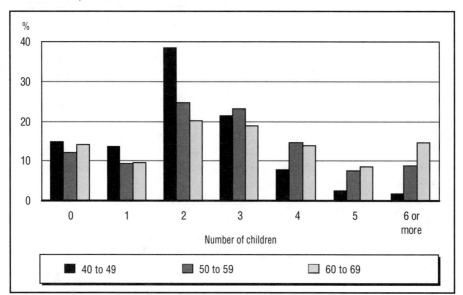

1. The data are taken from a 20% sample.
Note: The data for this figure are taken from Table 2.8.
Source: Census of Canada, 1991.

TABLE **2.9**

DISTRIBUTION OF EVER-MARRIED WOMEN, BY AGE AND NUMBER OF CHILDREN BORN,[1] 1991

	Age group		
	40–49	50–59	60–69
Number of women	1,731,920	1,208,635	1,105,110
Number of children		%	
0	10.1	8.0	9.4
1	13.7	9.4	10.0
2	40.9	25.9	21.3
3	22.8	24.3	19.9
4	8.2	15.3	14.7
5	2.6	8.0	9.2
6 or more	1.7	9.2	15.5
Total	**100.0**	**100.0**	**100.0**

1. These data are taken from a 20% sample.
Note: Percentages may not add to 100 due to rounding.
Source: Census of Canada, 1991.

FIGURE 2.8

DISTRIBUTION OF EVER-MARRIED WOMEN BY AGE AND NUMBER OF CHILDREN BORN, 1991[1]

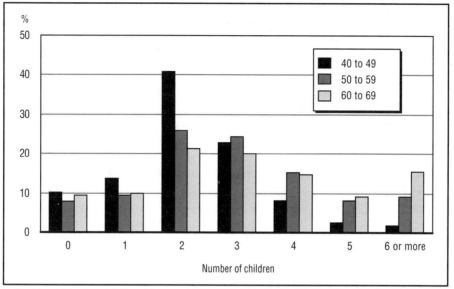

1. The data are taken from a 20% sample.

Note: The data for this figure are taken from Table 2.9.

Source: Census of Canada, 1991.

2.2   THE INCIDENCE OF FAMILY STATUSES

When a census is taken, the members of private households are classified into four groups, according to their family status at the time: husbands and wives; lone fathers and lone mothers; single sons and daughters living at home; and, finally, non-family persons. Husbands and wives are persons living with their spouse or common-law partner. Lone fathers and lone mothers are persons who head a lone-parent family—no spouse is present in the household, but they live with at least one single son or daughter. Single sons or daughters living at home are persons who have never been married and are living with either or both parents. Non-family persons are persons who do not fall into any of the above categories. Every five years, the census provides us with the data necessary to calculate and update the incidence of each status.

The incidences provided in this section have been calculated based on the Public Use Microdata File on Individuals (1990 GSS) excluding data for members of collective households and households outside Canada. The results show that, due to the changes that have occurred in union formation and dissolution, the trends observed before 1971 have been reversed (Wargon 1979a). There has been a decline in the popularity of marriage among young adults, an increase in lone parenthood among middle-aged adults, and an increase in the proportion of non-family persons among those under age 55.

2.2.1 The declining popularity of marriage among young adults

According to the information contained in the Public Use Microdata File on Individuals (1990 GSS), the proportion of husbands and wives among private household members has declined steadily among young people since the 1971 Census (see Table 2.10, and figures 2.9 and 2.10). The most marked declines were for the youngest age groups. Thus, in 20 years, the proportion of wives went from more than half (53.7%) to just one-third (33.1%) of women aged 20 to 24, and from more than three-quarters (79.3%) to less than two-thirds (64.4%) of women aged 25 to 29. Similarly, the proportion of husbands dropped from one-third (31.1%) to less than one-fifth (17.8%) of men aged 20 to 24, and from more than two-thirds (71.1%) to about half (52.0%) of men aged 25 to 29. Though not as pronounced, the declines observed among adults in their thirties were also substantial, in the order of 10%. In contrast, the proportions of husbands and wives remained relatively stable among people in their fifties, and even increased among the elderly. In short, it is at the very ages when people traditionally choose a spouse and settle down to have children that the popularity of married life drops off.

The reasons for this phenomenon have been clearly shown by retrospective family surveys. The fifth 1990 GSS revealed a one- or two-year increase in the median age on entering the first union, to age 23 for women and age 25 for men in the most recent generations (Beaujot et al. 1995). Accordingly, among the youngest generations, a growing proportion of men and women had not yet entered their first union, probably because of the universality of education and the longer time spent in school, as well as the difficulties young people have entering the labour market. Moreover, like the 1984 Retrospective Survey on Family, the 1990 GSS showed that conjugal life increasingly begins with a common-law union and that, in 25% or more of cases, this union lasts less than five years (Burch and Madan 1986; Wu and Balakrishnan 1994). When marriage does occur it comes later, and also breaks down earlier and more often than in the past (Dumas and Péron 1992). Therefore, at any given time, a high proportion of young adults find themselves without a spouse after the failure of their marriage or common-law union. In short, if fewer young people today live as husband and wife than their predecessors, it is because their unions occur later in life and are less stable. And, in some cases, the formation of a couple may not lead to the new spouses living together.

TABLE 2.10

PROPORTION OF WIVES AND HUSBANDS AMONG MEMBERS LIVING IN PRIVATE HOUSEHOLDS, 1971 TO 1991

Age group	1971	1976	1981	1986	1991
			Proportion of wives		
15–19	6.6	7.8	6.2	4.0	3.9
20–24	53.7	50.4	46.4	37.1	33.1
25–29	79.3	77.5	72.6	67.9	64.4
30–34	84.6	83.3	79.7	76.4	74.9
35–39	86.8	84.2	81.4	78.5	77.0
40–44	84.8	84.2	81.9	78.5	77.4
45–49	81.9	82.5	80.6	79.0	77.0
50–54	78.8	79.1	77.6	77.6	76.6
55–59	71.3	73.0	73.6	73.7	73.2
60–64	63.2	65.4	66.1	67.2	67.4
65–69	53.1	54.6	55.7	58.3	59.5
70–74	41.2	43.6	43.2	44.5	47.5
75–79	29.0	28.5	29.6	32.3	34.8
80–84	20.9	17.6	18.8	19.3	21.3
85 or older	11.4	10.3	10.8	8.6	10.6
All ages	**61.9**	**61.4**	**60.0**	**59.3**	**59.5**
	1971	1976	1981	1986	1991
			Proportion of husbands		
15–19	1.2	1.6	1.2	0.7	0.9
20–24	31.1	31.1	27.4	19.5	17.8
25–29	71.1	69.0	63.6	56.7	52.0
30–34	83.2	82.5	78.8	74.5	70.7
35–39	86.0	86.1	83.1	80.4	77.4
40–44	86.0	87.1	84.9	82.9	81.3
45–49	85.5	86.1	84.7	83.5	82.6
50–54	86.4	85.6	84.1	83.0	83.1
55–59	84.0	84.6	83.2	82.5	83.3
60–64	82.7	83.7	83.0	82.2	81.6
65–69	78.6	80.8	81.3	81.1	80.7
70–74	74.2	76.6	77.1	79.6	79.5
75–79	69.0	69.6	71.9	73.2	75.6
80–84	56.1	57.7	61.7	64.0	67.2
85 or older	47.0	44.8	48.8	52.9	52.6
All ages	**63.5**	**63.3**	**62.3**	**62.0**	**62.9**

Source: Census of Canada, Public Use Microdata Files, 1971 to 1991.

FIGURE 2.9

PROPORTION OF WIVES AMONG WOMEN LIVING IN PRIVATE HOUSEHOLDS, 1971 TO 1991

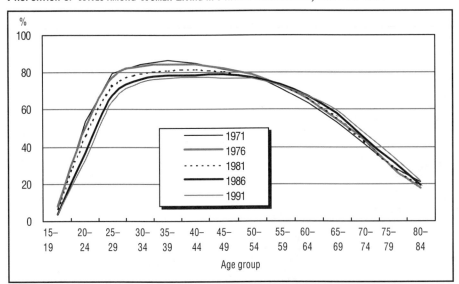

Note: The data for this figure are taken from Table 2.10.

Source: Census of Canada, Individual Public Use Microdata Files, 1971 to 1991.

FIGURE 2.10

PROPORTION OF HUSBANDS AMONG MEN LIVING IN PRIVATE HOUSEHOLDS, 1971 TO 1991

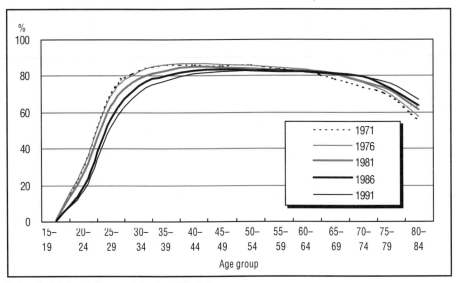

Note: The data for this figure are taken from Table 2.10.

Source: Census of Canada, Individual Public Use Microdata Files, 1971 to 1991.

Because their unions occur later in life, and are less official and more unstable, and because their circumstances are more precarious, an increasingly high proportion of young people are enumerated as single sons or daughters living with their parents (see Table 2.11). In the early 1970s, when people married fairly young, 28% of young women aged 20 to 24 were counted as "children" in a family. In 20 years, this proportion had increased by half to 42% in 1991. Among women aged 25 to 29 the proportion had nearly doubled, from 6% to 11%. The same trend can also be observed among men, at least since 1976. Thus, the proportion of men counted as single sons rose over a 15-year period, from 48% to 58% of those aged 20 to 24, and from 12% to 21% of those aged 25 to 29. In many cases, the young people enumerated had never left the parental home, while, in others, the young people had returned after an attempt at living on their own or after the dissolution of their common-law union.

TABLE 2.11

PROPORTION OF PERSONS CLASSIFIED AS DAUGHTERS OR SONS AMONG MEMBERS OF PRIVATE HOUSEHOLDS, 1971 TO 1991

Age group	1971	1976	1981	1986	1991
	Proportion of daughters				
15–19	86.5	83.9	85.1	87.7	87.8
20–24	28.0	28.2	30.8	39.7	42.3
25–29	6.1	6.0	6.3	9.2	11.0
30–34	3.2	2.9	2.7	3.2	3.9
	Proportion of sons				
15–19	93.4	91.5	91.1	92.9	92.5
20–24	50.3	47.7	49.5	58.1	58.0
25–29	12.5	12.1	13.7	18.0	20.5
30–34	5.2	4.7	5.2	6.3	7.7

Source: Census of Canada, Public Use Microdata Files, 1971 to 1991.

2.2.2 The increase in lone parenthood

Lone parenthood is usually the outcome of the break-up or dissolution of a marriage or common-law union. It generally ends either with the formation of a new union—in the majority of cases—or when the last child leaves home. This episode of parental life may be fairly brief, lasting only five years on average (Desrosiers, Le Bourdais and Péron 1993). Lone parenthood affects more women than men because women generally retain custody of the children following a separation.

From 1971 to 1991, as unions became increasingly unstable, the incidence of lone parenthood rose dramatically (see Table 2.12 and Figure 2.11). Among women under age 45 living in private households, the proportion of lone mothers nearly doubled. The highest proportions, in 1991, were from 10% to 11%, observed between ages 35 and 50. Male lone parenthood also increased, except for the youngest age groups. The highest proportion of lone fathers was about 3% in 1991, among men aged 40 to 55. It is worth noting that the incidence of lone parenthood would have been higher had it included only single parents with children living at home. In 1991, lone parents headed 20% of families with children (Public Use Microdata File on Family).

TABLE 2.12

PROPORTION OF LONE MOTHERS AND LONE FATHERS AMONG MEMBERS OF PRIVATE HOUSEHOLDS, 1971 TO 1991

Age group	1971	1976	1981	1986	1991
			Proportion of lone mothers		
15–19	0.3	0.6	0.5	0.6	0.9
20–24	2.4	2.8	3.4	3.8	4.5
25–29	4.2	4.7	5.8	6.7	7.0
30–34	5.3	6.2	7.6	8.5	8.6
35–39	5.6	8.2	9.5	10.2	10.4
40–44	6.4	7.8	9.8	11.6	11.0
45–49	7.2	8.2	9.5	9.8	9.9
50–54	7.3	7.7	9.4	9.3	7.9
55–59	7.3	7.6	7.4	8.3	7.2
60–64	6.1	5.6	6.5	6.5	6.3
65–69	5.2	5.7	4.9	5.2	5.2
70–74	5.9	5.4	4.9	4.5	5.1
75–79	7.2	7.2	5.4	5.5	5.3
80–84	9.0	9.3	7.3	7.2	5.6
85 or older	12.8	15.1	11.3	9.7	8.8
All ages	**4.9**	**5.5**	**6.3**	**7.0**	**7.2**
Age group	1971	1976	1981	1986	1991
			Proportion of lone fathers		
15–19	0.1	0.0	0.0	0.0	0.0
20–24	0.2	0.2	0.2	0.2	0.2
25–29	0.8	0.6	0.6	0.6	0.6
30–34	1.2	0.8	0.9	1.1	1.2
35–39	1.6	1.6	1.9	1.9	1.9
40–44	1.8	1.9	2.5	3.0	2.9
45–49	1.8	1.9	3.0	3.5	3.2
50–54	1.8	2.2	2.6	3.0	2.9
55–59	2.1	1.8	2.5	2.3	2.3
60–64	1.9	1.2	2.3	2.1	1.8
65–69	1.3	1.5	1.6	1.4	1.6
70–74	2.0	1.8	1.6	1.6	1.5
75–79	2.6	2.3	2.0	1.9	2.0
80–84	4.1	3.3	2.3	2.6	1.7
85 or older	4.7	5.9	5.7	4.6	3.8
All ages	**1.2**	**1.1**	**1.4**	**1.6**	**1.6**

Source: Census of Canada, Public Use Microdata Files, 1971 to 1991.

FIGURE 2.11

PROPORTION OF LONE MOTHERS AMONG WOMEN LIVING IN PRIVATE HOUSEHOLDS, 1971 TO 1991

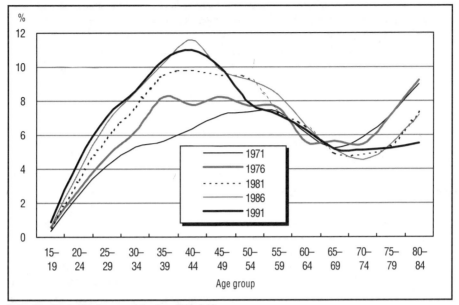

Note: The data for this figure are taken from Table 2.12.
Source: Census of Canada, Individual Public Use Microdata Files, 1971 to 1991.

2.2.3 Non-family persons

The status of non-family person is more common in early adulthood and old age than in the intermediate years (see figures 2.12 and 2.13). Many young people become non-family persons when they leave home, retain this status for a time, and then relinquish it when they form a union. Some acquire the status of non-family person a little later, when they separate from their spouse and do not retain custody of their children; but, again, they relinquish this status when they form another union. So, for most young people and middle-aged adults, the status of non-family person is only temporary—a pause between two phases of family life. At younger ages, men are more likely to have this status. More men than women leave their parents for reasons other than to form a union, and far fewer men than women retain custody of the children upon separation. In later years, after the children have left home, it is women who are more likely to acquire non-family status because they often outlive their husbands.

Because unions are being formed later in life, and particularly because unions are less stable, the proportion of non-family persons has increased among those under age 55 (see Table 2.13, figures 2.12 and 2.13). The greatest increases were observed among adults aged 25 to 34. In the 25-to-29 age group, the proportion of non-family persons rose from 10% to 18% among women, and from 16% to 27% among men. In the 30-to-34 age group, it rose from 7% to 13% among women, and from 10% to 20% among men. In contrast, the proportion of non-family persons generally decreased among those over age 55, doubtless owing to the increased life expectancy of older couples.

FIGURE 2.12

PROPORTION OF NON-FAMILY FEMALES AMONG WOMEN LIVING IN PRIVATE HOUSEHOLDS, 1971 TO 1991

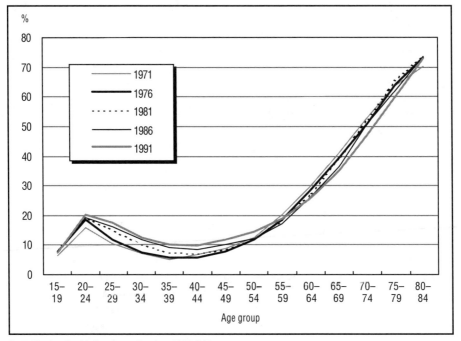

Note: The data for this figure are taken from Table 2.13.

Source Census of Canada, Individual Public Use Microdata Files, 1971 to 1991.

FIGURE 2.13

PROPORTION OF NON-FAMILY MALES AMONG MEN LIVING IN PRIVATE HOUSEHOLDS, 1971 TO 1991

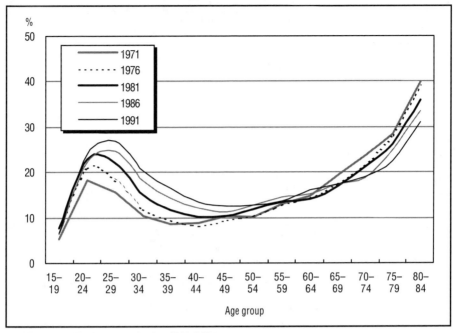

Note: The data for this figure are taken from Table 2.13.

Source: Census of Canada, Individual Public Use Microdata Files, 1971 to 1991.

THE EVOLUTION OF CENSUS FAMILIES FROM 1971 TO 1991

TABLE 2.13

PROPORTION OF NON-FAMILY FEMALES AND MALES AMONG MEMBERS OF PRIVATE HOUSEHOLDS, 1971 TO 1991

Age group	1971	1976	1981	1986	1991
			Proportion of females		
15–19	6.6	7.7	8.2	7.6	7.5
20–24	15.8	18.6	19.4	19.4	20.1
25–29	10.4	11.8	15.3	16.2	17.6
30–34	6.9	7.6	10.0	11.8	12.6
35–39	5.1	5.8	7.4	9.2	10.3
40–44	6.6	5.7	6.9	8.5	10.0
45–49	8.9	7.8	8.6	10.1	12.0
50–54	12.5	11.8	11.8	12.3	14.5
55–59	20.1	18.6	18.4	17.3	19.0
60–64	29.8	28.5	26.9	25.9	25.8
65–69	41.2	39.5	39.1	36.4	35.1
70–74	52.9	50.8	51.8	50.9	47.4
75–79	63.8	64.3	65.0	62.2	59.9
80–84	70.1	73.1	73.9	73.5	73.1
85 or older	75.8	73.4	78.0	81.7	80.5
All ages	**16.2**	**16.7**	**18.2**	**19.0**	**20.0**
			Proportion of males		
15–19	5.3	6.9	7.7	6.4	6.6
20–24	18.3	21.0	23.0	22.2	24.0
25–29	15.6	18.2	22.0	24.7	27.0
30–34	10.4	12.0	15.0	18.1	20.3
35–39	8.6	9.4	11.7	14.4	16.6
40–44	8.8	8.2	10.2	12.0	13.4
45–49	10.4	9.6	10.4	11.3	12.6
50–54	10.2	10.3	11.9	12.7	12.8
55–59	13.0	12.7	13.3	14.5	13.6
60–64	14.9	14.4	14.2	15.2	16.2
65–69	19.4	17.5	16.9	17.3	17.5
70–74	23.5	21.5	21.2	18.8	18.9
75–79	28.4	27.9	26.1	24.9	22.4
80–84	39.8	38.9	35.9	33.4	31.1
85 or older	48.3	47.7	45.5	42.5	43.5
All ages	**12.8**	**13.7**	**15.4**	**16.5**	**17.5**

Source: Census of Canada, Public Use Microdata Files, 1971 to 1991.

2.3 FAMILY STRUCTURE

The current definition of "census family" has been used since 1941. According to this definition, the census family is a family unit living in the same dwelling. It may be a couple, a couple and their never-married children, or a lone parent and their never-married children. Thus, since 1941, the number of family units and their distribution have periodically been classified by two broad categories: those that include a couple and those that do not.[4] Table 2.14 traces the evolution of these two family types over the last half century. Note that Newfoundland families are not included in 1941, and that the families of members of collective households and of Canadians enumerated abroad have not been included in the family census since 1976.

TABLE 2.14
DISTRIBUTION OF FAMILIES, BY TYPE, 1941 TO 1991

Year		Type of family			
		Husband–wife families			
		Total	Parents living common law	Lone-parent families	All families
1941	Number	2,202,707	..	306,957	2,509,664
	%	87.8		12.2	100.0
1951	Number	2,961,685	..	325,699	3,287,384
	%	90.1		9.9	100.0
1956	Number	3,393,061	..	318,439	3,711,500
	%	91.4		8.6	100.0
1961	Number	3,800,026	..	347,418	4,147,444
	%	91.6		8.4	100.0
1966	Number	4,154,381	..	371,885	4,526,266
	%	91.8		8.2	100.0
1971	Number	4,591,940	..	478,740	5,070,680
	%	90.6		9.4	100.0
1976	Number	5,168,560	..	559,335	5,727,895
	%	90.2		9.8	100.0
1981	Number	5,610,965	356,605	714,010	6,324,975
	%	88.7	6.4	11.3	100.0
1986	Number	5,881,330	486,940	853,645	6,734,980
	%	87.3	8.3	12.7	100.0
1991	Number	6,401,460	725,950	954,710	7,356,170
	%	87.0	11.3	13.0	100.0

.. figures not available

Note: Common-law unions are calculated as a percentage of all husband–wife families.

Source: Census of Canada, 1941 to 1991.

The number of census families more than doubled in 40 years, from 3.3 million in 1951 to 7.4 million in 1991. The number of husband–wife families also doubled, from 3.0 million in 1951 to 6.4 million in 1991. However, while these conjugal families consisted almost entirely of married couples until 1971, after 1976 they included a growing number of common-law unions (726,000 in 1991). The number of lone-parent families evolved differently, increasing just slightly from 1951 to 1966, and then significantly over the next 25 years, from 372,000 to 955,000. Therefore, as it grew, the pool of families also underwent major changes in composition.

The time series data shown in Table 2.14 cover a long enough period to show the reversal of the evolutionary trend of the percentage of lone-parent families: the percentage dropped from 12.2% in 1941 to 8.2% in 1966 before rising again to 13.0% in 1991, slightly above the 1941 value. The decline in lone-parent families during the 1940s and 1950s can be largely attributed to the decrease in mortality; during these decades it became increasingly unlikely that people would experience widowhood before their children had left home. However, the recovery of the percentage of lone parents, which begins in the mid-1960s, is mainly a result of the growing number of separations and divorces.

The change in the causes of lone parenthood can be seen in the distribution of lone parents by marital status (see Table 2.15). In 1951, two-thirds (66.5%) of lone parents were widows and widowers, the other third being primarily married couples who were separated, either in fact or in law. Forty years later, the vast majority of lone parents acquired this status following the dissolution of a marriage or common-law union, while widowers and widows constituted just under one-quarter (22.9%) of the total. Clearly, the recent increase in the proportion of lone-parent families is not a return to past trends. Forty years ago, the lone parent was often the sole surviving parent; today the absent parent is generally still living, and it is common for these parents to maintain contact with their children and contribute toward their maintenance and education.

TABLE 2.15
LONE-PARENT FAMILIES, BY LONE PARENT'S MARITAL STATUS, 1951 TO 1991

Marital status	1951	1961	1971	1981	1991
			Number		
Never married	4,831	9,326	36,950	70,050	167,305
Married, spouse absent	94,119	108,799	161,290	223,305	256,395
Widowed	216,641	213,657	222,625	233,180	218,945
Divorced	10,108	15,636	57,875	187,480	312,065
Total	**325,699**	**347,418**	**478,740**	**714,015**	**954,710**
			%		
Never married	1.5	2.7	7.7	9.8	17.5
Married, spouse absent	28.9	31.3	33.7	31.3	26.9
Widowed	66.5	61.5	46.5	32.7	22.9
Divorced	3.1	4.5	12.1	26.3	32.7
Total	**100.0**	**100.0**	**100.0**	**100.0**	**100.0**

Note: Percentages may not add to 100 due to rounding.

Source: Wargon, 1979a, 99; Census of Canada, 1951, 1961, 1971, 1981 and 1991.

A second major change concerns husband–wife families and the impact of the increased number of common-law unions on this family type. According to Statistics Canada, "common-law union" refers to two persons of the opposite sex who are not legally married to each other but live together as husband and wife in the same dwelling. Uncommon until 1971, except among native Aboriginal peoples, by 1976 such unions were fairly numerous. However, it was not until 1981 that their number could be estimated for the first time at 357,000. This number slightly more than doubled in the next decade, to 726,000 in 1991, representing more than 11% of the couples counted in private households.

The expression "common-law union" probably covers a wide range of situations, from temporary unions of convenience or gratification, to trial marriages involving longer-range family intentions. According to the 1984 and 1990 retrospective surveys, common-law union seems *a posteriori* to be a prelude to marriage in about half of cases (Burch and Madan 1986; Wu and Balakrishnan 1994). When there is no marriage, common-law union often ends in separation after a few months or years. In short, it is estimated that only 10% to 15% of common-law unions manage to survive without marriage or separation until the tenth anniversary of their formation. Consequently, the common-law unions counted at any given time are generally recent.

Most common-law unions are found among young couples (see Table 2.16). The younger the husband, the higher the proportion who are living common law: 79% of those under age 20, 53% of those aged 20 to 24, and 28% of those aged 25 to 29. The same is true of wives, the proportions being only slightly lower at any given age than those of husbands: 75%, 44% and 22%, respectively, for the three age groups. In Quebec, common-law union is still fairly widespread; the proportions of husbands are: 88% of those aged 15 to 19, 73% of those aged 20 to 24, 47% of those aged 25 to 29, and 30% of those aged 30 to 34 (Dumas and Péron 1992). These variations according to age primarily reflect the fact that the younger a person is, the more likely their union is to be recent, and, therefore, the more likely it is to be formed and maintained outside the bonds of marriage.

TABLE 2.16
HUSBANDS AND WIVES CURRENTLY MARRIED OR LIVING COMMON LAW, BY AGE,[1] 1991

Age group	Husbands			Wives		
	Now married	Living common law		Now married	Living common law	
	Number	Number	%	Number	Number	%
Under 20	1,725	6,570	79.2	8,910	26,135	74.6
20–24	77,755	89,200	53.4	180,210	138,485	43.5
25–29	427,115	163,840	27.7	591,615	169,065	22.2
30–34	706,540	140,405	16.6 ·	794,650	130,900	14.1
35–39	757,140	101,305	11.8	787,495	91,985	10.5
40–44	748,670	76,740	9.3	735,330	65,490	8.2
45–49	611,735	53,570	8.1	580,020	42,130	6.8
50–54	505,430	34,155	6.3	475,670	24,310	4.9
55–59	470,095	24,020	4.9	430,710	14,680	3.3
60–64	440,870	16,330	3.6	391,805	9,710	2.4
65–69	375,580	9,915	2.6	327,285	6,515	2.0
70–74	266,365	5,350	2.0	206,345	3,795	1.8
75 or older	286,495	4,560	1.6	165,465	2,755	1.6
All ages	**5,675,505**	**725,950**		**5,675,505**	**725,950**	

1. 100% data.

Source: Census of Canada, 1991.

In the next section of this chapter, we take a closer look at the evolution of each family category from 1971 to 1991. Section 2.4 is devoted to husband–wife families, while section 2.5 is devoted to lone-parent families. We begin the study of each category with an analysis of the effects various demographic factors have had on the increase in the number of families. We then present the main changes in the distribution of these families as they move through the life cycle, and conclude with a look at the changes that have occurred in their composition, that is, in the number and age of any children present in the home.

2.4   HUSBAND–WIFE FAMILIES

2.4.1   Irregular growth

To show the effect of several factors on the evolution of husband–wife families from 1971 to 1991, these families have been classified according to the wife's age. The three age groups used are those proposed by Priest (1982): 15 to 34, 35 to 54, and 55 and older. Age 35, older than the median age at completed fertility, is the age before which most families are likely to grow. Age 55, close to the median age of mothers when their last child leaves home, is the age after which only a small proportion of families have children living at home. Between these limits, most families have stopped growing and still have children living at home. Based on the woman's life cycle, this classification uses the wife as the family reference person, and three variation factors of the number of families are therefore used: the number of women in private households, their age distribution, and the proportion of wives at the various ages.

The method used is classic in demographics, and has been previously used in a study of Canadian households (Beaujot and Bland 1978). It consists of calculating the multiplier effect of the variation of each factor on the number of families, such that the product is equal to the variation in the number of families over a given period. For example, from 1971 to 1976, the number of wives under age 35 was multiplied by 1.180 (because of the increase in the number of young women counted in private households), then by 1.026 (because of the change in their distribution between the ages of 15 to 19 and 30 to 34), and finally by 0.977 (because of the decline in the popularity of married life at these same ages). The product of these three indices gives the total variation in the number of young families between the two censuses, for a multiplication factor of 1.182 (see Table 2.17). The calculations were first done by intercensal period, and then for the overall period 1971 to 1991 (for the forms used, see Beaujot and Bland 1978).

The number of youngest families—those in which the woman was under age 35—increased least over 20 years: 19.5%, compared with 44.9% and 77.2% for the other two family groups (see Table 2.17). In fact, their number rose until 1981, but then dropped. It would be tempting to attribute this slow increase in young families to the aging of the baby boom generations, because this aging led to a considerable increase in the number of young women until 1981, which was followed by a decrease in subsequent years. But this would ignore the fact that the decline in the number of young women beginning in 1981 was very slight, and that its unfavourable effect on the number of families was largely offset by the beneficial effect of an attendant change in the age distribution of these women in favour of younger women, that is, of women more likely to be living as part of a couple. Furthermore, looking at the period 1971 to 1991 as a whole, it can be seen that the evolution in the number of women aged 15 to 34 and their age distribution would have allowed for a greater increase in the number of young families over the 20-year period. All things being equal, the increase in the number of young women enumerated in households and the age distribution of these women would have resulted in a further increase of 18.5%, bringing the number of families to 2.6 million, that is, far above the counted number of just 2.0 million.

TABLE 2.17

EFFECT OF VARIOUS FACTORS ON VARIATION IN NUMBER OF HUSBAND–WIFE FAMILIES, 1971 TO 1991

Source of variation	1971–1976	1976–1981	1981–1986	1986–1991	1971–1991
			Wife's age 15–34		
Number of women	1.180	1.111	0.986	0.995	1.286
Age of women	1.026	1.046	1.061	1.040	1.185
Proportion of wives	0.977	0.934	0.904	0.952	0.784
All factors	**1.182**	**1.086**	**0.946**	**0.985**	**1.195**
			35–54		
Number of women	1.062	1.080	1.139	1.197	1.564
Age of women	0.999	1.002	1.001	1.000	1.003
Proportion of wives	0.993	0.974	0.974	0.982	0.923
All factors	**1.053**	**1.053**	**1.111**	**1.176**	**1.449**
			55 or older		
Number of women	1.162	1.179	1.123	1.114	1.714
Age of women	1.004	0.995	0.986	0.971	0.958
Proportion of wives	1.024	1.012	1.022	1.020	1.079
All factors	**1.193**	**1.188**	**1.132**	**1.105**	**1.772**
			All ages		
Number of women	**1.138**	**1.118**	**1.064**	**1.088**	**1.473**
Age of women	**0.999**	**1.013**	**1.031**	**1.023**	**1.065**
Proportion of wives	**0.993**	**0.966**	**0.958**	**0.981**	**0.903**
All factors	**1.129**	**1.094**	**1.051**	**1.091**	**1.417**

Note: To obtain a percentage variation, subtract 1 from the value of the index and multiply the result by 100.
Source: Census of Canada, Individual Public Use Microdata Files, 1971 to 1991.

Therefore, had it not been that unions were being formed later and were increasingly unstable, about 600,000 more young conjugal families would have been counted in 1991, for an increase since 1971 of 52.4%, rather than 19.5%.

The number of families in which the wife was aged 35 to 54 increased from nearly 2.0 million in 1971 to just over 2.8 million in 1991, a slightly higher-than-average increase: 44.9% versus 41.7%. This is due, of course, to the constant and increasingly rapid growth of the female population aged 35 to 54. But it is also owing to the fact that the decline in the popularity of conjugal life after age 35 was less marked than at younger ages. This declining popularity brought the number of families surveyed in 1991 down just 7.7% from what the count would otherwise have been. And this decrease is negligible compared with the 56.4% increase caused by the rise in the number of women aged 35 to 54 surveyed in private households.

It was, however, the oldest families (where the wife was aged 55 or older) that experienced the greatest increase in number (77.2%) in this 20-year period. This marked increase is essentially attributable to the steady, considerable rise in the female population aged 55 and older. The other two factors (the woman's age and the proportion of married women) had only a limited, and furthermore opposite, impact on the evolution of the number of families. We see, then, that the aging of the female population aged 55 and older somewhat stemmed the growth of the oldest families after 1976. This growth was stimulated by a slight increase in marriage among older women, with the result that in 1991, the number of families exceeded the anticipated number by 7.9% because of the evolution of the number and age distribution of older women.

In all, the number of husband–wife families increased 41.7% in 20 years, from 4.6 million in 1971 to 6.4 million in 1991. The increase is slightly less than that of the female population aged 15 and older, but not because of changes in the age composition of the female population since on the whole these changes led to a further 6.5% increase in the number of families. Rather, it was the changes that occurred in the proportions of wives at different ages that, taken together, stemmed the increase in the number of families. The 6.4 million families enumerated in 1991 represent only 90.3% of the families that would have been enumerated had there been no change in the incidence of marriage.

The number of families according to the wife's age increased quite erratically, contributing to major changes in the composition of the pool of families (see Table 2.18). After going from 37.4% in 1971 to 38.9% in 1981, the proportion of the youngest families dropped to 31.8% in 1991. The evolution of the proportion of families where the wife was aged 35 to 54 was the opposite; it went from 42.6% in 1971 to 38.6% in 1981, and then rose again to 43.8% in 1991. Only the proportion of the oldest families rose steadily, from 20.0% in 1971 to 22.5% in 1981, and then to 24.3% in 1991. If, from 1971 to 1981, families were getting both younger and older, from 1981 to 1991 rejuvenation gave way to aging at the bottom of the pyramid in addition to the aging at the top.

2.4.2 Smaller families

To provide a clearer picture of the evolution of the pool of families, we must complete the classification of families by accounting for the absence or presence of children in the home, as well as women's infertility or fertility. This analysis is presented in Table 2.18, which uses the data on family types published in 1971, 1981 and 1991. The families are divided into four groups using the classification method proposed by Priest (1982). The first group consists of couples with a wife aged 35 or older and no never-married children at home; in most cases, the wife has not yet had children, but is likely to in future (young couples without children). The second group consists of all couples with at least one never-married son or daughter at home (couples with children). The third group comprises couples with no single children at home where the wife is aged 35 or older and has had one or more children; these are mainly couples left on their own after the children have left home (couples in the postparental phase, or postparental couples). The fourth group consists of couples living on their own; the wife is aged 35 years or older and the couple has never had children; these are childless couples and will, for the most part, remain so given the wife's age (childless couples). This classification of families approximately corresponds with their classification by the wife's life-cycle stage.

TABLE 2.18

DISTRIBUTION OF HUSBAND–WIFE FAMILIES, BY WIFE'S AGE AND LIFE-CYCLE STAGE, 1971, 1981 AND 1991

Type of family	Wife's age			
	Under 35	35 to 54	55 or older	**All ages**
	Number ('000)			
Families with no children as yet				
1971	412	...	...	**412**
1981	688	...	...	**688**
1991	692	...	...	**692**
Families with children at home				
1971	1,310	1,659	266	**3,236**
1981	1,497	1,784	318	**3,599**
1991	1,346	2,157	327	**3,830**
Postparental families				
1971	...	181	519	**699**
1981	...	251	799	**1,051**
1991	...	413	1,084	**1,497**
Childless families				
1971	...	124	134	**259**
1981	...	128	146	**274**
1991	...	238	146	**383**
Husband–wife families				
1971	1,722	1,964	919	**4,605**
1981	2,184	2,163	1,264	**5,612**
1991	2,038	2,807	1,557	**6,402**
	%			
Families with no children as yet				
1971	8.9	...	...	**8.9**
1981	12.3	...	...	**12.3**
1991	10.8	...	...	**10.8**
Famlies with children at home				
1971	28.5	36.0	5.8	**70.3**
1981	26.7	31.8	5.7	**64.1**
1991	21.0	33.7	5.1	**59.8**
Postparental families				
1971	...	3.9	11.3	**15.2**
1981	...	4.5	14.2	**18.7**
1991	...	6.4	16.9	**23.4**
Childless families				
1971	...	2.7	2.9	**5.6**
1981	...	2.3	2.6	**4.9**
1991	...	3.7	2.3	**6.0**
Husband–wife families				
1971	37.4	42.6	20.0	**100.0**
1981	38.9	38.6	22.5	**100.0**
1991	31.8	43.8	24.3	**100.0**

...   amount too small to be expressed

Note: Percentages may not add to 100 due to rounding.

Source: Priest, 1982; Census of Canada, 1971, 1981 and 1991.

THE EVOLUTION OF CENSUS FAMILIES FROM 1971 TO 1991

Older on average than their 1971 counterparts, the husband–wife families surveyed in 1991 were also distributed differently between couples with children and couples without children (see Table 2.18). Although their number rose from 3.2 to 3.8 million in 20 years, couples with children represented less than 60% of conjugal families in 1991, while in 1971 they represented slightly over 70%. It was mainly young couples with children—the new guard, so to speak—whose number declined, their share of all families dropping from just over 28% in 1971 to 21% in 1991. In contrast, the proportion of young couples without children varied little over 20 years, no more than that of childless couples. Only the proportion of postparental couples rose considerably, from just over 15% in 1971 to just over 23% in 1991. This marked increase in the percentage of couples remaining on their own after their children's departure accounts for almost all of the percentage increase in couples without children.

The increase in the number of couples without children is one of two major characteristics of the change in distribution of husband–wife families by number of children living at home, the other being the near-disappearance of families with four or more children (see Figure 2.14). Couples without children, of which there were 1.4 million, made up almost 30% of conjugal families in 1971; 20 years later, the figure was 2.6 million, representing just over 40% (Public Use Microdata File on Individuals). In contrast, the number of families with four or more children dropped sharply, and their share of all families fell from nearly 15% in 1971 to less than 3% in 1991. Another less significant change than those mentioned above, but quite significant nonetheless, was the decrease in the proportion of families with three children. All of these changes led to a significant decrease in the average family size: after peaking at 1.9 in 1961 and 1966, the average number of children per couple was just 1.7 in 1971, and continued to decline to 1.4 in 1981, and then to 1.2 in 1991.

FIGURE 2.14

PROPORTION OF HUSBAND–WIFE FAMILIES, BY NUMBER OF CHILDREN PRESENT IN THE HOME, 1971, 1981 AND 1991

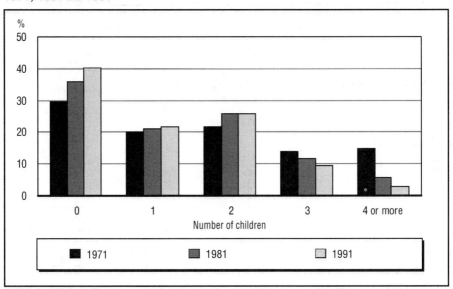

Note: The data for this figure are taken from Table 2.19.

Source: Census of Canada, 1971, 1981 and 1991, Family Public Use Microdata Files.

Table 2.19 shows the distribution of families for the three main age groups of the wife. For the youngest families, their distribution by the number of children present is very similar to the distribution of wives by number of children born. Changes in this distribution may be related to recent changes in the composition of offspring: an increase in the proportion of young couples without children following the rise of the mother's age at birth of the first child; a decrease in the number of young couples with three or more children owing to the lower incidence of children ranking third in the birth order, and the virtual absence of children ranking lower in birth order. For the other families, their distribution by number of children present differs from the distribution of wives by number of children born because of their children's departure from home. Even so, Table 2.19 provides evidence of earlier behavioural changes related to nuptiality and fertility. Thus, the fact that women born between the two world wars had had their last child at far younger ages than their predecessors is doubtless related to the high increase in the proportion of elderly postparental couples. Similarly, the fact that these same women married earlier than their elders probably explains the decline in the proportion of childless couples among couples where the wife was aged 55 or older. Finally, the near-disappearance of large- and medium-sized families marks the tapering off of the parental phase for women who had their offspring before the widespread use of effective methods of modern birth control, and their replacement by women who had their children more recently.

TABLE 2.19

DISTRIBUTION OF HUSBAND–WIFE FAMILIES, BY LIFE-CYCLE STAGE AND NUMBER OF CHILDREN PRESENT IN THE HOME, 1971, 1981 AND 1991

| Type of family | Wife's age | | | |
	Under age 35	Age 35 to 54	Age 55 or older	All ages
		%		
Young couples with no children				
1971	23.7	...	...	**8.8**
1981	31.4	...	...	**12.3**
1991	33.9	...	...	**10.8**
Couples with children				
1 child				
1971	24.6	16.9	18.2	**20.0**
1981	23.9	21.0	16.9	**21.2**
1991	24.5	23.0	15.4	**21.6**
2 children				
1971	27.1	24.4	6.5	**21.8**
1981	31.2	32.2	5.4	**25.7**
1991	29.2	35.1	4.1	**25.7**
3 children				
1971	14.3	18.6	2.5	**13.8**
1981	10.4	18.5	1.9	**11.6**
1991	9.8	14.1	1.0	**9.5**
4 children				
1971	6.2	11.2	1.2	**7.3**
1981	2.5	7.4	0.7	**3.9**
1991	2.2	3.5	0.2	**2.3**
5 children				
1971	2.5	6.6	0.4	**3.8**
1981	0.4	2.3	0.3	**1.1**
1991	0.4	0.7	0.1	**0.4**
6 or more children				
1971	1.6	6.7	0.3	**3.5**
1981	0.2	1.3	0.1	**0.6**
1991	0.1	0.3	0.0	**0.2**
Postparental couples				
1971	...	9.2	56.8	**15.3**
1981	...	11.4	63.4	**18.7**
1991	...	14.7	69.6	**23.3**
Childless couples				
1971	...	6.5	14.2	**5.6**
1981	...	6.0	11.4	**4.9**
1991	...	8.5	9.6	**6.1**

TABLE **2.19** (CONCLUDED)

DISTRIBUTION OF HUSBAND–WIFE FAMILIES, BY LIFE-CYCLE STAGE AND NUMBER OF CHILDREN
PRESENT IN THE HOME, **1971, 1981** AND **1991**

Type of family	Wife's age			
	Under age 35	Age 35 to 54	Age 55 or older	All ages
	%			
Couples with children				
Husband–wife families				
1971	1,685,400	1,941,800	910,000	**4,537,200**
1981	2,199,985	2,144,578	1,266,641	**5,611,204**
1991	2,043,231	2,820,064	1,552,532	**6,415,827**

... amount too small to be expressed

Source: Census of Canada, Public Use Microdata Files, 1971 to 1991.

2.4.3 Married couples and common-law unions

Of some 6.4 million couples surveyed in private households in 1991, 5.7 million (or 88.7%) were
married couples. Of wives under age 35, however, only 77.3% were married. The proportion was
far higher among women in the older age groups: 90.7% of wives aged 35 to 44, 94.2% of those
aged 45 to 54, and 97.6% of those aged 55 and older. Consequently, the proportion of young
wives was slightly smaller (7.3%) among married women than among all women living as part of
a couple (10.8%). The difference was especially marked in the under-35 age group; perhaps for
this reason a smaller proportion of couples without children, and a higher proportion of couples
with children, notably two, was noted among young married couples (see Table 2.20). All ages of
the wife combined, the distribution of married couples by family type was fairly similar to that of
all couples, the most notable difference being a smaller proportion of young couples without
children.

TABLE 2.20

DISTRIBUTION OF MARRIED COUPLES, BY LIFE-CYCLE STAGE, 1991

Type of family	Wife's age			
	Under age 35	Age 35 to 54	Age 55 or older	**All ages**
Young couples without children	26.3	...	...	**7.3**
		%		
Couples with children				
1 child	25.1	22.9	15.6	**21.5**
2 children	33.9	36.6	4.1	**27.2**
3 children	11.6	14.8	1.0	**10.2**
4 children	2.6	3.7	0.2	**2.5**
5 children	0.4	0.7	0.1	**0.4**
6 or more children	0.2	0.4	0.0	**0.2**
Postparental couples	...	13.7	69.5	**24.8**
Childless couples	...	7.2	9.4	**5.8**
Total	**100.0**	**100.0**	**100.0**	**100.0**
		Number		
All married couples	**1,579,865**	**2,597,531**	**1,515,032**	**5,692,428**

... amount too small to be expressed

Note: Percentages may not add to 100 due to rounding.

Source: Census of Canada, 1991, Family Public Use Microdata Files.

The distribution of common-law unions by family type evolved differently (see Table 2.21). In many respects, the distribution mirrored that of married couples. Of these couples, 58.4% had no children, and 41.6% had children, versus 37.9% and 62.1%, respectively, of married couples (see Table 2.20). Also, two-thirds of common-law unions without children were composed of young couples, while about two-thirds of married couples were composed of elderly postparental couples. However, common-law couples generally had fewer children, with most couples having just one child at home.

TABLE 2.21

DISTRIBUTION OF COMMON-LAW UNIONS, BY LIFE-CYCLE STAGE, 1991

Type of family	Wife's age			All ages
	Under age 35	Aged 35 to 54	Aged 55 or older	
Young couples without children	59.8	...	...	38.3
Couples with children				
1 child	22.5	24.4	6.7	22.3
2 children	12.9	17.5	1.3	13.7
3 children	3.6	5.7	0.4	4.1
4 children	0.8	1.6	0.1	1.0
5 children	0.2	0.5	...	0.3
6 or more children	0.1	0.1	...	0.1
Postparental couples	...	26.2	16.5	8.2
Childless couples	...	24.0	16.5	8.2
Total	**100.0**	**100.0**	**100.0**	**100.0**
	Number			
Husband–wife families	**463,366**	**222,533**	**37,500**	**723,399**

...   figures not applicable

Note: Percentages may not add to 100 due to rounding.

Source: Census of Canada, 1991, Family Public Use Microdata Files.

Another distinctive trait of unmarried couples was that the wives were younger: 64% were under age 35, 31% were aged 35 to 54, and only 5% were older. But the differences between common-law and married couples remained considerable regardless of the wife's age. In couples where the women was younger than 35, nearly 60% of common-law unions had no children, compared with 26% of married couples; this difference may be explained by the probable recentness of the common-law union and the youth of both partners. However, even when the wife was aged 35 to 54, the proportion of common-law unions without children was 50%, while for married couples the proportion was just 21%. In other words, at these ages, there were proportionally more postparental or childless women among common-law partners than among married couples. If we look at all ages combined, common-law unions with children usually had just one child compared with two children for married couples where the wife was under age 55.

Table 2.22 shows the distribution of wives by age, marital status and number of children born, allowing for a further comparison of marriages and common-law unions. Of unmarried wives under age 35, 8 in 10 were single and, of these, 6 in 10 had not yet had children, compared with just 1 in 4 married women. The difference was comparable with that already noted in the proportions of couples without children at home. Although smaller than that observed in wives, the proportion of mothers among these young single women was, all the same, highly indicative of the emergence of a very strong tendency not to legalize the common-law union until the birth of a child. In the 35-to-44 and 45-to-54 age groups, the vast majority of women living common law previously had been married and had formed a new common-law family comparable with that of married women. Only single women, now in the minority, differed from the others, with about 50% of them being childless. But while most common-law wives had had as many children as married women of the same age, it was more likely that their children were not living at home. Thus, according to the Public Use Microdata File on Family, 33% of divorced women aged 35 to 44 who had had a child had no children at home, compared with just 10% of their married counterparts. Similarly, among divorced women aged 35 to 44 with two children, 26% had no children at home and 24% had just one, while the corresponding proportions for married mothers of two children were 4% and 9%. This more frequent absence of children among divorced or separated women largely accounts for the small size of families of common-law wives aged 35 and older.

TABLE 2.22

DISTRIBUTION OF WOMEN BELONGING TO A COUPLE, BY NUMBER OF CHILDREN THEY HAVE HAD, SHOWING AGE AND MARITAL STATUS, 1991

Age group and number of children born	Marital status					
	Never-married women	Married women	Separated women	Divorced women	Widowed women	**All women**
	%					
Aged 15–34						
0	63.8	25.9	26.2	28.5	28.8[1]	**33.3**
1	22.0	24.8	22.5	28.9	20.3[1]	**24.3**
2	10.6	33.8	30.8	28.6	25.4[1]	**29.2**
3	2.9	11.9	14.5	10.5	18.6[1]	**10.2**
4 or more	0.7	3.5	6.0	3.5	6.8[1]	**3.1**
Total	**100.0**	**100.0**	**100.0**	**100.0**	**100.0**	**100.0**
	Number					
All women belonging to a couple	393,566	1,579,865	16,133	51,700	1,967[1]	2,043,231
	%					
Aged 35–44						
0	48.9	9.4	11.6	19.2	11.1	**11.3**
1	23.6	13.7	19.3	23.0	19.4	**14.5**
2	18.1	45.4	39.6	34.6	40.0	**43.9**
3	6.4	22.5	20.8	16.7	18.3	**21.7**
4 or more	3.0	8.9	8.6	6.4	11.1	**8.7**
Total	**100.0**	**100.0**	**100.0**	**100.0**	**100.0**	**100.0**
	Number					
All women belonging to a couple	57,900	1,534,465	17,267	76,100	6,000	1,691,732
	%					
Aged 45–54						
0	54.7	7.9	12.7	12.8	11.0	**8.6**
1	18.0	10.5	13.1	14.4	13.4	**10.8**
2	11.3	35.3	31.2	33.7	23.2	**34.9**
3	6.7	25.6	23.5	20.3	22.8	**25.2**
4 or more	9.4	20.6	19.5	18.8	29.4	**20.5**
Total	**100.0**	**100.0**	**100.0**	**100.0**	**100.0**	**100.0**

TABLE 2.22 (CONCLUDED)

DISTRIBUTION OF WOMEN BELONGING TO A COUPLE, BY NUMBER OF CHILDREN THEY HAVE HAD, SHOWING AGE AND MARITAL STATUS, 1991

Age group and number of children born	Marital status					
	Never-married women	Married women	Separated women	Divorced women	Widowed women	**All women**
	Number					
All women belonging to a couple	11,467	1,063,066	7,367	37,967	8,467	1,128,332
	%					
Aged 55 or older						
0	55.4	9.9	5.4[1]	9.7	13.5	**10.1**
1	15.5	9.9	10.9[1]	15.5	13.1	**10.0**
2	10.1	22.5	19.6[1]	20.3	18.8	**22.4**
3	4.1	21.0	25.0[1]	15.5	15.8	**20.8**
4 or more	14.8	26.8	39.1[1]	39.0	38.9	**36.8**
Total	**100.0**	**100.0**	**100.0**	**100.0**	**100.0**	**100.0**
	Number					
All women belonging to a couple	4,933	1,515,032	3,067[1]	12,667	16,833	1,552,532

1. Percentage was calculated from fewer than 100 cases in the sample.

Note: Percentages may not add to 100 due to rounding.

Source: Census of Canada, 1991, Family Public Use Microdata Files.

2.5   LONE-PARENT FAMILIES

2.5.1   Double the number in 20 years

Of all the family changes revealed by the censuses, the one that drew the most attention was undoubtedly the increase in the number of lone-parent families. This increase has been dramatic. According to the 1991 Census results (statistics from 20% of the sample), the number of lone-parent families included in private households doubled in 20 years, from 479,000 in 1971 to 955,000 in 1991. The number of lone mothers increased even more dramatically, from 377,000 in 1971 to 786,000 in 1991. After dropping from 100,000 in 1971 to 95,000 in 1976, the number of lone fathers, like that of lone mothers, rose to 168,000 in 1991. Such an increase in lone-parent households begs an explanation: To what extent is this increase attributable to the size and age composition of the population? And to what extent is it owing to the higher incidence of lone-parent households at various ages?

To provide this assessment, we used the same method as was used to examine the increase in the number of husband–wife families. Therefore, the lone-parent count at any given time depends on the following three factors:

1. the number of men and women aged 15 and older enumerated in private households
2. the age distributions of these men and women
3. the proportion of lone parents in the various five-year age groups.

The intercensal variation in the number of lone parents may be defined, then, as the product of three indices measuring, respectively, the multiplier effect of the increase in the population of private households, changes in the age composition of this population, and changes in the incidence in lone parenthood at the various ages. Table 2.23 shows the indices obtained for each intercensal period and for the 1971 to 1991 period as a whole.[5]

TABLE 2.23

EFFECT OF VARIOUS FACTORS ON THE VARIATION IN THE NUMBER OF LONE PARENTS, 1971 TO 1991

Source of variation	1971–1976	1976–1981	1981–1986	1986–1991	1971–1991
			Lone mothers		
Number of women	1.138	1.118	1.064	1.088	1.473
Age of women	0.990	1.014	1.039	1.035	1.079
Proportion of mothers	1.134	1.122	1.083	0.989	1.364
All factors	**1.278**	**1.272**	**1.197**	**1.114**	**2.166**
			Lone fathers		
Number of men	1.127	1.110	1.050	1.089	1.430
Age of men	0.974	1.008	1.046	1.064	1.087
Proportion of fathers	0.934	1.224	1.068	0.971	1.190
All factors	**1.024**	**1.370**	**1.172**	**1.125**	**1.850**

Source: Census of Canada, Individual Public Use Microdata Files, 1971 to 1991.

The growth in the number of lone mothers was especially rapid in the first two intercensal periods, reaching 28% for the period 1971 to 1976 and 27% for 1976 to 1981. It then slowed to just 20% for 1981 to 1986 and 11% for the period 1986 to 1991 (see Table 2.23). It is true that the number of women aged 15 and older also rose very rapidly before 1981 and far more slowly thereafter. However, with the aging of the baby boom generations, the slowed increase in the female population between 1981 and 1991 was largely offset by a change in the composition of this population in favour of those age groups with the highest proportions of lone mothers. In other words, the evolution of the incidence of lone parenthood among women greatly influenced the evolution of the number of lone mothers. In the 1970s, when separation and divorce were on the rise, the proportion of lone mothers grew rapidly in nearly all age groups, and this marked increase in the incidence of lone parenthood contributed as much to the rise in the number of lone mothers as did the population increase. In the 1980s, these variations in the incidence of female lone parenthood declined, contributing less to the increase in the number of lone mothers and even curbing it slightly between 1986 and 1991. For the entire 1971 to 1991 period, it can be estimated that the number of lone mothers increased 59% as a result of the evolution of the size and age composition of the population. Consequently, it is reasonable to believe that the female lone-parent count in 1991 was 36% higher than it would have been had there been no change in the incidence of female lone parenthood at the various ages.

The number of lone fathers evolved more irregularly, at least at the start of the period of study. Thus, according to the Public Use Microdata File on Individuals, the number of lone fathers increased little (2%) from 1971 to 1976, then dramatically (37%) from 1976 to 1981, owing to the unfavourable effect of the evolution of the incidence of male lone parenthood until 1976, and its extremely favourable effect thereafter. This irregular increase in the number of lone fathers is not confined to the small samples used here: it also appears in the 100% census data. In fact, according to the overall statistics, the number of lone fathers rose appreciably in the period 1966 to 1971, from 72,000 to 101,000 in all households, then dropped in 1971 to 1976 from 100,000 to 95,000 in private households, before climbing to 124,000 in 1981. It seems that this irregularity is due to an overestimate of the number of lone parents in the 1971 Census (Wargon 1979a). In the 1980s, however, the number of lone fathers grew steadily and fairly similarly to that of lone mothers, increasing 17% in the period 1981 to 1986, and then to 13% in 1986 to 1991. The results obtained for the entire 1971 to 1991 period show that the rise in the incidence of male lone parenthood boosted the number of lone fathers just 19% higher than it would otherwise have been in 1991.

While doubling in number, the lone-parent population remained predominantly female. According to the data reproduced in tables 2.24 and 2.25, the proportion of mothers among lone parents varied little over 20 years, rising only from 78.9% in 1971 to 82.6% in 1981, and to 82.4% in 1991. In contrast, the distribution of lone parents by age changed appreciably, notably between 1971 and 1981. In particular, the female lone-parent population became younger and included a higher proportion of young mothers—nearly one-third of lone mothers in 1991 were under age 35, compared with just one-quarter in 1971. The female lone-parent population also included a smaller proportion of mothers aged 55 and older—one-fifth in 1991 compared with one-third in 1971. The evolution of the male lone-parent population differed somewhat. This population now included a distinctly higher proportion of fathers aged 35 to 54 (58% in 1991 versus 44% in 1971) and a smaller proportion of fathers under age 35 (15% versus 20%) and fathers aged 55 and older (28% versus 36%).

2.5.2 One or two children

Not only the number, but also the proportion of lone-parent families increased. Owing to the rise in lone parenthood and the decline in the popularity of matrimony, their share of all families rose from 9.4% in 1971 to 11.3% in 1981, and 13.0% in 1991. Their share of the subset of families with children grew even more quickly—from 12.7% in 1971 to 16.6% in 1981, and to 20.0% in 1991. Thus, while in 1971 there were seven couples with children for every lone-parent family, there were just five in 1981, and four in 1991.

Like other families with children, among which they themselves had once been counted, lone-parent families became smaller (see Figure 2.15 for the evolution of the distribution of female lone-parent families by number of never-married children at home). There were more families with one child than ever and, as a proportion, the number with two children was slightly higher. In contrast, families with three children became less common, and those with four or more children became the exception. The same observation can be made of male lone-parent families, the only notable difference being that the proportion of families with two children tended to stabilize rather than increase (see Figure 2.16). In short, now nine-tenths of lone-parent families, not three-quarters, have just one or two children, there being twice as many families of one child as families of two children. The average number of children per family is therefore small: 1.5 for male lone-parent families and 1.6 for female lone-parent families.

FIGURE 2.15

DISTRIBUTION OF LONE MOTHERS, BY NUMBER OF CHILDREN PRESENT IN THE HOME, 1971, 1981 AND 1991

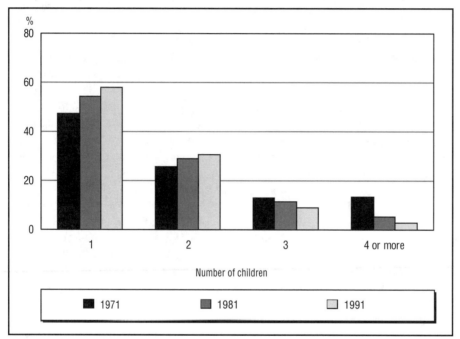

Note: The data for this figure are taken from Table 2.24.
Source: Census of Canada, 1971, 1981 and 1991, Family Public Use Microdata Files.

FIGURE 2.16

DISTRIBUTION OF LONE FATHERS, BY NUMBER OF CHILDREN PRESENT IN THE HOME,
1971, 1981 AND **1991**

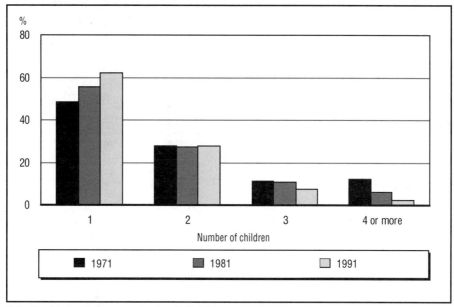

Note: The data for this figure are taken from Table 2.25.

Source: Census of Canada, 1971, 1981 and 1991, Family Public Use Microdata Files.

Tables 2.24 and 2.25 show the distribution of lone-parent families by number of children at home according to the sex and age of the lone parent. In 1971 and 1981, middle-aged parents (aged 35 to 54) clearly differed from younger parents in that they had more children. Thus, in 1971, 39% of lone mothers aged 35 to 54 had three or more children at home, compared with 27% of those under age 35; in 1981, the corresponding proportions were 26% and 13%. In contrast, in 1991, the distribution of families by size was about the same for these two age groups of the mother. Similarly, in 1991, there was no longer any difference in distribution by family size between lone fathers under age 35 and those fathers aged 35 to 54. The lone-parent families surveyed in 1991 were therefore far more similar in size than those surveyed 10 or 20 years earlier.

TABLE 2.24

DISTRIBUTION OF LONE MOTHERS, BY NUMBER OF CHILDREN PRESENT IN THE HOME AND MOHER'S AGE, 1971, 1981 AND 1991

Number of children present	Age group			All ages
	15–34	35–54	55 or older	
	%			
1971				
1	41.5	33.9	69.1	**47.4**
2	31.2	27.2	20.1	**25.8**
3	14.5	17.2	6.9	**13.2**
4 or more	12.8	21.6	3.9	**13.6**
Total	**100.0**	**100.0**	**100.0**	**100.0**
	Number ('000)			
All lone mothers	**87**	**158**	**122**	**367**
	%			
1981				
1	54.5	40.7	75.6	**54.3**
2	32.4	33.3	18.2	**29.0**
3	10.2	16.5	4.8	**11.4**
4 or more	3.0	9.5	1.4	**5.3**
Total	**100.0**	**100.0**	**100.0**	**100.0**
	Number ('000)			
All lone mothers	**187**	**247**	**155**	**589**
	%			
1991				
1	53.6	50.3	80.3	**58.0**
2	33.1	35.9	15.5	**30.5**
3	10.2	10.6	3.1	**8.8**
4 or more	3.1	3.1	1.1	**2.7**
Total	**100.0**	**100.0**	**100.0**	**100.0**
	Number ('000)			
All lone mothers	**240**	**362**	**173**	**775**

Note: Percentages may not add to 100 due to rounding.

Source: Census of Canada, 1971, 1981 and 1991, Family Public Use Microdata Files.

TABLE 2.25

DISTRIBUTION OF LONE FATHERS, BY NUMBER OF CHILDREN PRESENT IN THE HOME AND FATHER'S AGE, 1971, 1981 AND 1991

	Age group			
Number of children present	15–34	35–54	55 or older	**All ages**
	%			
1971				
1	40.3	39.0	65.0	**48.6**
2	35.3	29.3	21.5	**27.8**
3	15.9	13.6	6.0	**11.4**
4 or more	8.5	18.1	7.4	**12.3**
Total	**100.0**	**100.0**	**100.0**	**100.0**
	Number ('000)			
All lone fathers	**20**	**43**	**35**	**98**
	%			
1981				
1	63.8	45.1	71.3	**55.6**
2	27.5	32.3	18.2	**27.3**
3	7.4	13.8	6.8	**10.8**
4 or more	1.3	8.8	3.7	**6.3**
Total	**100.0**	**100.0**	**100.0**	**100.0**
	Number ('000)			
All lone fathers	**15**	**70**	**39**	**124**
	%			
1991				
1	56.9	57.0	74.6	**61.9**
2	31.9	31.2	19.3	**28.0**
3	8.5	9.2	4.1	**7.7**
4 or more	2.6	2.6	2.0	**2.4**
Total	**100.0**	**100.0**	**100.0**	**100.0**
	Number ('000)			
All lone fathers	**24**	**96**	**46**	**166**

Note: Percentages may not add to 100 due to rounding.

Source: Census of Canada, 1971, 1981 and 1991, Family Public Use Microdata Files.

2.5.3 Considerable diversity

Despite a number of shared characteristics, lone-parent families do not form a homogeneous group. For example, there are probably more differences than similarities between the situation of a young divorcee raising a small child alone and that of an elderly widow sharing her home with a grown son or daughter. The sex, age and marital status of the lone parent, the number of children born and the children's ages are all characteristics that create diversity. This section examines some aspects of the diversity of the families surveyed in 1991.

The distribution of lone parents by marital status varied greatly from one age group to another, notably among women (see Table 2.26). In the youngest age group, there were many singles because of the high incidence of separation among common-law couples. In fact, 45% of lone mothers under age 35 and 25% of lone fathers in the same age group had never been married. In contrast, of lone parents aged 35 to 44 and 45 to 54, most had previously been married, but their marriage had ended in separation or divorce. Divorced persons were the most common, accounting for nearly half of the lone parents. Finally, only among the oldest were the majority widowed—53% of fathers and 75% of mothers.

TABLE 2.26

DISTRIBUTION OF LONE PARENTS BY MARITAL STATUS, SHOWING PARENT'S AGE AND SEX, 1991

Age of lone parents	Marital status of lone parents					
	Never married	Married	Separated	Divorced	Widowed	All lone parents
	Lone mothers Number ('000)					
15–34	108	9	60	58	5	**240**
35–44	31	8	61	116	17	**233**
45–54	7	5	27	58	31	**128**
55 or older	3	6	12	23	129	**173**
All ages	**150**	**29**	**160**	**255**	**182**	**776**
	%					
15–34	45.0	3.8	25.0	24.2	2.1	**100.0**
35–44	13.3	3.4	26.2	49.8	7.3	**100.0**
45–54	5.5	3.9	21.1	45.3	24.2	**100.0**
55 or older	1.7	3.5	6.9	13.3	74.6	**100.0**
All ages	**19.3**	**3.7**	**20.6**	**32.9**	**23.5**	**100.0**
	Lone fathers Number ('000)					
15–34	6	5	6	6	1	**24**
35–44	4	8	14	23	3	**52**
45–54	2	7	11	20	6	**46**
55 or older	1	7	5	8	24	**45**
All ages	**13**	**26**	**37**	**57**	**34**	**167**
	%					
15–34	25.0	20.8	25.0	25.0	4.2	**100.0**
35–44	7.7	15.4	26.9	44.2	5.8	**100.0**
45–54	4.3	15.2	23.9	43.5	13.0	**100.0**
55 or older	2.2	15.6	11.1	17.8	53.3	**100.0**
All ages	**7.8**	**15.6**	**22.2**	**34.1**	**20.4**	**100.0**

Note: Percentages may not add to 100 due to rounding.

Source: Census of Canada, 1991, Family Public Use Microdata Files.

Another characteristic creating diversity is the number of children born (see Table 2.27). Obviously, the number of lone mothers who had not borne children was quite small: these were women who had adopted one or more children during a prior union or perhaps outside of any union. Relatively few in the younger age groups had had just one child: 48% of mothers under age 35, and 28% of mothers aged 35 to 44. The vast majority of lone mothers under age 45 had had just one or two children. By comparison, nearly half (48%) of those aged 45 to 54 and nearly three-quarters (74%) of those aged 55 and older had had three or more children. Compared with wives in the same age group who had had children (see Table 2.22), lone mothers in the youngest age group were more likely to have had one child, while lone mothers in older age groups tended to have had more children.

TABLE 2.27

DISTRIBUTION OF LONE MOTHERS BY NUMBER OF CHILDREN BORN AND MOTHER'S AGE, 1991

	Age group				
Number of children born	15–34	35–44	45–54	55 or older	**All ages**
			%		
0	0.9	1.1	2.0	1.9	**1.4**
1	48.1	27.7	16.0	8.2	**27.7**
2	33.8	42.8	33.8	16.0	**32.6**
3	12.4	18.6	23.0	18.8	**17.5**
4 or more	4.9	9.7	25.1	55.1	**20.9**
Total	**100.0**	**100.0**	**100.0**	**100.0**	**100.0**
			Number ('000)		
All lone mothers	**240**	**234**	**129**	**173**	**775**

Note: Percentages may not add to 100 due to rounding.
Source: Census of Canada, 1991, Family Public Use Microdata Files.

The difference between the number of children born and the number of children living at home was generally greater for lone mothers than for married women, except for those who had had just one child. Thus, according to the data taken from the Microdata File on Family (not reproduced here), the proportion of mothers of two children, both of whom were living at home, was 88% for lone mothers under age 35 and 95% for married women of the same age; 72% for lone mothers aged 35 to 44, and 86% for married women of the same age. Similarly, the proportion of mothers under age 35 with three children, all of whom lived at home, was 72% for lone mothers and 86% for married women; at ages 35 to 44, this percentage was 48% for lone mothers and 74% for married women. These results indicate a lesser tendency for there to be children in the home of lone-parent families headed by women, either because custody of the children is shared by the father and mother, or because the children leave home at an earlier age. Whatever the reasons, the lower rate of retention of children in the home was one of the reasons for the smaller size of lone-parent families.

Very similar in terms of size—most had just one or two children—female lone-parent families varied greatly by the children's age (see Table 2.28 for the age distribution of lone mothers according to the oldest child living at home). Mothers living only with children under age six accounted for only 16% of the total. For nearly twice as many (31%), the oldest child was aged 6 to 14. About half (47%) of lone mothers were therefore living only with children under age 15, and their families were truly young families. The rest, only somewhat fewer in number, had, in most cases, at least one child who had reached the age of majority (that is, aged 18 or older) living at home.

TABLE 2.28

DISTRIBUTION OF LONE MOTHERS, BY AGE OF OLDEST CHILD LIVING AT HOME AND MOTHER'S AGE, 1991

Mother's age	Age of oldest child					
	Under age 6	6–14	15–17	18–24	25 or older	All ages
	Number ('000)					
15–34	107	123	9	1	–	240
35–44	13	99	61	59	2	234
45–54	–	13	17	71	27	129
55 or older	–	1	3	26	142	173
All ages	**121**	**236**	**91**	**157**	**171**	**775**
	%					
15–34	44.4	51.2	3.9	0.4	–	100.0
35–44	5.8	42.2	26.0	25.2	0.9	100.0
45–54	–	10.5	13.6	54.9	21.0	100.0
55 or older	–	0.7	1.8	15.3	82.2	100.0
All ages	**15.6**	**30.5**	**11.7**	**20.2**	**22.1**	**100.0**

– nil or zero

Note: Percentages may not add to 100 due to rounding.

Source: Census of Canada, 1991, Family Public Use Microdata Files

Female lone-parent families differed considerably from husband–wife families by age of the oldest child living at home. The differences were greater for the youngest (under age 35) and oldest (age 55 and older) age groups (see tables 2.28 and 2.29). Young lone mothers tended more often than other mothers to have an oldest son or daughter over the age of five; while older lone mothers were more likely than other mothers to have an oldest son or daughter aged 25 or older. These differences occur mainly because, in both age groups, lone mothers were, on average, older than their cohorts. All ages of the mother combined, fewer lone-parent families had children only under age 15 (47% versus 55%), while far more had one child of majority age (42% versus 32%).

TABLE 2.29

DISTRIBUTION OF MOTHERS BELONGING TO A COUPLE, BY AGE OF OLDEST CHILD LIVING AT HOME,
SHOWING MOTHER'S AGE, 1991

Mother's age	Age of oldest child					
	Under age 6	6–14	15–17	18–24	25 or older	All ages
	Number ('000)					
15–34	711	594	39	7	0	1,351
35–44	104	643	340	351	8	1,446
45–54	3	59	93	429	134	717
55 or older	1	3	8	98	213	323
All ages	818	1,299	480	886	355	3,837
	%					
15–34	52.6	44.0	2.9	0.5	0.0	100.0
35–44	7.2	44.4	23.5	24.3	0.6	100.0
45–54	0.4	8.2	12.9	59.8	18.7	100.0
55 or older	0.3	0.9	2.4	30.4	66.0	100.0
All ages	21.3	33.8	12.5	23.1	9.3	100.0

Note: Percentages may not add to 100 due to rounding.

Source: Census of Canada, 1991, Family Public Use Microdata Files.

Lone fathers usually lived with even older children (see Table 2.30). Because the mother generally assumes custody of very young children, just 9% of lone fathers were living only with one or more children who were under six years of age. Just over one-third (35%) were living only with children under age 15. Half were living with at least one child of majority age. For all ages, however, there were few differences between lone fathers and lone mothers, except in the 45-to-54 and 55-and-older age groups. At these ages, the proportion of mothers living with at least one child aged 25 or older was higher than that of fathers, doubtless because women have their children at a younger age and live longer.

TABLE 2.30

DISTRIBUTION OF LONE FATHERS, BY AGE OF OLDEST CHILD LIVING AT HOME,
SHOWING FATHER'S AGE, 1991

Father's age	Age of oldest child					All ages
	Under age 6	6–14	15–17	18–24	25 or older	
	Number ('000)					
15–34	10	12	1	1	–	24
35–44	3	23	13	11	1	52
45–54	1	6	9	24	6	45
55 or older	–	1	2	11	30	46
All ages	15	43	25	47	37	166
	%					
15–34	43.7	50.6	3.2	2.2	0.3	100.0
35–44	6.3	45.4	25.6	21.7	1.0	100.0
45–54	1.5	12.8	19.2	53.7	12.8	100.0
55 or older	0.9	3.0	4.9	25.0	66.2	100.0
All ages	8.9	25.6	14.9	28.4	22.1	100.0

– nil or zero

Note: Percentages may not add to 100 due to rounding.

Source: Census of Canada, 1991, Family Public Use Microdata Files.

2.6 CONCLUSION

In the 1970s and 1980s, the behaviour of Canadian women and men related to union formation and dissolution changed profoundly. Long regarded as a prerequisite to forming a couple and starting a family, marriage gradually declined in popularity in relation to common-law unions and was entered into later in life and less often. Divorce, seldom granted and difficult to obtain before the 1968 *Divorce Act*, became common, even among couples that still had young children. A crack had appeared in the marriage mold that had previously ensured the stability of the family.

One of the first consequences of these behavioural changes was the decline in the popularity of married life among young adults and, to a lesser degree, middle-aged adults. And families where the wife was under age 35 registered the weakest increase in 20 years (the number even fell from 1981 to 1991), while those where the wife was aged 35 to 54 experienced slightly-higher-than-average growth. But the greatest increase is seen for families where the wife was aged 55 and older, mainly owing to the marked growth of the older population. While it went from 4.6 million in 1971 to 6.4 million in 1991, the number of husband–wife families increased less than might have been expected given the growth of the population and the changes in its age composition.

Another consequence of the behavioural changes referred to above was the sharp rise in the incidence of lone parenthood at ages when men and women generally have children living at home. The number of lone-parent families thus grew more than it otherwise might have because of the evolution in the size and age distribution of the population. The number of lone-parent families doubled in two decades, from 479,000 in 1971 to 955,000 in 1991, and rose from 9.4% to 13.0% as a proportion of all families. Also, unlike what had been observed in the 1950s and 1960s, lone parents were no longer mostly widows and widowers, but rather people whose marriage or common-law union had dissolved.

More diverse than the families of 1971, those of 1991 were also smaller. This was true of lone-parent families, nine-tenths of which had only one or two children at home. It was also true of husband–wife families. The proportion of couples without children rose from 30% to 40% in 20 years, owing essentially to the marked increase in the proportion of couples left on their own after their children had left home. The remaining couples generally had just one or two children living at home or, more rarely, three. Families with four or more children, still numerous in 1971, had virtually disappeared as the generations that had their offspring during the post-war baby boom left the postparental phase. These prolific generations had in effect been replaced by generations who had opted to keep their fertility low following the availability of modern methods of birth control. Also, two children became the norm for the majority of couples of the new generations, and few couples aspired to having more than three offspring.

Among the changes in the state of families from 1971 to 1991, the changes to family structure are the most striking in that they reveal a gradual abandonment of the family standards of the past. Accordingly, the place of common-law unions, which in 1991 represented 11% of all couples, and 23% of couples where the woman was under age 35, cannot be ignored. Similarly, one is struck by the growing place of lone-parent families, whose share of all families with children rose from 12.7% to 20.0% in 20 years. The increase in the incidence of these "anomalous" situations prompted Statistics Canada to conduct retrospective surveys on the family histories of Canadian men and women to more clearly identify the changes taking place. The chapters that follow present the analyses of the family biographies gathered through these retrospective surveys.

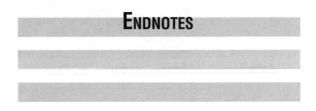

ENDNOTES

1. The "marriage market" refers to all persons of marrying age who are looking for a spouse.
2. See Duchesne (1993).
3. Completed fertility refers to the total number of children a woman bears in her lifetime.
4. The terms used to designate these two-family categories have changed over time, but only those used most recently are used here, that is, husband–wife families and lone-parent families.
5. The statistical data used to calculate the indices are taken from the Microdata File on Individuals after excluding data for members of collective households and for households outside Canada.

CHAPTER

3

FEMALE FAMILY PATHS

HÉLÈNE DESROSIERS, HEATHER JUBY

AND CÉLINE LE BOURDAIS

Since the mid-1960s, the demographic behaviours of Canadian men and women have altered profoundly, resulting in major changes in the composition of households and families. Based on the censuses of the last 40 years, the previous chapters attempt to shed light on the impact that the decline in fertility, the diminishing popularity of marriage, and growing marital instability have had on the family environment of Canadian men and women. These chapters also examine various developments, such as the increase in one-person households, the rise of lone-parent families after 1971, and the growing number of common-law unions.

The analysis of census data reveal some of the most notable changes in family life in Canada, but cannot take into account the extent of the changes taking place in the lives of individuals. First of all, in their current form, census data do not reflect the diversity of actual family statuses. For example, since respondents are asked to report a stepson, stepdaughter or adopted child as a son or daughter, it is impossible to identify "blended families" within the larger scope of "two-parent" families (Norris and Knighton 1995). This limitation becomes more constraining as marital instability and the number of blended families increase.

Secondly, the evolution outlined in the previous chapters is based on census "snapshots" and therefore provides only a glimpse of the changes taking place. "Purely cross-sectional observation has the disadvantage of skewing some observations by over-representing the most stable situations" [translation] (Léridon 1993, p. 57). Due to structural inertia, it always takes time before changes in individual behaviours are reflected, albeit imperfectly, in the cross-sections obtained from censuses. Also, being synchronous, census data obviously cannot describe the multiplicity and diversity of the individual life courses that flow from a given family environment. In order to document the past marital and family history of adults, it is therefore necessary to rely on retrospective survey data.

Without question, the main advantage of retrospective surveys is that they provide an in-depth look at the prior history of respondents (Léridon 1993). As these surveys are not constrained by a concern for completeness and continuity, they allow for a more profound analysis of the changes experienced by individuals. The surveys are not, however, without some of the problems previously mentioned. As a rule, the sampling method of these surveys is strictly cross-sectional, so there is a risk, as with all censuses, of underrepresenting the most mobile individuals and the most unstable situations. But the greatest limitation of these surveys is that the family configurations studied are often initially too uncommon in the population to allow for a very detailed analysis of the processes undergoing change. As a complement to the census, retrospective surveys do, however, reveal otherwise hidden situations and document their prior histories.

This chapter attempts to show how much the changes in fertility and conjugal life have played a role in altering and adding to the complexity of the family paths of Canadian women surveyed by the 1991 Census. Chapter 4 then examines how these changes have affected the lives of Canadian men. The data used are taken from the 1990 General Social Survey, cycle 5: Family and Friends (GSS), completed by Statistics Canada one year before the census.[1]

Specifically, this chapter first tackles the family statuses as defined in the census and observed on Census Day, and attempts to describe, retrospectively, the marital and family history of the women who experienced them. For example, we estimate, for all female respondents legally married at the time of the survey, the proportion who had lived common law, married their common-law partner, or remarried. We also examine the percentage of women who had children or raised the children of their spouse. Using these last figures, we then assess the significance of blended families within the female adult population.

The analysis in the next section of this chapter explores the dynamics of the formation and dissolution of various forms of family organization—the intact two-parent family, the lone-parent family, and the blended family—in women's lives. Using this study, it is possible to estimate the proportion of women likely to experience a given family status in their lifetime and the time women are likely to spend in these types of families, and to show the demographic events associated with the formation and dissolution of families with children.

The chapter's final section is devoted to describing female family paths. In addition to a general description, this section describes the specifics of the evolution of the various female family paths and estimates the proportion of women who will follow each.

In each of the analyses presented in this chapter, the comparison of women by age group reveals how much the profound changes in married life and fertility have variously affected the evolution of the family life of different generations of Canadian women. It should be said at the outset that the analysis covers all women aged 18 to 64 at the time of the 1990 GSS,[2] regardless of their family status at the time. A fair number of women aged 18 and older, namely, single women living with their parents, are still considered "children" in the context of the census. However, because some of these so-called children had already embarked on their conjugal and family life, and in spite of the fact that they were living with their parents at the time of the survey, we considered it both relevant and important to include them in our study of women's family life. This makes it possible to show the extent to which, in recent generations, the transition to adult life through the formation of a couple and a family tends increasingly to be marked by back-and-forth movements between the original family unit and the unit of destination. At the limit's other end, age 64 was chosen as the cut-off age to decrease the selection size and minimize the problems inherent in any analysis based on a retrospective survey of respondent's accurately remembering events that took place long ago.

3.1 PRESENTATION OF THE 1990 GENERAL SOCIAL SURVEY, CYCLE 5: FAMILY AND FRIENDS

The General Social Survey, cycle 5: Family and Friends (GSS) was conducted by Statistics Canada from January to March 1990. The GSS, a continuing program in which a survey is conducted on a different subject each year, was initiated to gather information on the long-term social trends of Canadian society and to provide information on specific policy issues concerning the lifestyles and material well-being of Canadians (McDaniel and Strike 1994). As its name indicates, the fifth GSS focused on the respondent's family and friends and on the relationships between them. Like the 1984 Family History Survey, it compiled the marital and parental histories of a large sample of respondents, establishing a chronology of common-law unions and marriages; separations, divorces and widowhood; and births and departures of children.[3] This GSS also explored other subjects related to family life, such as relationships with parents, grandparents and siblings; relationships with children no longer living at home; intentions with respect to fertility; contacts with friends; and several socio-economic characteristics. Although the sample was intended to be representative of the Canadian population, it excluded permanent residents of institutions. Nearly 13,500 people aged 15 and older in 1990, of whom 5,305 were women aged 18 to 64, were interviewed by telephone for this survey.

3.2 OVERVIEW OF THE MARITAL AND PARENTAL HISTORY OF WOMEN ACCORDING TO THEIR FAMILY STATUS

For the purposes of this section, the family status of women at the time of the survey corresponds with their living arrangements in a "census family."[4] Single (never-married) respondents, regardless of their age, who were living with one or both parents are considered "children." Women living with a spouse in a marriage or in a common-law union belong to a "couple," with or without children. Women with no spouse and living with one or more children are counted as "heads of lone-parent families." Finally, women not belonging to a census family, that is, who were not children, parents, nor members of a couple, as defined above, are classified as "non-family persons."

Before proceeding to the study of marital and parental histories, take a moment to examine the distribution of 1990 GSS respondents aged 18 to 64 by their family status at the time of the survey[5] (see Table 3.1). This table should provide a better sense of the magnitude of each of the groups just described.

TABLE 3.1

DISTRIBUTION OF WOMEN AGED 18 TO 64, BY FAMILY STATUS AND AGE AT THE TIME OF THE SURVEY, 1990

Family status[1] at the time of the survey	Age group					
	18–24	25–34	35–44	45–54	55–64	**All ages**
			%			
"Child" status	45	6	3	1	1	**10**
Women belonging to a couple	29	75	79	76	74	**68**
with no children	19	24	10	31	52	**24**
with children	10	51	69	45	22	**44**
Lone mothers	4	7	9	11	6	**8**
Non-family persons	22	12	9	12	19	**14**
Total	**100**	**100**	**100**	**100**	**100**	**100**
			%			
Distribution by age	16	29	24	17	14	**100**

1. Family status refers to the status held in relation to a census family.

Source: 1990 GSS, cycle 5, Public Use Microdata File.

At the time of the survey, just over two-thirds (68%) of respondents aged 18 to 64 were living with a spouse; 44% of these belonged to a couple with children, and 24% to a couple without children. Further, 8% of the women headed a lone-parent family, 10% had "child" status in a two-parent or lone-parent family, and 14% were not living in a census family, that is, they were classified as non-family persons. The highest percentage of women classified as children (45%) obviously was among respondents aged 18 to 24, while non-family persons were predominantly found (about 20%) among women aged 18 to 24 and 55 to 64. Finally, women were most likely to be a parent in a two-parent family between the ages of 35 and 44 (69%), and in a lone-parent family between the ages of 45 and 54 (11%).

These results provide a rather static picture of the family history of individuals, but do correspond fairly closely with their anticipated movement through the stages of life. Between the ages of 18 and 24, one enters adulthood and embarks on one's family and occupational life; however, while some respondents had a spouse or child, most were living with their parents or outside a parental or marital relationship. It is really between the ages of 25 and 44 that one embarks on the phase of forming and building a family. While a fair proportion of female heads of a lone-parent family showed that dissolved relationships contribute to considerable family mobility among this age group, even larger numbers of couples with children attest to the importance of this phase in a woman's life. After age 45, the number and size of families decrease considerably as the proportion of couples without children and the proportion of non-family persons increases. This, of course, is the time when children begin to leave the parental home and the effect of increased male mortality begins to be felt.

To what extent does this cross-sectional profile reflect female family paths? Or, conversely, to what extent does it camouflage the multiple, and sometimes contrasting, paths taken by the various groups of women? The following analysis attempts to answer these questions.

3.2.1 The history of "child" status

In the past, classifying single adults living with their parents as "children" did not pose a problem since, typically, these individuals had never left the parental home to live on their own. Unlike their "ever-married" siblings, these "children" had neither been involved in a union nor had they had children. The transition to adulthood is not as simple today as it was when the departure from home and marriage overlapped. Instead, it consists of a sequence of episodes that vary in number and are more or less interrelated (Lapierre-Adamcyk et al. 1995). The first departure from home is not always final, and the formation of a first union, often not legalized, does not necessarily rule out the possibility of a later return to the family of origin. The GSS data allow us to estimate the extent of these changes in the lives of young people. By looking at the proportion of "children" who temporarily left home, were involved in a couple, or had had children, we can better assess the degree to which the census classification is problematic.

Table 3.2 presents several indicators of the family history of female respondents aged 18 to 64 who had "child" status at the time of the survey. (Remember that this category includes all never-married women, regardless of age, living with one or both parents.) According to the data, 16% of female respondents living with their parents at the time of the survey had previously left home to live on their own. The percentage of "children" who had done so predictably increases with age: while 11% of respondents had left home once, this was true of just over 25% of women aged 25 to 34, and nearly 40% of those aged 35 and older. It was the youngest women who most often cited school attendance (45%) as the main reason for their most recent departure from home, while the oldest respondents usually cited a job (50%). A fair number of female respondents aged 25 to 34 (about 25%) said they had left home because of a job, to attend school, "to be independent/move into own place," or for some other reason, including to form a union (1990 GSS).

TABLE 3.2

INDICATORS OF THE RESIDENTIAL, CONJUGAL AND PARENTAL HISTORY OF WOMEN AGED 18 TO 64 HAVING "CHILD" STATUS, BY AGE GROUP AT THE TIME OF THE SURVEY, 1990

Indicators of residential, conjugal and parental history	Age group			
	18–24	25–34	35–64	All ages
Of all women having "child" status[1]				
Percent who had left the parental home	11	26	39	**16**
Percent who had experienced a common-law union	7	11	14	**8**
Percent who were single mothers (i.e., living with a child)	5	8	0	**5**
Of the women living with no children or spouse but with one or both of their parents				
Percent who had never been in a union	94	93	61	**90**
Percent who had lived common law but never been married	6	6	10	**6**
Percent who had been married	0	1	29	**4**

1. Since the subcategories are not mutually exclusive, the total may not equal 100%.

Source: 1990 GSS, cycle 5, Public Use Microdata File.

Five percent of women who were classified as children living in a census family were themselves parents (see Table 3.2). These women were young, single (never-married) mothers living in a three-generation household. In these situations, the census gave precedence to the "child" status of these women, which meant they were not identified as lone mothers. Furthermore, the census camouflages the parent–child relationship between these mothers and their children, the latter being regarded as non-family persons, that is, as not belonging to the family unit made up of the children's mother and her parents (Norris and Knighton 1995).[6] According to the 1990 GSS data, 5% of respondents aged 18 to 24 living with their parents were lone mothers, and this was also true of 8% of the smaller group of "children" aged 25 to 34 living with their parents. It is worth noting that slightly over one-quarter (28%) of single lone mothers aged 18 to 34 who were living with their parents had, in fact, had their child within a common-law union that subsequently ended in separation or with the death of their spouse. Since the births of their children occurred within a union, they cannot be considered births "outside of marriage" in the strict sense of the term.

The proportion of women who were living with their parents and had been in a common-law union is notable (see Table 3.2). According to the GSS data, 1 in 12 "children" had previously lived with a common-law partner. This phenomenon affected 7% of women aged 18 to 24 and 14% of those aged 35 and older. If we apply the principle that a person who has belonged to a couple is no longer considered a child, the census strategy of assigning "child" status to all never-married children has the effect, as Norris and Knighton (1995) point out, of overestimating their number in census families, given the significant increase in common-law unions observed over the last 20 years.

It is difficult to reconcile the fact that children who become separated after a common-law union, of any duration, and return home to live with their parents, regain "child" status, while those who return after the break-up of a legal marriage become "non-family persons." Insofar as common-law unions are gradually taking the place of marriage, as seen in the first two chapters of this monograph, the use of legal matrimony alone in determining "child" status may no longer be appropriate. Using the data at the bottom of Table 3.2, it is possible to compare the relative number of young women who returned to live with their family of origin after the dissolution of a common-law union or a marriage. These data are for all female respondents who had no spouse or children and who were living with their parents, regardless of whether they had been previously married.

These data show that 10% of respondents living without a spouse or children in their family of origin had been previously involved in a union. This proportion is decidedly higher among those aged 35 and older (39%) than among those aged 18 to 34 (6% to 7%). However, nearly all women aged 18 to 34 who had belonged to a couple had done so informally, while this is true of just one-third of those aged 35 and older. Several factors, including the deferral of marriage and the increase in and fragility of common-law unions in recent generations (Desrosiers and Le Bourdais 1993), explain this difference in distribution by age group. Furthermore, it is reasonable to assume that common-law wives are more likely than their married counterparts to return home to live with their parents after the break-up of their relationship. As common-law union covers a wide range of practices, which the terms "juvenile cohabitation" and "trial marriage" also attempt to convey, the importance (duration) of this type of union in the lives of individuals should be better defined. Given better terms and clearer definitions for common-law unions, we would be able to assess the degree to which giving "child" status to an ex-common-law wife who returns home to live with her parents is problematic. Here, keep in mind that behavioural changes in conjugal life may result in a relative overestimation of the number of children living in a census family in recent generations. Obviously, the spread of more informal conjugal living arrangements invites reflection about the very definition of the concept of "child" in the census and, more generally, the concept of family.

3.2.2 The history of women belonging to a couple

This section highlights the marital paths followed by the different generations of women living with a spouse (husband or common-law partner) at the time of the survey. The focus of the analysis then shifts to examine the parental life courses these women have followed.

3.2.2.1 Marital history

Several studies (Burch and Madan 1986; Dumas and Péron 1992; Le Bourdais and Desrosiers 1988; Le Bourdais and Marcil-Gratton 1996) describe the increase in common-law unions in Canada since the early 1970s and show that this phenomenon now affects not only young people at the start of conjugal life, but also a growing number of people entering a new union after the failure of their first marriage. These studies also underscore the decline in the rate of legal marriage and the increase in the number of unions that young people of recent generations are likely to experience. Table 3.3 clearly illustrates these developments across the generations.

TABLE 3.3

INDICATORS OF THE CONJUGAL HISTORY OF WOMEN AGED 18 TO 64 BELONGING TO A COUPLE, BY AGE AT THE TIME OF THE SURVEY, 1990

Indicators of conjugal history	Age group					
	18–24	25–34	35–44	45–54	55–64	All ages
Percent of married women	51	80	91	95	97	86
Percent of women living common law	49	20	9	5	3	14
Of the married women						
Percent in first marriage	100	94	90	91	89	92
with no previous union[1]	56	66	87	97	99	84
who married their common-law partner	43	33	12	2	1	16
who had lived common law with another partner	3	7	3	1	0	3
Percent remarried	0	6	10	9	11	8
who had never lived common law[1]	–	24	24	36	78	39
who married their common-law partner	–	65	71	64	21	57
Of the women living common law						
Percent in first common-law union	83	67	71	73	90[2]	73
never-married	100	78	27	9	0[2]	67
ever-married	0	22	73	91	100[2]	33
Percent in second or subsequent common-law union	17	33	29	27	10[2]	27
never-marrieds	98[2]	58	48	--	--	58
ever-married	2[2]	42	52	--	--	42

-- Percentage omitted (based on fewer than 10 cases in the sample). Expanded data reduced to the size of the initial sample.
– Nil or zero.
1. The subcategories are not mutually exclusive; therefore the total may not equal 100%.
2. Percentage calculated from fewer than 25 cases in the sample. Expanded data reduced to the size of the initial sample.
Source: 1990 GSS, cycle 5, Public Use Microdata File.

The top section of Table 3.3 shows the increase in the percentage of common-law unions observed at the time of the survey, from older to more recent generations. Based on the respondents' prior history, the next section of the table shows that about 1 in every 12 married women were in their second marriage at the time they were surveyed by the GSS. The percentage hovers at around 10% for women aged 35 and older, and clearly drops for younger ages. This is obviously related to the fact that the younger women were older on first marrying and, above all, were not as far along their marital life course.

Nearly all women aged 45 to 64 who were in their first marriage had not previously been in any other form of union, which is not surprising since many of them married before common-law unions became widespread. This situation changes as we approach more recent generations: 13% of women aged 35 to 44 and 44% of those aged 18 to 24 had cohabited before. In the vast majority of cases, these women had married their common-law partner (92.3% of those aged 35 to 44 and 97.7% of those 18 to 24).[7] Appreciably fewer women had lived with a partner other than their husband. It is interesting to note that about two-thirds of women had lived with their husband before legalizing the union. Only those aged 55 to 64 deviated from this model, with one-fifth of them reporting a prior common-law relationship.

The bottom section of Table 3.3 provides information about the marital history of women cohabiting at the time of the survey. Overall, just over one-quarter of common-law wives were in a second common-law union, while the percentage increases from 10% of those aged 55 to 64 to one-third of those aged 25 to 34. At younger ages, the marital paths of the women are not far enough advanced to allow accurate measurement of this phenomenon. Also, the proportion of ever-married women increases with the respondents' age, regardless of the rank (first, second, etc.) of the union in question. Thus, just under one-quarter (22%) of women aged 25 to 34 living common law for the first time had previously been married. This percentage climbs to 73% among those aged 35 to 44, and to more than 90% for women aged 45 and older. Common-law unions therefore occur later in life among older generations, generally following a marriage, while for younger generations it is more likely to be their first experience of conjugal life.

These data clearly illustrate the growing conjugal mobility of Canadian women today. The data otherwise tabulated show that 85% of female respondents aged 55 to 64 belonging to a couple had experienced only one union of a given type—in all cases, a direct marriage (a marriage not preceded by cohabitation). This percentage drops to 61% among those aged 25 to 34 who had only just begun their marital life.

3.2.2.2 The parental history of women belonging to a couple with children

The main purpose of this section is to shed light on the little-known phenomenon of blended families. Though not identifiable from census data, this form of family organization is gaining ground in a context of increased conjugal mobility.

Blended families that existed at the time of the survey are not directly identifiable in the GSS. This survey gathered information on natural, step- or adopted children, but their status was established only in relation to the respondents. Consequently, it is possible to identify women living with the children of their spouse, but not those living with a spouse who is not the father of their children. This makes it impossible to use the GSS to directly assess the magnitude of blended families (Norris and Knighton 1995). To do so, it is necessary to rely on the respondents' past history for information about the origin of the children living in the household (for more information, see Appendix 3.1; also see Desrosiers et al. 1994).

Table 3.4 illustrates the approach used to identify the various family types among couples with children. An "intact two-parent family" is a family unit that includes only those children[8] who are living with both of their natural or adoptive parents, whether their parents are married or common-law partners. A "blended family" refers to a family unit that includes at least one child who is living with his or her natural parent and a stepparent, again regardless of whether the couple are married or living common law. A blended family may include children from a previous union of either or both spouses, and may also include children born to the new couple. However, when the last child not born to the couple leaves the parental home, the blended family, strictly from the standpoint of living arrangements, becomes an "intact family." This family organization has been classified as a "re-created family" to distinguish it from both the original intact family and the blended family categories.

TABLE 3.4

DISTRIBUTION OF WOMEN BELONGING TO A COUPLE WITH CHILDREN, BY TYPE OF FAMILY AND AGE AT THE TIME OF THE SURVEY, 1990

Type of family[1]	Origin of children present	Age group			
		18–34	35–44	45–64	All ages
		%			
Intact families	All of the current couple	83	87	89	86
Blended families, no children common to the couple	All of a previous union	9	7	5	7
Blended families, with children common to the couple	Some children are of the current couple and others of a previous union	7	3	1	4
Re-created families[2]	All of the current couple	1	3	5	3
Total		100	100	100	100
		%			
Distribution by age		37	39	24	100

1. The type of family is determined according to the origin of the children present in the household at the time of the survey.
2. These are blended families which, strictly from the standpoint of living arrangements, become "intact" families once the last child not of the couple has left home, leaving behind a couple living with their own natural children.

Source: 1990 GSS, cycle 5, Public Use Microdata File.

At the time of the survey, nearly 9 in 10 women (86%) who belonged to a couple with children had formed a family with the father of their children, whereas 3% of couples belonged to a re-created family (see Table 3.4). Just over 10% of couples with children were living as a blended family and 4% of these couples had had a child together. The percentage of blended families increases slightly from older (6% of those aged 45 to 64[9]) to younger (16% of those aged 18 to 34) generations, a result obviously linked to the growing instability of conjugal life.

Note, however, that there are proportionally more re-created families among older women; this is no doubt because these older women had older children who were born outside the existing union and had left the home.

Table 3.5 provides a closer look at the composition of blended families surveyed by the GSS. Of families without children born to the couple, most (89.2%) include children of a single sibling relationship: in 49% of cases, the siblings were the wife's children; in 9% of cases, the siblings were the children of her spouse. Only 7% of families included stepbrothers and stepsisters— children of both spouses, born of previous unions. Of the blended families with children common to the couple, almost all included children of just one spouse, usually the woman's, thereby creating half-brother and half-sister sibling relationships. Barely 1% of blended families combined children of three different sibling relationships, that is, children of the wife, children of the husband, and children common to both spouses.

TABLE 3.5

DISTRIBUTION OF WOMEN LIVING IN A BLENDED FAMILY, BY FAMILY COMPOSITION, RANK OF THE EPISODE AND AGE AT THE TIME OF THE SURVEY, 1990

Family composition and rank of the episode	Age group			
	18–34	35–44	45–64	**All ages**
			%	
Family composition				
All children are of a previous union	56	69	82	**65**
of the respondent	39	55	66	**49**
of the husband	13	5	7	**9**
of both spouses	4	9	9	**7**
Some children are of the current couple and				
others are of a previous union	44	31	18	**35**
of the respondent	37	28	18	**31**
of the husband	6	1	0	**3**
of both spouses	1	2	0	**1**
Total	100	100	100	**100**
			%	
Rank of the episode				
1st episode	85	77	95	**84**
2nd episode	15	23	5	**16**
Total	100	100	100	**100**
			%	
Distribution by age	51	36	13	**100**

Source: 1990 GSS, cycle 5, Public Use Microdata File.

In all, nearly 9 in 10 women[10] brought their own children into the blended family, and only 9% were raising only the children of their spouse. This situation obviously attests to the fact that women are more likely to assume custody of their children after the break-up of a marriage.

Finally, the last section of Table 3.5 shows that the vast majority (84%) of women who belonged to a blended family were experiencing this situation for the first time. But this percentage varies depending on the women's age group. For example, of women aged 35 to 44 (the age group most affected by the changes in conjugal life), nearly one-quarter (23%) had experienced this type of family organization at least once before. Only 15% of women under age 35 had been in a blended family at least once before, but this percentage is likely to increase in the coming years.

The type of union chosen by women living in a two-parent family varies greatly depending on the type of family unit. Thus, 97% of women belonging to an intact two-parent family were married at the time of the survey. Of this percentage, 81% had entered directly into marriage with the father of their children, while 16% had lived with their spouse before marriage (see Table 3.6). In contrast, over one-third of women belonging to either a blended or re-created family were living common law, and nearly another third had married their spouse after living with him common law. The younger the age group, the more popular common-law union becomes; this is as true of intact families as it is of blended or re-created families.

TABLE 3.6

TYPE AND RANK OF THE UNION AND NUMBER OF CHILDREN PRESENT AMONG COUPLES WITH CHILDREN, BY TYPE OF FAMILY AND WOMAN'S AGE AT THE TIME OF THE SURVEY, 1990

| Type of family[1] | Age group | | | |
	18–34	35–44	45–64	All ages
Type of union[2]		%		
Intact families				
Direct marriage	63	87	98	**81**
Marriage preceded by a common-law union	29	12	2	**16**
Common-law union	8	1	0	**3**
Blended and re-created families				
Direct marriage	24	31	59	**34**
Marriage preceded by a common-law union	32	36	18	**31**
Common-law union	44	33	23	**35**
Rank of the union[3]		%		
Intact families				
1st union	91	94	98	**94**
2nd union	8	4	2	**5**
3rd or subsequent union	1	2	0	**1**
Blended and re-created families				
1st union	45	26	43	**37**
2nd union	47	56	57	**53**
3rd or subsequent union	8	18	0	**10**

TABLE **3.6** (CONCLUDED)

TYPE AND RANK OF THE UNION AND NUMBER OF CHILDREN PRESENT AMONG COUPLES WITH CHILDREN, BY TYPE OF FAMILY AND WOMAN'S AGE AT THE TIME OF THE SURVEY, **1990**

	Age group			
Type of family[1]	18–34	35–44	45–64	**All ages**
Number of children present[4]		%		
Intact families				
1 child	37	18	50	**33**
2 children	44	52	31	**44**
3 or more children	19	30	19	**23**
Average number of children	1.9	2.2	1.8	**2.0**
Blended and re-created families				
1 child	34	32	61	**39**
2 children	42	37	29	**37**
3 or more children	24	31	10	**24**
Average number of children	2.0	2.0	1.6	**1.9**

1. For analytical purposes "re-created" families have been grouped with blended families, with which they share a similar history in this table.

2. This refers to the type of the current union. The category "marriage preceded by a common-law union" refers to women who married their common-law partner.

3. When the marriage was to a common-law partner, it was considered a single union whose form had changed over time.

4. Includes natural, step- and adopted children.

Source: 1990 GSS, cycle 5, Public Use Microdata File.

Most women (94%) living in an intact family had not previously lived with a partner other than the father of their children.[11] In contrast, nearly two-thirds of women in a blended or re-created family had experienced two or more unions. The relatively high percentage (37%) of women in a blended or re-created family who had been involved in just one union may seem surprising, given the high proportion of women living with their own children. These are mostly women who had had a child outside of a union before forming a couple with a man assumed not to be the child's father.[12] The relative overrepresentation of these women in the 18 to 34 age group is doubtless owing to the fact that relatively few women had an opportunity, before age 35, to become part of a new couple after the dissolution of a union involving children. Among those aged 45 to 64, the distribution observed could be due to the small numbers involved. However, it is reasonable to assume that a proportion of first unions in the older age groups consists of women who were once young single mothers and who had married soon after the birth of their child.

The last section of Table 3.6 compares the distribution by number of children in the various types of family. It shows relatively little variation in the number of children living in all families considered: just under one in four families—two-parent or blended and re-created families—had three or more children, and about 4 in 10 families had two children. The differences are greater between the generations. Thus, the percentage of respondents aged 35 to 44 living with just one child is far lower among intact families (18%) than among blended or re-created families (32%), and the average number of children is therefore higher (2.2 versus 2.0). The same is true of those aged 45 to 64, where the average number of children is 1.8 for intact families and 1.6 for blended or re-created families. While blended families often include children of different sibling relationships, they do not appear to be any larger than intact families. In fact, they are smaller. This is probably due to the conjugal instability at the very root of the blended family phenomenon, which has the effect of delaying, even preventing, the birth of planned offspring. Also, several studies (Zhao et al. 1993) show that children in a blended family tend to leave the parental home at younger ages.

3.2.2.3 The parental history of women belonging to a couple without children

Women belonging to a couple without children account for a sizeable proportion (24%) of 1990 GSS female respondents aged 18 to 64 (see Table 3.1). Their age distribution largely follows a J curve; that is, the percentage is relatively high among young women who had not yet had children, then drops in the middle years, and then rises again, peaking among older women who had seen their children leave home.

From the census question on birth orders, it is possible to distinguish, among women with no children at home, those who had never had children from those whose children had left home or were deceased at the time they completed the census form. It is not possible, however, to identify women who had previously adopted children or raised the children of a spouse within a blended family, thereby fulfilling a parental role, or women living with the father of their children after the children's departure, thus constituting an "empty nest" in the strict sense used in the life-cycle approach. This section attempts to address some of these issues and shed light on the parental history of women who, at a certain time in their lives, find themselves without children.

Seventy-four percent (74%) of women who had had children belonged to a true "empty nest" at the time of the survey; that is, they were still living with the natural father of all their children after the children had left home (see Table 3.7). This was true of more than 8 in 10 respondents aged 55 to 64, but fewer than 2 in 10 respondents under age 45.[13] Conversely, nearly half of mothers aged 18 to 44 had never raised children with their current spouse; 34% had formed a blended family with their current spouse. These last two types of life courses were clearly less common among women aged 55 to 64, and in each case affected fewer than 10% of the respondents. The discrepancy between age groups is obviously related to the increase in conjugal instability in recent generations, but may be due more to the fact that mothers aged 18 to 44 whose children had already left home constitute a special group. These women either had their children at very young ages or lost custody of their children. Finally, we want to point out that 15% of female respondents aged 55 to 64 belonging to a couple without children and 25% of those aged 45 to 54 had previously experienced lone parenthood. Moreover, 9% of the older age group and 21% of the younger group had formed a blended family with either their current spouse at the time of the survey or with someone else.

TABLE 3.7

INDICATORS OF THE PARENTAL HISTORY OF WOMEN BELONGING TO A COUPLE WITH NO CHILDREN,
BY AGE AT THE TIME OF THE SURVEY, 1990

Indicators of parental history	Age group			
	18–44	45–54	55–64	All ages
Women who had had children	7	83	90	48
Women who had never had children	93	17	10	52
Of the women who had had children				
Women living with the father of all their children ("empty nest")	17	72	83	74
Women who had never raised children with their current spouse	49	10	8	12
Women who had lived in a blended family with their current spouse	34	18	9	14
Women who had experienced a lone-parent episode[1]	62	25	15	22
Women who had experienced a blended family episode[1]	47	21	9	16
Of the women who had never had children[1]				
Women still living with the adoptive father of all their adopted children ("empty nest")	0	6	22	2
Women who had never raised children with their current spouse	99	93	63	96
Women who had raised the children of their current spouse	1	1	15	2
Women who had experienced a blended family episode	2	1	15	3

1. The subcategories are not mutually exclusive; therefore the total may not equal 100%.
Source: 1990 GSS, cycle 5, Public Use Microdata File.

The second section of Table 3.7 concerns women who had never had a child and who belonged to a couple without children. The data show that the fact a woman has never had children does not necessarily mean she has never fulfilled a parental role, although in most cases it does. For example, slightly over 20% of wives aged 55 to 64 with no children belonged to an "empty nest" after raising children they had adopted with their current spouse; another 15% were living in a blended family with the father of children to whom they were stepmother. Even though the percentages are modest among the younger generations, there is every reason to believe they will increase as younger women, more affected by the changing trends in conjugal life, raise their spouse's children and see these children leave home.

3.2.3 The history of women who head a lone-parent family

The phenomenon of lone parenthood, which has surged since 1971, is described in Chapter 2 and in many earlier works (among the most recent, Hudson and Galaway 1993; Lindsay 1992). Censuses have in fact long provided socio-demographic data on lone-parent families. They have revealed a trend toward the declining age and the increased number of female lone parents over the last 20 years, as well as the growing impoverishment of women and children in lone-parent families (Dandurand and Saint-Jean 1988; Le Bourdais and Rose 1986; Lindsay 1992; Oderkirk and Lochhead 1992).

While census data provide information about the living conditions of persons in lone-parent families, they cannot be used either to examine the marital and parental history of lone mothers, or determine accurately the events that culminate in the forming of a lone-parent family.

Nevertheless, from the information gathered on the marital status of lone mothers, whether entry into lone parenthood follows the husband's death or the voluntary dissolution (separation or divorce) of a marriage can be determined. However, lone mothers who have had a child within a common-law union cannot be distinguished from those who have had a child outside of any union. Table 3.8 explores this issue as well as the marital history of lone mothers.

TABLE 3.8

INDICATORS OF THE CONJUGAL AND PARENTAL HISTORY OF FEMALE HEADS OF LONE-PARENT HOUSEHOLDS, BY AGE AT THE TIME OF THE SURVEY, 1990[1]

Indicators of conjugal and parental history	Age group					
	18–24	25–34	35–44	45–54	55–64	**All ages**
Percent of entries into lone parenthood by						
birth outside of a union	40	16	6	4	2	**11**
dissolution of a union	58	83	90	83	32	**77**
a marriage	28	50	71	66	28	**56**
a common-law union	30	33	19	17	4	**21**
spouse's death	2	1	4	13	66	**12**
Percent who had experienced no union[2]	28	9	4	2	0	**7**
Percent ever-married[2]	27	66	91	95	100	**81**
Percent who had experienced a common-law union[2]	58	63	34	26	9	**39**
Rank of the episode						
1st episode	77	62	72	69	76	**69**
2nd episode	23	29	24	26	24	**26**
3rd or subsequent episode	0	9	4	5	0	**5**

1. Excluded from this table are single (never-married) heads of lone-parent families living with their parents. In keeping with the census approach, they have been classified as "children" of a census family (see Section 3.2.1 and Table 3.2).
2. The subcategories are not mutually exclusive; therefore the total may not equal 100%.

Source: 1990 GSS, cycle 5, Public Use Microdata File.

First, recall that 8% of female GSS respondents aged 18 to 64 belonged to a lone-parent family; that is, they were living with no spouse and with one or more children (see Table 3.1).[14] Of this group, over three-quarters began their episode of lone parenthood following the voluntary dissolution of a marriage (56% of cases) or common-law union (21% of cases); 11% became lone parents following a birth outside of a union, and 12% became lone parents upon the death of their spouse (see Table 3.8).

Obviously, most women (two in three) enter lone parenthood between the ages of 55 and 64, following the death of their husband. At these ages, male mortality begins to affect women's family life course. In contrast, widowhood as the cause of lone parenthood touches 13% of those aged 45 to 54, and fewer than 4% of those aged 35 to 44. However, lone parenthood following a birth outside of a union predominated (40%) among women aged 18 to 24, still young enough to have experienced a fertile union followed by a separation. Finally, the dissolution of common-law unions and legal marriages were the source of more than 80% of episodes of lone parenthood among women aged 25 to 54 at the time of the survey, but the relative distribution of these two types of dissolution by generation was reversed relative to the type of union considered. Moreover, half of single (never-married) lone mothers experienced lone parenthood after the break-up of a common-law union and only half of these lone mothers had had a child outside of a union (and so had experienced "childbearing outside of marriage" in the strict sense of the term) (1990 GSS). On the whole, the variation in the distribution of means of entry into lone parenthood by age group is certainly due to the differing circumstances each generation of women experiences, and to the fact that lengthy episodes of lone parenthood, which are not unrelated to the means of entry (Le Bourdais et al. 1995; Moore 1989), may very well be over-represented in older persons.

A study of the marital history of lone mothers shows, moreover, that barely 7% of female heads of lone-parent families (28% of those aged 18 to 24) had never lived with a spouse, whether it was a husband or a common-law partner (see Table 3.8). About 8 in 10 lone mothers had been married, and nearly 4 in 10 had lived common law, regardless of whether these experiences were the cause of lone parenthood. As was true of women belonging to a couple, the proportion of lone mothers who had been married increases from more recent to older generations, reaching 100% among those aged 55 to 64. Conversely, the percentage of women who had cohabited increases from older to younger generations, to 58% of those aged 18 to 24.

Finally, the last section of the table shows that about 3 in 10 lone mothers were in their second or subsequent episode of lone parenthood. On the whole, the incidence of two or more episodes of lone parenthood increases from older to younger generations: among lone mothers aged 25 to 34, nearly 4 in 10 had experienced lone parenthood at least once, and nearly 1 in 10 had experienced it three or more times.

3.2.4 The history of women who are non-family persons

"Non-family persons" account for 14% of female respondents aged 18 to 64 (see Table 3.1). These women are more highly represented in both the youngest and oldest age groups, that is, before family life really gets underway and after it has begun to unravel. A certain percentage will have this status temporarily in their middle years, as they make the transition between two family episodes. The status of "non-family person" obviously applies to people with a wide variety of life experiences and is not limited to people with no family life.

Thus, slightly fewer than 5 in 10 women with non-family status had experienced no prior union, 39% of women with this status had been married, and 19% had lived with a common-law partner (see Table 3.9). Among women aged 45 and older, about one in six stated they had never cohabited with either a common-law spouse or a husband. As one would expect, the percentage of women who had cohabited was higher for women who were younger and at the beginning of their conjugal life. Conversely, while just 2% of women aged 18 to 24 said they had been married, the figure was 86% for those aged 55 to 64. Finally, the proportion of women who had lived with a common-law spouse before entering non-family status increases with age, peaking at 43% of those aged 35 to 44 before dropping to smaller percentages. The smaller percentage of cohabitants observed among those under age 35 can be attributed to the fact that many of these women had not yet begun their conjugal life at the time of the survey, while the low percentage among those aged 45 and older may be explained by the fact that common-law unions were less popular among these generations of women.

TABLE **3.9**

INDICATORS OF THE CONJUGAL AND PARENTAL HISTORY OF NON-FAMILY FEMALES, BY AGE AT THE TIME OF THE SURVEY, 1990[1]

| Indicators of conjugal and parental history[2] | Age group | | | | | |
	18–24	25–34	35–44	45–54	55–64	**All ages**
			%			
Women who had experienced no union	82	63	36	18	14	**47**
Women ever-married	2	15	45	77	86	**39**
Women who had experienced a common-law union	16	32	43	28	7	**19**
%						
Women who had had children	1	4	18	64	74	**28**
Women who had raised children[3]	2	4	20	67	75	**29**

1. As they were in the census, ever-married respondents who were not living with a spouse but were living with one or both parents at the time of the survey are classified as non-family persons.
2. The subcategories are not exclusive; the total may therefore not equal 100%.
3. Includes natural, step- and adopted children.
Source: 1990 GSS, cycle 5, Public Use Microdata File.

Nearly 30% of female respondents aged 18 to 64 with non-family status had had or raised a child at some point in their life. The percentages are distinctly higher among those aged 45 and older since many of these women's children had already left home. Until this age, the proportions are marginal given the very strong tendency of mothers to continue to live with their children after a separation or divorce.

3.3   DYNAMICS OF THE FORMATION AND DISSOLUTION OF DIFFERENT FORMS OF FAMILY ORGANIZATION

The previous section looks at different indicators of the marital and parental history of women according to their family status at the time of the 1990 GSS. The profile drawn from the current data sheds light on the diverse paths women follow in their life courses. However, this approach, based on persons at various stages of their life cycle, does not allow for a comparison of the actual extent of the changes that have occurred in the lives of various generations of women. For example, the life-cycle approach does not allow us to estimate the proportion of women who will experience a given family status in their lifetime. To do this, we must change perspective, placing ourselves at the start of women's life courses and following them as they progress.

This section adopts this new perspective and looks longitudinally at the dynamics of the formation and dissolution of first episodes of an intact two-parent family, a lone-parent family and a blended family, for various generations of women.[15] Using the attrition tables method, this analysis reveals the extent to which the frequency and timing patterns of the formation of a given family type differ from one generation to another, and estimates the proportion of women who will be affected by the phenomenon should the behaviours observed at the time of the survey continue in the coming years.

This analysis examines only family episodes involving children, regardless of their age. Unlike the census, which considers couples without children to be a "census family," only households including a female respondent (with or without a spouse) living with one or more children are considered. Therefore, in this study, the presence or absence of children determines whether a "family" exists. Because of insufficient data, all children present, regardless of their marital status, are included in the analysis. We should also note that this study covers the family paths of *all* female respondents, regardless of their living arrangements in a census family at the time of the survey. Finally, only data concerning first episodes (which account for most family episodes) of each family type are used.

For each type of family studied, the dynamics of the formation of first episodes is studied first for all women by means of entry into the family episode considered. Then the entry shifts by generation, all means of entry combined, are examined to assess the degree to which behaviours have changed over time. The same approach is then used to analyse exits from family episodes. The means of forming and dissolving family episodes are examined by generation to identify the variations that have occurred in recent decades.

The analysis is based on the establishment of multiple attrition tables.[16] This relatively straightforward method is used to determine the frequency and timing patterns of the transitions under study. The basic principle consists in calculating, for each interval considered, the probability that the respondents will experience a given family transition (for example, the probability of living in an intact two-parent family). This probability is determined by comparing the number of women making the transition during the interval considered with the number of women at risk of having the experience. In the case of entries into a family episode, all women who have not yet made the transition and are still under study are at risk.[17] The probabilities of entering into an episode are calculated and cumulated by "single year of age," starting at age 15. For exits from episodes, the probabilities are calculated by "duration" from the time of entry into the family episode; only women living in the family status concerned are at risk of exiting from it. The various means of exiting a given family status (for example, the break-up of a relationship or the children's departure) are treated as concurrent risks, and the table provides the "net" probability of each one occurring.

The advantage of the attrition tables principle is that all information gathered can be used and benefited from, including incomplete family histories, that is, histories that are currently unfolding. The number of respondents at risk of making a transition thus excludes those cases for which there is incomplete information. The assumption is that cases excluded from the analysis would adopt the same behaviour as those that are included. This has some effect on the interpretation of exits from episodes, particularly in the case of younger generations, where a particular subgroup of women who began their family path very early may well be over-represented, and their behaviours are probably not representative of the group as a whole. We will revisit this issue in 3.3.1.2.

Based on some of our earlier studies, the analysis includes all female respondents who were aged 18 to 65 at the time of the survey and for whom there is sufficient information to reconstitute this marital and parental history (see Desrosiers et al. 1994).

3.3.1 Intact two-parent families

After reaching its peak with the life-cycle approach in the 1970s, the study of the dynamics of intact two-parent families, also known as "nuclear families" or "simple two-parent families" (Le Gall 1992), was gradually abandoned in favour of analysing newly emerging family forms, such as lone-parent families formed by the dissolution of a union. However, the study of intact two-parent families is relevant here since the changes noted in fertility and conjugal life affected the formation and dissolution processes of these families across generations.

In this analysis, an episode in an intact two-parent family refers to any period during which a woman lives only with a spouse and the children (natural or adopted) of their relationship.[18] The woman's age at the birth or adoption of the couple's first child (rather than her age on the formation of the union) marks the start of the family episode.[19] There are three distinct means of entry into the spouses' conjugal relationship before the arrival of the first child: direct marriage, marriage after a phase of cohabitation, and common-law union. The episode may, moreover, end in one of three distinct ways: the departure from the home (or the death) of the last child, separation or divorce, or the death of the husband.

3.3.1.1 Formation of intact two-parent families

Figure 3.1A presents, by age, the cumulative probabilities for women who have experienced an intact two-parent family episode. The figure shows that, if the behaviours of the various generations of women surveyed in 1990 continue, nearly 8 in 10 Canadian women will, at some time in their life, experience an episode in an intact two-parent family. Two-thirds of women will enter this form of family life through direct marriage, 8% after marrying their common-law husband, and 5% on giving birth to a child within a common-law union.

Regardless of the means of entry, women are typically involved in an intact two-parent family before age 40, as shown in Figure 3.1A by the levelling off of the curves at this age. This of course reflects the fact that most women begin their parental life before reaching their forties; only a very small proportion of women have their first child after this age. Most women enter an intact two-parent family in their twenties, that is, around the average age when women have their first child (see Figure 3.1A). The analysis shows that a significant proportion of women had this experience early in life: at age 20, nearly 1 in 10 respondents had already experienced this form of family life. Almost all of these young mothers married their spouse without first living with him; as discussed below, most of these women were in the older generations. Finally, women who lived with their spouse before marrying them formed their families a little later. The average age was 28.5, compared with 26.8 for direct marriages and 25.6 for families formed within a common-law union (1990 GSS).

A study of the curves by generation, all conjugal statuses combined, reveals some changes over time in the formation of intact two-parent families (see Figure 3.1B). The delayed entry of women into this type of family is quite evident. For example, over half of women aged 45 and older at the time of the survey had already experienced an intact two-parent family episode by age 25, while just over 40% of those aged 35 to 44 and only about 3 in 10 of those aged 25 to 34 had had a similar experience by this age. By age 35, only two-thirds of those aged 35 to 44 at the time of the survey had experienced this form of family life, compared with three-quarters of women aged 45 and older—a considerable difference.

Not only are younger generations delaying having their first child, but they are also doing so in quite a different context than in the past. A study of the table of entry into an intact two-parent family broken down by cause and by generation (see Appendix 3.2, Table 1) shows a marked increase in common-law unions and decrease in marriage as the way in which younger generations form families. For example, fewer than 3% of respondents aged 35 to 44 at the time of the survey had established a family within a "paperless marriage"; by age 30, the proportion nearly tripled (8%) among those aged 25 to 34. In older generations, this situation is extremely rare: fewer than 1% of female respondents aged 45 and older had experienced this situation. The rise in cohabitation as a prelude to marriage, or as the context for starting a family, therefore does not entirely offset the marked decline in marriage seen in younger generations (see Appendix 3.2, Table 1). It is possible, however, that the difference observed between generations will narrow slightly in the years to come, as younger women age and advance further in their childbearing years.

Figure 3.1a

Cumulative Probabilities for Women of Living in an "Intact" Two-parent Family, by Conjugal Status on Entry[1, 2]

1. Refers to the conjugal status on arrival (birth or adoption) of the first child.
2. Excludes eight cases for which the type of union is not known.
3. Female respondents who married their common-law spouse before the arrival (birth or adoption) of the first child.
4. Includes some respondents who would ultimately marry their common-law spouse.
Source: 1990 GSS, cycle 5, Public Use Microdata File.

FIGURE 3.1B

CUMULATIVE PROBABILITIES FOR WOMEN OF LIVING IN AN "INTACT" TWO-PARENT FAMILY,
BY AGE AT THE TIME OF THE SURVEY

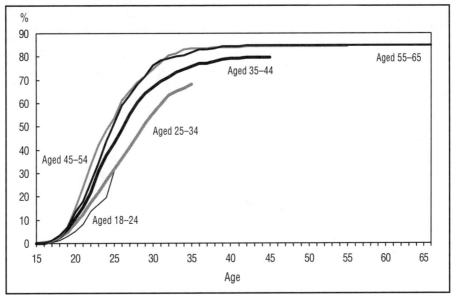

Source: 1990 GSS, cycle 5, Public Use Microdata File.

3.3.1.2 Dissolution of intact two-parent families

Figure 3.2A shows the cumulative probabilities of exiting an intact two-parent family for the three means of dissolution considered. At a glance, it appears that nearly all women (90%) will have exited this family status 40 years after the family unit was initially formed if the behaviours of the respondents observed in 1990 continue. Nearly 60% of these episodes will end with the departure of the children, while about one-quarter will end following the dissolution of the marriage, and 10% with the death of the husband. From the standpoint of living arrangements, these family units will then become either couples without children or lone-parent families.[20]

The curves that emerge from the tables (see Appendix 3.2, Table 2) show that unions are ending sooner: over one-quarter of dissolutions occurred within five years of cohabitation, and half of all separated women experienced the dissolution of their union before having completed 12 years of cohabitation. Exits from intact two-parent families associated with the children's departure occurred much later. It was only after 18 years of conjugal life that this type of exit really began to increase, replacing death as the cause of family dissolution. Only after 27 years of cohabitation did the children's departure from home become the main cause of the end of the intact two-parent family.

FIGURE 3.2A

CUMULATIVE PROBABILITIES FOR WOMEN WHO HAVE EXPERIENCED AN "INTACT" TWO-PARENT
FAMILY OF EXITING THIS FAMILY STATUS,[1] BY MEANS OF EXIT

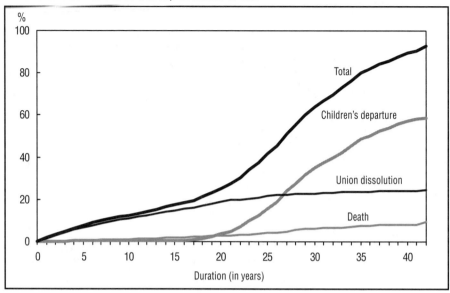

1. Excludes 120 cases for which the date of the end of the episode is not known.
Source: 1990 GSS, cyle 5, Public Use Microdata File.

Presenting the data from the exit tables by generation, all causes combined, Figure 3.2B shows the very distinct variations between generations.[21] As this figure illustrates, episodes in an intact two-parent family tend to be shorter among younger generations: after 10 years in an intact two-parent family, 13% of female respondents aged 35 to 44, when surveyed, had exited this family status, compared with 9% of those aged 45 to 54, and just 5% of those aged 55 to 65. Among those women aged 25 to 34, 19% are likely to leave an intact two-parent family after this time, but it is uncertain whether this result accurately reflects the behaviour of this generation because it is partially based on women who formed their family at a relatively young age. The remarkable acceleration of the rate of exit after longer durations (17 years or more) observed among those aged 35 to 44 is probably related to this same phenomenon.

The decrease in the time spent in an intact two-parent family seen across generations is linked to the marked increase in union dissolutions among younger cohorts (see Appendix 3.2, Table 2). For example, after 10 years of cohabitation, 12% of respondents aged 35 to 44, when surveyed, had gone through a separation or divorce—four times the rate (3%) noted for unions of the same duration among respondents aged 55 to 65. By comparison, deaths dropped slightly over the generations, the demarcation tending now to be between the 55 to 65 age group and the under-55 age group. This is somewhat related to the fact that men's life expectancy increased well before this period of family transformation.

FIGURE 3.2B

CUMULATIVE PROBABILITIES FOR WOMEN WHO HAVE EXPERIENCED AN "INTACT" TWO-PARENT FAMILY OF EXITING THIS FAMILY STATUS,[1] BY AGE AT THE TIME OF THE SURVEY[2]

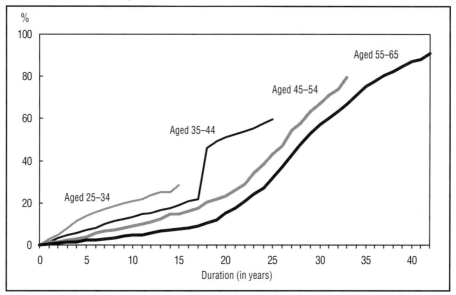

1. Excludes 120 cases for which the date of the end of the episode is not known.
2. The curves are discontinued when the number of respondents likely to experience the transition at the duration in question is less than 20.

Source: 1990 GSS, cycle 5, Public Use Microdata File.

To what extent will the spread of "paperless marriages," recognized as being more unstable than legal marriages (Desrosiers and Le Bourdais 1996; Le Bourdais and Marcil-Gratton 1996), intensify the trend toward the weakening of the family? The phenomenon is probably still too recent to provide a conclusive answer. One thing is certain: the trends described suggest a very definite decrease in the duration of an intact two-parent family, from older to younger generations, in favour of other forms of family organization.

3.3.2 Lone-parent families[22]

In Canada, of all families with children living at home, it is undoubtedly lone-parent families that have been studied the most in recent years. The emergence of a "new lone parenthood" as a result of union dissolutions (Dandurand and Saint-Jean 1988) and the economic hardship of female lone-parent families are among the reasons for the growing number of such studies. Most, however, are based on census data and basically provide a series of snapshots of the evolution of the phenomenon. In Canada, Moore (1988; 1989) was among the first investigators to begin studying lone parenthood longitudinally, using data from the Family History Survey taken by Statistics Canada in 1984 (see also Desrosiers et al. 1993, 1994). Moore's studies have shown that lone parenthood is clearly more widespread than the current data would lead us to believe, and that the time spent in this type of family is related to the woman's means of entry.

A "lone-parent episode" refers to any period during which a woman lives without a spouse and with at least one child.[23] In the following analysis, those who experienced lone parenthood include young single mothers who live with their parents and are regarded by the census as "children." Three events likely to lead to the formation of a lone-parent household are identified: births outside of a union,[24] voluntary dissolution of a marriage (via separation or divorce) or common-law union, and widowhood. Three means of exit are identified: marriage, common-law union, and the departure (or death) of the last child.

3.3.2.1 Formation of lone-parent families

Figure 3.3A presents the cumulative probabilities at each age for women who have experienced an initial lone-parent episode, by means of entry. If the behaviours of the different generations of women surveyed in 1990 continue, just over one-third (35%) of Canadian women will experience lone-parent status at some point in their life. This percentage is more than four times that noted at the time of the survey (8%), illustrating the persistence of this phenomenon in women's lives. As Figure 3.3A shows, the largest proportion of women (18%) will enter lone parenthood following the dissolution of a common-law union or marriage, and 10% will do so after their husband's death. Births outside of a union will be the means of entry for 7% of women if the trends observed in 1990 continue.

FIGURE 3.3A

CUMULATIVE PROBABILITIES FOR WOMEN OF EXPERIENCING A LONE-PARENT EPISODE, BY MEANS OF ENTRY

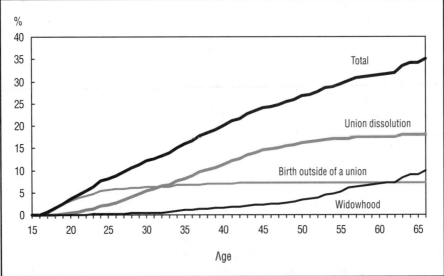

Source: 1990 GSS, cycle 5, Public Use Microdata File; figure adapted from Desrosiers et al., 1994, 20, graph 3.1.

FIGURE 3.3B

CUMULATIVE PROBABILITIES FOR WOMEN OF EXPERIENCING A LONE-PARENT EPISODE, BY AGE AT THE TIME OF THE SURVEY

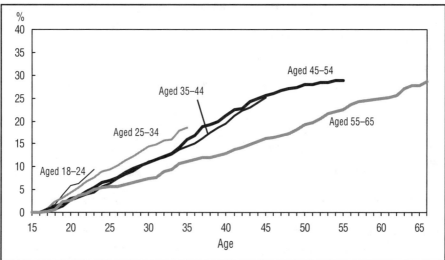

Source: 1990 GSS, cycle 5, Public Use Microdata File; figure adapted from Desrosiers et al, 1994, 22, graph 3.2.

The curves presented in Figure 3.3A show that the timing patterns of entries into lone parenthood are closely linked to the event that is the source of the episode. Lone parenthood episodes following a birth outside of a union generally occur early in a woman's life; a very small proportion of women experience this means of entry after age 25, as shown by the levelling off of the curve after this age. In contrast, lone-parent episodes following the death of the spouse occurred later and increased steadily after women reached their mid-forties. Finally, the phases of lone parenthood caused by voluntary dissolution of a marriage or common-law union generally occurred between these two age ranges, that is, between a woman's mid-twenties and late forties. These results attest to the diversity of female lone-parenthood experiences and the variable circumstances (for example, life-cycle phase, parental responsibility) associated with them.

Figure 3.3B shows a sharp increase in the phenomenon of lone parenthood, all circumstances combined, across all generations. On the whole, age for age, more women in younger than in older generations had headed a family. For example, by age 35, 15% of respondents aged 35 to 44 at the time of the survey had experienced a first lone-parent episode, while only 11% of respondents aged 55 and older had done so; among those aged 25 to 34, only a fraction of whom were in their mid-thirties at the time of the survey, this proportion was nearly 20%.

Also, relatively more respondents aged 45 to 54 had experienced lone parenthood than those aged 35 to 44. This was no doubt caused by the particular context in which the women of this generation (aged 45 to 54) evolved. When Canada's *Divorce Act* was adopted in 1968, the average age of these women was 28. In the 15 years that followed this legislation, their rate of entry into lone parenthood accelerated as a result of marriage dissolution, as though a fair number of couples had been waiting for this legislation in order to divorce. By their mid-forties, the likelihood of this generation entering into lone parenthood seems to have levelled off—a trend that may not be followed by women aged 35 to 44, who have clearly been less affected by the adoption of the *Divorce Act*. In light of the trends observed in the younger generations, the number of lone-parent families may therefore continue to rise in the coming years.

3.3.2.2 Dissolution of lone-parent families

The impact of lone parenthood on women's living conditions is related not only to the way in which the family unit is formed, but also to the duration of the episode. The means of exiting this family status, whether it is the formation of a union or the children's departure from the parental home, also affects women's standard of living since, in the first instance, women will continue to have custody of their children with a new spouse, while in the second, they will find themselves on their own (with no spouse or children), and this often occurs at a later stage in their life.

To explain these aspects of lone parenthood, Figure 3.4A presents first, for all female respondents who had experienced a first lone-parent episode, the cumulative probabilities of exiting this family status for the three means of exit considered. The figure shows that if the behaviours observed in 1990 continue, nearly all (92%) of women will have left this status 22 years after it began. The duration of the lone-parent family is, however, quite variable. Regardless of the means of exit, female lone-parent status will have been very transitory in 22% of cases, lasting less than one year; nearly 6 times in 10, lone-parent status will have lasted less than five years, and 1 time in 4, more than 10 years.

FIGURE **3.4A**

CUMULATIVE PROBABILITIES FOR WOMEN WHO HAVE EXPERIENCED A LONE-PARENT EPISODE OF EXITING LONE-PARENT STATUS, BY MEANS OF EXIT[1]

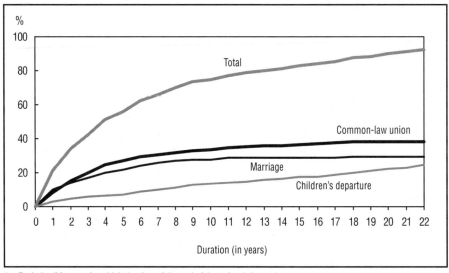

1. Excludes 38 cases for which the date of the end of the episode is not known.

Source: 1990 GSS, cycle 5, Public Use Microdata File; figure adapted from Desrosiers et al. 1994, 24, graph 3.3.

FIGURE 3.4B

CUMULATIVE PROBABILITIES FOR WOMEN WHO HAVE EXPERIENCED A LONE-PARENT EPISODE OF EXITING LONE-PARENT STATUS, BY AGE AT THE TIME OF THE SURVEY[1]

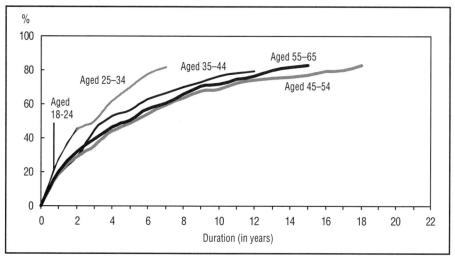

1. The curves are discontinued when the number of respondents likely to experience the transition at the duration in question is less than 20.

Source: 1990 GSS, cycle 5, Public Use Microdata File; figure adapted from Desrosiers et al., 1994, 27, graph 3.4.

Entry into a union (or the formation of a blended family) is the most common means of exiting lone-parent episodes (see Figure 3.4A). If the observed trends continue, more than two-thirds of first experiences of lone parenthood will end in either a common-law union (38% of cases) or in marriage (30% of cases). Relatively less common, exits from lone parenthood after the children leave home occur later in women's lives; for the 24% of episodes that end in this way, the mean duration is about eight years.

Figure 3.4B illustrates the data from the tables of exit from lone parenthood by generation, showing generally that younger birth cohorts tend to leave female lone-parent status sooner than older birth cohorts. In fact, 7 in 10 respondents aged 25 to 34 left their first lone-parent episode within five years of entering it; of respondents aged 45 and older, about half no longer headed a lone-parent family. The acceleration of the rate of exit from lone parenthood in younger generations is striking: after two years at the head of a lone-parent family, nearly 1 in 2 women under age 35 had left this family status, compared with about 3 in 10 respondents aged 35 and older.

Respondents aged 45 to 54 tended to exit lone-parent status less quickly than their elders (see Figure 3.4B). This discrepancy between the two oldest generations can be attributed, at least in part, to the greater tendency of women aged 55 to 65 to marry in the initial years following the start of their lone-parent episode, and also to the later entry of these women into a lone-parent family, with the result that more of them will soon see their youngest child leave home (see Appendix 3.2, Table 3). A different dynamic is at work in younger generations of lone mothers. The strong tendency of those under age 35 to exit lone parenthood quickly is probably tied to the early onset of their lone-parenthood experiences. The results of an earlier study show that young lone mothers are generally more inclined to form a new union quickly than women who had this experience later in life (Le Bourdais et al. 1995). The data, broken down by cause and by generation, illustrate the swiftness with which common-law unions were formed by the younger generations of the women surveyed in 1990 (see Appendix 3.2, Table 3). Also, the rise in "paperless marriages" more than offset the observed decline in the popularity of marriage among the more recent cohorts of lone mothers.

Overall, this brief analysis of the dynamics of female lone parenthood shows that union dissolution is now the principal means of entry into lone-parent status, and that this phenomenon is on the rise among younger generations of Canadian women. Meanwhile, the duration of lone-parent episodes seems to be declining in recent generations of lone mothers, as more of them choose common-law union when forming a new family. The next section looks at the formation of blended families.

3.3.3 Blended families

Blended families, though not a recent phenomenon, have been the subject of very few socio-demographic studies outside the United States. In Canada, the lack of research until quite recently is related to the lack of data for identifying these families. By combining the marital and parental histories provided by 1990 GSS female respondents, it is now possible to identify blended families and determine where they occur in the life course of Canadian women (see Section 3.2.2.2 and Appendix 3.1).

Unlike the American studies, which are based mainly on the study of remarriages, the following analysis is based on a broad definition of the concept of blended family. Here, a blended family episode designates any period during which a woman lives with a spouse and at least one child not born of their union. A blended family may therefore include children born (or adopted) outside of the current union, children of one or both spouses, and sometimes children the couple has had together.

Entries into a blended family are first examined according to the type of union (marriage or common law) that exists when the family unit is formed, then according to the family status of the respondents. Four statuses are identified. The first, "without children," comprises women who had no children or whose children were not living with them when the blended family was formed, that is, those who entered a blended family as the stepmother. The other three categories distinguish women living with their children according to whether they formed a union after a birth outside of a union, a separation or divorce, or the death of their spouse. Two types of exit are considered: the dissolution of the union,[25] and the departure from the parental home of the last child not born to the couple.

3.3.3.1 Formation of blended families

Figure 3.5A presents the cumulative probabilities of living in a blended family by type of union entered into by the spouses. Seventeen percent (17%) of women will live in a blended family at some point in their life if the trends observed in 1990 continue: 11% in the context of a common-law union,[26] and about half that (6%) in the context of a marriage. Also, most women form a blended family before they reach age 45.

FIGURE 3.5A

CUMULATIVE PROBABILITIES FOR WOMEN OF EXPERIENCING A BLENDED FAMILY, BY TYPE OF UNION ON ENTRY

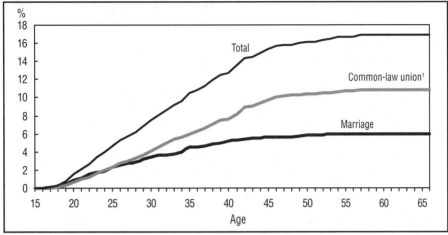

1. Includes a certain number of respondents who will ultimately marry their common-law spouse.

Source: 1990 GSS, cycle 5, Public Use Microdata File.

FIGURE 3.5B

CUMULATIVE PROBABILITIES FOR WOMEN OF EXPERIENCING A BLENDED FAMILY, BY FAMILY STATUS ON ENTRY[1]

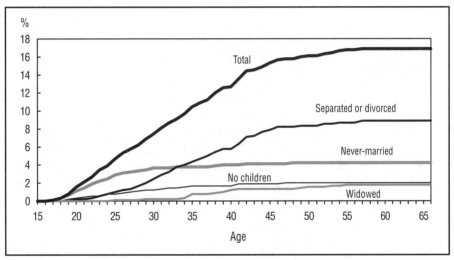

1. The categories "never-married," "separated or divorced" and "widowed" pertain to women who were living with their children at the time of entry into the blended family. The category "never-married" includes women who were not living with the father when their child was born, that is, who had a child outside of a union. The category "no children" refers to women with no children or whose children were no longer living with them when they entered the blended family.

Source: 1990 GSS, cycle 5, Public Use Microdata File; figure adapted from Desrosiers et al., 1994, 30, graph 4.1.

Once again, common-law unions are clearly more prevalent among the more recent generations, although nearly all female cohorts who had experienced a blended family seem to have been affected by this ground swell. The detailed analysis of probabilities of entry by cause and by generation show a particularly marked upsurge in common-law unions at the start of the 1980s in all generations of women who were under age 55 when surveyed (1990 GSS).

Figure 3.5B illustrates the probabilities of entry into a blended family by respondents' family status, all types of union combined, and shows that most women (88.2%) brought at least one dependent child into the blended family; only 2% had no children when they set up house with a spouse and his children. Of the women who had children, most (9%) formed a blended family following a separation or divorce, 4% did so following a birth outside of a union, and 2% did so after being widowed. On the whole, the blended family episode therefore begins, in more than half of cases, following a separation or divorce, which implies that the other natural parent (in this case, the father) remains, to some extent, accessible to his children.

Most women who have belonged to a blended family following a birth outside of a union (without having lived with the father of their child) have generally done so at a relatively young age; this is illustrated by the rapid rise of the never-married curve after age 20 and its levelling off at about age 35 (see Figure 3.5B). Conversely, blended family episodes following widowhood occurred later; the curve for this family status does not really begin to climb until women reach their mid-thirties. The formation of a blended family following the voluntary dissolution of a union occurred for women in the intervening ages. The likelihood of a blended family associated with this family status increased dramatically from age 27 on; starting at age 34, separation and divorce were the most common means of entry into a blended family. Finally, note that the entry timing patterns of women without children extend over some time, as illustrated by the gradual and steady rise of the curve (see Figure 3.5B).

Figure 3.6 shows the probability of entry into a blended family by age group, all family statuses combined. Women of recent generations are more likely than their elders to experience a blended family, with the exception of those aged 18 to 24 who generally begin conjugal life at older ages. This development is the result of increases in both the number of union dissolutions and the swiftness with which lone mothers of recent generations form a union (see previous section). By age 35, for example, 11% of respondents aged 35 to 44 had already experienced a blended family episode, compared with 8% of women aged 45 and older. Among those aged 25 to 34, only a fraction of whom were in their mid-thirties when surveyed, this proportion was 15%. Note the relatively high proportion of respondents aged 55 to 65 who had experienced a blended family episode before reaching their thirties. This result could be attributable, as has been seen, to the strong tendency of this generation of women to marry quickly in the initial years following entry into a lone-parent episode.

FIGURE 3.6

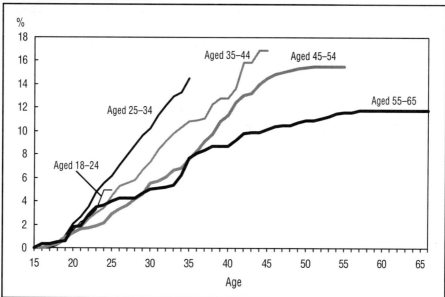

Source: 1990 GSS, cycle 5, Public Use Microdata File; figure adapted from Desrosiers et al., 1994, 32, graph 4.2.

3.3.3.2 Dissolution of blended families

Figure 3.7A shows, for all respondents who had experienced a blended family episode, the cumulative probabilities of exiting this family status, by means of exit. About 90% of women will have exited this family status 23 years after the start of the first episode if the respondents' behaviours observed in 1990 continue. Nearly one-third of these episodes will end with the dissolution of the union, over half will end when the children leave home, and a very small percentage (2%) will end upon the husband's death.

Union dissolutions occur fairly soon after the blended family is formed: four years after the start of the union 16% of couples had ended their relationship, and more than one-quarter of women experienced a dissolution of the union before completing 10 years of conjugal life. Exits from blended families associated with the children's departure occurred a little later. After 13 years, it was the departure of children not born to the current union that most often ended the blended family, resulting in a couple without children or a re-created two-parent family—that is, a couple living only with the children they had had together.

The data from the attrition table, sorted by generation, all means combined (see Appendix 3.2, Table 4), show that women aged 25 to 54 at the time of the survey had a similar likelihood of exiting a blended family episode (see Figure 3.7B).[27] Only the 55 to 65 age group, who were less inclined to exit this family status quickly, differed markedly from the other age groups. This result is doubtless related to the socio-historical context of these women. A number of these families had been formed long ago, and were therefore less affected by the marital instability of the last 20 years (see Appendix 3.2, Table 4). The detailed data in this table show that the relative homogeneity of the behaviour of women aged 25 to 54 camouflages the marked increase of marriage dissolutions from older to younger generations, resulting in fewer exits caused by the children's departure from the home.

In short, the study of the dynamics of blended families shows that common-law union is clearly more common than marriage as the means of entry to the blended family; it also shows the phenomenon's evolution over time. For women, blended families often follow a period, of varying duration, as the head of a lone-parent family; indeed, in most cases, blended families are organized around separated or divorced women who have child custody. While the study of exits from blended families shows few variations by generation at first glance, a shortening of the duration of this type of family can be expected because of the greater conjugal instability noted among younger generations of women.

FIGURE 3.7A

CUMULATIVE PROBABILITIES FOR WOMEN WHO HAVE EXPERIENCED A BLENDED FAMILY OF EXITING THIS FAMILY STATUS, BY MEANS OF EXIT[1]

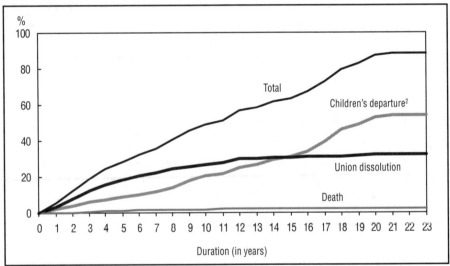

1. Excludes 18 cases for which the date of the end of the episode is not known.
2. Refers to the departure of the last child not born to the couple. The blended family then becomes either an "intact" two-parent family, that is, one where all children present are of the current union, or a couple with no children.

Source: 1990 GSS, cycle 5, Public Use Microdata File; figure adapted from Desrosiers et al., 1994, 34, graph 4.3.

FIGURE **3.7**B

CUMULATIVE PROBABILITIES FOR WOMEN WHO HAVE EXPERIENCED A BLENDED FAMILY OF
EXITING THIS FAMILY STATUS, BY AGE AT THE TIME OF THE SURVEY[1]

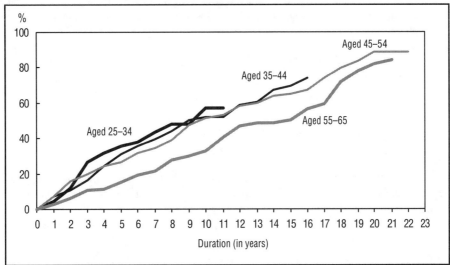

1. The curves are discontinued when the number of respondents likely to experience the transition at the duration in question is less than 20.

Source: 1990 GSS, cycle 5, Public Use Microdata File; figure adapted from Desrosiers et al., 1994, 35, graph 4.4.

3.4 THE FAMILY PATHS OF WOMEN[28]

The previous section presented an analysis of how the three types of family with children, considered separately, formed and dissolved. This section looks at the overall family paths of women, that is, the sequence of the various periods spent in an intact two-parent family, a lone-parent family or a blended family, in the lives of the Canadian women surveyed by the 1990 GSS. Attrition tables once again are used to support the analysis and, as in the previous section, the study concerns only family episodes involving children, regardless of their age. Since the subject of interest is the overall family history of women, this analysis confines itself to those female respondents who were aged 35 to 64, that is, already well into their parental life at the time of the survey.

3.4.1 Analytical method

Figure 3.8 shows the family-paths tree studied, which combines four types of family organizations: the intact family, the lone-parent family, the blended family, and the re-created family. Besides the preparental status from which all women depart, six distinct family statuses are identified:

a) The intact two-parent family

b) The first lone-parent family episode

c) The first blended family episode

d) The re-created two-parent family[29]

e) The second lone-parent family episode

f) The second blended family episode.

The analysis does not consider all possible transitions between all statuses. To begin with, some transitions are illogical; for example, a transition from a second to a first lone-parent family episode is impossible. Secondly, other transitions are excluded from the analysis quite simply because they are too uncommon; this is the case, for example, for a direct transition from a first to a second blended family.

The family episodes studied do not always lead to a new family phase. They may end when the respondent's children leave home, resulting in a transition to a non-parental status. Two scenarios are then possible. First, the children's departure will sometimes mark the end of the respondents' parental path; this is the case, for example, of women heading a lone-parent family or living in an intact two-parent family, who will grow old alone or with their spouse after the last child leaves home.[30] This type of life course is represented by perpendicular arrows leading to no other family destination (see Figure 3.8). Secondly, the children's departure will sometimes mark instead an interlude in the histories of women; for example, female heads of lone-parent families will live alone for a time after their children leave home before forming a blended family with a spouse and his children. This type of interrupted life course is rather uncommon in the lives of women, the vast majority of whom assume custody of their children after the dissolution of a union. Because analysis was discontinued when there were fewer than 25 people[31] with the same family status, this type of path is never followed beyond the non-parental episode; it ends at "non-family" status (see Figure 3.8). The analysis therefore does not cover all possible life courses, and including only sufficiently developed paths probably masks to some degree the diversity of the histories experienced by a limited, though growing, number of women.

FIGURE 3.8
FAMILY PATHS OF WOMEN AGED 35 TO 64

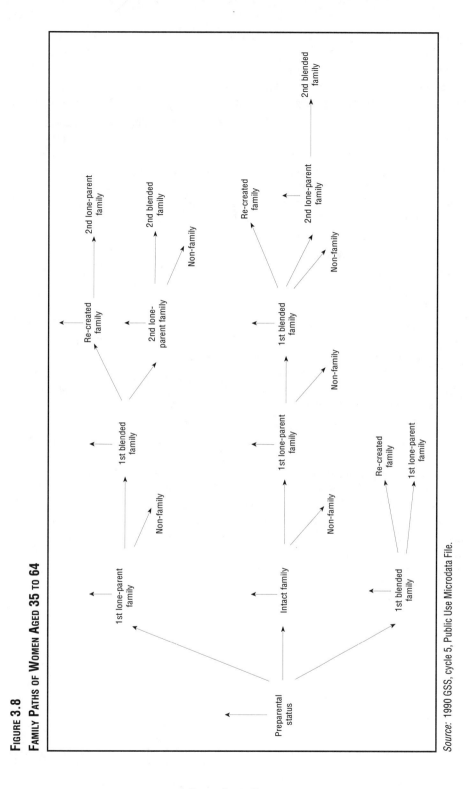

Source: 1990 GSS, cycle 5, Public Use Microdata File.

In the previous section, the probabilities of women experiencing a first episode in a given family type were taken from multiple attrition tables calculated for all women. In the following analysis, the probabilities of experiencing a particular family status take into account the women's prior history; in other words, these probabilities are established based solely on women who have followed a certain common family path.

In concrete terms, the approach used may be expressed as follows. All respondents who depart from "preparental" status are initially exposed to the risk of making a first transition into one of the following three family destinations: an intact two-parent family, a lone-parent family, or a blended family. Each of these statuses then becomes, in turn, the new point of departure for other destinations. The attrition tables are therefore established based only on those women who reached the first family status considered. Thus, the probabilities of living in a lone-parent family following the dissolution of an intact two-parent family are calculated only for those women who began their parental life in this latter situation.[32]

All women are at risk of experiencing a first family transition beginning at age 15; the probabilities are calculated and cumulated for each year of age. For subsequent transitions, the probabilities are calculated by duration from the time of entry into the first family status, and cumulated yearly.

The cumulative transitional probabilities established for each family status are shown in Figure 3.9 (italicized numbers on the arrows). They indicate the proportion of women who will experience the transition in question if the behaviours observed at the time of the survey continue, as well as the proportion of women who will remain in this situation (the sum of the cumulative probabilities for each situation being equal to 1). For example, the risk of lone parenthood for women living in a two-parent family is 0.318 (about one in three); conversely, their likelihood of still being with their husband when the last child leaves home is 0.678.

The estimated overall proportion of women who will follow a given family path (also called the "life course probability") is obtained simply by multiplying all transitional probabilities leading to the final destination considered. For example, the proportion of women who will experience a first lone-parent episode after a period in an intact two-parent family, which is 26.1% (in bold in Figure 3.9), corresponds with the product of the probabilities of first moving from the initial preparental status to an intact two-parent family (0.822), and then to a lone-parent family (0.318).

FIGURE 3.9

FAMILY PATHS OF **WOMEN AGED 35 TO 64**[1], **SHOWING TRANSITION AND PATH PROBABILITIES**

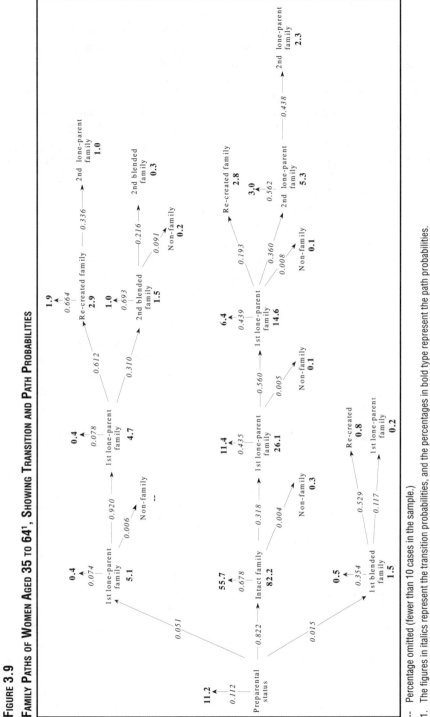

-- Percentage omitted (fewer than 10 cases in the sample.)

1. The figures in italics represent the transition probabilities, and the percentages in bold type represent the path probabilities.

Source: 1990 GSS, cycle 5, Public Use Microdata File.

3.4.2 The family paths of women

The overall picture that emerges from the life-course tree studied is that of a family life starting out in a fairly traditional way, and quite often leading to other forms of family organization defined according to the presence or absence of a husband. Figure 3.9 clearly shows that the preferred means of entering motherhood is still through a couple made up of the two natural (or adoptive) parents of the child, the couple being married more than 9 times out of 10 (1990 GSS). While more than four in five women took this path, only 5.1% began their parental life course as a lone mother; even fewer (1.5%) entered parenthood as a stepmother. Slightly more than 10% of women will remain childless if the observed trends continue. Clearly, a very small proportion of women who have been a parent will experience an episode in a non-family situation, as defined in section 3.4.1. Thus, the instability of the conjugal relationship contrasts with the obviously indissoluble bond between women and their children.

The sum of the life-course probabilities recorded for each family episode of a given rank gives the percentage of women who will go through at least the listed number of transitions in their lifetime.[33] The data show that the vast majority of women (88.8%) will experience at least one parental episode in their lifetime. Nearly one in three women[34] will experience at least a second family episode, one in five will experience a third, and 1 in 10 a fourth.

More than 80% of women will live in an intact two-parent family if current trends continue; 31.4% (5.1% + 26.1% + 0.2%) will have at least one experience of lone parenthood, 20.8% will form a blended family, and 6.5% will belong to a re-created two-parent family (see Figure 3.9).[35] The distribution of women who will belong to the various family types is similar to that of women who will experience a given number of family episodes, since most follow similar paths. Thus, a very high proportion of first family episodes are experienced in an intact two-parent family, a significant percentage of second episodes are experienced in lone-parent families, and so on.

At first glance, intact two-parent families seem relatively stable compared with other family types: if the observed trends continue, more than two-thirds (67.8%) of female respondents living in this type of family will see their last child leave home while still living with the father of their children. In contrast, a woman is decidedly less likely to remain in a lone-parent situation until the children leave home, and the chances of exiting this type of family episode are appreciably higher than are the chances of entering it, regardless of the path previously travelled. For example, of the 26.1% of women who will enter a lone-parent family episode from an intact two-parent family, more than half (56.0%) will form a new couple before their children leave home. The chances of a woman growing old in a lone-parent situation increase with the rank of the episode, but the likelihood she will form a new union is still considerable.

Episodes in an intact two-parent family may initially appear more stable than blended family episodes: female respondents were more likely to remain in the former situation than in the latter (0.678 versus 0.354). However, when blended families that become re-created two-parent families are taken into account, the similarity in the behaviours of the two groups becomes more apparent. Women who have experienced a blended family at some time in their life do not seem more likely to experience a separation than their counterparts in an intact two-parent family. The likelihood of women from a blended family entering a re-created two-parent family after all children not of the current union have left home varies, depending on their prior family history.

For women whose blended family episode is the first parental experience with a spouse (women who entered this family status directly or following a lone-parent episode), the chance of forming this family type (greater than one in two) is more than twice that of respondents who have previously lived in an intact two-parent family (0.193). This is doubtless related to the fact that the respondents who took the first path were generally younger when they entered a blended family and, because they were not far along in their parental life, they were more likely to have had children with their partner.

3.5 CONCLUSION

The analysis at the start of this chapter revealed how, in a context of growing marital mobility, the status observed at any given time tells us less and less about the past family path of individuals. We can appreciate the diversity of the marital and parental histories that emerge from the picture provided by the census. At the same time, the analysis allows us to assess to some degree how the changes that have occurred in recent decades have affected the various generations of women.

One of the salient findings of the study is that a fair proportion of women who neither belonged to a couple nor were a parent at the time of the survey, and who were classified as "children" or "non-family persons" according to the census classification, had already fulfilled the role of spouse or mother at some point in their lives. Among older women (aged 55 to 64), the distinction between their current and former statuses certainly reflects, as we have seen, the fact that many women in this age group are old enough to have experienced the death of their spouse or their children's departure from home. Among younger women, marital mobility is certainly a factor worth mentioning; a relatively large proportion of "non-family persons" and "children" living with their parents have been involved in a common-law union, and these statuses are temporary as these women wait for their family life to really get underway.

In the middle years (ages 35 to 44), the preference is still to live as part of a couple, but this apparent stability masks the sizeable proportion of women (1 in 10) who belonged to a blended family. In most cases, blended families organize around women and their children; only 9% of women in a blended family were raising only the children of their spouse. These results attest to the indissolubility of the mother–child bond following the dissolution of a union; very few mothers under age 45 reported living apart from their children, either as "non-family persons" or with a childless spouse.

In an attempt to document further the real extent of the changes experienced by different generations of women, the next section focused on how various types of family organization involving children are formed and dissolved. The analysis shows that the intact two-parent family (father, mother and their children) is still the path followed by most women. However, the means of forming this family type have changed; common-law union is the choice of a growing number of women of more recent generations. Episodes in an intact two-parent family also begin later, last for a shorter time than before, and usually end with the break-up of the couple. These family dissolutions are the cause of a growing number of lone-parent family episodes, which in turn lead to a subsequent conjugal involvement sooner than in the past. More often than not, common-law union is the context for the formation of blended families, which themselves are also marked by instability. Overall, if the trends observed in 1990 among respondents aged 18 to 65 continue, one in three women will experience lone parenthood at least once in their life, and one in six will live in a blended family.

The family paths approach used in the last section made it possible to determine the impact of changes in conjugal life on the sequence of family episodes in women's lives. As in the previous section, the analysis shows that the vast majority of women aged 35 to 64 experience parenthood and do so first in an intact two-parent family; only 5% embark on their parental path as a lone mother, and even fewer (1.5%) experience parenthood initially as a stepmother. It also shows that one in three women will experience at least two family episodes in their lifetime if the observed behaviours for respondents aged 35 to 64 continue; one in five women will experience at least three, and 1 in 10 at least four. Moreover, one in four lone mothers will go through at least two phases of lone parenthood in their lifetime.

Already fairly high, the probability that women will experience more than one family type could increase for recent generations (under age 35), which are more affected by conjugal instability. This is what an initial study of all family paths followed by the various generations of women suggests. The younger the generation, the more paths taken and the higher the number of episodes experienced, even though these women are not as far along in their conjugal and parental path (Juby and Le Bourdais 1995).

The life-course approach is certainly worthy of being pursued further. To ensure a sufficient number of cases for analysis, it was necessary to form groupings, for example, by combining legally married couples and common-law partners in the same category. This reduced the diversity of family histories, since distinct forms of conjugal life, for which behaviours may differ, were classed together and treated as though they were the same. For example, families formed within a common-law union are more likely to end in dissolution than those formed in the context of a marriage (Desrosiers and Le Bourdais 1996; Le Bourdais and Marcil-Gratton 1996), but the men and women in common-law relationships share housework more evenly (Le Bourdais and Sauriol 1995; Shelton and John 1993). Given the growing popularity of common-law unions, the distinction between types of union will therefore become very relevant to the study of family life courses in the years ahead.

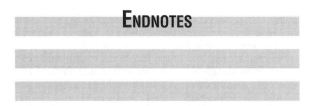

1. For a description of the survey, see Section 3.1.

2. Some analyses, taken from previous studies, include women aged 18 to 65.

3. The 1990 General Social Survey, cycle 5: Family and Friends (GSS) compiled data on two types of unions: marriages and common-law unions. For each union the female respondents entered into, we know their age (in years to one decimal point) at the start and end of the union and, where applicable, we know the reason for dissolution (separation, divorce, or death of the spouse). For common-law unions ending in marriage, we know the respondents' age at marriage. The survey also gathered data on the children—natural or adopted, or stepchildren (children of a previous union of the husband)—raised by the respondents. For each child, we know the respondent's age when the child was born and the place of residence at the time of the survey, and the child's age on final departure from the parental home, if applicable. (For more information about the data, see Appendix 3.1. See also Desrosiers et al. 1994; McDaniel and Strike 1994.)

4. See Appendix 3.1 of this chapter, which presents the method used, based on 1990 GSS data, to determine the living arrangements of respondents in a "census family."

5. For a comparison of the distribution by family status of women aged 18 to 64 based on the 1991 Census and the 1990 GSS, see Appendix 3.1.

6. Obviously, when this approach is used, the numbers of lone-parent families tend to be underestimated, particularly among young people. Using 1990 GSS data, Norris and Knighton (1995) estimate that 32% of lone parents aged 15 to 24 and 9% of lone parents aged 25 to 34 were not identified by the 1991 Census.

7. These percentages are obtained by subtracting from 100% the proportion of married women who had experienced no union prior to this marriage.

8. Unlike the children identified in the census, these children may be either single or once married. The GSS compiled the marital status of each member present in the households sampled in order to select the respondents. Unfortunately, this information is provided only for respondents and their spouse in the public microdata file produced by Statistics Canada.

9. As the numbers were quite small, age groups had to be regrouped to form the youngest and oldest age groups.

10. This is the total of percentage of families with children born to the woman or to both spouses.

11. The marriage of both partners of a common-law union is regarded here as a single union whose form has changed over time.

12. With the GSS data, it is impossible to know whether the husband is really the child's father. To avoid classifying an "intact" family as "blended," we assumed that the respondent married the father of the child if the union occurred within six months of the child's birth.

13. In view of the small number of mothers under age 45 not living with their children, the first three age groups were combined.

14. Unlike the children identified in the census, these may be either single or once-married children.

15. From the retrospective data on unions and children compiled by the 1990 GSS, it is possible to reconstruct the family episodes experienced by the respondents. Thus, for each respondent, we know the number of past episodes in a particular family type, the duration of these episodes, and the demographic events marking the beginning and end of each. (For more details about the reconstitution of family episodes, see Desrosiers et al. 1994.)

16. For a detailed presentation of the method, see Burch and Madan (1986) and Desrosiers et al. (1993).

17. In this analysis, all respondents aged 18 to 65, regardless of their marital or parental status, are considered, at each age, likely to experience the transitions considered. All women are therefore at risk of becoming heads of a lone-parent family. If they have no children and no spouse, they are likely to experience a birth outside of a union. If they belong to a couple, they are at risk of becoming the sole household maintainer following the dissolution of the union

at any time (it is possible for the husband's death or separation to occur during pregnancy). Similarly, a woman on her own (with no spouse or children) could enter a blended family as a stepmother. Keeping all women in the at-risk group may be less justifiable when analysing entries into an intact two-parent family, as it is quite rare for a woman to experience such an episode after having been, at some time, the head of a lone-parent family. In principle, then, it would be justifiable to exclude women from the group likely to live in an intact two-parent family from the time (age) at which they experience a birth outside of a union. Separate analyses have shown, however, that this strategy did not affect the results presented below. The proportion of women who experienced a birth outside of a union is not high enough to shift the probabilities of entering into an intact two-parent family calculated at the different ages.

18. It should be noted that women belonging to a re-created family, that is, those living with a spouse and their common children after having experienced a blended family phase, are excluded from the analysis.

19. Because of insufficient data to verify this, it was assumed that women forming a union within six months of the birth of a child outside of a union had formed an "intact" two-parent family with the father of their child. For these women, their age at the formation of the union, rather than at the birth of their child, marks the start of the family episode.

20. For a very small number of women living in an intact two-parent family, the episode will end simultaneously with the children's departure and the dissolution of the union; in these instances, precedence was given to the dissolution of the union as the cause of family dissolution.

21. Because they are based on a very specific subgroup of women who began their family life at a very young age, the cumulative probabilities of exiting an intact two-parent family are not provided for those aged 18 to 24.

22. The next two sections are modelled largely on the report "Vivre en famille monoparentale et en famille recomposée: portrait des Canadiennes d'hier et d'aujourd'hui" (Desrosiers et al. 1994).

23. The very small number of lone-parent episodes begun before age 16 were excluded from the analysis. We felt that these very early experiences resulted from distinct circumstances and probably brought different strategies into play (see Desrosiers et al. 1994).

24. All such births, whether or not they were followed by a union within six months, are regarded as leading to an episode of lone parenthood, however brief.

25. Women who formed a union within six months of the birth are excluded from this group; although this cannot be confirmed by the GSS data, it is assumed that these women formed a union with the father of the child and therefore did not form a blended family.

26. Of this group, a certain number of respondents will eventually marry their common-law spouse.

27. The cumulative probabilities of exiting the blended family are not provided for those aged 18 to 24 since they are based on a very specific subgroup of women who began their family life at a very young age.

28. This section is inspired in part by the article "Les parcours familiaux des Canadiennes" by Juby and Le Bourdais (1995).

29. The term "re-created two-parent family" refers to a woman and her spouse living with children they had or adopted together after experiencing a blended family phase (see Section 3.2.2.2 of this chapter).

30. For very few women living in an intact two-parent family, the parental life course ends simultaneously with the departure of the children and the dissolution of the union. In Figure 3.8, these cases are included in the "non-family persons" category to distinguish them from those where the couple survives following the children's departure.

31. The analysis is discontinued when the numbers are too small to provide reliable estimates.

32. These probabilities were calculated using the "non-markovian" version of the LIFEHIST computer program developed by Rajulton (Rajulton 1992; Rajulton and Balakrishnan 1990).

33. Note that second and subsequent episodes may be slightly underestimated, as certain life course paths were not continued because the numbers were too small.

34. This percentage represents the sum of path probabilities for second episodes: from top to bottom in the figure, 4.7% in a first blended family (after a first lone-parent episode) + 26.1% in a first lone-parent family + 0.8% in a re-created two-parent family + 0.2% in a first lone-parent family.

35. These figures differ somewhat from the percentages provided in the previous section (78.6% of women will belong to an intact two-parent family, 35.0% to a lone-parent family, and 16.9% to a blended family). Besides the fact that different populations were studied (women aged 35 to 64, and those aged 18 to 65), the discrepancy is owing to the differences in the methodology used, that is, the fact of considering overall family paths and taking into account the interdependence of family episodes.

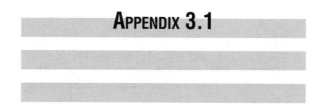

APPENDIX 3.1

APPROACH USED TO DETERMINE THE RESPONDENTS' LIVING ARRANGEMENTS IN A "CENSUS FAMILY"

The public use microdata file of the 1990 General Social Survey, cycle 5: Family and Friends (GSS) contains no single variable for determining the living arrangements of respondents within a "census family." One of the survey's variables does indicate who the respondent was living with at the time of the survey. But the information provided is not detailed enough to allow for respondents to be classified into categories consistent with those taken from the 1991 Census. For example, there is no indication of the marital status of persons living in the household.[1] The family status of respondents at the time of the survey was therefore determined by combining all information provided about their marital and parental status: marital status, number of children in the household, presence or absence of a husband or common-law spouse, and so on.

Thus, regardless of their age, respondents, including single mothers, are classified as "children" if they were living with one or both parents at the time of the survey[2] and had been reported as "single/never-married." All persons living with a spouse (within a marriage or common-law union) belong to a couple; couples are therefore distinguished according to whether any children were living with them at the time of the survey.[3] Heads of lone-parent families are persons living with one or more children at the time of the survey and having no spouse (husband or common-law partner). Finally, all respondents not belonging to a census family, that is, who were not a child, a parent, or part of a couple, according to the information provided by the census, are classified as "non-family persons." Thus, as in the census, an ever-married respondent living with one or both parents at the time of the survey is considered a non-family person.

The following table therefore provides an overview of the distribution of Canadian women aged 18 to 64 by family status at the time of the 1990 GSS and 1991 Census. As can be seen, the distribution of women according to the GSS data is fairly consistent with the profile drawn from census data. Note, however, that the proportion of GSS respondents living as a couple without children seems higher (24% versus 22%). Conversely, except for those aged 18 to 24, the proportion of non-family persons seems relatively higher among 1991 Census female respondents. Thete is also an appreciably smaller proportion of "children" among 1990 survey respondents aged 18 to 24 than couples without children and non-family persons. These slight variations may be attributable to the differences in the populations covered by the two sources (McDaniel and Strike 1994).

TABLE 1

COMPARISON OF THE DISTRIBUTION OF WOMEN AGED 18 TO 64, BY FAMILY STATUS AND
AGE AT THE TIME OF THE SURVEY (S) AND THE CENSUS (C), 1990 AND 1991

Family status		Age group					
		18–24	25–34	35–44	45–54	55–64	All ages
				%			
"Child" status	(s)	45	6	3	1	1	10
	(c)	52	7	2	1	1	11
Women belonging	(s)	29	75	79	76	74	68
to a couple	(c)	26	70	77	77	70	66
with no children	(s)	19	24	10	31	52	24
	(c)	16	19	11	28	49	22
with children	(s)	10	51	69	45	22	44
	(c)	10	51	66	49	21	44
Lone mothers	(s)	4	7	9	11	6	8
	(c)	4	8	11	9	7	8
Non-family persons	(s)	22	12	9	12	19	14
	(c)	18	15	10	13	22	15
Total	(s)	16	29	24	17	14	100
	(c)	16	28	25	17	14	100

Source: 1990 GSS, cycle 5, Public Use Microdata File; Census of Canada, 1991, Individual Public Use Microdata Files.

IDENTIFICATION OF BLENDED FAMILIES

So-called "blended" families existing at the time of the survey are not immediately identifiable from the GSS data. The status of children living in the household is established in relation to the respondents only. It is therefore possible to identify women who are raising their children with their spouse, but not respondents living with a spouse other than the father of their children. To identify these families, it is therefore necessary to reconstitute the respondents' family histories retrospectively by combining the retrospective data they have provided about their marital path (formation and dissolution of common-law unions and marriages) and parental life course (births, adoptions, stepchildren, and departure of children from the home).

This exercise does, however, raise some difficulties. Some of the information needed to reconstruct family episodes was not gathered within the scope of the GSS. For example, the survey does not give the arrival date in the respondents' home of step- or adopted children. Only the birth date of these children is known.[4] Moreover, there was no question about the age at death of children reported in the survey as deceased. Because it is impossible to determine how long these children lived with the respondents, it is therefore impossible to reconstruct with any certainty the various phases of the respondent's family life. The survey also has no information about periods during which children temporarily left home to live on their own. We only know their final departure date from the parental home.

Despite the difficulty of accurately determining when step- or adopted children came into the respondents' life, a strategy for allocating arrival dates was developed. Stepchildren have been allocated to the union following their birth and when their presence in the union is borne out by the child's date of departure from the respondent's home. Adopted children have been allocated to the union coinciding with their birth or immediately following it, unless the union lasted less than two years, in which case it was assumed the child was adopted in the context of the subsequent union. Owing to a lack of sufficient data, it was also assumed that all children, including "natural" children, were present in the family until their final departure.[5]

Using all of these data, it was possible to reconstitute the female respondents' episodes in a blended family. Current blended families were used to determine the family status of respondents at the time of the survey.

APPENDIX 3.2

TABLE 1

CUMULATIVE PROBABILITIES FOR WOMEN OF EXPERIENCING AN "INTACT" TWO-PARENT FAMILY AT VARIOUS AGES, BY MARITAL STATUS ON ENTRY AND AGE AT THE TIME OF THE SURVEY, 1990

Age[1] and marital status[2]		Age group					
		18–24	25–34	35–44	45–54	55–65	**All ages**
				%			
Age 20	P_m	1.6	5.1	9.5	14.8	13.3	**8.6**
	P_{cm}	0.5	1.2	0.3	0.1	0.0	**0.5**
	P_c	3.1	2.5	0.9	0.3	0.0	**1.4**
	P	5.2	8.8	10.7	15.2	13.3	**10.5**
Age 25	P_m	10.2	21.0	39.0	53.0	51.1	**35.6**
	P_{cm}	10.2	5.2	2.2	0.1	0.1	**2.7**
	P_c	10.5	5.6	1.9	0.4	0.0	**3.2**
	P	30.9	31.8	43.1	53.5	51.2	**41.5**
Age 30	P_m		35.3	59.2	73.5	75.7	**55.8**
	P_{cm}		12.4	5.4	0.6	0.4	**6.0**
	P_c		8.1	2.4	0.6	0.1	**4.1**
	P		55.8	67.0	74.7	76.2	**65.9**
Age 35	P_m		43.0	65.9	82.4	81.4	**63.9**
	P_{cm}		15.8	6.9	0.6	0.4	**7.1**
	P_c		9.4	3.0	0.6	0.1	**4.5**
	P		68.2	75.8	83.6	81.9	**75.5**
Age 40	P_m			67.8	82.8	83.6	**65.7**
	P_{cm}			8.0	0.8	0.5	**7.7**
	P_c			3.3	0.6	0.1	**4.7**
	P			79.1	84.2	84.2	**78.1**
Age 45	P_m			68.5	82.8	84.1	**66.2**
	P_{cm}			8.0	0.8	0.5	**7.7**
	P_c			3.3	0.6	0.1	**4.7**
	P			79.8	84.2	84.7	**78.6**
Age 50	P_m				82.8	84.1	**66.2**
	P_{cm}				0.8	0.5	**7.7**
	P_c				0.6	0.1	**4.7**
	P				84.2	84.7	**78.6**

TABLE 1 (CONCLUDED)

CUMULATIVE PROBABILITIES FOR WOMEN OF EXPERIENCING AN "INTACT" TWO-PARENT FAMILY AT VARIOUS AGES, BY MARITAL STATUS ON ENTRY AND AGE AT THE TIME OF THE SURVEY, 1990

Age[1] and marital status[2]		Age group					
		18–24	25–34	35–44	45–54	55–65	**All ages**
					%		
Age 55	P_m				82.8	84.1	**66.2**
	P_{cm}				0.8	0.5	**7.7**
	P_c				0.6	0.1	**4.7**
	P				84.2	84.7	**78.6**
Age 60	P_m					84.1	**66.2**
	P_{cm}					0.5	**7.7**
	P_c					0.1	**4.7**
	P					84.7	**78.6**
Age 65	P_m					84.1	**66.2**
	P_{cm}					0.5	**7.7**
	P_c					0.1	**4.7**
	P					84.7	**78.6**
N[3]		105	786	998	745	677	**3,311**

1. Exact age.
2. P^m: cumulative probabilities following a direct marriage.

   P^{cm}: cumulative probabilities following a marriage preceded by a common-law union.

   P^c: cumulative probabilities following a common-law union.

   P: cumulative probabilities for all marital statuses.

3. Expanded data reduced to the size of the initial sample. Excludes eight cases for which the type of union is not known.

Source: 1990 GSS, cycle 5, Public Use Microdata File.

TABLE 2

CUMULATIVE PROBABILITIES FOR WOMEN WHO HAVE EXPERIENCED AN "INTACT" TWO-PARENT FAMILY OF EXITING THIS FAMILY STATUS AT VARIOUS DURATIONS, BY MEANS OF EXIT AND AGE AT THE TIME OF THE SURVEY, 1990

Duration[1] and means of exit[2]		Age group				All ages
		25–34	35–44	45–54	55–65	
				%		
Age 1	P_b	2.8	0.9	1.1	0.0	1.5
	P_d	0.0	0.1	0.1	0.2	0.1
	P_c	0.3	0.2	0.0	0.2	0.2
	P	3.1	1.2	1.2	0.4	1.8
2 years	P_b	4.6	2.9	1.3	0.5	2.9
	P_d	0.0	0.1	0.1	0.2	0.1
	P_c	0.3	0.2	0.0	0.2	0.2
	P	4.9	3.2	1.4	0.9	3.2
3 years	P_b	7.9	4.0	2.2	0.6	4.4
	P_d	0.0	0.3	0.1	0.4	0.2
	P_c	0.4	0.3	0.0	0.2	0.2
	P	8.3	4.6	2.3	1.2	4.8
4 years	P_b	10.7	4.9	2.9	0.6	5.5
	P_d	0.1	0.4	0.1	0.8	0.4
	P_c	0.5	0.2	0.0	0.2	0.3
	P	11.3	5.5	3.0	1.6	6.2
5 years	P_b	12.4	6.2	3.6	0.9	6.5
	P_d	0.1	0.6	0.1	1.2	0.6
	P_c	1.1	0.2	0.0	0.2	0.3
	P	13.6	7.0	3.7	2.3	7.4
10 years	P_b	19.0	12.3	8.3	2.6	11.1
	P_d	0.4	0.8	0.4	1.9	1.0
	P_c	1.5	0.2	0.1	0.2	0.4
	P	20.9	13.3	8.8	4.7	12.5
15 years	P_b	22.7	16.9	12.8	4.6	14.8
	P_d	1.1	1.6	1.5	2.9	2.0
	P_c	4.5	0.5	0.3	0.2	0.6
	P	28.3	19.0	14.6	7.7	17.4
20 years	P_b		24.9	17.9	7.0	19.0
	P_d		2.5	2.3	3.8	2.7
	P_c		1.7	3.3	4.3	3.6
	P		29.1	23.5	15.1	25.3
25 years	P_b		28.6	21.7	9.5	21.9
	P_d		2.5	3.6	5.6	4.1
	P_c		6.3	18.0	16.6	15.5
	P		37.4	43.3	31.7	41.5
30 years	P_b			22.4	10.8	22.9
	P_d			4.5	8.5	6.1
	P_c			40.3	37.8	35.1
	P			67.2	57.1	64.1

TABLE 2 (CONCLUDED)

CUMULATIVE PROBABILITIES FOR WOMEN WHO HAVE EXPERIENCED AN "INTACT" TWO-PARENT FAMILY OF EXITING THIS FAMILY STATUS AT VARIOUS DURATIONS, BY MEANS OF EXIT AND AGE AT THE TIME OF THE SURVEY, 1990

Duration[1] and means of exit[2]		Age group				All ages
		25–34	35–44	45–54	55–65	
				%		
35 years	P_b				11.8	23.8
	P_d				10.7	7.7
	P_c				53.1	48.8
	P				75.6	80.3
40 years	P_b				12.0	24.0
	P_d				11.0	8.0
	P_c				64.0	57.6
	P				87.0	89.6
N[3]		117	200	358	523	1,230

1. Duration in exact years.
2. P^b: cumulative probabilities following voluntary breakdown of a union.

   P^d: cumulative probabilities following the death of the spouse.

   P^c: cumulative probabilities following the children's departure.

   P: cumulative probabilities for all episodes.
3. Expanded data reduced to the size of the initial sample. Excludes 120 cases for which the date of exit from the episode is not known. The total includes 32 female respondents aged 18 to 24 for whom the cumulative probabilities are not shown separately.

Source: 1990 GSS, cycle 5, Public Use Microdata File.

TABLE 3

CUMULATIVE PROBABILITIES FOR WOMEN WHO HAVE EXPERIENCED A LONE-PARENT EPISODE OF EXITING LONE-PARENT STATUS AT VARIOUS DURATIONS, BY MEANS OF EXIT AND AGE AT THE TIME OF THE SURVEY, 1990

Duration[1] and means of exit[2]		Age group					All ages
		18–24	25–34	35–44	45–54	55–65	
				%			
1 year	P_m	4.2	8.3	7.4	10.7	15.5	**9.9**
	P_{cl}	18.5	14.2	9.0	6.5	0.9	**8.5**
	P_c	5.0	4.8	1.9	1.7	3.7	**3.1**
	P	27.7	27.3	18.3	18.9	20.1	**21.5**
2 years	P_m	6.1	12.6	11.1	13.6	22.2	**14.1**
	P_{cl}	29.1	27.4	15.9	11.1	3.3	**15.3**
	P_c	10.5	4.8	2.0	3.8	6.4	**4.5**
	P	45.7	44.8	29.0	28.5	31.9	**33.9**
3 year	P_m		13.8	16.2	16.0	26.1	**17.2**
	P_{cl}		30.3	26.4	14.6	3.7	**19.7**
	P_c		5.7	2.0	4.9	9.6	**5.7**
	P		49.8	44.6	35.5	39.4	**42.6**
4 years	P_m		17.7	18.6	18.8	29.6	**20.2**
	P_{cl}		38.6	31.7	19.2	5.9	**24.6**
	P_c		5.7	2.6	6.1	10.8	**6.5**
	P		62.0	52.9	44.1	46.3	**51.3**
5 years	P_m		19.1	20.1	21.9	30.9	**22.0**
	P_{cl}		45.3	33.4	20.6	7.9	**27.2**
	P_c		5.7	2.7	6.4	12.0	**6.9**
	P		70.1	56.2	48.9	50.8	**56.1**
10 years	P_m			27.4	28.5	36.8	**27.8**
	P_{cl}			43.5	27.4	8.7	**33.7**
	P_c			5.6	13.0	26.3	**13.4**
	P			76.5	68.9	71.8	**74.9**
15 years	P_m				30.3	38.6	**29.1**
	P_{cl}				30.9	10.1	**36.3**
	P_c				16.0	34.1	**17.4**
	P				77.2	82.8	**82.8**
20 years	P_m						**29.5**
	P_{cl}						**38.5**
	P_c						**22.2**
	P						**90.2**
N^3		29	144	166	186	163	688

1. Duration in exact years.
2. P^m: cumulative probabilities following a marriage.
   P^{cl}: cumulative probabilities following a common-law union.
   P^c: cumulative probabilities following the children's departure.
   P: cumulative probabilities for all episodes.
3. Expanded data reduced to the size of the initial sample. Excludes 38 cases for which the date of exit from the episode is not known.
Source: 1990 GSS, cycle 5, Public Use Microdata File.

TABLE 4

CUMULATIVE PROBABILITIES FOR WOMEN WHO HAVE EXPERIENCED A BLENDED FAMILY OF EXITING THIS FAMILY STATUS AT VARIOUS DURATIONS, BY MEANS OF EXIT AND AGE AT THE TIME OF THE SURVEY, 1990

Duration[1] and means of exit[2]		Age group				All ages
		25–34	35–44	45–54	55–65	
				%		
1 year	P_b	4.3	3.4	4.1	0.0	**3.2**
	P_d	0.0	0.0	0.0	0.0	**0.0**
	P_c	0.0	3.6	3.5	2.8	**2.4**
	P	4.3	7.0	7.6	2.8	**5.6**
2 years	P_b	11.4	7.2	8.8	1.4	**7.9**
	P_d	0.3	0.0	0.6	0.0	**0.2**
	P_c	0.4	3.6	6.1	5.0	**3.9**
	P	12.1	10.8	15.5	6.4	**12.0**
3 years	P_b	21.6	11.1	11.1	1.4	**12.2**
	P_d	2.2	0.0	0.6	0.0	**0.7**
	P_c	2.7	5.3	8.0	9.0	**6.2**
	P	26.5	16.4	19.7	10.4	**19.1**
4 years	P_b	25.5	16.8	15.0	1.4	**15.8**
	P_d	2.2	0.0	0.6	1.0	**0.9**
	P_c	4.2	7.8	8.9	9.0	**7.5**
	P	31.9	24.6	24.5	11.4	**24.2**
5 years	P_b	29.4	20.2	15.6	2.6	**18.1**
	P_d	2.2	0.0	2.1	1.0	**1.3**
	P_c	4.2	10.8	8.9	11.8	**8.9**
	P	35.8	31.0	26.6	15.4	**28.3**
10 years	P_b	44.3	31.8	22.4	6.4	**26.5**
	P_d	2.2	0.5	2.1	2.8	**1.9**
	P_c	10.4	19.7	22.8	23.6	**20.4**
	P	56.9	52.0	47.3	32.8	**48.8**
15 years	P_b		35.9	26.9	11.8	**30.6**
	P_d		0.5	2.4	2.8	**2.0**
	P_c		33.1	35.9	35.8	**30.9**
	P		69.5	65.2	50.4	**63.5**
20 years	P_b				13.8	**32.0**
	P_d				3.7	**2.3**
	P_c				6.4	**52.7**
	P				81.9	**87.0**
N[3]		152	161	128	91	553

1. Duration in exact years.
2. P^b: cumulative probabilities following voluntary breakdown of a union.
   P^d: cumulative probabilities following the death of the spouse.
   P^c: cumulative probabilities following the children's departure.
   P: cumulative probabilities for all episodes.
3. Expanded data reduced to the size of the initial sample. Excludes 18 cases for which the date of exit from the episode is not known. The total includes 21 female respondents aged 18 to 24 for whom the cumulative probabilities are not shown separately.

Source: 1990 GSS, cycle 5, Public Use Microdata File.

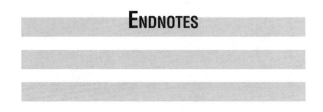

ENDNOTES

1. It was also found that this variable did not always reflect accurately enough the family status of respondents in unusual living arrangements. For example, some women raising stepchildren at the time of the survey were classified as living with "a spouse and other relatives" rather than with "a spouse and children."

2. The household may also include brothers and sisters and other persons, related or not.

3. Unlike children identified in the census, these may be never-married or ever-married children. The GSS microdata file provides no information about the marital status of the children present.

4. It is important to point out that in this survey, information is available for up to 10 natural children, three stepchildren, and two adopted children. In the case of natural children, dated information is therefore provided for the nine oldest children and the youngest child; in the case of stepchildren, it has been gathered for the two oldest children and the youngest child; and in the case of adopted children, it has been gathered for the oldest child and the youngest child (Statistics Canada 1991).

5. When the respondent did not report the age of a child or specify when the child left home, or when the child's age at death is not known, it is impossible to classify the child with any certainty in a family episode. These children, and not the respondent, were therefore excluded from the analysis. (For a detailed presentation of the method used to constitute family episodes, see Desrosiers et al. 1994.)

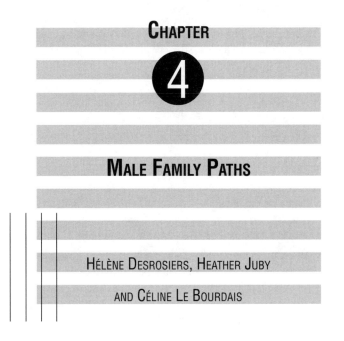

CHAPTER

4

MALE FAMILY PATHS

HÉLÈNE DESROSIERS, HEATHER JUBY

AND CÉLINE LE BOURDAIS

Chapter 3 describes the marital and family history of Canadian women. Based on the retrospective data of the 1990 General Social Survey, cycle 5: Family and Friends (GSS), the analysis of women's family paths reveals the multiplicity and diversity of individual life courses that have emerged over the last 30 years, which can be attributed to the major demographic changes that have occurred during that period.

This chapter looks at the family life of men. Using the same approach as in Chapter 3, it attempts to show the extent to which the changes noted in fertility and conjugal life have played a part in altering and complicating the family paths of Canadian men. It also compares the family paths of men and women, highlighting the most striking differences.

Given the in-depth analysis of female paths in Chapter 3, one might well wonder what additional information this study of male family paths could reveal. Since both the men and women aged 18 to 64 surveyed by the 1990 GSS lived through the same socio-historical period, does it not seem likely that their demographic behaviours would be altered in appreciably the same way? Is it not therefore logical to assume that the family histories of men replicate those of women, except for certain well-known differences in timing patterns (such as men's later entry into marital and parental life)?

While these assumptions are true at a general analytical level, a closer study of the individual paths of men and women does in fact show differences by sex. Recent studies have shown, for example, that the impact of union dissolution on the subsequent evolution of family life is not the same for men and women. Following separation or divorce, women are more likely than men to assume custody of their children, and therefore to experience a period of lone parenthood (Oderkirk and Lochhead 1992). On the other hand, studies show that men tend to enter into new unions sooner than women after a marital breakdown (Villeneuve-Gokalp 1991), and that these new unions quite often lead to the formation of a blended family centred around the woman and her children. We can therefore expect these sex-based behavioural differences to be reflected in the sequencing of men and women's family statuses.

Until quite recently, most demographic studies of the family focused primarily on women. This meant that, for years, the data needed to study male family paths were sadly lacking. However, a number of longitudinal surveys of both men and women have now been completed in several countries and the required data are now available. Why then are there still so few studies of male family paths (Kuijsten 1995)?

First, retrospective data on male fertility are less reliable, and there is little doubt that this has contributed to the lack of interest in pursuing the study of male family paths (Furstenberg 1988). Secondly, the theory, long accepted in family sociology, that the family universe and the custody of children essentially concern women has also contributed to men's exclusion as subjects in this field of analysis. Finally, the notion that men's family paths mirror those of women within two or three years has supported the practice of studying family paths from a single perspective.

To counter the current lack of studies of male family paths, we decided to devote an entire chapter of this monograph to this subject, despite the obvious risk of repeating information already presented in the chapter on female family paths. To present as complete a profile as possible, comments are provided for each table and figure presented in this chapter. However, in the interest of brevity, the reader is frequently referred to Chapter 3 regarding matters of methodology and context. While the text is primarily concerned with those aspects of the profile that are related specifically to men, each section concludes with a presentation of the factors that distinguish the family paths of men from those of women.

Like Chapter 3, this chapter begins with a brief presentation of the data, this time emphasizing the inherent limitations of the information obtained from men. The chapter's second section provides a retrospective description of the marital and family history of men in various family situations at the time of the survey. In this section we estimate, for example, the proportion of men, among non-family persons, who were in a previous union or fathered children with whom they no longer live. The third section uses the attrition tables method to look specifically at the dynamics of the formation and dissolution of various forms of family organization—such as the intact two-parent family, the lone-parent family and the blended family—in men's lives. The chapter's concluding section describes the evolution of male family paths and attempts to estimate the proportion of men who will follow each type of path over the course of their lives.

All analyses in this study use 10-year age groupings to illustrate behavioural changes over generations. This study includes all 1990 GSS male respondents, regardless of their family status, who were aged 18 to 64 in 1990.[1]

4.1   SOME CLARIFICATIONS ABOUT THE DATA GATHERED FROM MEN

The data are taken from the 1990 General Social Survey, cycle 5: Family and Friends (GSS), conducted by Statistics Canada between January and March 1990.[2] The sample is representative of the Canadian population aged 15 and older, excluding institutional residents. Of the nearly 13,500 people aged 15 and older who were interviewed, 4,498 were men aged 18 to 64 at the time of the survey.

The 1990 GSS gathered data on the marital and parental histories of the respondents—that is, information on the chronology of the respondents' common-law unions and marriages, separations, divorces and widowhood, as well as the births and final departures from the family home of their children (natural, step- or adopted). By combining these various chronologies, we can reconstruct the respondents' family paths and identify their family status at the time of the survey (see Chapter 3, Section 3.1 and Appendix 3.1).

To ensure the reconstruction of family paths based on retrospective data is reliable, all events (unions, dissolutions, and children's births and departures) experienced by the respondents must be accurately listed and dated. The omission of events (or the inclusion of erroneous dates) would result in incomplete or inaccurate histories. On this issue, past studies all make the same observation: men appear to be more inclined than women to provide an incomplete account of their marital (Bumpass et al. 1991) or reproductive (Furstenberg 1988) histories by neglecting to report particular past experiences. If such omissions occur when men are questioned about their own offspring, it can be readily assumed that this will occur even more often when men report the history of stepchildren who lived with them in a blended family for a relatively brief time. Because the 1990 GSS contains no data about the family life of respondents' wives and ex-wives, it unfortunately cannot be used to assess the extent of this undercount. For now, we can only note that the parental histories of men are likely to be slightly less reliable than those of women.

The way in which the data are used to identify various family statuses, in particular parenting arrangements, also requires further explanation. Like all data collections centred on the household (including the census), the 1990 GSS provides no information about the custody arrangements adopted following a separation. Since only the birth date and final departure date of each child are known, we are forced to assume that the children lived continuously with the respondent until they left home, however long that may have been.[3] The available data therefore compel us to restrict the notion of family to parent–child or stepparent–child cohabitation, without regard to the actual parenting arrangements involved. This constraint posed little difficulty in the study of the family paths of women, most of whom assume custody of their children following separation or divorce. It does, however, lead to inaccuracies with respect to men, who are less likely to obtain sole custody of their children after the dissolution of a union (La Novara 1993), and who maintain varying ties with their children over time (Seltzer 1991).

Due to constraints such as these, the family statuses described in this chapter may at times conceal quite different realities. For example, lone-parenthood episodes may in fact cover a wide range of arrangements—from the "weekend dad," who sees his children every second weekend, to the lone father who has sole custody of his children. Lone fathers are a diverse group. However, they do share some characteristics, the most interesting perhaps being that they do not consider their children to have left home for good. Similarly diverse are blended families, which may encompass various forms of family organization, such as the separated father who lives on his own with a new spouse and occasionally cares for his children from a previous union, or the stepfather who shares daily responsibility for his wife's children. This diversity of family forms, covered by the notions of lone-parent and blended families, should be kept in mind when conducting analyses of family status.

4.2 OVERVIEW OF THE MARITAL AND PARENTAL HISTORY OF MEN ACCORDING TO THEIR FAMILY STATUS

This section begins by documenting the living arrangements of the male respondents at the time of the survey in relation to the "census family,"[4] then explores the marital and parental history of the men living in these various arrangements. Before we begin this discussion, a brief review of the definitions used in this section (and in Chapter 3) is in order. "Child" status is assigned to all single (never-married) respondents, regardless of age, who were living with their parents at the time of the survey. "Couple" status is assigned to respondents who were living with a partner, with or without children, whether in a marriage or a common-law union. "Heads of lone-parent families" status includes respondents who had no spouse, but were living with one or more children. Finally, "non-family person" status includes respondents who did not belong to a census family—that is, those people who the census did not consider to be a "child," a parent, or part of a couple as defined above.

Table 4.1 shows the distribution of GSS male respondents aged 18 to 64 according to these family statuses.[5] Two-thirds of the respondents were living with a spouse at the time of the survey, slightly more than one-fifth belonged to a couple without children, and 45% to a couple with children. A very small percentage of respondents (2%) headed a lone-parent family. "Child" status was assigned to 16%, while a similar proportion (17%) were not living in a census family and were therefore classified as "non-family persons." Predictably, those aged 18 to 24 had the highest proportion of "children" (66%), while the status of "non-family person" was dominant (about 20%) among those under age 35. Finally, more men (more than 60%) were a parent in a two-parent family between the ages of 35 and 54 than at any other age, and in a lone-parent family (5%) after age 55.

TABLE 4.1

DISTRIBUTION OF MEN AGED 18 TO 64, BY FAMILY STATUS AND AGE AT THE TIME OF THE SURVEY, 1990

Family status[1] at the time of the survey	Age group					All ages
	18–24	25–34	35–44	45–54	55–64	
	%					
"Child" status	66	11	3	3	1	16
Men belonging to a couple	15	66	82	83	82	66
with no children	12	23	11	22	47	21
with children	3	43	71	61	35	45
Lone fathers	0	0	2	3	5	2
Non-family persons	19	23	13	11	12	17
Total	**100**	**100**	**100**	**100**	**100**	**100**
	%					
Distribution by age	18	28	24	16	14	**100**

1. Family status refers to the status held in relation to a census family.

Source: 1990 GSS, cycle 5, Public Use Microdata File.

How accurately does this cross-sectional profile reflect male family paths? Or to what extent does the profile camouflage the multiple, and sometimes contrasting, paths taken by the various groups of male respondents? The following analysis tackles these questions.

4.2.1 The history of "child" status

Today the transition to adulthood is not as easy as it once was, when the departure from home and marriage overlapped. Instead, it is a sequence of episodes that vary in number and are more or less interrelated (Lapierre-Adamcyk et al. 1995). The first departure from home is not always final, and the formation of a first union, which often is not legalized, does not rule out the possibility of a later return to the family of origin (see Table 4.2).

TABLE 4.2

INDICATORS OF THE RESIDENTIAL, CONJUGAL AND PARENTAL HISTORY OF MEN AGED 18 TO 64 HAVING "CHILD" STATUS, BY AGE AT THE TIME OF THE SURVEY, 1990

Indicators of residential, conjugal and parental history	Age group			All ages
	18–24	25–34	35–64	
			%	
Of all men having "child" status[1]				
Men who had left the parental home	12	30	34	**17**
Men who had experienced a commonlaw union	5	15	21	**8**
Men who were single fathers (i.e., living with a child)	0	2	0	**0**
Of the men living with no children or spouse but with one or both of their parents				
Men who had never been in a union	95	81	73	**90**
Men who had lived common law but who had never married	5	13	19	**8**
Men who had been married	0	6	8	**2**

1. The subcategories are not mutually exclusive, therefore the total may not equal 100%.
Source: 1990 GSS, cycle 5, Public Use Microdata File.

The data show that 17% of "children" who lived with their parents at the time of the survey had previously left the parental home to live on their own. As expected, this percentage increases with age: although a little more than 1 in 10 respondents aged 18 to 24 had already left home once, this was true of almost one-third of men aged 25 and older living with their parents. Economic reasons—men aged 25 to 34 reported leaving because of a job, while men aged 35 and over reported leaving to attend school—were usually cited as the main motives for their final departure from home after age 25. Almost the same proportion (about 25%) of "children" aged 18 to 24 reported having left the parental home because of a job, to attend school, "to be independent/move into own place," or for some other reason, including to form a union (1990 GSS).

Very few men with "child" status in a census family were living with a child (see Table 4.2). The few cases identified were young, single, never-married fathers, aged 25 to 34, who were living in a three-generation family.[6] In these instances, the census gave precedence to the "child" status of these men, which means they were not identified as single fathers (Norris and Knighton 1995). However, this approach had little effect on the estimate of lone-parent status among men who, unlike women, rarely assume the custody of children born outside of marriage.

Table 4.2 also shows that 1 in 12 single male respondents who were living with their parents had previously lived in a common-law union. This phenomenon affects 5% of "children" aged 18 to 24, and about 20% of "children" aged 35 and older. As Norris and Knighton (1995) point out, the significant increase in common-law unions observed over the last 20 years could have resulted in an overestimation in recent censuses of the number of "children." As common-law unions gradually take the place of marriage, the census strategy of using only legal matrimony to determine "child" status no longer seems appropriate. In fact, it may prevent us from identifying, among all single persons living with their parents, "children" who have returned to the home after the dissolution of their common-law union. The data in the lower part of Table 4.2 allow for a comparison of the relative number of young men who have returned to live with their family of origin after the break-up of a common-law union or marriage. Unlike the data presented in the top section of the table, these data are for *all* respondents with no wife or children who are living with their parents. So the data include men who had previously been married and returned to live with their parents following a separation.

The data show that 10% of respondents who were living in their family of origin, without children or a spouse, had previously been in a union. This proportion is decidedly higher among men aged 35 and older (27%), who had had time to form a union (and to experience its dissolution), than among men aged 18 to 34 (5%). Regardless of their age at the time of the survey, most men who were living with their parents and had belonged to a couple were not legally married. Clearly, the changing patterns of conjugal life, coupled with the inclusion of men who had previously cohabited in the category of "child," may result in a significant overestimation of the number of men with "child" status living in census families.

4.2.2 The history of men belonging to a couple

This section highlights the marital paths followed by the different birth cohorts of men who belonged to a couple (that is, who had a common-law partner or wife) at the time of the survey. The focus of the analysis then shifts to an exploration of the parental paths followed by these men.

4.2.2.1 Marital history

Like previous studies (Burch and Madan 1986; Dumas and Péron 1992; Le Bourdais and Desrosiers 1988; Le Bourdais and Marcil-Gratton 1996), the analyses in Chapter 3 show that there is not only an increase in common-law unions by young people at the start of their conjugal life, but also a growing proportion of people who enter a new union after the failure of their first marriage. The analyses presented in Chapter 3 also confirm the declining popularity of legal marriage and the increasing number of common-law unions in recent generations of women. Table 4.3 clearly illustrates these same developments among men.

TABLE 4.3

INDICATORS OF THE CONJUGAL HISTORY OF MEN AGED 18 TO 64 BELONGING TO A COUPLE, BY AGE AT THE TIME OF THE SURVEY, 1990

Indicators of conjugal history	Age group					
	18–24	25–34	35–44	45–54	55–64	**All ages**
			%			
Married men	39	77	90	92	96	**86**
Men living common law	61	23	10	8	4	**14**
Of the married men						
Men in a first marriage	100	97	89	87	88	**91**
with no previous union[1]	57	69	83	95	99	**84**
who married their common-law partner	41	29	15	4	1	**14**
who had lived common law with another partner	3	7	5	2	1	**4**
Men having remarried	0	3	11	13	12	**9**
who had never lived common law[1]	–	50	30	42	68	**45**
who married their common-law partner	–	50	60	55	28	**50**
Of the men living common-law						
Men in a first common-law union	90	65	45	67	65	**65**
never-married	100	91	40	8	15	**72**
ever-married	0	9	60	92	85	**28**
Men in second or subsequent						
common-law union	10	35	55	33	35	**35**
never-married	--	66	20	0[2]	--	**41**
ever-married	--	34	80	100[2]	--	**59**

– Nil or zero.

-- Percentage omitted (based on fewer than 10 cases in the sample). Expanded data reduced to the size of the initial sample.

1. The subcategories are not mutually exclusive therefore the total may not equal 100%.

2. Percentage calculated for fewer than 25 cases in the sample (expanded data reduced to the size of the initial sample).

Source: 1990 GSS, cycle 5, Public Use Microdata File.

The top section of Table 4.3 shows the increase in the percentage of common-law unions reported by men who belonged to a couple at the time of the survey, from 4% for older generations to 61% for younger generations. Based on the prior history of the respondents, the next section of the table shows that nearly 1 in 10 married men were in their second marriage when surveyed. The percentage of men in their second marriage hovers at around 10% beginning at age 35, and drops sharply below that age. This result is evidently linked to the fact that the younger men were older when they first married and, more importantly, had not been married as long as those aged 35 and older.

Nearly all men aged 45 to 64 who were in their first marriage in 1990 had never been in any other form of union, perhaps because a high proportion of them married before common-law unions became widespread. This changes when we consider more recent generations: 17%[7] of respondents aged 35 to 44 in their first marriage had cohabited before; the figure jumps to 43% for those aged 18 to 24. In the vast majority of cases, these men had wed their common-law partner (88.2% of those aged 35 to 44, and 95.3% of those aged 18 to 24). Indeed, a much smaller proportion of men had cohabited with a partner other than their wife. Finally, it was noted that between 50% and 60% of remarried men had wed their common-law partner; only those aged 55 to 65 did not follow this model, with fewer than 3 in 10 remarried men marrying their common-law partner.

The bottom section of Table 4.3 provides information about the marital history of the men who were living in common-law unions at the time of the survey. Overall, one in three common-law husbands were in a second common-law union. This proportion was clearly higher among men aged 35 to 44, affecting half of these cohabitants. Overall, the proportion of cohabitants previously married increases with the respondents' age, regardless of the rank of the union in question. For example, just under 10% of men aged 25 to 34 and living common law for the first time had previously been married. This percentage climbs to 60% among those aged 35 to 44, and to about 90% for husbands aged 45 and older. A common-law union, which generally follows a marriage, therefore occurs later in life among older than among younger birth cohorts, for whom it is generally the first experience.

4.2.2.2 The parental history of men belonging to a couple

Using women's responses to the census question about birth parity, it is possible to distinguish women who have never had children from women whose children had left home or died. But because this question is never asked of men, it is impossible to make this distinction in order to identify those who have fathered children. The census data, therefore, do not allow us to estimate the proportion of men living without children after all of their natural children had left home or the percentage still living with the mother of these children and thus forming a true "empty nest" as defined in the life-cycle approach. Since censuses do not ask individuals about their parental history, they do not allow us to identify those men who had adopted or raised the children of a spouse within a blended family, and had therefore fulfilled a parental role in their lifetime.

In a context of marital stability, one would expect the vast majority of men aged 18 to 64 who had had children to be living with them. The discrepancy between the proportion of men who had fathered children and the proportion of men living with their children should be minimal at younger ages, increasing gradually over the years as the children grow up and leave the parental home. Similarly, the difference observed between the number of natural children present in the respondent's household and the total number of children present should be minimal, and is attributable to adopted children or stepchildren of a union that ended with the death of the mother. However, in the current context of conjugal mobility, the family status of men may differ appreciably from this theoretical distribution. Because women are more likely to assume custody of the children following a separation or divorce, men are therefore more likely to experience, for a period of time, life episodes without their children. Conversely, men are probably more inclined than women to form a blended family around the children of their new spouse.

Table 4.4 attempts to illuminate these aspects of the family life of men, using indicators that describe men's parental status at the time of the survey. The data in this table show that the distribution of married men is appreciably similar to that expected of a marital-stability model: a very small proportion of men under age 45 who had children were not living with them; and the percentage of men living without their children increases as the respondent's age increases and the grown children leave the family home. However, beginning at age 25, a small proportion of married men were living with children they had not fathered. With the exception of those men who were living with children they had adopted, such cases are probably the result of men living with a spouse and her children from a previous union.

TABLE 4.4

PARENTAL STATUS OF MEN AGED 18 TO 64 BELONGING TO A COUPLE, BY AGE AT THE TIME OF THE SURVEY, 1990

Indicators of parental status	Age group					
	18–24	25–34	35–44	45–54	55–64	**All ages**
			%			
Married men[1]						
who had had natural children	31	73	89	94	92	**85**
living with natural children	28	71	86	73	41	**70**
living with children, all types	28	74	90	75	44	**73**
Men living common law[1]						
who had had natural children	12	27	80	82	74[2]	**49**
living with natural children	10	27	42	28	7[2]	**27**
living with children, all types	20	38	64	51	7[2]	**50**

1. The subcategories are not mutually exclusive; therefore the total may not equal 100%.
2. Percentage calculated for fewer than 25 cases in the sample (expanded data reduced to the size of the initial sample).
Source: 1990 GSS, cycle 5, Public Use Microdata File.

The profile of men living in a common-law union is far more heterogeneous (see the bottom section of Table 4.4). Before age 35, men who had fathered children generally lived with them. This group of men includes a sizeable proportion of respondents (about 10%) who lived with children they had not fathered. However, after age 35, the profile changes dramatically. This is probably because marital mobility begins to emerge after this age. At ages 35 to 44, for example, nearly half of fathers (47.5%) were no longer living with their natural children. These children were probably still too young to have left home to live on their own, therefore it can be assumed that they were living with their mother after the dissolution of their parents' marriage. Moreover, a relatively large segment (just over 20%) of middle-aged cohabitants who had had children were living with children other than their own: although 64% of common-law partners aged 35 to 44 and about 50% aged 45 to 54 reported living with children, only 42% and 28% reported living with their natural children. In cases where men lived with children that were not their own, the children had been adopted. In most cases, however, they were the partner's children from a previous union. As other studies have shown (Furstenberg 1988; Jacobsen and Edmondson 1993), marital instability seems to result for men in "serial fatherhood." In other words, for a variety of reasons, men seem unable to remain closely involved with their own children after a marriage breakdown, and so tend to exercise a parental role with the children who enter their lives as their marital histories unfold. Our study of the profiles of men living common law supports this hypothesis.

4.2.2.3 The parental history of men belonging to a couple with children

The main purpose of this section is to measure the magnitude of blended families among the men who were living in a couple with children at the time of the survey. Blended families cannot be identified from census data, so few studies of these families have previously been undertaken. Blended families also cannot be immediately identified using GSS data. Therefore, for our analysis, it was necessary to combine the information gathered on the respondents' family status with their past history at the time of the survey. (For more information on this method, see Appendix 3.1.) Table 4.5 illustrates the approach used.

TABLE 4.5

DISTRIBUTION OF MEN BELONGING TO A COUPLE WITH CHILDREN, BY TYPE OF FAMILY AND AGE AT THE TIME OF THE SURVEY, 1990

| Type of family[1] | Origin of children present | Age group | | | |
		18–34	35–44	45–64	All ages
		%			
Intact families	All of the current couple	84	83	86	84
Blended families, no children common to the couple	All of a previous union	9	9	8	9
Blended families, with children common to the couple	Some children are of the current couple and others of a previous union	7	7	2	5
Re-created families[2]	All of the current couple	0	1	4	2
Total		100	100	100	100
		%			
Distribution by age		28	39	33	100

1. The type of family is determined according to the origin of the children present in the household at the time of the survey.
2. These are blended families that (strictly from the standpoint of living arrangements) become "intact" families once the last child not of the couple has left home, leaving behind a couple living with their own natural children.
Source: 1990 GSS, cycle 5, Public Use Microdata File.

Table 4.5 shows that more than 8 in 10 men (86%) living in a couple with children[8] at the time of the survey formed a family with the mother of these children: 84% belonged to an intact two-parent family[9] and 2% to a re-created family—that is, a family unit that had previously gone through a blended family phase. The table also reveals that one in seven couples with children were living as a blended family—that is, a family where one of the two spouses was not the natural or adoptive parent of one or more of the children and that 5% of couples had given birth to a child within this type of family.

The percentage of blended families increases somewhat from older generations (10% of those aged 45 to 64[10]) to younger generations (16% of those aged 35 to 44 and those under age 35), a result clearly linked to growing marital instability. Note, however, that there are proportionally more re-created families among older men. This may be explained by the fact that these men had had children, born outside of the existing union, who were old enough to have left the home.

Table 4.6 takes a closer look at the composition of the blended families to which the surveyed men belong. Of the families with no children common to the couple, the great majority (85.5%) included children of a single sibling relationship. In 17% of cases, the siblings were the respondent's children, and in 36% of cases they were those of his wife. Only 9% of the blended families included stepbrothers or stepsisters (children of each spouse born of previous unions). Of the blended families with half-brother and half-sister sibling relationships, most blended children of just one spouse (usually the husband's) with children common to the couple. For the men surveyed, fewer than 1% of all blended families identified blended children from three different sibling relationships: the husband's children, those of his wife, and those common to both. In all, about half of the men[11] brought their own children into the blended family, while nearly 4 in 10 men raised only the children of their spouse.

TABLE 4.6

DISTRIBUTION OF MEN LIVING IN A BLENDED FAMILY, BY FAMILY COMPOSITION, RANK OF THE EPISODE AND AGE AT THE TIME OF THE SURVEY, 1990

Family composition and rank of the episode	Age group			
	18–34	35–44	45–64	**All ages**
			%	
Family composition				
All children are of a previous union	56	55	81	**62**
of the respondent	12	11	32	**17**
of the wife	40	33	38	**36**
of both spouses	4	11	11	**9**
Some children are of the current couple and others				
are of a previous union	44	45	19	**38**
of the respondent	23	27	19	**24**
of the wife	20	16	0	**13**
of both spouses	1	2	0	**1**
Total	**100**	**100**	**100**	**100**
			%	
Rank of the episode				
First episode	97	86	79	**88**
Second episode	3	14	21	**12**
Total	**100**	**100**	**100**	**100**
			%	
Distribution by age	32	44	24	**100**

Source: 1990 GSS, cycle 5, Public Use Microdata File.

The last section of Table 4.6 reveals that the vast majority (88%) of men belonging to a blended family were experiencing this status for the first time. However, this percentage decreases from younger to older generations. Thus, 21% of respondents aged 45 to 64 at the time of the survey had been a member of this type of family at least once, compared with 14% of those aged 35 to 44 and less than 5% of those aged 18 to 34. However, given the climate of increasing marital instability, it is reasonable to expect the proportion of men who will have more than one such experience in their lifetime to increase as younger generations advance through their marital histories.

The type of union—married or common-law—favoured by men living in a couple with children varies depending on the type of family unit in which they are living. Nearly all men (96%) belonging to an intact two-parent family were married at the time of the survey: 83% had entered directly into marriage with the mother of their children, while 13% had first lived with their partner before marriage (see Table 4.7). In contrast, slightly more than one-third (34%) of men belonging to a blended or re-created family were living common law, and more than one-quarter (27%) had married their spouse after living with her common law. In general, common-law unions become increasingly popular the younger the generation, and this is as true of intact families as it is of blended or re-created families.

TABLE 4.7

TYPE AND RANK OF THE UNION AND NUMBER OF CHILDREN PRESENT AMONG COUPLES WITH CHILDREN, BY TYPE OF FAMILY AND MAN'S AGE AT THE TIME OF THE SURVEY, 1990

Type of family[1]	Age group			
	18–34	35–44	45–64	All ages
Type of union[2]				
Intact families				
direct marriage	65	84	97	83
marriage preceded by a common-law union	26	14	3	13
common-law union	9	2	0	4
Blended and re-created families				
direct marriage	28	37	54	39
marriage preceded by a common-law union	25	31	22	27
common-law union	47	32	24	34
Rank of the union[3]				
Intact families				
first union	91	91	94	92
second union	7	8	5	7
third or subsequent union	2	1	1	1
Blended and re-created families				
first union	64	40	29	44
second union	29	35	61	41
third or subsequent union	7	25	10	15
Number of children present[4]				
Intact families				
1 child	42	18	47	35
2 children	48	58	36	48
3 or more children	10	24	17	17
Average number of children	1.7	2.1	1.8	1.9
Blended and re-created families				
1 child	32	35	41	36
2 children	44	22	39	33
3 or more children	24	43	20	31
Average number of children	1.9	2.3	1.8	2.1

1. For analytical purposes, in this table "re-created" families have been grouped with blended families, with which they share a similar history.
2. This refers to the type of the current union. The category "marriage preceded by a common-law union" refers to men who married their common-law partner.
3. When the marriage was to a common-law partner, it was considered a single union whose form had changed over time.
4. Includes natural, step- and adopted children.
Source: 1990 GSS, cycle 5, Public Use Microdata File.

The vast majority (92%) of men living in an intact family had never lived with a partner other than the mother of their children.[12] In contrast, more than 5 in 10 men in a blended or re-created family had experienced two or more previous unions. The percentage (44%) of men belonging to a blended or re-created family who had experienced only one union is very likely made up of men who had had no children when they formed a blended family with their partner and her children. Note that, the younger the generation, the more this percentage increases.

The final section of Table 4.7 compares the distribution of the number of children by type of family. These data show little variation in the number of children from one family type to the next; blended or re-created families observed from the men's perspective are, on the whole, slightly larger than intact two-parent families. Nearly one in three blended or re-created families had three or more children, while only one in six intact two-parent families had as many, making the average number of children in blended families higher (2.1 versus 1.9). However, these differences vary by generation. The percentage of respondents aged 18 to 34 and living with three or more children is distinctly lower among intact families (10%) than among blended or re-created families (24%). In contrast, more men aged 35 to 44 were living with two children than their counterparts living in a blended or re-created family (58% versus 22%). By comparison, little difference separates those aged 45 to 64 by type of family unit (36% and 39%, respectively). The more marked differences in behaviour observed among those under age 45 may be attributable to the fact that the marital instability at the very root of blended families affects them earlier in life, and therefore has more of an impact on their reproductive and parental history.

4.2.2.4 The parental history of men belonging to a couple without children

Men belonging to a couple without children represent a sizeable proportion (21%) of 1990 GSS male respondents aged 18 to 64 (see Table 4.1). While about 25% of men aged 25 to 34 were in this category, the percentage of men belonging to a couple without children drops to 11% among those aged 35 to 44 before peaking at 47% among men aged 55 to 64.

As for the parental history of these men, slightly less than half (47%) of those aged 18 to 64 who belonged to a couple without children had fathered a child (see Table 4.8). Obviously, the proportion of men in this situation varies according to their age: 77% of those aged 45 to 54 and 88% of those 55 to 64 had had a child with whom they no longer lived, while this was true of only 12% of men under age 45,[13] whose parental histories were far from complete.

TABLE 4.8

INDICATORS OF THE PARENTAL HISTORY OF MEN BELONGING TO A COUPLE WITH NO CHILDREN, BY AGE AT THE TIME OF THE SURVEY, 1990

Indicators of parental history	Age group			
	18–44	45–54	55–64	**All ages**
			%	
Men who had had children	12	77	88	**47**
Men who had never had children	88	23	12	**53**
Of the men who had had children				
percent still living with the mother of all their children ("empty nest")	6	65	74	**62**
percent who had never raised children with their current spouse	74	13	11	**20**
percent who had lived in a blended family with their current spouse	20	22	15	**18**
percent who had experienced a lone-parent episode[1]	51	23	23	**27**
percent who had experienced a blended family episode[1]	28	24	17	**20**
Of the men who had never had children[1]				
percent still living with the adoptive mother of all their adopted children ("empty nest")	0	2	26	**2**
percent who had never raised children with their current spouse	99	93	60	**96**
percent who had raised the children of their current spouse	1	5	4	**2**
percent who had experienced a blended family episode	2	5	4	**2**

1. The subcategories are not mutually exclusive; therefore the total may not equal 100%.

Source: 1990 GSS, cycle 5, Public Use Microdata File.

Of the men who had had children, 62% belonged to a true "empty nest"; that is, they were still living with the natural mother of their children after the children had left home (see Table 4.8). This situation affected nearly three-quarters of respondents aged 55 to 64, but barely 6% of men under age 45. In contrast, nearly three-quarters of fathers aged 18 to 44 had never raised children with their current spouse, but 20% had raised children with their current spouse during a previous blended family episode. The magnitude of the last type of path varies relatively little by generation; however, the proportion of fathers who had never raised children with their current spouse is markedly higher among those aged 18 to 44. This high proportion must be seen in relation to the rise in marital instability and, in particular, the lesser likelihood of men to take custody of the children following a separation. Finally, note that 23% of respondents aged 55 to 64 who belonged to a couple without children, as well as 51% of those aged 18 to 44, had experienced lone parenthood in the past. Moreover, 17% of the former and 28% of the latter had lived within a blended family, either with or without their current spouse.

The second section of Table 4.8 concerns men belonging to a couple without children and who had had no children. The data show that some men who have never fathered children have in fact been parents. For example, slightly more than one-quarter (26%) of men aged 55 to 64 who had not fathered a child belonged to an "empty nest" after having raised the children they had adopted with their current spouse, another 4% were stepfathers to the children of the women they were living with in a blended family. Although this last percentage is modest among the most recent generations (ages 18 to 44), there is every reason to believe it will increase in the years to come.

4.2.3 The history of men who head a lone-parent family

The phenomenon of lone-parent families, which has surged since 1971, is one of the few family types that has been studied from the male perspective. In fact, the census has long provided socio-demographic data on lone-parent families by sex of the lone parent. These data show that one in five lone-parent families are today headed by a man (Oderkirk and Lochhead 1992). Like the studies done in other western countries, such as France (Le Gall and Martin 1987) and Great Britain (Hardey and Crow 1991), the studies done in Canada show the situation of lone fathers is generally more favourable than that of lone mothers. For example, the former are more educated than the latter and, because more lone fathers are employed, they also have higher incomes (Oderkirk and Lochhead 1992).

Although the census data shed some light on the phenomenon of lone parenthood among men, they do not provide an accurate picture of the situation experienced by lone fathers. For example, the data do not allow us to accurately determine the events leading to men's entry into a lone-parent family. Table 4.9 illuminates this aspect of lone parenthood and provides a more general look at the marital history of lone fathers.

TABLE 4.9

INDICATORS OF THE CONJUGAL AND PARENTAL HISTORY OF MALE HEADS OF LONE-PARENT HOUSEHOLDS, BY AGE AT THE TIME OF THE SURVEY, 1990[1]

	Age group		
Indicators of conjugal and parental history	18–44	45–64	**All ages**
Entries into lone-parenthood by			
Birth outside of a union	0	3	**2**
Dissolution	92	66	**76**
of a marriage	61	62	**61**
of a common-law union	31	4	**15**
Spouse's death	8	31	**22**
Men who had not experienced a union[2]	0	3	**2**
Ever-married men[2]	95	91	**92**
Men who had experienced a common-law union[2]	66	19	**37**
Rank of the episode			
First episode	64	78	**73**
Second episode	16	17	**16**
Third or subsequent episode	20	5	**11**

1. Excluded from this table are single (never-married) heads of lone-parent families living with their parents. In keeping with the approach taken by the census, they have been classified as "children" of a census family (see Section 4.2.1 and Table 4.2 of this chapter).

2. The subcategories are not mutually exclusive; therefore the total may not equal 100%.

Source: 1990 GSS, cycle 5, Public Use Microdata File.

First, recall that barely 2% of GSS male respondents aged 18 to 64 belonged to a lone-parent family; that is, they were living with no spouse and one or more children (see Table 4.1).[14] Of the total, just over three-quarters began their episode of lone parenthood following the voluntary dissolution of a union, either a marriage (61% of cases) or common-law union (15% of cases); only 2% had become lone parents following a birth outside of a union, and more than one in five following the death of their spouse (see Table 4.9).

Certainly, most men who had become lone parents through widowhood were aged 45 to 64—ages when the impact of the female death rate begins to be felt. Close to one in three fathers in this age group had taken this path, compared with 8% of those aged 18 to 44. In contrast, lone parenthood following the break-up of a common-law union or marriage predominated among those aged 18 to 44:[15] 92% of lone fathers in this age group had experienced the voluntary dissolution of a union, compared with about 66% (or two in three) lone fathers aged 45 to 64. As might be expected, the dissolution of a common-law union affected significantly more lone fathers in recent generations, causing 31% of lone-parent episodes among men aged 18 to 44 at the time of the survey (versus 4% of those aged 45 to 64).

A study of the marital history of lone fathers shows, moreover, that barely 2% of male heads of lone-parent families had never lived with a spouse, whether a wife or a common-law partner. About 9 in 10 lone fathers had been married, and nearly 4 in 10 had lived common law. The proportion of lone fathers who had previously been married is relatively stable from one generation to another; the percentage of men who had lived common law is markedly higher (66%) among those aged 18 to 44.

Finally, the last section of the table shows that just over one in four fathers (27%) were in their second or subsequent episode of lone parenthood. The incidence of two or more episodes of lone parenthood increases over time. For example, of those aged 18 to 44, only one in three lone fathers had experienced lone parenthood more than once, and one in five had experienced it three times or more.

4.2.4 The history of men who are non-family persons

"Non-family persons" represented 17% of the male respondents aged 18 to 64 at the time of the survey (see Table 4.1). There are more non-family persons among the youngest age groups (under age 35)—that is, at ages before family life really gets underway. Some respondents experience this status only temporarily in their middle years, as they make the transition between two family episodes; others experience this status when they are older and their "family life" ends (at least from the standpoint of their living arrangements). The status of "non-family person" therefore does not apply only to persons who have no family life. Far from it.

Just over 5 in 10 men with non-family status had never experienced a prior union; however, 28% had been legally married, and nearly one-third had lived with a common-law partner (see Table 4.10). On the whole, the percentage of respondents who had never experienced a union decreases as the age of the respondents increases, because men are not as far along in their marital life. Conversely, the proportion of ever-married men increases with age and stabilizes (slightly more than two in three men) after age 45. Similarly, the number of common-law unions in men's lives increases over the generations, peaking (at around 40%) between ages 25 and 54, and then dropping back down to 19% of men aged 55 to 64. The smaller percentage of men living common law observed among those aged 55 to 64 (19%) is doubtless due to the fact that common-law union is less popular with this generation. Furthermore, proportionally fewer men at these ages than those aged 45 to 54 had belonged to a couple at least once in their life. The discrepancy between these two groups is quite likely an effect of selection. For example, men aged 45 to 54 are more affected by marital instability and thus more likely to fall temporarily into the category of non-family persons while they are in transition between two unions.

TABLE 4.10

INDICATORS OF THE CONJUGAL AND PARENTAL HISTORY OF NON-FAMILY MALES, BY AGE AT THE TIME OF THE SURVEY, 1990[1]

Indicators of conjugal and parental history[2]	Age group					
	18–24	25–34	35–44	45–54	55–64	All ages
			%			
Men who had experienced no union	88	57	36	21	30	53
Men ever-married	1	13	41	69	67	28
Men who had experienced a common-law union	12	39	42	43	19	32
Men who had had children	1	13	27	63	60	24
Men who had raised children[3]	2	14	30	65	61	25

1. As they were in the census, ever-married respondents who were not living with a spouse but were living with one or both parents at the time of the survey are classified as non-family persons.
2. The subcategories are not exclusive; therefore the total may not equal 100%.
3. Includes natural, step- and adopted children.
Source: 1990 GSS, cycle 5, Public Use Microdata File.

About one-quarter of respondents aged 18 to 64 living in a non-family situation fathered or parented children at some point in their life. These percentages are distinctly higher among those aged 45 and older who were old enough to have seen their children leave home. But the proportions are sizeable for men between the ages of 25 to 44 and this result is clearly linked to increasing marital mobility.

4.2.5 Male–female comparison

The previous section explored the diverse marital and parental histories that emerged from our analysis of census data. The analysis shows that a significant proportion of men who were neither members of a couple nor parents at the time of the survey, and who were classified as "children" or "non-family persons" by the census, had been a husband or father at some point in their lives. From the analysis, it is also possible to document the marital mobility of men who were part of a couple (with or without children) and to estimate the proportion who had formed a blended family.

This section highlights the main differences in the family life of men and women.[16] While the proportion of respondents belonging to a couple (with or without children) at the time of the survey was almost identical for both groups, in 1990 lone parenthood was still a reality that clearly affected women (8%) more often than men (2%) (see tables 3.1 and 4.1). However, relatively more men than women had "child" status and, although to a lesser degree, more men than women lived outside a census family. Men usually had these statuses before age 35, whereas, by age 35, a significant proportion of women were already wives or mothers. And while 5% of women classified as "children" by the census were themselves the parent of a child, this situation was extremely rare among men. However, in later years (ages 55 and older) more men than women were living in a couple with children (35% versus 22%), while more women than men had the status of "non-family person" (19% versus 12%).

The distribution by type of union of men and women who belonged to a couple at the time of the survey is appreciably the same. A difference in behaviour between the sexes is seen only in those under age 25; common-law union was dominant among these men as they were still quite young to be married (see tables 3.3 and 4.3). Overall, the marital history of married men is quite similar to that of married women. Among those living common law, the differences by sex are slightly more marked, particularly in the middle years (that is, ages 35 to 44). At these ages, men were clearly more inclined to have experienced more than one common-law union than women (55% versus 29%), and to have entered into such unions after previously being married.

Men's greater marital mobility, combined with women's greater tendency to assume custody of the children following a separation, are reflected in the different distribution, by sex, of the various types of two-parent family with children. A slightly higher proportion of men than women who belonged to a couple with children at the time of the survey belonged to a blended family: 14% versus 11% (see tables 3.4 and 4.5). Compared with women, men were definitely more often the stepparent in a blended family. Nearly 60% of men living in a blended family were living with at least one child of which they were neither the natural nor adoptive father. In contrast, barely 12% of those women living in a blended family were not living with at least one of their natural or adopted children from a previous marriage (see tables 3.5 and 4.6).

Aside from a few expected random variations, the differences observed in the distribution of male and female respondents living in various types of blended families raise many questions. For example, the fact that 41% of men belonging to a blended family reported living only with their own children is surprising, as only 12% of women living in such a family reported raising only the children of their spouse (see tables 3.5 and 4.6). Aside from the age effect—men with children being generally older than their female counterparts—the discrepancy between the two sexes is likely due in part to men and women reporting differently. Recall that blended families were identified by combining the marital and parental histories of the respondents. Thus, given the variable involvement of men and women with their children and stepchildren, some of the male–female discrepancies may well derive from the different reporting of the two groups when responding to the questionnaire.[17]

As for the couples who had had no children at the time of the survey, the analysis shows, on the whole, little difference in the propensity of men and women to have previously had children. Only at ages 18 to 44 were the men who reported having had a child outnumbered by their female counterparts (see tables 3.7 and 4.8). Of the respondents who had had children, a smaller proportion of men than women (62% versus 74%) were still living with the natural parent of these children and thus formed an "empty nest," according to the strict definition of the term. In contrast, a higher percentage of fathers than mothers were living with a spouse with whom they had never raised children (20% versus 12%).

Of the respondents who were non-family persons at the time of the survey, the only difference by sex worthy of note is the distinctly higher proportion of men than women aged 25 to 44 who reported having previously had or raised children (see tables 3.9 and 4.10). This result clearly attests to the lesser involvement of fathers in the custody of their children following the break-up of a union.

The differences observed in the family profiles drawn of men and women are the result of the greater mortality of men at older ages, their later entry into married life and parenthood, and their propensity to form a new couple sooner after a marital breakdown. Consequently, despite a later start, men generally experience greater marital mobility than their female counterparts. Once they become fathers, they are more likely than women to live, at least for a time, apart from their children and to play the role of stepparent in a blended family. Here, the "serial fatherhood" some men experience is in stark contrast to the indissolubility of the mother–child bond noted in Chapter 3.

4.3 DYNAMICS OF THE FORMATION AND DISSOLUTION OF DIFFERENT FORMS OF FAMILY ORGANIZATION

The previous section looks at different indicators of the marital and parental history of men according to their family status at the time of the survey. However that approach, which is based on individuals at various stages of their life cycle, does not allow for the comparison of the extent of the changes that have occurred in the lives of various generations of men. For example, using that approach, it is impossible to estimate the proportion of men who will experience a given family status in their lifetime. To do this, we must change perspective, placing ourselves at the start of men's trajectories and following their marital and parental histories as they unfold.

Here, as in Chapter 3 on women, we examine the dynamics of the formation and dissolution of various forms of family organization for different generations of men over time.[18] Three types of family are considered: the "intact" two-parent family, the lone-parent family and the blended family. Based on the attrition tables method,[19] this analysis reveals how much the frequency and timing patterns of the formation and dissolution of a given family type differ from one generation to another, and estimates the proportion of men who will be affected by the phenomena if the behaviours observed at the time of the survey continue in the coming years.

Only family episodes involving children, regardless of age, are examined here. Unlike the census, which considers couples without children to be a census family, only households consisting of a male respondent (with or without a spouse) living with one or more children are considered in this analysis. Therefore, the presence or absence of children determines the existence or non-existence of a family. Because there are not enough data, all children present, regardless of their marital status and the time spent in the respondent's household, are considered to belong to the family unit. It is important to remember that the various types of family studied may cover a variety of arrangements, as the GSS contains no information about the terms of child custody following marriage dissolution. Finally, only first episodes, which account for the vast majority of episodes experienced in the various family types, are considered. This analysis covers all respondents aged 18 to 65.[20]

For each family type considered, the dynamics of the formation of first episodes is studied first for all men, by means of entry into the episode considered. Then, entry-shifts by generation, all means combined, are examined to assess how much men's behaviour has changed over time. The same approach is then used to analyse exits from family episodes. How family episodes are formed and dissolved is examined by generation, and the variations that have occurred in recent decades are identified. And, as in the previous section, this section concludes with a comparison of men's and women's experiences.

4.3.1 Intact two-parent families

In recent years, a number of studies have described various facets of fatherhood and pointed out many issues related to recent marital and social transformations (see, for example, Björnberg 1991; Bozett and Hanson 1991; Gauthier 1987; Moxnes 1991). However, studies that have used demographics to define the impact of these changes on male family paths are less common. For example, very little is known about the extent to which the transformations noted in fertility and conjugal life affect the process of the formation and dissolution of intact two-parent families within various generations of men. This analysis attempts to clarify this aspect of male family paths.

In this analysis, an episode in an intact two-parent family refers to any period during which a man lives only with his spouse and the children (natural or adopted) of their relationship.[21] The man's age at the birth or adoption of the couple's first child (rather than on the formation of the union) marks the start of the episode.[22] Three means of entry, each of which describes the conjugal relationship of the spouses before the arrival of their first child, are examined: direct marriage; marriage following a phase of cohabitation; and common-law union. Finally, three distinct means of exit from the episode are considered: the departure from the home (or death) of the last child; separation or divorce; and the death of the wife.

4.3.1.1 Formation of intact two-parent families

Figure 4.1A presents men's cumulative probabilities of experiencing an episode in an intact two-parent family. Almost 8 in 10 Canadian men will experience an episode in an intact two-parent family before age 66, if the behaviours of the men surveyed in 1990 continue. Two-thirds of the respondents will enter this type of family following a direct marriage, 8% will enter an intact two-parent family after marrying their common-law wife and about 5% will do so within the context of a common-law union.

Most men will enter an intact two-parent family before age 45. Conversely, very few will begin their parental life after that age, as shown in the leveling off of the curves for men in their mid-forties. In fact, a very high proportion of men will have their first child between the ages of 25 and 35, or at an average age of about 30—at age 31.6 for men who have cohabited with their spouse before marrying her, 29.8 for those marrying without first living common law, and 30.0 for those men who formed such families in the context of a common-law union (1990 GSS). (See Figure 4.1A.)

FIGURE 4.1A

CUMULATIVE PROBABILITIES FOR MEN OF EXPERIENCING AN "INTACT" TWO-PARENT FAMILY, BY CONJUGAL STATUS ON ENTRY[1,2]

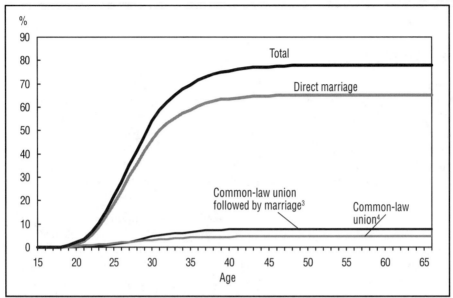

1. Refers to the conjugal status on arrival (birth or adoption) of the first child.
2. Excludes two cases for which the type of union is not known.
3. Male respondents who married their common-law spouse before the arrival (birth or adoption) of the first child.
4. Includes some respondents who would ultimately marry their common-law spouse.
Source: 1990 GSS, cycle 5, Public Use Microdata File.

A study of the curves (Figure 4.1B) by generation, all conjugal statuses combined, reveals some changes over time, including men's later entry into an intact two-parent family. For example, at age 25, more than one-quarter of men aged 35 and older when surveyed had already experienced an episode of this family type, while this was true of only about one in six male respondents aged 25 to 34. The discrepancy between generations increases in older generations: barely 70% of those aged 35 to 44 at the time of the survey reported having formed an intact two-parent family by age 35, compared with nearly 80% of respondents aged 55 to 65 who reported having done so by age 35.

FIGURE 4.1B

CUMULATIVE PROBABILITIES FOR MEN OF EXPERIENCING AN "INTACT" TWO-PARENT FAMILY,
BY AGE AT THE TIME OF THE SURVEY

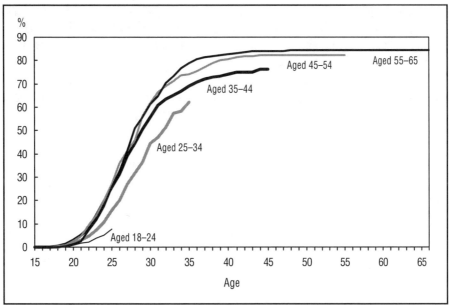

Source: 1990 GSS, cycle 5, Public Use Microdata File.

A study of the table of entry into an intact two-parent family (by means of entry and by generation) also reveals that men's marital status when their first child is born has changed appreciably in recent decades (see Appendix 4.2, Table 1). In particular, a marked increase in common-law unions as the context in which families are formed, causing a decrease in the incidence of marriage, is evident in recent generations of men. At age 30, for example, less than 3% of male respondents aged 35 to 44 at the time of the survey had entered fatherhood in the context of a "paperless marriage," while this proportion nearly doubled (to 7%) among those aged 25 to 34. Among older generations, this means of entry into an intact family remains the exception: fewer than 1% of respondents aged 45 and older had experienced such a situation. The rise in common-law unions noted among younger generations, therefore, only partially offsets the decline in marriage as the context for forming intact two-parent families. It is reasonable to assume, however, that this intergenerational gap will narrow slightly in the years to come as younger men advance further along their life courses.

4.3.1.2 Dissolution of intact two-parent families

Figure 4.2A shows the cumulative probabilities of leaving an intact two-parent family by the three means of dissolution considered. Nearly two-thirds (64%) of episodes in an intact two-parent family will end following the departure of the children, while about one-sixth will end with the dissolution of the union, and 5% will end with the death of the wife.[23] From the standpoint of living arrangements, these family units will then become either couples without children or lone-parent families.

The curves that emerge from the attrition tables (see Appendix 4.2, Table 2) show that voluntary dissolutions occur quite early on: nearly one-quarter occurred after five years of cohabitation, and half of the men who were separated at the time of the survey witnessed the dissolution of their union before completing 13 years of cohabitation.

Exits from intact two-parent families associated with the children's departure from home occur much later; this means of exit only begins to increase 18 years after the family is formed. But after 21 years, the children's departure from home becomes the primary cause of the end of this family status (see Figure 4.2A).

FIGURE 4.2A

CUMULATIVE PROBABILITIES FOR MEN WHO HAVE EXPERIENCED AN "INTACT" TWO-PARENT FAMILY OF EXITING THIS FAMILY STATUS,[1] BY MEANS OF EXIT

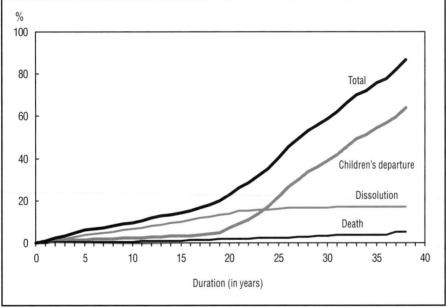

1. Excludes 113 cases for which the date of the end of the episode is not known.
Source: 1990 GSS, cycle 5, Public Use Microdata File.

Figure 4.2B highlights the variations between generations of men[24] using data from the tables of exit by generation, all causes combined. This figure illustrates that the duration of episodes in an intact two-parent family tends to become shorter from older to younger generations: after 10 years in an intact two-parent family, 12% of male respondents aged 35 to 44 at the time of the survey had exited this family status, compared with 8% of those aged 45 to 54, and just 3% of those aged 55 to 65. Among those aged 25 to 34, the likelihood of leaving an intact two-parent family by age 35 reaches 18%, but it is uncertain whether this result accurately reflects the behaviour this generation will adopt because it includes men who formed their family at a relatively young age. Moreover, the acceleration in the rate of exit among those aged 45 to 65 after 20 years in an intact two-parent family is doubtless closely related to the gradual departure of children from the parental home. However, it is also related to the increase in marriage dissolutions that affected these generations after the adoption of the *Divorce Act* in 1968 (see Appendix 4.2, Table 2).

FIGURE 4.2B

CUMULATIVE PROBABILITIES FOR MEN WHO HAVE EXPERIENCED AN "INTACT" TWO-PARENT FAMILY OF EXITING THIS FAMILY STATUS,[1] BY AGE AT THE TIME OF THE SURVEY[2]

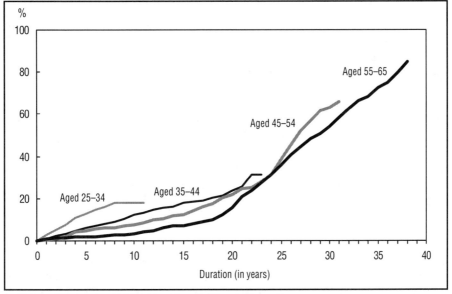

1. Excludes 113 cases for which the date of the end of the episode is not known.
2. The curves are discontinued when the number of respondents likely to experience the transition at the duration in question is less than 20.

Source: 1990 GSS, cycle 5, Public Use Microdata File.

As was the case for female respondents, the decreased amount of time spent in an intact two-parent family seen across the male generations is linked to the marked increase in the dissolutions of unions among younger cohorts (see Appendix 4.2, Table 2). For example, after 10 years in an intact two-parent family, 9% of respondents aged 35 to 44 had gone through a separation or divorce. This is nine times the rate noted, for the same duration, among respondents aged 55 to 65 at the time of the survey (1%). By comparison, deaths dropped slightly as a factor of family dissolution over the generations, the demarcation now being between those aged 55 to 65 and those aged under 55. This situation is related to the fact that women's life expectancy had increased before the period studied, and therefore had little effect on the post-war generations.

4.3.2 Lone-parent families[25]

In Canada, there have been few longitudinal studies of lone parenthood among men. Both the relatively small proportion of men among all lone parents and the lack of reliable data to enable the study of male family paths doubtless contribute to the scarcity of demographic studies on this subject.[26] However, the appreciable increase in the number of male lone-parent families since the early 1980s (Lindsay 1992) and the changes surrounding the expression of fatherhood today warrant an attempt to better define the place of lone parenthood in male family paths (Desrosiers and Le Bourdais 1995).

In this analysis, an episode of lone parenthood refers to any period during which a man without a spouse lives with one or more children, regardless of the custody arrangements adopted when lone parenthood was the result of a separation or divorce. Lone parenthood, as defined at the beginning of this chapter, includes the sole physical custody of the children by the respondent, custody shared by the spouses, and even partial custody of the children. Recall that, to be considered head of a lone-parent family, the respondent need only consider that his children have not left the family home for good. In this analysis, three means of formation of a lone-parent family are considered: a birth outside of a union,[27] the voluntary dissolution of a common-law union or marriage (through separation or divorce), and widowhood. Three types of exit from lone parenthood are also considered: the departure (or death) of the last dependent child from the parental home, the marriage of the respondent, and the respondent's entry into a common-law union.

4.3.2.1 Formation of lone-parent families

Figure 4.3A shows men's cumulative probabilities of experiencing a first lone-parent episode through this family status. If the behaviours of the various generations of men surveyed in 1990 continue, nearly one-quarter (23%) of men will experience their first episode of lone parenthood before age 66. This percentage is much higher than the proportion (2%) of men who were lone fathers at the time of the survey. The discrepancy may be attributed in part to the very restrictive nature of the concept of lone parenthood at the time of the survey: the survey assigned the status of lone parent only to those respondents who could claim the "usual" presence of children in their family home. However, this discrepancy may also be attributed to the fact that men who find themselves on their own at the head of a family generally remain so for a relatively brief time, as will be discussed later.

FIGURE 4.3A

CUMULATIVE PROBABILITIES FOR MEN OF EXPERIENCING A LONE-PARENT EPISODE, BY MEANS OF ENTRY

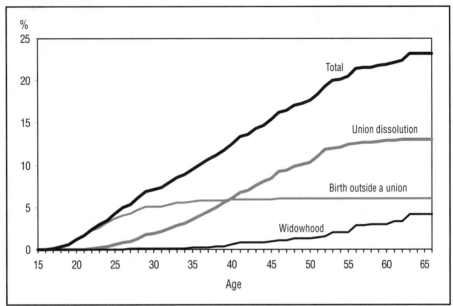

Source: 1990 GSS, cycle 5, Public Use Microdata File; figure adapted from Desrosiers and Le Bourdais, 1995, 52, Figure 1.

The first episode of lone parenthood usually (in more than half of all cases) follows the voluntary dissolution of a union: 13% of men entered lone parenthood after a separation or divorce, while 4% entered this status following the death of their wife, and 6% entered following the birth of a child outside of a union—in other words, with no union reported (see Figure 4.3A). The episodes of lone parenthood attributable to a birth outside of a union occurred early in the life of the respondents. Few experienced such an event after age 30, as the leveling off of the curve (Figure 4.3A) after this age shows. Conversely, entering into lone parenthood by becoming a widower occurs later in men's lives, gradually increasing as they enter their forties. Finally, separation and divorce as the causes of entry into lone parenthood occurred in men's middle years—that is, between the ages of 30 and 50.

The number of lone-parent episodes experienced by men following a birth outside a union may seem surprising considering that men are less likely to assume the custody of young children (Cloutier 1990; La Novara 1993). These may include, however, a number of episodes reported by men who formed a couple with the mother of the child in the months following the birth. Unfortunately, these cases cannot be identified from the GSS data. Probably relatively few lone fathers assume full custody of their child at birth. In such cases, it is reasonable to think that lone parenthood among men will be short-lived or that the custody arrangements will change over time.[28]

Figure 4.3B, which illustrates the data for the table of entry into lone parenthood by generation, all means combined, shows that men's likelihood of experiencing at least one episode of lone parenthood has varied little over time. Regardless of age, a very slight growth is observed from the generation of men aged 55 to 65, to those aged 35 to 44. However, note the acceleration in the rate of entries into lone parenthood between the early thirties and mid-forties among men aged 45 to 54 at the time of the survey. It is important to consider this acceleration in light of the adoption of the *Divorce Act* in 1968, which affected more men of this generation. Finally, men under age 35 are relatively unlikely to have experienced lone parenthood. As discussed in the previous section, this phenomenon may be explained in younger generations of men by their more advanced age at the time of their first union and later entry into fatherhood.

FIGURE 4.3B

CUMULATIVE PROBABILITIES FOR MEN OF EXPERIENCING A LONE-PARENT EPISODE, BY AGE AT THE TIME OF THE SURVEY

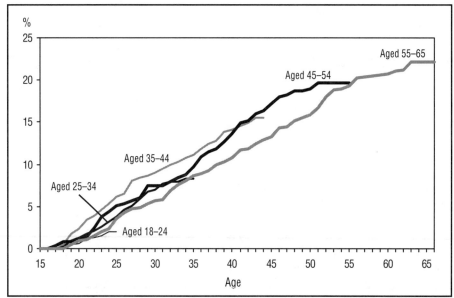

Source: 1990 GSS, cycle 5, Public Use Microdata File: figure adapted from Desrosiers and Le Bourdais, 1995, 53, Figure 2.

4.3.2.2 Dissolution of lone-parent families

Do men who experience lone parenthood leave this family status sooner? Which event usually brings the episode of lone parenthood to an end: the departure of the children, or the formation of a union with a new spouse?

To find the answers to these questions, we considered the cumulative probabilities, for all respondents who experienced a first episode of lone parenthood, of leaving this family status by the three means of exit considered: marriage, common-law union, and the children's departure (see Figure 4.4A). We found that nearly all lone fathers (94%) will leave this status 15 years after the start of their lone parenthood if the behaviours observed in 1990 continue. The swiftness with which men leave lone parenthood is striking: all types of exit considered, nearly 4 in 10 men had left lone-parent status after one year, and only about 1 in 10 men experienced lone parenthood for 10 years or more.

The formation of a couple is the means of exiting lone parenthood most often reported by men (see Figure 4.4A). In all, two-thirds of men's first experience of lone parenthood had ended in a union before the 17th year: by marriage in 40% of cases, and by a common-law union in 26% of cases. Lone fathers form new unions at a very rapid rate. After two years as head of a lone-parent family, nearly 40% of men had formed a union.

Exits from lone parenthood related to the children's departure also occur relatively often. Of the 28% of episodes that ended with the children's departure, nearly half (13%) of these men's lone-parent episodes had lasted less than one year, and nearly all had lasted less than five years.

FIGURE 4.4A

CUMULATIVE PROBABILITIES FOR MEN WHO HAVE EXPERIENCED A LONE-PARENT EPISODE OF EXITING LONE-PARENT STATUS, BY MEANS OF EXIT[1]

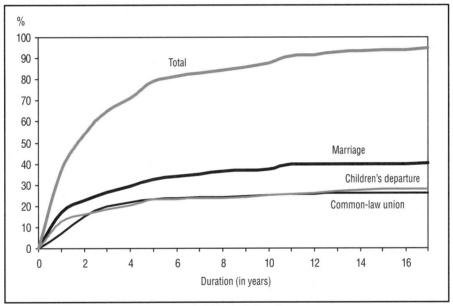

1. Excludes 15 cases for which the date of the end of the episode is not known.

Source: 1990 GSS, cycle 5, Public Use Microdata File; figure adapted from Desrosiers and Le Bourdais, 1995, 54, Figure 3.

The data from the tables on exits from lone parenthood by generation, all means combined, show a distinct shortening of periods of lone parenthood from the older to the younger generations of males (see Figure 4.4B). For example, three years after the start of the first lone-parent family episode, 82% of lone fathers aged 25 to 34 had left this family status, compared with 72% of those aged 35 to 44, and 66% of those aged 45 to 54. However, during the same period, only 43% of men aged 55 to 65 had left this family status.

FIGURE 4.4B

CUMULATIVE PROBABILITIES FOR MEN WHO HAVE EXPERIENCED A LONE-PARENT EPISODE
OF EXITING LONE-PARENT STATUS, BY AGE AT THE TIME OF THE SURVEY[1]

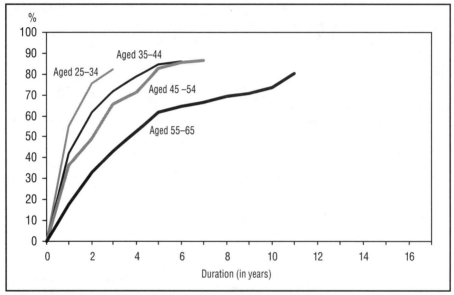

1. The curves are discontinued when the number of respondents likely to experience the transition at the duration in question is less than 20.

Source : 1990 GSS, cycle 5, Public Use Microdata File; figure adapted from Desrosiers and Le Bourdais, 1995, 55, Figure 4.

The discrepancy between those aged 55 to 65 and younger generations is largely attributable to the marked increase in common-law unions in the most recent generations, given that the inclination of lone fathers to marry remained appreciably unchanged over the years (see Appendix 4.2, Table 3). However, the brief duration (three years or less) of lone parenthood observed in men aged 45 and younger can be attributed to the greater likelihood of these men to see their children leave the family home. Thus, the proportion of lone fathers who, after three years at the head of their family, experienced their children leaving home was three times greater among respondents aged 25 to 34 than among their counterparts aged 55 to 66 (33% versus 11%). It is safe to assume that most of these departures concerned children whose parents had dissolved their unions. These children had probably left the father's parental home to go live with their mother, or had left the family home and were simply no longer in contact with the father.

Conversely, having experienced lone parenthood later in life and more often following the death of their wife, older lone fathers are more likely to assume custody of their children until they reach adulthood.

4.3.3 Blended families

Owing to a lack of data, the blended family has, until recently, been the subject of very few studies in Canada, and little is known about the dynamics of the formation and dissolution of this type of family. Yet blended family experiences are not new. Remarriages of couples who bring their children from one or more previous marriages into the new family have existed for some time. Indeed, it was not unusual to see a widower quickly form a new union after his wife died in childbirth. Today, there is a surge in the number of blended families formed as the result of a new union of one or two separated parents (Théry 1993).

In general, women form blended families following an episode of lone parenthood, however brief. Many men, however, experience this form of family without having previously experienced lone parenthood. What, then, is the path taken by the men experiencing a blended family for the first time?

Before we answer this question, we should first review the definition of a blended family episode, which here refers to any period during which a man lives with a spouse and at least one child not born of their relationship. Therefore, a blended family may include the children of either or both spouses, born (or adopted) outside of the current union, and may additionally include the children born of the current union. To explore the paths followed by men in blended families, we first examine the dynamics of the formation of blended families, in terms of the type of union (common-law or marriage) entered into when forming the family unit, and in terms of the respondents' family status. Four categories of blended family status are identified for men. The category "without children" refers to men without children or whose children were not living with them in the blended family. The remaining three categories of family status apply to men who were living with children when they formed a union. "Never-married" refers to fathers who were living with children born outside of a union; "separated or divorced" refers to men who were living with children born of a union that ended in separation or divorce; and "widowed" identifies those men whose union dissolved following the death of their wife.

Two means of exit are identified in the study of exits from a blended family: dissolution of the union (separation, divorce or widowhood),[29] and the departure from home of the last child not born to the couple.

4.3.3.1 Formation of blended families

According to the cumulative probabilities of men living in a blended family by type of union formed by the husbands, one in six respondents will experience at least one blended family episode in their lifetime if the behaviours observed in 1990 continue. Nine percent of men will form a blended family in the context of a common-law union, and a slightly smaller proportion (8%) will do so through marriage. The data also show that nearly all men experience blended family episodes before their mid-fifties, as shown by the leveling off of the curve at that age (see Figure 4.5A).

FIGURE **4.5A**

CUMULATIVE PROBABILITIES FOR MEN OF EXPERIENCING A BLENDED FAMILY,
BY TYPE OF UNION ON ENTRY

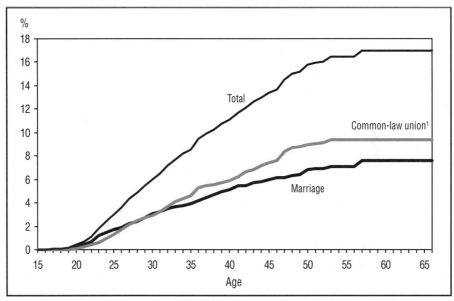

1. Includes a certain number of respondents who will ultimately marry their common-law spouse.
Source: 1990 GSS, cycle 5, Public Use Microdata Files.

The detailed analysis of the cumulative probabilities by cause and generation shows that common-law union was the most common form of entry into a blended family across all generations of respondents; only men aged 55 to 65 were little affected by this phenomenon (1990 GSS). The propensity to marry, however, remained unchanged over the generations, reflecting the same tendencies noted in the discussion on exits from lone parenthood.

As for the family status of men at the time of entering a blended family, an appreciable proportion (5.5%) did not bring any children into the blended family (this would include men without children, as well as men whose children were not living with them at the time of the survey). A slightly higher proportion of men (6.4%) brought one child or more into a new blended family after a separation or divorce; 4% brought one child born outside of a union, while barely 1% brought children of a union ended by widowhood (see Figure 4.5B).

FIGURE 4.5B

CUMULATIVE PROBABILITIES FOR MEN OF EXPERIENCING A BLENDED FAMILY,
BY FAMILY STATUS ON ENTRY[1]

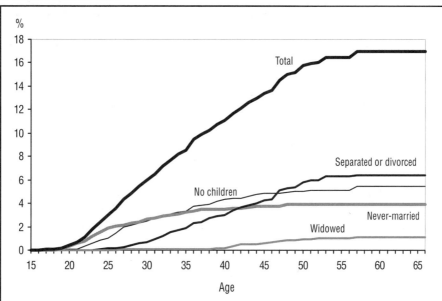

1. The categories "never-married," "separated or divorced" and "widowed" pertain to men who were living with their children at the time of entry into the blended family. The category "never-married" includes men who had never lived with the mother of their child, that is, who had a child outside of a union. The category "no children" refers to men with no children or whose children were no longer living with them when they entered the blended family.

Source: 1990 GSS, cycle 5, Public Use Microdata File; figure adapted from Desrosiers and Le Bourdais, 1995, 56, Figure 5.

Most men who form a blended family after the birth of their child outside of a union ("never-married" men), or enter this family status without children, generally do so at a relatively young age. This is shown by the steady rise of the "never-married" and "no children" curves when men reach their mid-thirties, and the more gradual increase thereafter. In contrast, blended family episodes linked to the death of the wife occur later in men's lives, and the curve does not really begin to climb until men reach their early forties. Most blended families created following the voluntary dissolution of a union occur, for men, between the ages of 30 and 50. The probability of entering a blended family following the dissolution of a union increases steadily and continuously for men from their early thirties onward and, after age 47, the cumulative probability of entering into blended family after the dissolution of a union exceeds that of any other means.

As with lone parenthood, the magnitude of blended family episodes in men's lives following the arrival of a child born outside of a union is surprising, particularly as episodes resulting from the formation of a union within six months of the child's birth were not counted as blended families (in such cases the "never-married" fathers were assumed to have formed a couple with the mother of the child.)[30] The nature and frequency of contacts between a father and his child born outside of a union may very well change profoundly after the father forms a union; however, the GSS data do not tell us about this aspect of men's family paths.

The cumulative probabilities of living in a blended family, by generation, all means combined, suggest on the whole an increase in the frequency of the blended family phenomenon from older to more recent generations (see Figure 4.6). Only men younger than age 35 deviate from this trend. As previously discussed, this is probably attributable to the later formation of first unions in these generations, and the later separations and divorces that result. Except for this group, it is clear that recent generations are more likely than the older generations to experience a blended family: 12% of men aged 35 to 44 at the time of the survey had, by age 35, experienced a blended family, compared with 7% of respondents aged 45 to 54 and just 4% of those aged 55 to 65.

This development is obviously linked to the marked increase in union dissolutions observed over the past 25 years. The number of blended families formed after a separation or divorce has increased, and men of recent generations have been affected at ever younger ages. A detailed study by cause and generation suggests that the propensity of men to form a blended family unaccompanied by children has also increased over the generations (1990 GSS). This last result is surely related to the higher incidence of lone parenthood among women, described in Chapter 3.

FIGURE 4.6

CUMULATIVE PROBABILITIES FOR MEN OF EXPERIENCING A BLENDED FAMILY, BY AGE AT THE TIME OF THE SURVEY

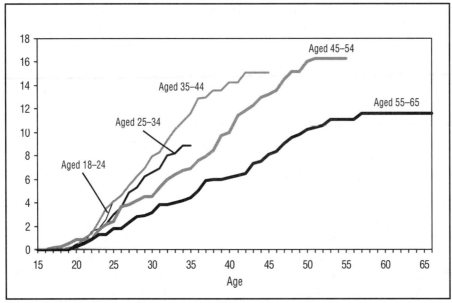

Source : 1990 GSS, cycle 5, Public Use Microdata File; figure adapted from Desrosiers and Le Bourdais, 1995, 57, Figure 6.

4.3.3.2 Dissolution of blended families

The analyses presented in Chapter 3 show that, from the perspective of women, blended family experiences seem to be increasingly transitory. Are these experiences evolving in a similar fashion for men?

To attempt to answer this question, let us first examine, for all male respondents who experience a first blended family episode, the cumulative probabilities of leaving this family status by two means of exit: the dissolution of the union, and the departure of the last child not born to the couple (see Figure 4.7A). More than three-quarters of men who belonged to a blended family will have left this status 20 years after the start of the episode if the behaviours observed in 1990 continue. More than half (55%) of episodes will end when the children not common to the couple leave home, and 22% will end with the dissolution of the union. It is interesting to note that there are few differences in the timing patterns of these two means of exit for episodes of short duration, as the overlapping of the curves after eight years shows: 11% of family episodes will end by one of these two means before the completion of five years. However, over the long term, children's departures far exceed union dissolutions as the means of exiting this type of family.

FIGURE 4.7A

CUMULATIVE PROBABILITIES FOR MEN WHO HAVE EXPERIENCED A BLENDED FAMILY OF EXITING THIS FAMILY STATUS, BY MEANS OF EXIT[1]

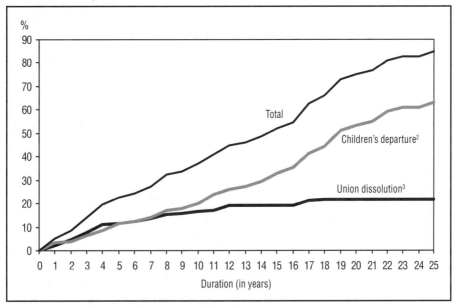

1. Excludes 15 cases for which the date of the end of the episode is not known.
2. Refers to the departure of the last child not born to the couple. The blended family then becomes either a "re-created" two-parent family, that is, one where all children present are of the current union, or a couple with no children.
3. Includes a very small percentage of deaths.

Source: 1990 GSS, cycle 5, Public Use Microdata File; figure adapted from Desrosiers and Le Bourdais, 1995, 58, Figure 7.

FIGURE 4.7B

CUMULATIVE PROBABILITIES FOR MEN WHO HAVE EXPERIENCED A BLENDED FAMILY OF EXITING
THIS FAMILY STATUS, BY AGE AT THE TIME OF THE SURVEY[1]

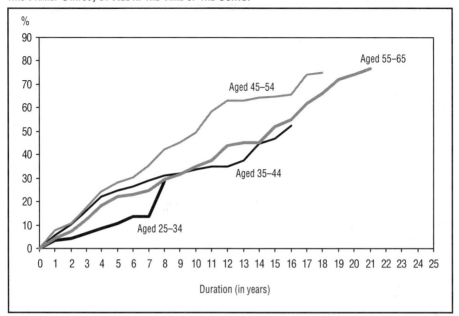

1. The curves are discontinued when the number of respondents likely to experience the transition at the duration in question is less than 20.

Source: 1990 GSS, cycle 5, Public Use Microdata File; figure adapted from Desrosiers and Le Bourdais, 1995, 59, Figure 8.

These data, presented for all male respondents, mask certain variations between the generations. First, the generational data show a similar duration of blended family episodes among respondents aged 35 to 44 and those aged 55 and older (see Figure 4.7B). In contrast to these two generations, those aged 45 to 54 leave the blended family sooner and in proportionally greater numbers; those aged 25 to 34, on the contrary, seem to enjoy greater family stability. This latter group represents a distinct subgroup of men who were still young while in the blended family episode and whose behaviours are probably not representative of their generation.

Ten years after the start of the first blended family episode, just over one-third of respondents aged 35 to 44 and 55 to 65 had exited this family status, compared with nearly half of those aged 45 to 54. A close study of the data by means of exit and by generation suggests that the distinctive behaviour of men aged 45 to 54 is attributable to the particular context in which their family history evolved (see Appendix 4.2, Table 4). Finding themselves in the very midst of the family transformations that followed the coming into force of the *Divorce Act*, these men present behavioural traits characteristic of the generations that came both before and after them. Like those before them, they have a high propensity to exit a blended family following the departure of children not of the current union; like those after them, they have a high propensity to leave this type of family after the voluntary dissolution of a union.

4.3.4 Male–female comparison

Our analysis of the dynamics of the formation and dissolution of various forms of family organization allows us to assess the extent of the changes that have taken place in the lives of various generations of men and to shed light on the conditions underlying these changes. The analysis shows that, even today, the vast majority of men experience life in an intact two-parent family. However, among younger recent generations, there has been an increase in common-law unions—and a decrease in marriages—as a means of entering into this type of family. Further, the intact two-parent family episode now begins at a more advanced age and does not last as long as it once did, usually ending with the dissolution of the union (see figures 4.1A and 4.1B).

In several respects, the family profile that emerges for men is identical to that of women.[31] Men, however, experience parenthood in an intact two-parent family later in life, on average about three years after their female counterparts (at age 30.0 versus age 26.9). The duration and type of exit from these family episodes also vary by sex (see figures 3.2 and 4.2). The intact-family episodes reported by men seem to last a little longer than those reported by women, and end less often with the death of their partner (married or common-law), or with marital breakdown; conversely, men's episodes end slightly more often following the children's departure from the family home.

Several factors contribute to these differences. The small proportion of episodes among men ended by the wife's death is of course related to the fact that women die at relatively older ages. The fewer incidences of separations and divorces among men and, conversely, the slightly higher proportion of children's departures, may be because male marital and reproductive histories are less reliable or, quite simply, due to the inherent biases of a retrospective survey that considers only surviving spouses at the time of the survey. Thus, the men surveyed may have had longer to see their children leave home than the women, whose unions were more often ended by widowhood.

Aside from these differences in the paths followed by men and women, the trends suggest that the time spent in an intact two-parent family decreases from older to younger generations for both sexes. Does this growing fragility of intact two-parent families place both men and women at greater risk of living in a lone-parent family?

Our analysis of the dynamics of lone parenthood shows that a significant proportion (23%) of men will, at some point in their life, head a lone-parent family if the observed trends continue (see Figure 4.3A). This high proportion is surprising at first glance. It is, however, markedly lower than the percentage of women (35%) who will experience lone parenthood (see Figure 3.3A), and probably covers very different realities for men than for women. For example, we know that a very small proportion of men, in particular, younger men, gain sole custody of their children following the dissolution of a union (Cloutier 1990; La Novara 1993). Further, we know that most children in their father's custody maintain continuous ties with their mother, while the reverse is less common (Dandurand 1994). Thus, in contrast to women's experience of lone parenthood, a large proportion of male episodes of lone parenthood likely refer to a situation in which the father shares joint, and even occasional, custody of his children with his ex-wife.

For both men and women, lone parenthood does not seem to last as long today as it once did (see figures 3.4 and 4.4). However, males experience this family type for a distinctly shorter duration than their female counterparts: fewer than half as many lone fathers (12% versus 25% of lone mothers) will experience lone parenthood for at least 10 years. In contrast, the proportion of very brief episodes of lone parenthood (less than one year) is nearly twice as high among men as among women (37% versus 22%). The briefness of these male episodes probably explains in part the difference noted between the proportion of lone fathers observed at the time of the survey (2%) and the percentage of those who will experience this status in their lifetime (23%) (see figures 4.1 and 4.3A).

Besides their variable duration, episodes of lone parenthood often end differently depending on the sex of the lone parent (see figures 3.4 and 4.4). Thus, lone fathers choose a common-law union less often than their female counterparts following an episode of lone parenthood (26% versus 38%), and more of them opt for marriage (40% versus 30%). Furthermore, lone fathers are clearly more inclined than lone mothers to leave an episode of lone parenthood soon after their children leave home: 19% of lone fathers will exit lone parenthood in this way within three years of the beginning of the episode, compared with 6% of lone mothers.

These results attest to the very different conditions of lone parenthood experienced, depending on whether the parent is male or female. While the formation of a union does not necessarily mean the end of parental responsibilities, the final departure of children from the family home does radically alter the conditions of parenthood. These departures may involve children leaving home to live on their own. But given the generally short duration of lone parenthood, it can be assumed they involve mostly children who leave to live with their mother or have lost contact with their father after living with him fairly regularly (Furstenberg 1988). These paths, seen more often among the younger generations of lone fathers, may partially reflect the fact that many "part-time dads" prefer to sever their ties with their children completely rather than see them only periodically and thus be deprived of a favoured link with them. At least, this is what some studies suggest (Lund 1987).

The subsequent analysis of the dynamics of blended families shows that nearly one in six men will eventually live in a blended family if the behaviours observed in 1990 continue (see Figure 4.5A). This proportion is about the same as the estimated percentage for women (see Figure 3.5A). As was the case with women, the phenomenon of blended families grew over time, meaning more men of recent generations have experienced a blended family than their predecessors. However, we observed that men tend to favour marriage slightly more than do women (8% versus 6%).

Other than this difference, men generally experience a blended family at slightly older ages than women, on average at about age 35.0 (versus age 32.3 for women) (1990 GSS). They enter this type of family less often accompanied by children from a previous marriage that ended in separation or divorce than women—nearly 6%, versus 9% (see figures 3.5A and 4.5A); conversely, they enter blended families far more often without children (6% versus 2%). The increase in the proportion of men who find themselves "with 'parental status' without [themselves] being parents" [translation] (Théry 1986, p. 60) or, in any case, not actively exercising this role, must be considered in light of the marked increase in lone parenthood among women observed in recent generations. Some studies argue that this also reflects the tendency of non-custodial fathers to lose contact with their own children over time and to devote themselves instead to the children of their new partners (see Jacobsen and Edmondson 1993).

The analysis of exits from blended families showed the greater fragility of the family units in which men aged 45 to 54 lived. Nevertheless, generally speaking, blended families observed from the male perspective seem more stable than those studied from the female perspective (see figures 3.7A and 4.7A). Not only did fewer men than women leave this family status 20 years after entering it (75% versus 87%), but they were also less likely to have seen their family status altered following the dissolution of a union: 10 years after the start of a blended family episode only 17% of men had experienced a separation or divorce, while more than one in four women had. Of the factors that may explain these differences by sex, the type of family organization (family with a stepfather or stepmother) in which the men and women live plays a significant role. Various studies have pointed out that blended families with a stepmother (that is, those that include only the man's children) are more stable than those with a stepfather (Ambert 1986; Desrosiers et al. 1995; Ferri 1995). However, today the former type of organization is relatively more common among blended family episodes as seen from the male perspective.[32]

4.4 THE FAMILY PATHS OF MEN

The previous section analyses how the three types of family, considered separately, are formed and dissolved. We will now take an overall look at the family paths of men to examine the sequence in their lives of the various periods spent in an intact two-parent family, a lone-parent family or a blended family.

To conduct this analysis properly, multiple attrition tables are again used, but the probabilities of experiencing a given family transition is determined this time by taking into account the men's past experience. In other words, the probabilities of transition are calculated only for those men who have travelled a certain common family path.[33] In concrete terms, all respondents begin with "preparental" status and are initially considered to be at risk of making an initial transition to one of the three family destinations (an intact two-parent, lone-parent or blended family). Then, each of these situations, in turn, becomes the departure point to other destinations, and the attrition tables are established based only on the men who have experienced the first family status considered.[34] All men are at risk of experiencing an initial family transition as of age 15; these probabilities are calculated and cumulated by single year of age. For subsequent transitions, the probabilities are calculated by duration from the time of entry into the initial family status, and cumulated yearly.

As in the previous section, the analysis concerns only family episodes involving children, regardless of their age. As we are interested in the whole family history of the men, the analysis is limited to respondents who were aged 35 to 64 at the time of the survey—that is, those who were already well into their parental life.

4.4.1 The family life courses of men

Figure 4.8 presents the cumulative probabilities of transition from one family status to another (illustrated by the italicized figures in the arrows) and the path probabilities (represented by bold figures)—that is, the overall proportion of men who will follow a given family path. For example, the risk to men living in a two-parent family of experiencing lone parenthood is 0.217 (or about one in five). The percentage of men who will experience a first episode of lone parenthood after a period in an intact two-parent family (17.3%) corresponds with the product of the probability of going first from the initial preparental status to an intact two-parent family (0.798), and then to a lone-parent family (0.217).

Of course, family episodes do not always lead to a new family phase. They may end when the respondent's children leave home, resulting in a transition to a non-parental situation. This type of path is represented by perpendicular arrows when the children's departure marks the end of the respondents' parental path. It is considered to lead to "non-family" status when the children's departure represents an interruption in the family history, or when it coincides with the dissolution of the respondent's union.

The transitions tree developed for men is appreciably the same as that for women, shown in Chapter 3. About one in eight men (12%) will remain without children if the trends observed in the survey data continue. Nearly 80% will first experience parenthood in the context of an intact two-parent family, 4.6% will experience it as a lone parent following the birth of a child outside of a union, and 3.6% as the stepfather in a blended family.

Moreover, 22.3%[35] of men will, at least for a time, experience a lone-parent family, 18.1% will be either the father or stepfather at least once in a blended family, and 8.5% will belong to a re-created family; that is, they will live only with their spouse and the children they had or adopted together, after passing through a blended family phase (see Figure 4.8). Although the vast majority (nearly 90%) of men will experience at least one parental episode, slightly less than one-quarter (23.8%) will experience at least two different parental episodes, and 15% will experience three or more.[36]

Intact two-parent families seem relatively stable compared with the other family types. If the observed trends continue, more than three in four respondents (77.2%) living in this type of family will still be married to the mother of their children when their last child leaves home. In contrast, the chances of exiting lone parenthood are still far greater than the risk of entering it, regardless of the path previously travelled. For example, of the 17.3% of men who will experience a period of lone parenthood after an episode in an intact two-parent family, nearly three in five (59.4%) will form a couple before their children leave home.

At first glance, blended family episodes may seem less stable than episodes of intact two-parent families, respondents in the first being less likely to retain their status than those in the second (0.369 versus 0.772). This apparent instability hides the fact that a significant proportion of blended families, which will serve as the context for having children, will become re-created two-parent families after the children not common to the couple leave home. Thus, when these blended families are taken into account, the similarity in the behaviours of the two groups is more striking, and men who have experienced a blended family do not seem more at risk of a separation than their counterparts who have experienced an intact two-parent family episode.

FIGURE **4.8**
FAMILY PATHS OF MEN AGED **35** TO **64**

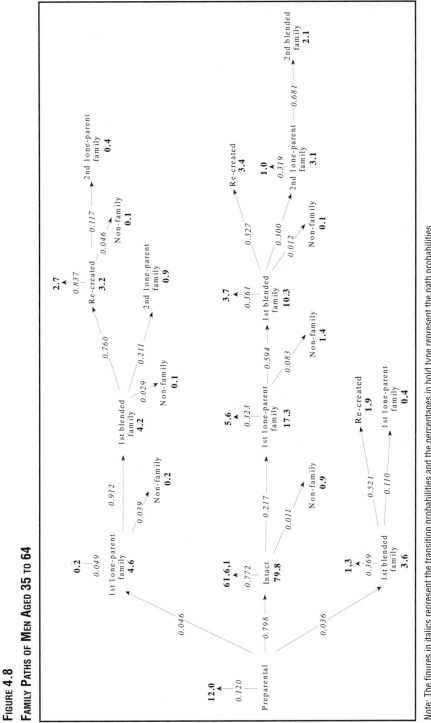

Note: The figures in italics represent the transition probabilities and the percentages in bold type represent the path probabilities
Source: 1990 GSS, cycle 5, Public Use Microdata File.

4.4.2 Male–female comparison

By means of the family paths approach used in this section, it is possible to illustrate the sequences of family episodes in men's lives. As in the previous section, the analysis shows that most men experience parenthood, and do so first in the context of an intact two-parent family.

While the proportion of men and women who experience parenthood in their lifetime is very similar (88.0% of men versus 88.8% of women), some differences are worth noting (see figures 3.9 and 4.8). A marginally smaller proportion of men begin their family life in an intact family, and men are somewhat more inclined than women (3.6% versus 1.5%) to enter parenthood as a stepparent. Also, they are slightly more inclined than women (2.8% versus 0.7%) to experience a "non-family" episode, that is, to live without a spouse or children, at least for a time, following the failure of a union. Finally, once their parental life begins, men seem less inclined than women to experience several family episodes in their lifetime. Just under one-quarter will experience at least two different family episodes, compared with nearly one-third of women, and 6.9% (versus 9.4%) will go through at least four family episodes.

This last result is rather unexpected, given the greater marital mobility displayed by recent generations of men. However, the paths tree shown here cannot illustrate the behavioural differences between the men and women of these generations. First, because of a lack of sufficient numbers, it is possible to show only the most common paths. That is, we can follow the paths taken by an appreciable proportion of male respondents, but not the more diversified paths of men, such as their family paths after a "non-family" episode. Secondly, as our analysis is based on the histories of respondents aged 35 to 64 at the time of the survey, it tends to overestimate the family paths of older generations—a fact that helps to explain the lesser family mobility of these men according to the paths tree. This lesser mobility must be seen in light of men's higher mortality rates, later entry into marital and parental life, and tendency to provide incomplete marital histories. Consequently, the paths tree shown here does not shed light on the behavioural differences in more recent generations by sex. This would require a comparative study of the family paths of men and women by generation, which would exceed the scope of this study.

4.5 CONCLUSION

The analysis conducted in this chapter shows that, in a context of increasing marital mobility, the profile of family situations drawn on the basis of cross-sectional data provide a fair amount of information about the past family paths of individuals. It also shows the particular features of situations experienced by men compared with those of women. These variations, as stated many times, must be seen in light of men's later entry into marital and parental life, and higher mortality rates, and the lesser participation of fathers in the custody of their children following a separation.

The life courses of men, like those of women, no longer appear to be as linear as they once were. Thus, an appreciable proportion (17%) of never-married men who were classified as "children" by the census had, in fact, already left the family home once to live on their own, and nearly 10% of these men had lived with a partner in a common-law union. Also, a fair percentage of middle-aged cohabitants had fathered children with whom they were no longer living at the time of the survey, and a relatively large proportion were living with children other than their natural children. In this last respect, men clearly differ from their female counterparts, who are more inclined to assume custody of their children following a separation. Men are therefore more likely to find themselves in a blended family and in the role of stepfather. Conversely, they are far less likely to be counted, at any given time, as head of a lone-parent family.

From the subsequent analysis of the dynamics of the formation and dissolution of various family types, it is possible to assess the extent of family changes in the life of various generations of men and to show the mechanisms underlying these changes. According to the analysis, even today, the vast majority of men experience living in an intact two-parent family (father, mother and children), but entry into this type of family happens increasingly through common-law union rather than marriage; it also occurs later in life for men than for women. A result of the increase in marital instability, episodes in an intact two-parent family do not last as long as they once did, and more often lead to the formation of lone-parent families, whose duration is diminishing.

While, on the whole, the evolutions of men and women are similar, when compared, some differences nevertheless emerge. First of all, lone parenthood affects a markedly higher proportion of women than men, and is generally of far greater duration for women than for men, who are more likely to see their children leave home sooner or to form a new union more quickly. In contrast, the episodes in an intact two-parent family and a blended family reported by men appear slightly more stable than those reported by women, and the discrepancy is slightly more pronounced for the latter family type. Finally, the analysis of family paths showed that while about 60% of men aged 35 to 64 will experience just one parental episode, spent in an intact two-parent family, nearly one-quarter will have to adapt to at least one change in their family status during the course of their lifetimes. Already quite high, men's tendency to experience more than one family type should increase in the coming years, as the more recent generations, which are more affected by family instability, move along their paths. At least this is what an initial analysis of male family paths by generation suggests (Juby and Le Bourdais 1997).

The comparative study of family paths by sex shows that while very similar proportions of men and women will experience parenthood in their lifetime, men are slightly more inclined than women to enter this status as a stepparent.

The analysis done in this chapter, based on 1990 GSS data, allows us to describe demographically the family paths of men aged 18 to 64 at the time of the survey. It also shows, statistically, the main differences in the conjugal and parental behaviours of men and women. But because of a lack of data, the analysis says nothing about the way in which the changes noted affected people's lives in concrete terms, for example, in terms of the day-to-day child custody arrangements men and women make as they go through various family episodes. Today the differences between the sexes may very well be far more pronounced in this regard than would appear merely from a measurement of the frequency and timing patterns of family transitions, owing to the decidedly greater tendency of women to assume custody of the children after a separation and their greater capacity to maintain close ties with their children over time.

Despite these limitations, our analysis of male family life is nevertheless relevant, to the extent that it shows some of the differences observed in male and female family paths. The male–female differences detected, for example, in the tendency to form a new couple or to assume custody of the children following a marriage breakdown are not without consequences for the living conditions of adults and children today and pose challenges to the social policy responsible for ensuring the well-being and custody of children after a separation. In this sense, the study of the marital and family history of men is worthy of continuation.

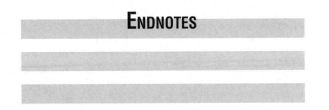

ENDNOTES

1. For an explanation of the age groups used, see the introduction to Chapter 3. Note, however, that some analyses, taken from earlier studies, also include men aged 65.

2. For a presentation of the survey, see Chapter 3.

3. The survey does not provide information on the periods during which children were temporarily absent from the parental home. Given insufficient data, we must therefore assume that the children were present in the family until their final departure.

4. See Chapter 3, Appendix 3.1 for a presentation of the method used, based on 1990 GSS data, to determine the respondents' living arrangements in a "census family."

5. For a comparison of the distribution by family status of men aged 18 to 64 based on the 1991 Census and the 1990 GSS, see Appendix 4.1, Table 1.

6. Note that the length of time the children spent in this household reported by the single respondent cannot be verified using the 1990 GSS data.

7. This percentage is obtained by subtracting from 100% the proportion of married men who had no experience of a prior union.

8. Unlike the children identified in the census, these children may be either single or once married. The GSS compiled the marital status of each member present in the households sampled in order to select the respondents. Unfortunately, this information is provided only for respondents and their spouses in the public microdata file produced by Statistics Canada.

9. See Section 3.2.2.2 of Chapter 3 for the exact definitions of the various family types considered.

10. As the numbers were quite small, age groups had to be combined for the youngest and oldest age groups.

11. This is a total of percentages of families with children of the respondent or of both spouses.

12. The marriage of both partners of a common-law union is regarded here as a single union whose form has changed over time.

13. In view of the small number of fathers under age 45 not living with their children, the first three age groups were combined.

14. Unlike the children identified in the census, these children may be either single or once married.

15. As the numbers were quite small, the age groups had to be grouped into two broad categories.

16. The figures for women are taken from Chapter 3.

17. For example, it is quite reasonable to assume that a fraction of respondents did not report "having raised" their spouse's children with whom they were not living on a regular basis, owing to the stronger likelihood of women to assume custody of the children following the dissolution of a union. It is reasonable to think, however, that the fathers of these children did not consider the children to have left home for good, regardless of the time spent with them. The former will therefore not be considered as belonging to a blended family, while the latter will.

18. From the retrospective data on unions and children compiled by the 1990 GSS, it is possible to reconstruct the family episodes experienced by the respondents. Thus, for each respondent, we know the number of past episodes in a particular family type, the duration of these episodes, and the demographic events marking the beginning and end of each. (For more details about the reconstitution of family episodes, see Desrosiers et al. 1994; Desrosiers and Le Bourdais 1995.)

19. For a brief presentation of the method, see Section 3.3 of Chapter 3.

20. For the sake of comparability with some of our earlier studies, the analysis also includes respondents aged 65 at the time of the survey.

21. It should be noted that men belonging to a re-created family; that is, those living with a spouse and their common children after having experienced a blended family phase are excluded from the analysis.

22. See Chapter 3 for more details about the reconstitution of these episodes.

23. For a very small number of men living in an intact two-parent family, the episode will end simultaneously with the children's departure and the dissolution of the union. In these instances, precedence was given to the dissolution of the union as the cause of family dissolution.

24. As they are based on a very specific subgroup of men who began their family life at a very young age, the cumulative probabilities of exiting an intact two-parent family are not provided for those aged 18 to 24.

25. The next two sections are modelled largely on the report "Vivre en famille monoparentale et en famille recomposée: portrait des Canadiennes d'hier et d'aujourd'hui," (Desrosiers and Le Bourdais 1995).

26. The 1984 Family History Survey conducted by Statistics Canada using a large sample of men and women did not allow for family transformations from the male perspective to be studied. Specifically, because the questions on fertility were worded differently for male and female respondents, men did not report children born of a previous union who were not living with them at the time of the survey, which makes a study of their family paths impossible.

27. It should be noted that all births outside of a union, whether or not they were followed by a union within six months, are regarded as leading to an episode of lone parenthood, however brief.

28. Owing to a lack of sufficient data on the actual presence of children in the respondents' home, it is difficult to support these assumptions.

29. Unlike the section on intact two-parent families, no distinction is made here between voluntary dissolutions and deaths, owing to the very small number of deaths observed.

30. It is, however, impossible to be certain, as the GSS provides no information about respondents' wives or ex-wives.

31. The figures for women are taken from Chapter 3.

32. It should be noted, however, that the relative distribution of blended family episodes by type according to the respondents' sex may be affected by the different ways in which men and women interpreted the retrospective questions about the children they have raised (see Section 4.2.5 of this chapter).

33. For a more detailed presentation of the method, see Section 3.4.1 of Chapter 3.

34. These probabilities were calculated using the "non-markovian" version of the LIFEHIST computer program developed by Rajulton (Rajulton 1992; Rajulton and Balakrishnan 1990).

35. This percentage represents the sum of life course probabilities for first lone-parenthood episodes (4.6% + 17.3 + 0.4%).

36. These percentages represent the sum of path probabilities for each family episode of a given rank. For example, the sum of path probabilities ranking second is calculated as follows: from top to bottom of Figure 4.8, 4.2% in a first blended family + 17.3% in a first lone-parent family + 1.9% in a re-created two-parent family + 0.4% in a first lone-parent family.

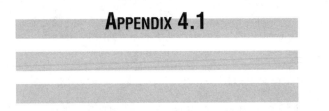

APPENDIX 4.1

COMPARISON OF THE FAMILY STATUS OF MEN ACCORDING TO THE 1990 GSS AND 1991 CENSUS

Table 1 provides an overview of the distribution of Canadian men aged 18 to 64 by their family status at the time of the 1990 GSS and the 1991 Census.[1] The table shows that the distributions are quite similar from one source to another. Note, however, that the percentage of men aged 18 to 24 surveyed by the GSS is slightly higher than that obtained from the census (18% versus 15%). Also, proportionally more GSS respondents aged 25 to 34 belonged to a couple, with or without children (66% versus 61%), while, in the census, men of the same age tended slightly less often to be classified as "children" (14% versus 11%). Finally, it will be seen that the proportion of GSS male respondents belonging to a couple with children was slightly higher among those aged 35 to 44 (71% versus 67%), causing a decrease, this time, in the number of non-family persons (13% versus 15%). These variations, however, are never more than five percentage points and are slightly less marked than those observed for women.

TABLE 1

COMPARISON OF THE DISTRIBUTION OF MEN AGED 18 TO 64, BY FAMILY STATUS AND AGE AT THE TIME OF THE SURVEY (S) AND THE CENSUS (C), 1990 AND 1991

Family status		Age group					
		18–24	25–34	35–44	45–54	55–64	All ages
				%			
"Child" status	(s)	66	11	3	3	1	16
	(c)	66	14	3	1	1	15
Men belonging to	(s)	15	66	82	83	82	6
a couple	(c)	14	61	79	83	82	65
with no children	(s)	12	23	11	22	47	21
	(c)	9	21	12	23	50	21
with children	(s)	3	43	71	61	35	45
	(c)	5	40	67	60	32	44
Lone fathers	(s)	0	0	2	3	5	2
	(c)	0	1	3	3	2	2
Non family persons	(s)	19	23	13	11	12	16
	(c)	20	24	15	13	15	18
Total	(s)	18	28	24	16	14	100
	(c)	15	28	26	17	14	100

Source: 1990 GSS, cycle 5, Public Use Microdata File; 1991 Census Public Use Microdata File on Individuals.

---

[1]   For a presentation of the approach used to determine the living arrangements of respondents in relation to a "census family," based on 1990 GSS data, see Appendix 3.1 of Chapter 3.

APPENDIX 4.2

TABLE 1

CUMULATIVE PROBABILITIES FOR MEN OF EXPERIENCING AN INTACT TWO-PARENT FAMILY AT VARIOUS AGES, BY MARITAL STATUS ON ENTRY AND AGE AT THE TIME OF THE SURVEY, 1990

Age[1] and marital status[2]		Age group					
		18–24	25–34	35–44	45–54	55–65	**All ages**
				%			
20 years	P_m	0.2	0.9	2.3	2.4	1.2	**1.4**
	P_{cm}	0.2	0.2	0.2	0.0	0.0	**0.1**
	P_c	0.4	0.7	0.6	0.0	0.0	**0.4**
	P	0.8	1.8	3.1	2.4	1.2	**1.9**
25 years	P_m	3.4	9.5	22.5	27.1	25.6	**18.6**
	P_{cm}	1.9	2.9	1.3	0.1	0.1	**1.4**
	P_c	2.5	3.4	1.8	0.0	0.0	**1.8**
	P	7.8	15.8	25.6	27.2	25.7	**21.8**
30 years	P_m		28.0	48.0	59.8	60.8	**46.0**
	P_{cm}		9.9	4.8	1.1	0.2	**4.7**
	P_c		6.6	2.8	0.8	0.2	**3.2**
	P		44.5	55.6	61.7	61.2	**53.9**
35 years	P_m		37.6	57.8	70.8	78.4	**58.9**
	P_{cm}		13.7	7.8	1.7	0.2	**6.6**
	P_c		10.8	3.5	1.8	0.2	**4.1**
	P		62.1	69.1	74.3	78.8	**69.6**
40 years	P_m			60.8	76.1	82.1	**63.5**
	P_{cm}			9.2	2.7	0.2	**7.6**
	P_c			4.3	1.8	0.2	**4.4**
	P			74.3	80.6	82.5	**75.5**
45 years	P_m			62.7	76.6	83.3	**64.7**
	P_{cm}			9.2	3.2	0.4	**7.9**
	P_c			4.3	2.3	0.2	**4.6**
	P			76.2	82.1	83.9	**77.2**
50 years	P_m				77.0	83.7	**65.3**
	P_{cm}				3.2	0.4	**7.9**
	P_c				2.3	0.2	**4.6**
	P				82.5	84.3	**77.8**

MALE FAMILY PATHS

TABLE 1 (CONCLUDED)

CUMULATIVE PROBABILITIES FOR MEN OF EXPERIENCING AN INTACT TWO-PARENT FAMILY AT VARIOUS AGES, BY MARITAL STATUS ON ENTRY AND AGE AT THE TIME OF THE SURVEY, 1990

Age[1] and marital status[2]		Age group					
		18–24	25–34	35–44	45–54	55–65	All ages
				%			
55 years	P_m				77.0	83.7	**65.3**
	P_{cm}				3.2	0.4	**7.9**
	P_c				2.3	0.2	**4.6**
	P				82.5	84.3	**77.8**
60 years	P_m					83.7	**65.3**
	P_{cm}					0.4	**7.9**
	P_c					0.2	**4.6**
	P					84.3	**77.8**
65 years	P_m					83.7	**65.3**
	P_{cm}					0.4	**7.9**
	P_c					0.2	**4.6**
	P					84.3	**77.8**
N[3]		947	1,494	1,290	859	767	**5,357**

1. Exact age.
2. P^m: cumulative probabilities following a direct marriage.

   P^{cm}: cumulative probabilities following a marriage preceded by a common-law union.

   P^c: cumulative probabilities following a common-law union.

   P: cumulative probabilities for all marital statuses.
3. Expanded data reduced to the size of the initial sample. Excludes two cases for which the type of union is not known.

Source: 1990 GSS, cycle 5, Public Use Microdata File.

TABLE 2

CUMULATIVE PROBABILITIES FOR MEN WHO HAVE EXPERIENCED AN INTACT TWO-PARENT FAMILY OF EXITING THIS FAMILY STATUS AT VARIOUS DURATIONS, BY MEANS OF EXIT AND AGE AT THE TIME OF THE SURVEY, 1990

Duration[1] and means of exit[2]		Age group				
		25–34	35–44	45–54	55–65	**All ages**
				%		
1 year	P_b	1.1	0.1	0.2	0.0	**0.3**
	P_d	0.0	0.0	0.0	0.8	**0,2**
	P_c	1.5	0.7	0.1	0.0	**0.6**
	P	2.6	0.8	0.3	0.8	**1.1**
2 years	P_b	2.7	1.6	0.9	0.0	**1.3**
	P_d	0.0	0.0	0.0	1.1	**0.3**
	P_c	2.6	0.9	0.1	0.1	**0.9**
	P	5.3	2.5	1.0	1.2	**2.5**
3 years	P_b	3.9	1.9	1.8	0.2	**1.9**
	P_d	0.0	0.0	0.0	1.1	**0.3**
	P_c	3.5	1.2	0.2	0.1	**1.2**
	P	7.4	3.1	2.0	1.4	**3.4**
4 years	P_b	6.8	2.9	3.1	0.6	**3.0**
	P_d	0.0	0.0	0.5	1.1	**0.4**
	P_c	4.0	1.7	0.5	0.1	**1.5**
	P	10.8	4.6	4.1	1.8	**4.9**
5 years	P_b	8.3	4.4	3.8	0.6	**3.9**
	P_d	0.3	0.0	0.5	1.2	**0.5**
	P_c	4.3	1.7	0.6	0.1	**1.6**
	P	12.9	6.1	4.9	1.9	**6.0**
10 years	P_b	11.9	9.0	6.4	1.2	**6.8**
	P_d	0.7	0.0	0.5	1.8	**0.7**
	P_e	5.4	3.1	0.8	0.3	**2.2**
	P	18.0	12.1	7.7	3.3	**9.7**
15 years	P_b		11.5	9.9	4.6	**9.8**
	P_d		1.4	0.9	2.0	**1.2**
	P_c		5.0	1.5	0.5	**3.1**
	P		17.9	12.3	7.1	**14.1**
20 years	P_r		15.7	15.9	7.7	**14.0**
	P_d		1.6	1.2	2.8	**1.7**
	P_c		6.2	4.9	5.4	**6.9**
	P		23.5	22.0	15.9	**22.6**

TABLE 2 (CONCLUDED)

CUMULATIVE PROBABILITIES FOR MEN WHO HAVE EXPERIENCED AN INTACT TWO-PARENT
FAMILY OF EXITING THIS FAMILY STATUS AT VARIOUS DURATIONS, BY MEANS OF EXIT
AND AGE AT THE TIME OF THE SURVEY, 1990

Duration[1] and means of exit[2]	Age group				
	25–34	35–44	45–54	55–65	All ages
			%		
25 years P_b			16.6	10.8	**16.1**
P_d			1.5	4.0	**2.5**
P_c			20.8	21.3	**21.7**
P			38.9	36.1	**40.3**
30 years P_b			16.6	11.8	**16.7**
P_d			1.9	4.9	**3.3**
P_c			44.7	37.6	**38.8**
P			63.2	54.3	**58.8**
35 years P_b				12.3	**17.2**
P_d				5.7	**3.9**
P_c				54.5	**54.5**
P				72.5	**75.6**
N[3]	596	876	671	619	**2,785**

1. Duration in exact years.
2. P^b: cumulative probabilities following voluntary breakdown of a union.
   P^d: cumulative probabilities following the death of the spouse.
   P^c: cumulative probabilities following the children's departure.
   P: cumulative probabilities for all episodes.
3. Expanded data reduced to the size of the initial sample. Excludes 113 cases for which the date of exit from the episode is not known. The total includes 23 male respondents aged 18 to 24 for whom the cumulative probabilities are not shown separately.

Source: 1990 GSS, cycle 5, Public Use Microdata File.

TABLE 3

CUMULATIVE PROBABILITIES FOR MEN WHO HAVE EXPERIENCED A LONE-PARENT EPISODE OF
EXITING LONE-PARENT STATUS AT VARIOUS DURATIONS, BY MEANS OF EXIT AND
AGE AT THE TIME OF THE SURVEY, 1990

Duration[1] and means of exit[2]		25–34	35–44	45–54	55–65	All ages
				%		
1 year	P_{cl}	20.0	19.4	17.1	13.0	**17.3**
	P_m	8.8	7.4	12.4	1.4	**7.2**
	P_c	26.2	15.4	6.9	3.1	**12.6**
	P	55.0	42.2	36.4	17.5	**37.1**
2 years	P_{cl}	22.7	22.8	22.8	22.7	**22.8**
	P_m	22.4	20.5	17.5	3.3	**15.3**
	P_c	30.3	18.6	9.1	7.2	**15.9**
	P	75.4	61.9	49.4	33.2	**54.0**
3 years	P_{cl}	27.3	25.6	27.9	25.2	**26.4**
	P_m	22.6	25.4	25.8	6.5	**19.8**
	P_c	32.5	20.6	12.0	11.4	**18.7**
	P	82.4	71.6	65.7	43.1	**64.9**
4 years	P_{cl}		30.0	29.5	29.6	**29.2**
	P_m		27.7	29.5	7.1	**21.6**
	P_c		21.1	12.3	16.0	**20.5**
	P		78.8	71.3	52.7	**71.3**
5 years	P_{cl}		35.1	32.1	34.5	**32.7**
	P_m		27.7	31.9	10.0	**23.3**
	P_c		21.7	18.8	17.5	**23.2**
	P		84.5	82.8	62.0	**79.2**
10 years	P_{cl}				38.8	**37.5**
	P_m				11.5	**25.3**
	P_c				23.4	**25.1**
	P				73.7	**87.9**
15 years	P_{cl}					**39.7**
	P_m					**26.3**
	P_c					**27.8**
	P					**93.8**
N^3		98	163	157	157	**586**

1. Duration in exact years.
2. P^{cl} : cumulative probabilities following a common-law union.

   P^m: cumulative probabilities following a marriage.

   P^c: cumulative probabilities following the children's departure.

   P: cumulative probabilities for all episodes.
3. Expanded data reduced to the size of the initial sample. Excludes 15 cases for which the date of exit from the episode is not known. The total includes 11 male respondents aged 18 to 24 for whom the cumulative probabilities are not shown separately.

Source: 1990 GSS, cycle 5, Public Use Microdata File.

TABLE 4

CUMULATIVE PROBABILITIES FOR MEN WHO HAVE EXPERIENCED A BLENDED FAMILY OF
EXITING THIS FAMILY STATUS AT VARIOUS DURATIONS, BY MEANS OF EXIT AND
AGE AT THE TIME OF THE SURVEY, 1990

Duration[1] and means of exit[2]		Age group				
		25–34	35–44	45–54	55–65	**All ages**
				%		
1 year	P_b	0.7	3.4	1.8	1.0	**2.0**
	P_d	0.0	0.0	0.4	0.0	**0.1**
	P_c	2.6	2.2	5.4	3.3	**3.2**
	P	3.3	5.6	7.6	4.4	**5.3**
2 years	P_b	1.3	7.8	5.0	1.0	**4.5**
	P_d	0.0	0.0	0.4	0.0	**0.1**
	P_c	3.0	2.5	5.4	6.2	**3.9**
	P	4.3	10.3	10.8	7.2	**8.5**
3 years	P_b	3.3	12.7	8.2	1.0	**7.5**
	P_d	0.0	0.0	0.4	0.0	**0.1**
	P_c	3.0	3.6	9.0	11.4	**6.3**
	P	6.3	16.3	17.6	12.4	**13.9**
4 years	P_b	4.4	17.7	11.8	2.2	**10.8**
	P_d	0.0	0.0	0.4	0.0	**0.1**
	P_e	4.3	4.2	12.2	16.2	**8.5**
	P	8.7	21.9	24.4	18.4	**19.4**
5 years	P_b	4.4	18.3	12.1	2.7	**11.2**
	P_d	0.0	0.0	0.4	0.0	**0.1**
	P_c	6.2	6.5	15.7	19.7	**11.4**
	P	10.6	24.8	28.2	22.4	**22.7**
10 years	P_b		22.8	20.4	3.9	**16.6**
	P_d		0.0	0.4	0.0	**0.1**
	P_c		10.7	28.8	31.1	**20.2**
	P		33.5	49.6	35.0	**36.9**
15 years	P_b		24.3	24.9	3.9	**18.6**
	P_d		0.0	0.4	2.1	**0.7**
	P_c		22.6	39.4	46.2	**32.7**
	P		46.9	69.7	52.2	**52.1**
20 years	P_b				4.7	**21.0**
	P_d				2.1	**0.7**
	P_c				67.5	**53.4**
	P				74.3	**75.1**
N[3]		94	166	122	78	**471**

1. Duration in exact years.
2. P_b: cumulative probabilities following voluntary breakdown of a union.

   P_d: cumulative probabilities following the death of the spouse.

   P_c: cumulative probabilities following the children's departure.

   P: cumulative probabilities for all episodes.
3. Expanded data reduced to the size of the initial sample. Excludes 16 cases for which the date of exit from the episode is not known. The total includes 11 male respondents aged 18 to 24 for whom the cumulative probabilities are not shown separately.

Source: 1990 GSS, cycle 5, Public Use Microdata File.

CHAPTER

5

FAMILY STATUS FROM THE CHILDREN'S PERSPECTIVE

ÉVELYNE LAPIERRE-ADAMCYK

AND NICOLE MARCIL-GRATTON

Sylvia Wargon was the first in Canada to point out the usefulness of analysing census data from the perspective of children. In view of the profound changes in marital and reproductive behaviours, which, as early as 1976, had altered the face of family life, she determined to underscore their impact on children's lives. When the United Nations declared 1979 the International Year of the Child, Statistics Canada published *Children in Canadian Families* in which Sylvia Wargon skilfully used the available data to outline how the living environment of Canadian children had evolved since the 1931 Census (Wargon 1979b). But, by her own admission, major time and budgetary constraints prevented her from extracting the special tabulations that would have allowed her to highlight further the significant changes the new marital behaviours of adults were imposing on childhood. In her preface, Sylvia Wargon encouraged further study along the lines of her work—work that can still be described as groundbreaking today. In Canada, it would be 10 years before the torch was taken up. In the context of a study of demographic development and its impact on economic and social policy (Marcil-Gratton 1988), the relevance of studying the impact of family changes on the evolution of children's lives was again put forward.

There are two reasons for the special consideration of childhood in this monograph about the family based on the 1991 Census. Firstly, complex tables have become much easier to obtain, thanks to the greater accessibility of microdata files. Second, the phenomena responsible for the changes in the family environment of children, first noted in 1976, continued to evolve at rates and in directions that could not easily have been predicted 15 years ago. The decline in fertility, the remarkable increase in the participation of mothers in the labour market, the declining popularity of marriage, the growing phenomenon of cohabitation, and the increase in marital instability are some of the impetuses for the changes children continue to experience in their family environment.

This chapter first shows the relevance of analysing family life from the children's perspective, then examines the indicators of the changes that have occurred. This study is based primarily on 1991 Census data, in light of observations from the 1990 General Social Survey, cycle 5: Family and Friends (GSS).

5.1   THE CHILDREN'S PERSPECTIVE: A RELEVANT APPROACH?

How is the observation of family life enhanced by an analysis whose reference population comprises neither the adults who are adopting the new marital and reproductive behaviours nor the resulting family units, but instead is composed only of the children affected by these new behaviours? Essentially, using children as the basis of measurement provides a far more reliable estimate of how much the environment of younger generations is being altered by their parents' behaviour. The analysis therefore involves determining how many children were experiencing various situations, by age at the time of the census. By comparing children of different age groups, we can establish a relationship between the family status of children and the profound changes the family has undergone, and to interpret this relationship, in the light of census data, as the outcome of family paths experienced at different times by different generations of children. Measurements of the family environment of children based on census data are no doubt less refined than those based on GSS data, particularly as the former are not retrospective. However, the advantage is that these measurements can be compared with various aspects of children's living conditions, which are inevitably affected by the family environment that prevails at any given time.

The dramatic decline in family size over 30 years, a direct outcome of the decline in fertility, effectively illustrates the usefulness of adopting the analytical perspective of children. Table 5.1 shows, for the various decennial censuses of Canada since 1951, the distribution of families with children by number of children present in the family, as well as the distribution of these children according to the same criterion. Thus, in 1951, while only 6.8% of families had six or more children living at home, no less than 20.1% of children were growing up with at least five brothers or sisters. Conversely, again in 1951, while 34.7% of families with children had just one child at home, they represented just 13.9% of children. The second proportion in each case therefore provides a far more accurate view than the first of the true reality of the family environments of children. Also, to the extent that sibling relationships are an important factor of child development, the usefulness of accurately measuring the presence or absence of siblings must be acknowledged. This illustration should convince the reader of the relevance of analysing family realities from the children's perspective.

TABLE 5.1

DISTRIBUTION OF FAMILIES WITH CHILDREN AND DISTRIBUTION OF CHILDREN UNDER AGE 25,
BY NUMBER OF CHILDREN IN THE HOME, 1951 TO 1991

	Number of children						
	1	2	3	4	5	6 or more	Total
	%						
1951							
Families with children	34.7	29.2	16.1	8.5	4.7	6.8	**100.0**
Children	13.9	23.5	19.4	13.7	9.4	20.1	**100.0**
1961							
Families with children	28.6	29.2	19.0	10.6	5.5	7.0	**100.0**
Children	10.8	22.0	21.5	16.0	10.4	19.3	**100.0**
1971							
Families with children	29.6	30.6	19.2	10.4	5.3	4.9	**100.0**
Children	11.8	24.3	22.9	16.6	10.5	13.9	**100.0**
1981							
Families with children	35.2	39.3	17.4	5.8	1.6	0.8	**100.0**
Children	17.3	38.7	25.8	11.4	3.8	2.9	**100.0**
1991							
Families with children	38.5	41.9	15.1	3.6	0.7	0.3	**100.0**
Children	20.6	44.8	24.1	7.6	1.8	1.1	**100.0**

Note: Percentages may not add to 100 due to rounding.

Source: Census of Canada, 1951, 1961 and 1971, Family Public Use Microdata Files; Census of Canada, 1981 and 1991, unpublished compilation.

5.2 THE CONCEPT OF FAMILY ENVIRONMENT, THE DEFINITION OF "CHILD" AND THE SOURCES USED

In this chapter, the term "family environment" refers to a close classification of family types present in the census, which includes the parents' legal marital status. Thus, not only are two-parent families distinguishable from lone-parent families, but parents living common law, one of whom had previously been married, are also distinguishable from those families where neither parent had ever been married. Similarly, lone parents are further identified by their legal marital status, that is, as single, divorced or widowed. Using these categories, each child is described according to the type of family in which they live. While very detailed, this classification is still imperfect as blended families cannot be identified. First, remarried couples cannot be distinguished from couples married for the first time. Second, it is not possible to distinguish, from the question on the relationship between the reference person and household members, natural, step- and adopted children. When the relationship to the reference person is given as "son or daughter," the child is considered to be the child of the couple to which the reference person belongs. Thus, the presence in the household of children who are not the natural children of both members of the couple, an essential feature of blended families, cannot be detected. This imprecision grows in magnitude with the increase in the number of blended families, reported in other sources. Moreover, this classification is valid only for the 1991 Census. In previous censuses, parents in a common-law union could not be identified; until June 1991, common-law couples were classified among married couples, either because, during data collection, respondents living common law were instructed to declare themselves as married, or because of how the data were processed.

The census defines as a "child" any person present in a household on Census Day who is not married and declares a filial bond with an adult in the same household. The published data often reflect only those "children" under age 25, and provide a fairly reliable picture of the child population from the time they are born until they leave home. Most children continue to live with their parents until age 18; then a significant number leave home to move into their own place (see Table 5.2). Needless to say, our first step was to remove young people aged 18 to 24 from the child population studied since 40% no longer lived with their parents.

TABLE 5.2

PERCENTAGE OF PERSONS UNDER AGE 25 WHO HAVE "CHILD" STATUS ACCORDING TO THE 1991 CENSUS

		Age group		
Under 6	6–14	15–17	18–24	**All ages**
		%		
97.1	98.0	94.9	59.2	**86.6**

Source: Census of Canada, 1991, Individual Public Use Microdata Files, unpublished compilation.

Also, to satisfy the methodological imperatives, we decided to remove those aged 15 to 17 from some measurements, even though 94.9% of these young people were classified as children living in the household of at least one of their parents. Data from the 1990 GSS were sometimes consulted in order to shed light on certain phenomena not covered by the census data, but which a present-day analysis of the family environment of children could not ignore. While the GSS data do not invalidate the fact that young people aged 15 to 17 still have "child" status, these same young people are eligible to be respondents of the general social surveys of Statistics Canada. Those aged 15 to 17 declared to be children of respondents of these surveys therefore do not represent the entire population of young people in that age group. So caution dictates that they not be included in calculations when comparing the two data sources.

Having said this, as the family environment is of special interest to the extent that it provides information about how children in our society are cared for, this shortcoming seems secondary, and we believe our objectives can be achieved by limiting our analysis to children under age 15. This approach also simplifies our task when consulting the Public Use Microdata Files on Family, which identifies families with children under age 15.

5.3 HISTORICAL EVOLUTION OF THE FAMILY ENVIRONMENT OF CHILDREN

Before beginning our in-depth analysis of the environment of children in 1991, it might be helpful to place it in the context of its longer term evolution, taking into account the family categories used over the past four decades from 1951 to 1991.

Table 5.3 shows the evolution, since 1951, of the proportion of children under age 25 by family type. Most evident is the decrease in the proportion of children living in a two-parent family, from 92% to 85%. This apparently modest decrease masks the impact of the increase in common-law unions as the living environment of children; for example, 1991 Census data tells us that 6% of children under age 25 belonged to a family where the couple was living common law. It also masks the ever-growing incidence of children who are living in a "blended" family. The main purpose of this chapter is to reveal the heterogeneity of this family category.

TABLE 5.3

DISTRIBUTION OF CHILDREN UNDER AGE 25, BY MARITAL STATUS OF PARENT OR PARENTS, 1951 TO 1991

	1951	1961	1971	1981	1991
			%		
Husband–wife families					
Married	92.0	93.6	90.4	87.3	79.0
Common law	..	..	..	..	6.0
Lone-parent families					
Lone fathers, total	1.8	1.4	2.1	2.2	2.6
Married (wife absent)	0.6	0.7	0.4	0.4	0.5
Widowed	1.1	0.6	0.6	0.5	0.3
Divorced	0.1	0.1	0.3	0.6	0.9
Separated	..	..	0.6	0.7	0.7
Never married	0.0	0.0	0.3	0.1	0.2
Lone mothers, total	6.2	5.0	7.5	10.5	12.5
Married (husband absent)	2.5	2.1	0.4	0.4	0.5
Widowed	3.4	2.6	2.9	2.5	1.3
Divorced	0.2	0.3	1.0	3.2	4.7
Separated	..	..	2.7	3.3	3.4
Never married	0.1	0.1	0.5	1.1	2.6
Total	**100.0**	**100.0**	**100.0**	**100.0**	**100.0**

.. not available

Note: Totals may not add to 100 due to rounding.

Source: Census of Canada, 1951, 1961 and 1971, Family Public Use Microdata Files; Census of Canada, 1981 and 1991, unpublished compilation.

Obviously, this decrease was accompanied by an increase in the percentage of children living in a lone-parent family (from 8% to 15%), usually with their mother (78% of cases in 1951, 83% in 1991). Also, of those children living in either a male or female lone-parent family, the number living with a widowed parent has declined over the decades: while in 1951, 56% of children living in a lone-parent family were doing so following the death of a parent, this was true of just

11% in 1991. This change is almost entirely due to the increase in the number of voluntary union dissolutions; the greater life expectancy of parents merely bolstered the trend. Also note that the proportion of children who, when the various censuses were taken, were in a lone-parent family does not take their complete history into account, as those whose parents formed a new union were reclassified as children living in a two-parent family.

This seemingly uneventful historical evolution from the children's perspective seems to be marked primarily by the increase in the proportion of children in a lone-parent family. But, on close examination of 1991 Census and 1990 GSS data, this evolution proves to be more diversified. In fact, the impact of new behaviours, already revealed in earlier chapters by observing families and adults, is seen even more clearly.

5.4 THE FAMILY ENVIRONMENT OF CHILDREN IN 1991

In section 5.2, the classification of the family environment of children is determined based on 1991 Census data. Basically, it is possible to distinguish two-parent families from lone-parent families; families of a married couple from families of a common-law couple; and lone-parent families, where the parent's status is the result of widowhood, separation or divorce, from those where the parent's marital status is single. Blended families, however, cannot be taken into account, as they are hidden in the census among the various types of two-parent families. Survey data are therefore helpful in assessing the extent of this phenomenon.

5.4.1 From childhood to early adulthood

Two observations can be made about the changes that have occurred over time in the family environment of children. First, the percentage of children living in a two-parent family has gradually declined since 1951 (see Table 5.3). Secondly, in looking at the situation of children at the time of the 1991 census, taking age into account, it is clear that, from early childhood to the start of adulthood, children experience several changes in their family environment. For the reasons mentioned in section 5.2, the following analysis concerns children under age 18.

The percentage of children living in a two-parent family dropped from 87.8% among preschool children to 84.9% among school-age children and 83.1% among adolescents (see Table 5.4). On closer examination of this group, whose family environment seems fairly traditional and homogeneous, it is interesting to note that, of the children living with two adults, 5.3% of adolescents aged 15 to 17, 6.5% of school-age children, and nearly twice as many (11%) preschool children lived with an unmarried couple (see Table 5.5A). This variation reflects the fact that common-law unions had become an increasingly common form of union and context in which to raise children. It is mostly children born since the mid-1980s who had parents living common law. Also, of the children whose parents lived common law, the percentage of those under age six living with parents who had never been legally married was far greater than that of older children: 65% of preschool children, 29% of those aged 6 to 14, and just 11% of those aged 15 to 17. These results reflect the rise in unmarried cohabitation as a context for forming families, hence the higher proportion of recent generations of children who now belong to a non-traditional family from birth. This phenomenon is not evenly spread across Canada. Section 5.5 looks at the specific case of Quebec, where this behaviour is far more prevalent.

TABLE 5.4

DISTRIBUTION OF CHILDREN UNDER AGE 18, BY AGE AND FAMILY ENVIRONMENT, 1991

| Family environment | Age group | | | | |
	Under 6	6–14	Sub-total	15–17	All ages
Parents married	78.1	79.3	78.9	78.7	**78.8**
Parents living common law:					
At least one spouse ever married	3.4	3.9	3.7	3.9	**3.8**
Both spouses never married	6.3	1.6	3.5	0.5	**3.0**
Subtotal	87.8	84.9	86.1	83.1	**85.6**
Mothers never married	4.9	2.4	3.4	1.1	**3.1**
Mothers divorced	5.7	9.6	8.0	10.5	**8.4**
Mothers widowed	0.2	0.8	0.6	1.7	**0.7**
Subtotal	10.9	12.7	12.0	13.4	**12.2**
Fathers never married	0.3	0.2	0.2	0.2	**0.2**
Fathers divorced	1.0	2.0	1.6	3.0	**1.8**
Fathers widowed	0.0	0.2	0.1	0.4	**0.2**
Subtotal	1.3	2.4	2.0	3.5	**2.2**
Total	**100.0**	**100.0**	**100.0**	**100.0**	**100.0**
Number of cases	**66,337**	**99,518**	**165,855**	**31,321**	**197,176**

Note: Percentages may not add to 100 due to rounding.

Source: Census of Canada, 1991, Family Public Use Microdata Files, unpublished compilation.

TABLE 5.5A

DISTRIBUTION OF CHILDREN LIVING IN A TWO-PARENT FAMILY, BY AGE AND PARENTS' MARITAL STATUS, 1991

| Family environment | Age group | | | |
	Under age 6	6–14	15–17	All ages
		%		
Parents married	89.0	93.5	94.7	**92.1**
Parents living common law:				
At least one spouse ever married	3.9	4.6	4.7	**4.4**
Both spouses never married	7.1	1.9	0.6	**3.5**
Total, two-parent families	**100.0**	**100.0**	**100.0**	**100.0**
% of children in two-parent families	87.8	84.9	83.1	**85.6**

TABLE 5.5B

DISTRIBUTION OF CHILDREN LIVING IN A LONE-PARENT FAMILY, BY AGE AND PARENT'S SEX AND MARITAL STATUS, 1991

Family environment	Age group							
	Under age 6		6–14		15–17		All ages	
					%			
Lone mothers	89.1	100.0	84.2	100.0	79.1	100.0	**84.7**	**100.0**
Never married		45.6		18.9		8.4		**25.1**
Divorced		52.2		75.1		78.6		**68.8**
Widowed		2.3		6.0		13.0		**6.1**
Lone fathers	10.9	100.0	15.8	100.0	20.9	100.0	**15.3**	**100.0**
Never married		23.4		8.7		4.4		**10.6**
Divorced		73.1		83.4		84.8		**81.7**
Widowed		3.5		7.9		10.8		**7.8**
Total lone-parent families	**100.0**		**100.0**		**100.0**		**100.0**	
% of children in lone-parent families	12.2		15.1		16.9		**14.4**	

Note: Percentages may not add to 100 due to rounding.

Source: Census of Canada, 1991, Family Public Use Microdata Files, unpublished data.

These results show only part of the reality. As mentioned in section 5.2, the categories defined here do not reveal the precise nature of the parent–child relationship. There is no way of knowing what proportion of children were living with both natural parents. Studies based on 1990 GSS data show that, by their sixth birthday, nearly 20% of children born between 1981 and 1983 were no longer living with both natural parents; about half of these belonged to a blended family (Marcil-Gratton 1993). We discuss this further in section 5.4.5. First, we continue our look at the situation as revealed by the 1991 Census, focusing on children in a lone-parent family.

5.4.2 Children who live, or have ever lived, in a lone-parent family

Living part of one's childhood in a lone-parent family is becoming a more and more common reality for Canadian children. Also, children experience life in lone-parent families increasingly early on in their childhood. These realities, brought to light by the GSS data, are only partially evident in the census.

The percentage of children in a lone-parent family increases with age; this increase only partly reflects the effect of the duration of unions on the proportion of broken families (see Table 5.4). Also, this cross-sectional datum gives no indication of the growing magnitude of the lone-parent experience for children, or the ever-younger age at which it occurs. A study of the 1990 GSS data by generation confirmed that not only will greater proportions of children born in the 1980s experience a lone-parent episode, but they will also do so at an increasingly younger age (see Figure 5.1). Thus, nearly 25% of children born in the early 1960s experienced a lone-parent family before age 20, while 20% did so before they reached age 16. The experiences of divorce in the families of these children are largely a result of the liberal views concerning divorce at the end of that decade. The acceleration of the phenomenon is evident among children born 20 years later, in the early 1980s: about 18% had experienced a lone-parent family before age six.

FIGURE 5.1

CUMULATIVE PERCENTAGE OF CHILDREN WHO WERE BORN TO A PARENT LIVING ALONE OR WHO SAW THEIR PARENTS SEPARATE AT VARIOUS AGES AND FOR VARIOUS GENERATIONS

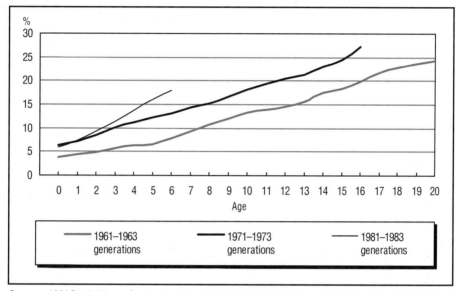

Sources: 1984 Family History Survey, for 1961–1963 generations; 1990 General Social Survey for 1971–1973 and 1981–1983 generations, Marcil-Gratton, 1993, unpublished compilation.

According to the census, a sizeable proportion (about half, as the data in Figure 5.3 show) of the children whose parents dissolved their union and then formed a new household "disappear" in the census into the two-parent family categories: "married parents"; "common-law parents, at least one spouse ever-married"; or even just "common-law parents, both spouses never-married" (applied if neither parent has ever been married). Here is another instance where the census data do not reflect a reality that is becoming extremely complex. Past events cannot be taken into account, only the situation as of Census Day can be observed.

Table 5.5B does, however, provide useful information about the family environment of the proportion of children (14.4% of children under age 18) living in a lone-parent family at the time of the census. It is not surprising to see that most children in a lone-parent family lived with their mother, since, as we outlined earlier, this is the historical trend. However, the proportion declines as age increases, from 89.1% of the youngest age group to 79.1% of those aged 15 to 17, which means that one-fifth of adolescents in a lone-parent family were living with their father. Among the youngest children, the proportion whose mother was single is markedly higher (45.6% versus 18.9% of those aged 6 to 14, and fewer than 10% of those aged 15 to 17). This can likely be attributed to two types of behaviour: children born to single mothers living without a spouse fall into this category until their mother forms a union; the proliferation of births among common-law couples is probably another contributing factor, since separations are more common among these young couples. Finally, in most cases where children are living with just their mother, the mother is divorced; widowhood is not a significant factor among young adults until later. A similar variation is seen among the small minority of children who live with their father.

In short, the study of the family environment of children by age highlights the growth of common-law union as the family environment of young children, the increase in the proportion of those living in a lone-parent family from early childhood until late adolescence, and a similar increase in the proportion of those living with their father. The importance of divorce as the point of departure into lone parenthood should also be mentioned.

In order to assess the magnitude of the proportion of children living in a blended family, we must first explore the presence of siblings in the family environment of children.

5.4.3 The presence of siblings: another dimension of family environment

The experience of growing up in a family is mainly about the relationships between parents and children. But from the child's perspective, relationships with siblings are almost as important a part of childhood development. Having or not having siblings, having several or just one, being the oldest or youngest child in the family, growing up with or without children close in age— these are all factors that significantly affect children's family landscape and, according to psychologists, their development.

One of the most dramatic effects of the sharp decline in fertility over the last 30 years, but probably one of those that has received the least media attention, is the remarkable decline in sibling relationships. Table 5.1 illustrates this by showing the disappearance of large families. According to the 1951 Census, nearly one in three children (29.5%) had at least four siblings; in 1991, this figure was barely 2.9%. Conversely, in 1991, one in five children (20.6%) were the "only child," and it was typical for a child to share his or her family environment with just one sibling (44.8%); this proportion is nearly double that observed in 1951. Today, most Canadian children are born the eldest or youngest in the family, remain an only child, or have just one sibling.

The implications are numerous. Today, children are often born to parents who have little or no experience in childrearing. They grow up surrounded by fewer, if any, siblings. Inevitably, their parents' expectations of them have changed accordingly. And at day-care or in school, they constitute quite a different clientele than in the recent past. Educators often deal with children who, until this point in their lives, have been the focus of their family and for whom fitting into a group doubtless requires more of an adjustment.

The situation of children in relation to their siblings varies from younger to older ages but, overall, two-thirds (64.4%) of school-age children (aged 6 to 14) and preschoolers (under age 6) are an only child (17.3%) or have just one sibling (47.1%) (see Table 5.6). Also, given the narrow age difference between the first and second child, most children under age six are the only child (25.9%) or have one sibling also of preschool age (32.2%). Finally, the presence of older children—brothers and sisters who, in families with more children, no doubt play a certain role in relation to the smaller children—is less and less common, as can be seen by the small percentage of school-age or preschool-age children who have a sister or brother at home over age 15.

TABLE 5.6

DISTRIBUTION OF CHILDREN UNDER AGE 15, BY AGE AND CHARACTERISTICS OF SIBLING RELATIONSHIP,[1] 1991

		Age group of children		
Number	Age	Under age 6	6–14	**All ages**
1	Under 6	25.9	–	**10.4**
	6–14	–	11.5	**6.9**
	Subtotal	25.9	11.5	**17.3**
2	Both under 6	32.2	–	**2.9**
	Under 6; 6–14	14.4	9.6	**11.5**
	Under 6; 15 or older	0.6	–	**0.3**
	Both 6–14	–	28.7	**17.2**
	6–14; 15 or older	–	8.7	**5.2**
	Subtotal	47.2	47.0	**47.1**
3 or more	All under 6	4.5	–	**1.8**
	Youngest under 6; oldest 6–14	19.4	15.0	**16.7**
	Youngest under 6; oldest 15 or older	3.0	2.1	**2.5**
	All 6–14	–	11.1	**6.7**
	Youngest 6–14; oldest 15 or older	–	13.3	**8.0**
	Subtotal	26.9	41.5	**35.7**
	Total	**100.0**	**100.0**	**100.0**
	Number of cases	**66,337**	**99,518**	**165,855**

1. Sibling relationship refers to the number of children in the home and age of these children.
– nil or zero
Note: Percentages may not add to 100 due to rounding.
Source: Census of Canada, 1991, Family Public Use Microdata Files, unpublished compilation.

5.4.4 Family environment and children's sibling relationships

While it is inappropriate to examine the causes of the decline in fertility in this chapter, readers should recall that the evolution of marital behaviours is closely linked to that of reproductive behaviours. It is not important to know here whether couples are having fewer children because their relationships are less stable, or are less stable because they are having fewer children. One thing is certain: the sibling relationships of the children they have or raise highly depend on their marital history.

Table 5.7 makes this clear by showing the distribution of children by number of siblings (expressed here as the number of children present in the family) and by family environment. The number of children present in the family is interpreted as follows: children in a family where there are two children live with just one sibling, those in a family of three children live with two siblings, and so on. The children's age is related to the life cycle of the family, and the differences between preschool and school-age children partly reflect this reality. For example, the higher percentage among preschoolers of children who are an only child is related to the fact that these children are usually the first child of a couple who have not yet had time to have their second, while for those aged 6 to 14 there has been more time for younger siblings to have been born.

TABLE 5.7

DISTRIBUTION OF CHILDREN UNDER AGE 6 AND AGED 6 TO 14, BY FAMILY ENVIRONMENT AND NUMBER OF CHILDREN PRESENT IN THE HOME, 1991

| | Number of children | | | | |
	1	2	3	4 or more	Total
Children under 6					
Parents married	22.0	49.4	20.6	8.0	**100.0**
Parents living common law					
At least 1 spouse ever-married	31.6	40.0	19.6	8.8	**100.0**
Both spouses never married	46.2	40.8	10.4	2.5	**100.0**
Lone-parent families					
Lone mothers					
Never married	50.4	33.1	11.8	4.6	**100.0**
Divorced	29.0	43.0	20.2	7.8	**100.0**
Widowed	21.8	41.2	21.2	15.8	**100.0**
Lone fathers					
Never married	49.9	34.3	12.2	3.5	**100.0**
Divorced	34.3	40.9	17.3	7.4	**100.0**
Widowed	39.3	34.0	20.1	6.6	**100.0**
Total	**25.9**	**47.2**	**19.4**	**7.5**	**100.0**
Children aged 6–14					
Parents married	8.1	47.6	31.0	13.3	**100.0**
Parents living common law					
At least 1 spouse ever-married	22.4	42.8	22.6	12.2	**100.0**
Both spouses never married	22.4	47.7	21.5	8.4	**100.0**
Lone-parent families					
Lone mothers					
Never married	40.4	35.5	16.0	8.1	**100.0**
Divorced	21.3	47.7	22.5	8.4	**100.0**
Widowed	19.0	47.5	23.4	10.0	**100.0**
Lone fathers					
Never married	41.9	36.5	10.3	11.3	**100.0**
Divorced	27.1	43.5	20.2	9.1	**100.0**
Widowed	16.5	37.2	28.2	18.2	**100.0**
Total	**11.5**	**47.0**	**29.0**	**12.5**	**100.0**

Note: Percentages may not add to 100 due to rounding.

Source: Census of Canada, 1991, Family Public Use Microdata Files, unpublished compilation.

The main characteristics that emerge from a study of Table 5.7 can be summarized as follows:

a) Most children of married couples live in a household where there is at least one other child (78.0% of those under age 6 and 91.9% of those aged 6 to 14).

b) Children whose parents are single, that is, living either common law or alone, tend more often to be an only child. Similarly, they tend more often to have no more than one sibling in the home.

c) Children in a lone-parent family created following a divorce or widowhood have a similar number of siblings as children of married couples, and more siblings than children in a lone-parent family where the parent is single.

d) Finally, children of married two-parent families tend more often to have several brothers or sisters. However, they are closely followed by children of common-law couples where at least one spouse has been previously married. There is a concentration of blended families here, which by definition have more children.

It should again be pointed out that the picture presented here is a snapshot of family status, which changes as the life cycle unfolds and transitions are made from one family type to another. Thus, the status of only child may not be permanent for many children. An older sibling may already have left home or a younger sibling may be added to the family. Similarly, children who experience a lone-parent episode may find themselves in a blended family accepting a new parent and perhaps a "brother" or "sister" with whom they will form a new family. The main point to keep in mind is that the sibling environment of children depends on the marital path of the parents, and changes accordingly.

In Figure 5.2, the children are grouped not only by number of siblings, as in Table 5.7, but also by age composition of the sibling relationship. They are then distributed by family environment according, it will be recalled, to the marital status of the "parents." The figure provides a clearer picture of the nature of the sibling relationships that surround children as they grow up, and of their family environment. At a glance, a connection can be seen between having more siblings and having parents who are married. The fewer the number of siblings, the more likely the child will be in the household of a lone parent or common-law couple. In larger families (three or more children), at least 80% of the children have a married couple at the head of the household, regardless of the age difference between siblings or their age group. The variation is far greater for children who are an only child or have just one sibling. Thus, only 60% of children who are the only child in the home, as distinguished from children who are truly an only child, belong to households headed by a married couple. It is not surprising to find the highest proportions of children in a lone-parent family among children who are an only child: 18.1% of young children (under age 6) and 33.1% of older children (aged 6 to 14). Section 5.4.6 reveals other ties between the composition of sibling relationships and the incidence of blended families.

FIGURE 5.2

DISTRIBUTION OF CHILDREN UNDER AGE 15, BY SIBLING RELATIONSHIP AND FAMILY ENVIRONMENT, 1991

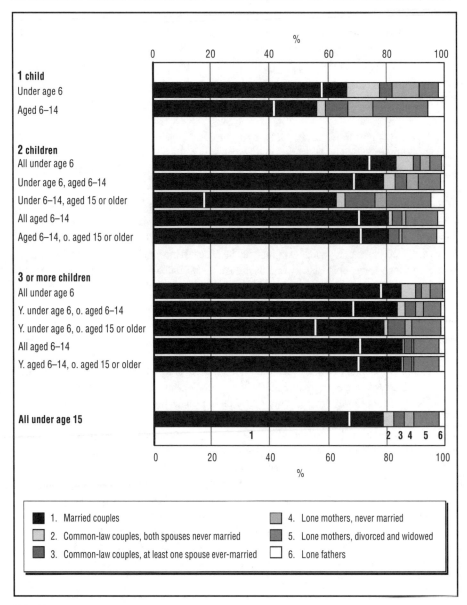

Note: Y. = youngest; o. = oldest

White line = intact families (percentage estimated from the 1990 GSS).

Source: Census of Canada, 1991, Family Public Use Microdata Files, unpublished compilation.

5.4.5 What about children in blended families?

Because it was developed at a time when blended families resulted only from widowhood, the census cannot be used to evaluate the extent of the recent phenomenon of new families formed following a union ended by separation or divorce. This limitation is specifically due to the fact that only the relationship to the reference person is reported, and the natural or adopted children of either spouse or common-law partner are classified, where applicable, as children of the couple, without further distinction.

It can sometimes be deduced that a family is blended when one member of the common-law couple declares his or her status as single and that of the partner as separated, widowed or divorced. Again, this cannot be confirmed since, in the census, all children present will be attributed to the couple, whether or not they are their natural children. The fact remains that today blended families are hidden in the census within the categories of "married couples" and "spouses living common law." The survey results may therefore supplement the census data.

The family environment categories used in the census analysis for the child population under age 15 has been recreated based on 1990 GSS data (see Table 5.8). The remarkable similarity of the two distributions attests to the quality of Statistics Canada survey design, and allows us to estimate quite confidently some of the parameters not revealed in the official statistics.

TABLE 5.8

COMPARISON OF THE DISTRIBUTION OF CHILDREN UNDER AGE 15, BY FAMILY ENVIRONMENT, DETERMINED ACCORDING TO THE 1991 CENSUS AND THE 1990 GENERAL SOCIAL SURVEY (GSS)

Family environment	Age group					
	Under age 6		Aged 6–14		All ages	
	1991 Census	1990 GSS	1991 Census	1990 GSS	1991 Census	1990 GSS
	%		%		%	
Married couples	78.1	79.5	79.3	78.4	78.9	78.8
Couples living common law	9.7	9.3	5.6	6.7	7.2	7.7
Lone mothers	10.9	10.8	12.7	12.0	12.0	11.6
Lone fathers	1.3	0.4	2.4	2.9	2.0	1.9
Total	100.0	100.0	100.0	100.0	100.0	100.0
Number of cases	66,337	2,809	99,518	4,249	165,855	7,058

Note: Percentages may not add to 100 due to rounding.
Source: Census of Canada, 1991; 1990 GSS.

As the 1990 GSS contains all the information about the marital and fertility histories of the adults surveyed, it is possible to create family categories that include a blended family category on the basis of two criteria: the parents' marital status at the start of the current union, and the fact that all children present in the home were born within the current union. It is thus possible to distinguish families of married parents from families of parents living common law (see Table 5.9); this distinction is common to both the census and the 1990 GSS. Based on the 1990 GSS, these two categories are then divided into the following three groups:

a) Intact families, where both spouses have never previously been married and all children present are their natural or adopted children.

b) Blended couples, where one spouse had previously been married before the start of the current union, but all children present are their natural or adopted children.

c) Blended families, where at least one child present was born outside of the current union, regardless of the parents' marital history.

TABLE 5.9

DISTRIBUTION OF CHILDREN UNDER AGE 15, BY FAMILY ENVIRONMENT, 1990

Family environment	Age group					
	Under age 6		6–14		All ages	
	%		%		%	
Married couples	79.5	100.0	78.4	100.0	**78.8**	**100.0**
Intact families	68.4	86.1	65.7	83.7	**66.8**	**84.7**
Blended couples	6.0	7.6	4.2	5.4	**5.0**	**6.3**
Blended families	5.0	6.3	8.5	10.9	**7.1**	**9.0**
Couples living common law	9.3	100.0	6.7	100.0	**7.7**	**100.0**
Intact families	4.6	49.2	0.9	13.7	**2.4**	**30.9**
Blended couples	1.6	17.6	0.2	3.5	**0.8**	**10.2**
Blended families	3.1	33.2	5.5	82.7	**4.6**	**58.9**
Lone mothers	10.8	–	12.0	–	**11.6**	–
Lone fathers	0.4	–	2.9	–	**1.9**	–
Total	**100.0**	–	**100.0**	–	**100.0**	–
Number of cases	2,809	–	4,249	–	**7,058**	–

– nil or zero

Note: Percentages may not add to 100 due to rounding.

Source: 1990 GSS.

These categories do not cover all blended families, as some spouses may have children from a previous union who live elsewhere, for whom they are still responsible, and who occasionally come to live for awhile with their parent's new family. The advantage is that it fits neatly with the information provided by the census while supplementing it, so that a more accurate profile can be drawn of the family status of children at a given point in time.

Table 5.9 shows that 86.5% of children live in a two-parent family. Not all these families, however, are "traditional": the figure falls to 78.8% when only families where the couple is married are counted; 7.7% of children live in a two-parent family where the couple is living common law. Even more importantly, according to the 1990 GSS, only two-thirds (66.8%) of children live with parents married for the first time and with siblings born of the same union (intact family).

Nearly 1 in 10 children living with a married couple belongs to a blended family. For families formed around a common-law union, the proportion climbs to nearly 6 in 10 children, whether the couple consists of two single persons or includes a spouse who has previously been married. This already tells us that, although common-law union is chosen by more and more couples forming a new family, the children who live in this type of family environment are more often in a blended family than in an "intact" family. This is far more apparent among children aged 6 to 14 (82.7% versus 33.2% of those under age 6).

Common-law union has been chosen by young couples primarily as a way to begin their conjugal life. In the early 1980s, the number of "paperless" first unions rose rapidly, with half of young couples reporting in the 1984 Survey of Fertility in Canada (Balakrishnan et al. 1993) that they had lived together before marrying. Marriage, however, remained on the horizon, and when it came time to start a family and have children they did not hesitate to legalize the union. Since then, common law has become a form of union that also includes families, whether newly formed by young people or formed when older partners blend their existing family units. From the children's perspective, common-law union has therefore become an integral part of the family landscape.

Finally, the extent of the phenomenon of blended families can perhaps be more accurately assessed by taking into account the proportion of children living with a blended couple (a couple where at least one spouse has previously been married and all children in the household are of the current union). This is not to suggest that, although they may not be reported as living in the household at the time of data collection, children of a previous marriage of either spouse do not periodically intervene in the life of the household, at least in terms of economic or emotional support provided by the natural parent living there.

Moreover, the breakdown by age group reflects the effects of both the duration of the parents' union and the stages of the children's environment. Thus, more school-age children (aged 6 to 14) live in a lone-parent or blended family situation, while the youngest children (under age 6) are more likely to live in the context of a common-law union. These common-law unions will more often comprise intact families when the children are of preschool age, and blended families when the children are over age six.

On the whole, 12% of children under age 15 live in a blended family, while another 14% live in a lone-parent family (see Table 5.9). A further 6% have a sibling not living in the same household but with whom they share a natural parent. Section 5.4.7 attempts to uncover the hidden life courses of these children, which provide an even more accurate picture of the extent of the changes in family environment experienced by children today.

5.4.6 Composition of sibling relationships and the blended family

Various studies have shown the relationships between the fertility of couples and their fairly strong tendency to dissolve and blend family units. For example, it is known that, on average, couples that split up have slightly fewer children than stable couples, and the blended family often results in a greater number of sibling relationships than would otherwise be the case (Léridon and Villeneuve-Gokalp 1994).

From the children's perspective, the composition of sibling relationships is closely linked to the parents' marital history (see Figure 5.2). The previous section uses census data to provide a better estimate of the proportion of children raised in an intact family by a stable couple. This estimate can now be further refined. The results are shown in Figure 5.2: to the proportions of children living with a married couple observed in the census, we applied the fraction of these same children who were identified as children in a first stable marriage in the 1990 GSS.

The vertical white line shows, for each type of sibling relationship by number and by age of the children, the proportion of those living in a family defined as "intact." Children raised in the context of a first stable marriage are unlikely to be an only child and usually have siblings fairly close to them in age. Thus, only 58.4% of children under age six who are an only child grow up with both natural parents, who married once and are living together; the proportion drops to 41.1% among older children who are an only child (aged 6 to 14). Also, the blended family tends to encompass more sibling relationships and greater age differences. For example, only 55% of children raised in sibling relationships of three or more children, where the youngest was preschool-age and the oldest was over 15, can claim they have the same parents united in a first marriage. In contrast, children who are very close in age to their siblings, however many there may be, clearly belong more often to intact families.

5.4.7 Behind the census profile: the diversification of children's family paths

Previous sections show that, in addition to the census-based profile of the family context in which children live at a given point in time, we must rely on survey data to understand the new fluidity of the family life of children and to show the ever-increasing diversity of the episodes that make up their family paths.

Thus, the longitudinal retrospective view provided by the 1990 GSS shows that more and more children experience lone-parent families, and at an increasingly young age. By comparing children's situations according to the census with the information gathered by the 1990 GSS about the life courses leading to them, we gain a far better understanding of rapidly growing phenomena. This part of the analysis concludes with another illustration of the soundness of this approach.

Let us look, for example, at children born in the early 1980s, whose family life courses to age six are already known (Marcil-Gratton 1993). In the analyses based on the 1990 GSS data, the children studied were born over a three-year period, covering the generations born in 1981, 1982 and 1983. For purposes of comparison, those children who were aged six to eight at the time of the 1991 Census were identified from the Public Use Microdata File on Individuals. Although, on average, these two groups of children were separated by almost a year, their family situations at the time of data collection were similar enough to estimate that they had experienced similar life courses from birth until age six. This makes it possible to reveal to some extent the complexity of children's lives which, from the census data alone, appear rather uneventful.

Let us take a closer look at what the census tells us about the family environment of children aged six to eight and see how this information can be supplemented by data from the 1990 GSS (see Figure 5.3).

FIGURE 5.3

DISTRIBUTION OF CHILDREN AGED 6 TO 8, BY FAMILY ENVIRONMENT AND FAMILY PATH, 1990

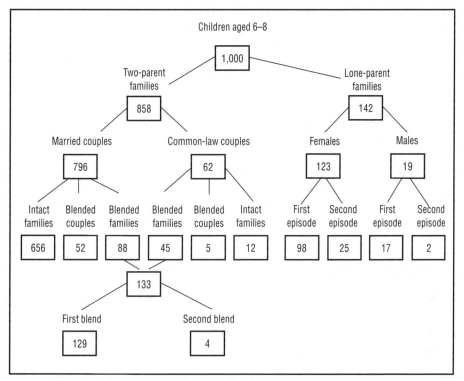

Source: Census of Canada, 1991, Individual Public Use Microdata Files; 1990 GSS, unpublished compilation.

Both sources confirm that, at the time of data collection, 86% of these children were living in a two-parent family, 9 in 10 times with married "parents" and 1 in 10 with common-law "parents." The remaining 14% were living in a lone-parent family: 12% of them with their mother and 2% with their father.

Figure 5.3 makes it possible to delve more deeply. First of all, among two-parent families, it distinguishes married couples from common-law couples; each of these two categories includes intact families, blended couples and blended families. The children belonging to this last category represent 13% of all children in this age group: two-thirds (88 of 133) come from blended families where the couple is married; the remaining third (45 of 133) come from a household where the couple is living common law.

The paths of these children, reconstituted from the 1990 GSS, can be extended even further. By age six, most of these children in a blended family had experienced just one blended family episode. Only 3% (4 out of 133) were already in their second such episode; that is, they had already seen their second family break up, experienced a second lone-parent family, and were in a third two-parent family environment. All of this by the age of six! One can only hope that the proportion of children that experience these record-setting paths grows no further!

A fair number of children in a lone-parent family also had multiple-episode paths behind them. At age six, one-fifth of children (27 out of 142) were in their second lone-parent family episode. This means they had experienced a first lone-parent family episode, either because they were born into it or because they had seen the dissolution of their natural parents' union, leading to a new union of the parent with whom they lived, and this new union also did not survive. All before age six.

This is just one example of the usefulness of relying on cross-sectional data on the family status of children, without losing sight of the paths travelled to get there. The phenomena responsible for the growing complexity of these life courses of children—the instability of couples, the fragility of "free union," the ease with which paperless unions are dissolved, and the swiftness with which new unions are formed—have continued to evolve toward a new flexibility of conjugal ties. In such a context, we must try to make all sources available for analysis more meaningful. This is a small price to pay to gain a better understanding of the direction of new trends in family life, from the perspective of both the adults who form families and of the children who grow up within these families.

5.5   CANADIAN DIVERSITY

Canadian society is very socially and culturally diverse, as shown by different behaviours in various regions of the country. When parents adopt different attitudes about conjugal life, this necessarily translates into differences in the family environment of children.

The spectacular increase in births outside of a union since the mid-1980s is no doubt one of the most widespread phenomena of new reproductive and family behaviours. In Canada, the proportion of births outside of a union rose from about 5% of all births in the 1960s to 10% in the early 1970s, then climbed to more than 20% in the early 1990s, peaking at 29% in 1993. These births, until 1974 referred to as "illegitimate," are now more appropriately termed "births outside of marriage." This new vocabulary corresponds with a new reality in the Canadian family landscape: the birth of children to unmarried parents, most of whom are living common law. This new reality is the most widespread in Quebec. In 1993, 46% of all births were classified as "outside of marriage," but in only 5% of cases the father was reported as "not known" on the birth certificate (Duchesne 1993). Analyses have shown that, in actual fact, these children born "outside of marriage" could unequivocally be classified as children born into a two-parent family (Marcil-Gratton 1993).

This appearance of common-law union in the family environment of children is the focus of Figure 5.4, which shows the relative magnitude of the phenomenon in the various regions of Canada. It is generally more common among younger children. This reflects both its recentness and the tendency of couples to marry eventually, something that happened fairly often in the late 1980s. The Atlantic and Prairie provinces and British Columbia do not differ appreciably, with about 8% of young children and 5% of older children living with unmarried parents. However, in Quebec, the Yukon and Northwest Territories, relatively more children live with parents who are in a common-law union, and this reality is clearly more striking among young children (under age six) (the figures are 20.1% and 24.5%, respectively). Ontario, however, is distinctly conservative, having the smallest proportions in Canada: 5.2% of children under age 6 and 3.9% of those aged 6 to 14. These differences reflect distinct cultural behaviours whose explanation exceeds the scope of this census monograph. It is worth mentioning, however, that the causes of these behaviours probably differ between Quebeckers and the Aboriginal peoples who make up much of the population of the Yukon and Northwest Territories; the ways of life of these peoples are quite different from each other and from those of other Canadians.

Finally, across all regions, a remarkable similarity can be seen in the number of children living in a lone-parent family at the time of the census. The proportion of these children increases with age, more markedly in Quebec and the Yukon and Northwest Territories. Everywhere, the vast majority of these children live with their mother, but the proportion living in male lone-parent families increases with age: only 1 in 10 children under age six in a lone-parent family lived with their father, while the figure is double, or one in five, for adolescents aged 15 to 17 (see Table 5.5B).

FIGURE 5.4

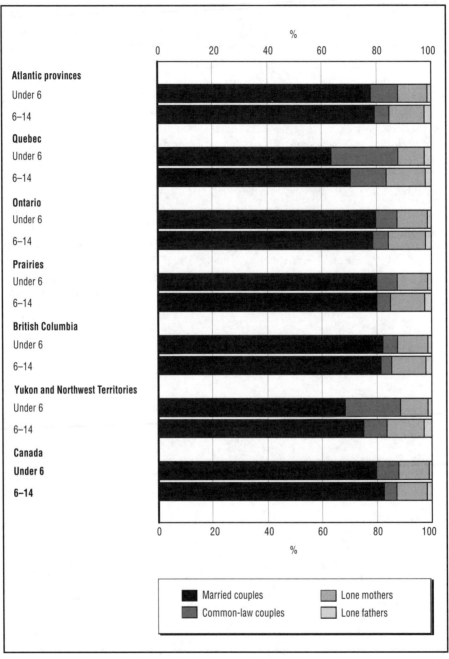

Source: Census of Canada, 1991, Family Public Use Microdata Files, unpublished compilation.

5.5.1 Common-law unions in Canada's regions: a means of forming or blending families?

Throughout Canada, most children (86%) are in two-parent families. Within these families, 14% of children are in a blended family and 7% live with both their parents who form a blended couple. There is a distinct possibility that there are other children outside the household who intermittently or regularly intervene in the life of their intact family (see Table 5.10).

TABLE 5.10

DISTRIBUTION OF CHILDREN UNDER AGE 15, BY PARENTS' MARITAL STATUS IN TWO-PARENT FAMILIES AND BY TYPE OF FAMILY, 1990

| | Parents' marital status | | | | | | | | |
| | Canada | | | Atlantic | | | Quebec | | |
Type of family	Married couples	All couples living common law	Two-parent families	Married couples	All couples living common law	Two-parent-families	Married couples	All couples living common law	Two-parent families
Intact families	84.7	30.9	79.9	82.5	14.9	78.9	88.4	47.1	81.3
Blended couples	6.3	10.2	6.6	5.5	12.6	5.9	2.9	6.8	3.6
Blended families	9.0	58.9	13.5	12.0	72.5	15.2	8.7	46.1	15.2
Total	**100.0**	**100.0**	**100.0**	**100.0**	**100.0**	**100.0**	**100.0**	**100.0**	**100.0**
Number of cases	5,564	546	6,110	551	31	582	1,257	263	1,520
% of all families	78.8	7.7	86.6	84.8	4.8	89.5	70.4	14.7	85.1
	Ontario			Prairies			British Columbia		
Intact families	85.7	7.3	81.0	82.2	27.2	78.7	80.3	21.2	76.2
Blended couples	7.6	23.3	8.5	6.5	3.5	6.3	9.2	3.3	8.8
Blended families	6.7	69.4	10.5	11.3	69.3	15.0	10.4	75.5	15.0
Total	**100.0**	**100.0**	**100.0**	**100.0**	**100.0**	**100.0**	**100.0**	**100.0**	**100.0**
Number of cases	2,011	128	2,139	1,120	77	1,197	625	47	672
% of all families	82.6	5.3	87.8	81.4	5.6	87.0	77.4	5.8	83.2

Note: Percentages may not add to 100 due to rounding.
Source: 1990 GSS.

This distribution of two-parent families hardly varies from region to region, except perhaps for Ontario where only 10% children live in a blended family, compared with about 15% children elsewhere in the country. This difference is somewhat reduced when considering that Ontario children in two-parent families are more likely to have a blended couple at the head of their household. It may be that, in Ontario, fewer blended families include children of previous marriages in the new household.

It should be recalled that about 1 in 10 two-parent families (13%) are headed by a common-law couple. However, the children in these families will usually have to fit in with half-brothers or half-sisters living in the same household. In fact, only 1 in 10 children (9.0%) belong to a blended family where the couple is married, compared with 6 in 10 (58.9%) where the couple is living common law (see Table 5.10).

The 1990 GSS did not provide a sufficiently large sample to allow for a closer analysis of regional differences in family behaviours, but it is possible, nonetheless, to look at the circumstances of entry into common-law union. There appears to be a marked difference between Quebec and the rest of Canada (see Table 5.10). In Quebec, common-law unions are more evenly distributed between intact families and blended families: there are as many children of common-law couples whose family is intact (47.1%) as there are in a blended family (46.1%). This reflects the increasingly evident phenomenon of young couples who choose to form a family and have children without legalizing their union through a civil or religious ceremony. In the rest of Canada, the tendency is clearly otherwise: couples who choose common-law union are far more likely to be about to merge into a second family, such that 7 in 10 children living with an unmarried couple belong to a blended family.

5.5.2 The increase in lone parenthood in Canada's regions

To conclude this outline of the regional differences in the family environment of children, we look at the 1990 GSS data to assess whether the phenomenon of lone parenthood is growing at the same rate for all Canadian children. Figure 5.5 echoes the results, reported for all of Canada in Figure 5.1, regarding the increasing frequency and early occurrence of lone parenthood among generations of young Canadians for the two largest regions, Quebec and Ontario. Overall, it too shows that the Canadian situation truly represents a midpoint between clear-cut regional diversities, with Quebec and Ontario at either pole.

On the whole, over a 30-year period, children in Canada's regions have experienced a growing frequency and early occurrence of the lone-parent family. Apart from this general observation, there are differences.

Some regions, such as British Columbia and Ontario, have a longer experience of divorce, with the result that children born in the early 1960s experienced a lone-parent family earlier and more often than children in Quebec, the Atlantic provinces or the Prairies born in the same period (see Table 5.11). Thus, nearly 30% of Ontario children of these generations, and more than 40% of those in British Columbia, experienced a lone-parent family before age 20, while for the corresponding generations in Quebec, the Atlantic provinces and the Prairies, the proportion was less than 20%.

FIGURE 5.5

CUMULATIVE PERCENTAGE OF CHILDREN IN QUEBEC AND ONTARIO WHO WERE BORN TO A
PARENT LIVING ALONE OR WHO SAW THEIR PARENTS SEPARATE

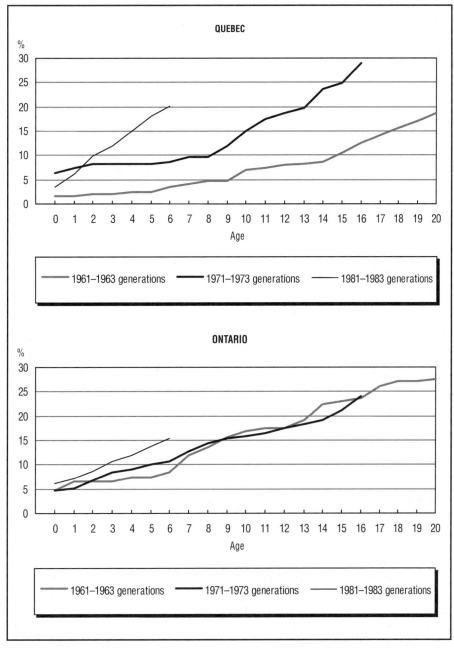

Source: 1984 Family History Survey, for the 1961–1963 generation; 1990 GSS for 1971–1973 and 1981–1983 generations, unpublished compilation.

FAMILY STATUS FROM THE CHILDREN'S PERSPECTIVE

TABLE 5.11

CUMULATIVE PERCENTAGE OF CHILDREN IN VARIOUS REGIONS OF CANADA WHO WERE BORN TO A
PARENT LIVING ALONE OR WHO SAW THEIR PARENTS SEPARATE BY AGE 6 AND BY AGE 20, 1990

Region	1981–1983 generations	1961–1963 generations	
	By age 6	By age 6	By age 20
Atlantic provinces	13.4	8.0	19.5
Quebec	20.1	3.5	18.8
Ontario	15.4	8.5	27.6
Prairie provinces	16.4	6.8	17.0
British Columbia	26.3	16.5	42.5
Canada	**18.1**	**7.8**	**24.2**

Source: 1990 GSS.

However, while the trends seem to have continued upward in British Columbia, they levelled off more quickly in Ontario. For the most recent generations observed (those of 1981 to 1983), children in British Columbia were most likely to experience a lone-parent family (26% before age six); children in Ontario and the Atlantic provinces were most likely to be spared the experience (15% and 13%, respectively, before age six).

Quebec stands apart because of the notable difference between the life course of children born 30 years ago and that of children born in the early 1980s. For the former, the lone-parent family was rarely a part of the family landscape, as they were born at a time when the Catholic church's teaching of the indissolubility of marriage was adhered to, like it or not. The latter belonged to the first generations for whom cohabitation became an acceptable context for having and raising children. The link has been shown elsewhere (Marcil-Gratton 1993; Le Bourdais and Marcil-Gratton 1996) between the growing incidence of cohabitation and the increasing fragility of marriages. The result, of course, has been a more fragile family environment for the children born of these unions. Today this link is strongest in Quebec.

5.6   CONCLUSION

In social demographics, the study of the impact of new adult family behaviours on the family environment of children is in the very early stages. Until recently, childhood *per se* had rarely been a subject of study, probably because once the perils linked to the mortality of infants and young children had been eliminated, modern society believed it had sheltered this part of human existence from the ups and downs of life. Children had only to concern themselves with growing up; their parents would provide the daily environment in which to do so properly, and society would lend a hand by providing them with an education to make them into tomorrow's productive citizens. But the last 30 years have seen very significant changes in adult behaviour related to fertility, conjugal life and labour force activity, which have radically altered the way in which parents, and therefore modern society, will care for children in future.

Specifically, growing marital instability and shorter unions are having a critical impact on the family environment of children. Whether through the declining popularity of marriage, the growing number of common-law unions, the higher incidence of separation, the greater number of lone-parent episodes, the incidence of blended families, or the growing phenomenon of families where both parents work outside the home, the disintegration of the "traditional" family unit significantly affects the daily living environment of children and their relationships with their parents. In future, the family paths of children should be studied separately from those of their parents, as family life no longer follows a single path from the union of the two parents until the death of one, as it did in the model that applied until the 1960s. The growing complexity of parents' lives necessarily translates into the growing complexity of their children's lives, perhaps to an even greater degree.

Today, childhood is the focus of several investigations in various countries by those who have recognized the need to adopt the child's perspective. Such initiatives have sprung up virtually everywhere and almost simultaneously, whether in the form of symposia (Festy 1994; Dandurand et al. 1996), publications (Le Bourdais and Marcil-Gratton 1994), or research projects gathering data on childhood in various societies (Furstenberg 1994). This chapter, and some sections of chapters 6 and 7, which dwell on the connections between the family environment of children and their living conditions, are a modest contribution to these initiatives. In addition, the Canadian government recently launched a major initiative focusing on children; within its scope, Human Resources Development Canada and Statistics Canada created the National Longitudinal Survey of Children and Youth. This survey will allow for a far more in-depth and meaningful analysis of the relationship between the evolution of the family environment of children and their personal development. These data, recently made available, will help answer the growing number of questions raised by the changes taking place in family life and their impact on child development.

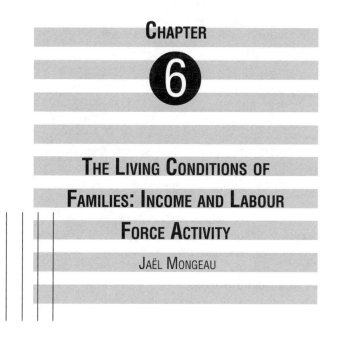

CHAPTER

6

THE LIVING CONDITIONS OF FAMILIES: INCOME AND LABOUR FORCE ACTIVITY

JAËL MONGEAU

Chapters 1 and 2 describe how the structure and composition of households and families have changed over the years. Among other trends, the studies presented in these chapters reveal that more and more census families and non-family persons are living alone (leading to the increased autonomy of households). Families are having fewer children, but children are living at home longer. Couples are opting increasingly for a common-law union before or instead of marriage. The increase in the number of union dissolutions has resulted in a larger proportion of lone-parent families and non-family persons. Common-law unions, less stable than unions sanctioned by marriage, have caused much of the increase of lone-parent families headed by a single parent.

These significant changes in households and families have taken place in the context of women's liberation. Women have benefited, first and foremost, from the democratization of education; thus, since 1981, in the 15-to-24 age group more women than men have completed postsecondary studies or have graduated from university.[1] They have flooded the labour market: of women aged 15 and older, 53% worked outside the home in 1991 compared with just 41% in 1975 (Statistics Canada 1994f). In the same period, the percentage of men dropped from 74% to 70%. Also, from 1970 to 1990, women's earnings rose appreciably more than those of men (Rashid 1991). Women have therefore played a part in helping families cope with the steady increase in the cost of living and unemployment. Since 1971, the rise in the cost of living has hit especially hard; prices were four times higher in 1991 than they were in 1971 (Statistics Canada 1995). And unemployment has continued to rise since the end of the war (Gera and McMullen 1991).

Of course, census data cannot be used to establish causal connections between living conditions and the structure and composition of households and families. Moreover, these connections can as easily go in either direction. To demonstrate this conundrum, take, for example, the connection between the decline in fertility and women's employment outside the home: Do women tend to work outside the home because they are having fewer children, or are they having fewer children because they work outside the home?

As these causal links cannot be determined, we instead look to the living conditions of households, families and family persons, who have experienced all of the changes referred to above. Have these changes improved the material well-being of all household and family types, or have they increased the disparities? Has the massive entry of women into the labour market brought the living conditions of single women (who have experienced the dissolution of a union and become lone mothers or non-family persons) into line with those of women who live with their partner? Are the living conditions of common-law couples the same as those of married couples?

This chapter looks at income and its links to labour force activity. The parents' labour force activities are also be considered from the children's perspective. This chapter is followed by a companion study that looks at the housing conditions of families.

6.1   HOUSEHOLD AND FAMILY INCOME

In the census, income data pertain to the calendar year preceding the census; for example, the 1991 Census reflects 1990 incomes. Total household income is the total of all incomes of all household members, and total family income is the total of all incomes of all family members. Thus the employment income of students who live with their parents is included in the total family income, even though quite often young peoples' income goes toward paying only some of their personal expenses and none of the family expenses. This should be kept in mind when interpreting the data on household and family income.

The average income of a Canadian household was $46,137 in 1990. This is about $5,200 less than the average family income ($51,342). The fact that families are better off than households is due to the different composition of households and families. As Chapter 1 shows, most non-family households are made up of persons living alone. On average, a one-person household has a lower income than a family, the latter quite often benefiting from two incomes—the husband's and the wife's. Thus, when only households consisting of more than one person are considered, the average household income climbs to $52,752.[2] This is greater than the average family income because, while most families live on their own and the household income is therefore the same as the family income, some families may cohabit with another family (multiple-family household) or with non-family persons, and this may help to raise the level of household income.

Figure 6.1 shows a general upward trend in income since 1960.[3] However, from 1970 to 1980 (there are no data on average household income for 1960), the average household income rose less than the average family income, although the evolution of both was virtually identical thereafter. The period 1970 to 1980 was a particularly favourable time for the formation of non-family households compared with the period that followed (see Chapter 1). As non-family households are composed mainly of persons who live alone, their greater number widens the gap between average household income and average family income. After 1980, the two curves show that average income suffered as a result of the recession in the early 1980s, dropping from 1980 to 1985 before rising again. Thanks to this recovery, the average income of households and families was higher in 1990 than in 1980, but income did not pick up its pre-1980 rate of increase such that the effects of the recession in the early 1980s were not completely offset. Family income dropped slightly less than household income between 1980 and 1985, and rose slightly more from 1985 to 1990. The higher proportion of wives on the labour market allowed family incomes to rise, at least in part, more than household incomes in the latter period. In fact, the proportion of wives holding paid employment rose from 56% in 1980 to 66% in 1990 (see Appendix 6, Table 6).

FIGURE 6.1

AVERAGE INCOME OF FAMILIES, OF MALES AND FEMALES, 1960 TO 1990, AND HOUSEHOLDS, 1970 TO 1990

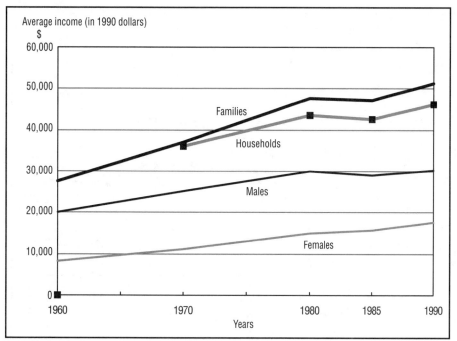

Note: The data for this figure are from Appendix 6, Table 1.
Source: Census of Canada, 1961, 1971, 1981, 1986 and 1991.

Figure 6.2 shows the difference in income between families and non-family persons, and by type of family (husband–wife family, male lone-parent family, and female lone-parent family). In 1990, as in 1960, husband–wife families fared best. In 1990, their average income was $55,000. Lone-parent families headed by a male earned only three-quarters of this amount, and those headed by a female received only half as much. Non-family men and women earned even less. Of course, husband–wife families have, on average, more members, so in principle their needs are greater. The same is true of lone-parent families compared with non-family persons. There are, however, *a priori*, no differences in the needs of lone fathers and lone mothers or even of non-family men and non-family women. Yet there is a considerable difference in the average incomes of these paired categories, and this difference is largely related to sex since men, on average, have higher incomes than women.

The classification of categories was identical in 1960 and 1990 but, over time, the gap widened between husband–wife families and lone-parent families, perhaps because more and more wives held paid employment. According to Dooley (1988), the growth in the incomes of husband–wife families is attributable to the increase in the employment income of wives and in income from government transfers. Also, generally speaking, women do not seem to have been hit as hard by the recession of the early 1980s:[4] the average income of lone mothers dropped less than that of their male counterparts, and the average income of non-family women even rose, though only slightly.

FIGURE 6.2

AVERAGE INCOME, BY TYPE OF FAMILY, **1960** TO **1990**

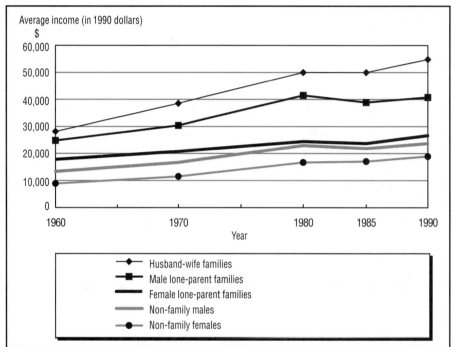

Note: The data for this figure are from Appendix 6, Table 1.
Source: Census of Canada, 1961, 1971, 1981, 1986 and 1991.

It is only after age 45 that the average income of female lone-parent families was higher than that of non-family persons (see Figure 6.3). At younger ages, that is, while these women were responsible for small children, their average income was lower than that of non-family persons, who, in principle, must provide only for themselves. Fewer lone mothers than non-family persons held paid employment: under age 45, 69% did so in 1990, only 54% worked full time, compared with 81% of non-family women (67% full time) and 84% of non-family men (75% full time).[5] Also, the jobs they held were less well paid; their average employment income was $12,025 compared with $13,834 for non-family women.[6] It is reasonable to think that lone mothers may have been more inclined than non-family persons to stop working; not only would they be inclined to stop working to have and be with children, but lone mothers may also have more possible sources of income to afford this step: widow's pensions, support payments from an ex-husband, full- or part-time employment of older children, and greater participation in the labour force because their children are older, as Section 6.3 shows. Children's income is included in family income, whether or not it is used to help pay family expenses, but it is reasonable to think it is more often used in this way in a lone-parent family, where it is needed, than in a husband–wife family.

There is a connection between the increase in average income by age (of the wife, lone parent or non-family person) and the presence of children in the home. When there are no children, that is, in the cases of husband–wife families with no children and of non-family men and women, average income is highest between ages 30 and 44. It then drops as labour force activity declines (see Table 6.1). In the case of husband–wife families, only 68% of husbands are in the labour market when their wife is aged 45 to 64, and only 16% when she is over age 64, while this is true of more than 90% of husbands when their wife is younger. The percentages are similar for non-family persons of both sexes. No doubt a generational effect is also at work: older persons have less schooling than younger persons. Thus, in 1991, 22% of the population aged 45 to 64 had not completed Grade 9, while this was true of just 5% of those aged 25 to 44. And only 11% of those aged 45 to 64 had graduated from university, compared with 16.5% of those aged 25 to 44.[7]

FIGURE 6.3

AVERAGE INCOME, BY TYPE OF FAMILY AND AGE OF WIFE, LONE PARENT OR NON-FAMILY PERSON, 1990

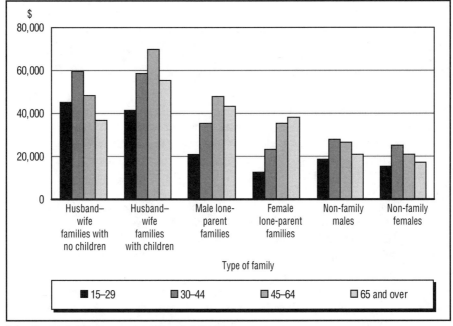

Note: The data for this figure are from Appendix 6, Table 2.

Source: Census of Canada, 1991, Family Public Use Microdata Files.

There is currently a strong link between educational attainment and income (Demers 1991), and since older persons have less schooling, fewer occupy high-income jobs. Another factor may also come into play in the case of women: even when they have the same schooling, they earn less than men (Statistics Canada 1994f). They have made progress in occupations that were virtually closed to them in the past, but older women have benefited less from this progress (Boulet and Lavallée 1984).

TABLE 6.1

PROPORTION OF HUSBANDS, WIVES AND NON-FAMILY PERSONS GAINFULLY EMPLOYED, BY AGE, 1990

			15–29	30–44	45–64	65 and older
				%		
Husband–wife families without children	Husbands		96.8	94.5	68.2	16.4
	Wives	Full-time	78.5	77.7	37.4	3.8
		Part-time	15.1	11.5	16.3	4.1
		Total	**93.7**	**89.1**	**53.7**	**7.9**
Husband–wife families with children	Husbands		95.5	96.4	85.6	22.7
	Wives	Full-time	48.9	53.2	47.1	7.0
		Part-time	22.2	24.5	20.1	4.0
		Total	**71.1**	**77.7**	**67.2**	**10.9**
Non-family	Males		88.9	88.6	68.2	14.0
	Females		87.4	88.2	58.4	5.6

Note: Families where one of the spouses was a non-permanent resident have been excluded, as have non-family persons who were non-permanent residents.

Source: Census of Canada, 1991, Family Public Use Microdata Files.

When children are present, that is, in the case of husband–wife families and lone-parent families, the average income continues to rise until age 64, and even beyond in the case of lone mothers. This difference is no doubt due to the fact that when parents are between the ages of 45 and 64, their children may hold part- or full-time paid employment. According to our estimates based on the 1991 Census Public Use Microdata File on Family, in husband–wife families with children, when the wife is aged 45 to 64, 18% of family income comes from the children's employment earnings, while this percentage is just 3% when the wife is aged 30 to 44. If only the income of the two spouses were counted as family income, average family income would be lower when the wife is aged 45 to 64 ($55,960) than when she is aged 30 to 44 ($56,929). The lower income observed among persons not living with their children is more than offset by the income contributed by children's employment.

At young ages, the difference in income according to whether children are present is the reverse for husband–wife families. When the wife is aged 15 to 29, the average family income is slightly lower when there are children present, probably because fewer of these wives hold paid employment (see Table 6.1). Seventy-one percent (71%) are gainfully employed, nearly one-third of them part time, compared with 94% of wives with no children, only 15% of whom work part time. Not only are the wives with children less likely to hold paid employment, but, when they do, it is also usually part-time. When the wife is aged 30 to 44, the family incomes of these two family types are the same, regardless of whether children are present. Wives with children are still less likely to hold paid employment than those with no children at home (see Table 6.1), but the difference is not as great as for the 15-to-29 age group. Also, as shown earlier, some children hold paid employment; their earnings help boost the family income to the level enjoyed by families with no children.

FIGURE **6.4**

AVERAGE INCOME OF HUSBAND–WIFE FAMILIES, BY WIFE'S AGE, TYPE OF UNION AND PRESENCE OF CHILDREN, **1990**

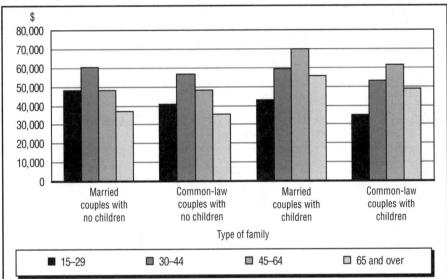

Note: The data for this figure are from Appendix 6, Table 2.
Source: Census of Canada, 1991, Family Public Use Microdata Files.

In 1990, the average income was lower for families of common-law spouses than for families of married spouses, particularly when there were children present (see Figure 6.4). The difference was about $7,000, regardless of the wife's age. When there were no children, married couples and common-law couples differed only before age 44. It is reasonable to think that some couples do not commit to marriage precisely because they feel they do not have the financial stability that stable employment brings. This does not, however, explain the difference in income when there are children: parenthood is a long-term commitment, whether or not the union is sanctioned by marriage. But we have learned that after divorce it is usually the mother who obtains custody of the children, and that she is not as likely as her ex-husband to remarry (Beaujot et al. 1995; Dumas and Bélanger 1996). We also know that common-law union is a phenomenon now seen in second unions formed after the failure of a first marriage, not just among young people beginning their conjugal life (see Chapter 3). It is therefore reasonable to think that the children in a common-law union are often from a previous marriage, and that parenthood came about in the context of a marriage. The rejection of long-term commitment might therefore also apply to some common-law couples living with children.

Lone-parent families can also be subdivided. The family income of lone mothers may well vary depending on their marital status, a once-married mother possibly having access to resources not available to the never-married mother, such as support payments if the husband is still living, her husband's life insurance benefits, or a widow's pension if the husband is deceased. But regardless of her marital status, on average, the lone mother has a lower income than the lone father (see Figure 6.5). Women generally earn less than men and lone mothers are not as likely as their male counterparts to be in the labour market, as shown in Section 6.4. Further, lone fathers seem to be employed more continuously than lone mothers, and their income is therefore more likely to increase. Very few fathers take paternity leave and probably fewer still quit their job to care for their children full time, even if they have sole custody. To our knowledge, no study has been done on the subject, but we observe that lone fathers, whose socio-economic situation is more favourable than that of lone mothers, can more easily reconcile parenthood and a career (Dulac 1993, p. 57).

FIGURE **6.5**

AVERAGE INCOME OF LONE-PARENT FAMILIES, BY LONE FATHER'S AGE AND LONE MOTHER'S AGE AND MARITAL STATUS, **1990**

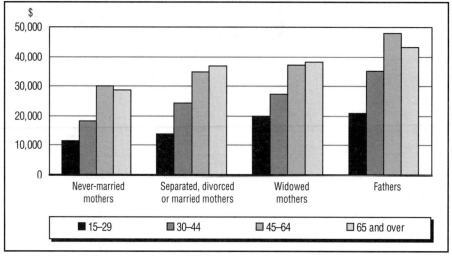

Note: The data for this figure are from Appendix 6, Table 2.
Source: Census of Canada, 1991, Family Public Use Microdata Files.

As might be expected, the single mother is at the bottom of the income ladder, regardless of her age. Up one rung is the mother who has previously been married, followed by the widowed lone mother. Income does not decline for these last two situations at age 65 and older, as it does for other single mothers and fathers, perhaps, at least in the case of widows, because of pensions and insurance.

Figure 6.6 shows the evolution of the source of family income by age of the lone parent. The highest proportion of income transfer is among lone parents aged 15 to 29, followed by those aged 60 and older. In each age group, lone-parent families receive more in government transfers when the parent is female than when he or she is male, regardless of the mother's marital status, but the difference by parent's sex is far greater in the 15-to-29 age group than in the other age groups. For single mothers in this age group, more than half the average income is from this source. The proportion of income transfer is highest among single mothers, except for the 45-to-64 age group which is replaced by widows. At ages 30 to 44 and 45 to 64, the parent's employment income is the main income source, except for widowed mothers aged 45 to 64. However, the older the parent, the more weight the children's employment income has among sources of family income. When the parent is over age 64, between 40% and 50% of family income comes from children's job earnings and the sources of income are thus more diversified. Therefore, as of ages 45 to 64, when children who still live with their parents are gainfully employed and contributing to the family income, the differences in sources of income by parent's sex and mother's marital status become less distinct.

Except at age 65 or older, the proportion of family income that comes from gainful employment is higher for male than for female lone-parent families, probably because, on average, men still earn more than women, and lone fathers are more likely to hold paid employment than lone mothers.

FIGURE 6.6

SOURCE OF INCOME OF LONE-PARENT FAMILIES, BY AGE OF LONE FATHER AND AGE AND MARITAL STATUS OF LONE MOTHER, 1990

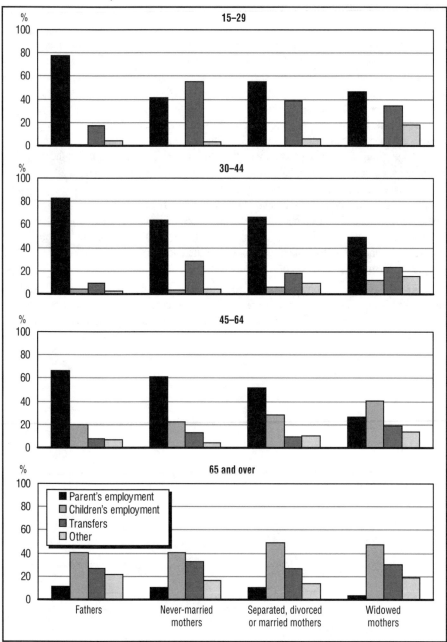

Note: The data for this figure are from Appendix 6, Table 3.

Source: Census of Canada, 1991, Family Public Use Microdata Files.

6.2   INCOME, LIFE CYCLE AND EMPLOYMENT

Precisely which husband–wife families are at the top of the income ladder? In Figure 6.7, husband–wife families in the first and fifth quintiles of family income are distributed by "life cycle," as defined in Chapter 2.[8] Over half (53%) of husband–wife families in the fifth quintile (the 20% of families with the highest incomes) are families with children where the wife is aged 35 to 54. The employment incomes of older husbands are higher than those of younger husbands. Probably more women work after age 35 than before, because their children are older and therefore more independent. Further, some of these older children may contribute to the family income. At the bottom of the income ladder, that is, in the first quintile (the 20% of families with the lowest incomes), one category dominates, though to a lesser degree than in the case of the fifth quintile, namely, families where the children have left home and the wife is aged 55 or older (36% of husband–wife families in the first quintile). It helps to explain here that this category dominates the first quintile because it is made up mainly of retired couples where the wife is older. In the first quintile, 61% of wives aged 55 and older were actually aged 65 and older, while this was true of only 39% of wives in the fifth quintile (Public Use Microdata File on Family). The second largest category, constituting 20% of the first quintile, is of families with children present where the wife is under age 35. The three largest categories alone—the third being families with children present where the wife is aged 35 to 54—account for nearly three-quarters (72%) of husband–wife families in the first income quintile. Husband–wife families are concentrated among the poorest when they are raising their children and after the children have left home to live on their own.

These observations concerning the connection between income and the life-cycle stage reached by families raise questions about the situation with respect to children, again from the perspective adopted in Chapter 5. Of the least affluent two-parent families (the first quintile in Figure 6.7), 39% have children. Of the most affluent families (the fifth quintile in Figure 6.7), 72% have children.

FIGURE **6.7**

COMPOSITION OF **1**ST AND **5**TH FAMILY INCOME QUINTILES AMONG HUSBAND–WIFE FAMILIES, **1990**

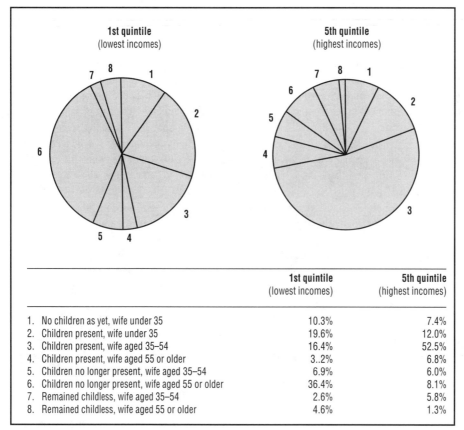

	1st quintile (lowest incomes)	5th quintile (highest incomes)
1. No children as yet, wife under 35	10.3%	7.4%
2. Children present, wife under 35	19.6%	12.0%
3. Children present, wife aged 35–54	16.4%	52.5%
4. Children present, wife aged 55 or older	3..2%	6.8%
5. Children no longer present, wife aged 35–54	6.9%	6.0%
6. Children no longer present, wife aged 55 or older	36.4%	8.1%
7. Remained childless, wife aged 35–54	2.6%	5.8%
8. Remained childless, wife aged 55 or older	4.6%	1.3%

Note: The data for this figure are from Appendix 6, Table 4.

Source: Census of Canada, 1991, Family Public Use Microdata Files.

One might therefore wonder how children are dispersed in terms of the income of their family. If all children under age 18 are considered, they are found to be fairly evenly distributed among the income quintiles (see Table 6.2). This distribution varies from one age group to another, children under age six are overrepresented in families in the first and second quintiles and therefore underrepresented in the fifth quintile. Similarly, those aged 15 to 17 are over-represented in the highest income quintiles and less numerous in the lowest income quintiles. These results are consistent with the connection observed between the parents' life cycle and income. When the children are small, the parents are young and their incomes lower; when the children reach adolescence, their parents are older, further along in their careers and earning higher incomes.

TABLE 6.2

CHILDREN UNDER AGE 18, BY AGE GROUP AND FAMILY INCOME QUINTILE,[1] 1990

	Income quintile					Total	Total
	1st	2nd	3rd	4th	5th	%	sample
Under 18	18.4	18.8	21.6	21.8	19.4	100.0	197,175
Under 6	21.4	20.7	22.9	20.6	14.6	100.0	66,337
6–14 years	17.6	18.4	21.6	22.3	20.1	100.0	99,518
15–17 years	14.6	16.0	19.2	23.0	27.2	100.0	31,321

1. Families have been classified by income in ascending order. Thus the 1st quintile represents the 20% of families with the lowest incomes.

Note: Figures may not add to 100 due to rounding.

Source: Census of Canada, 1991, Family Public Use Microdata Files.

It is also interesting to look at the distribution of children in families in different income quintiles according to their family environment as defined in Chapter 5. Figure 6.8 shows this distribution for the first and fifth quintiles. Note that the distribution of children under age 18 by family environment is as follows: 78.8% have married parents; 3.8% have parents living common law, one of whom has previously been married; 3.0% have parents living common law, both of whom have never been married; 3.1% have a never-married lone mother; 9.1% have an ever-married lone mother; and 2.2% have a lone father (see Table 5.4 of Chapter 5). In Figure 6.8, the contrast is striking. Of children whose family is in the first quintile (18.4% of children under age 18), fewer than half have parents who are married (44.1%); about the same percentage of children live in a lone-parent family with their mother. At the other end of the income ladder (19.4% of children under age 18), the picture is totally different, as virtually all parents of children in affluent families are legally married, the other family categories accounting for only very small proportions. The very diversified picture presented here for all children under age 18 does not vary according to the children's age.

It is also interesting to note that, while 18.4% of children live in families whose income is in the first quintile, this is true of only 10.3% of children whose parents are married. In contrast, this is the case for 84.5% of those living with their single mother; 60.4% of those living with their separated, divorced or widowed mother; and about 30% of those whose parents are single and living common law, or living with a lone father (Public Use Microdata File on Family). These observations shed light on the situation of children in the most precarious economic circumstances according to the type of family environment in which they live.

FIGURE 6.8

DISTRIBUTION OF CHILDREN UNDER AGE 18 WHOSE FAMILIES ARE IN THE 1ST AND 5TH INCOME QUINTILES, BY FAMILY ENVIRONMENT,[1] 1990

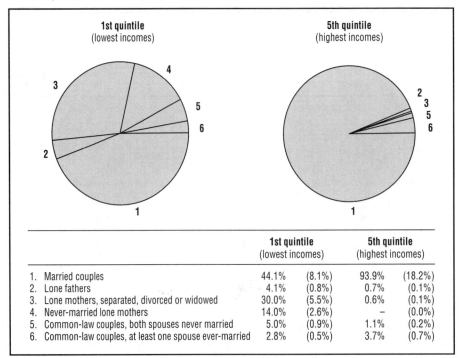

1st quintile (lowest incomes)

5th quintile (highest incomes)

		1st quintile (lowest incomes)		5th quintile (highest incomes)	
1.	Married couples	44.1%	(8.1%)	93.9%	(18.2%)
2.	Lone fathers	4.1%	(0.8%)	0.7%	(0.1%)
3.	Lone mothers, separated, divorced or widowed	30.0%	(5.5%)	0.6%	(0.1%)
4.	Never-married lone mothers	14.0%	(2.6%)	–	(0.0%)
5.	Common-law couples, both spouses never married	5.0%	(0.9%)	1.1%	(0.2%)
6.	Common-law couples, at least one spouse ever-married	2.8%	(0.5%)	3.7%	(0.7%)

– nil or zero

1. In brackets is the percentage each group represents of all children under age 18.

Source: Census of Canada, 1991, Family Public Use Microdata File.

At each life-cycle stage, the proportion of families where both spouses hold paid employment is higher in the fifth than in the first quintile (see Figure 6.9). To progress to the fifth income quintile, in nearly all young couples still without children both spouses must hold paid employment. The proportion of two employment incomes in the fifth income quintile is close to 90% for all other categories of couples where the wife is under age 55.

FIGURE 6.9

PROPORTION OF HUSBAND–WIFE FAMILIES WHERE BOTH SPOUSES ARE GAINFULLY EMPLOYED, BY LIFE CYCLE AND 1ST AND 5TH INCOME QUINTILES, 1990

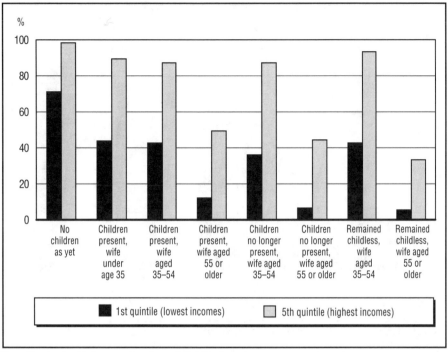

Note: The data for this figure are from Appendix 6, Table 4.

Source: Census of Canada, 1991, Family Public Use Microdata File.

From 1970 to 1990, the proportion of husband–wife families where both spouses held paid employment, whether full- or part-time, rose from 42% to 63%. This increase was seen in all regions of the country, such that in 1990 the proportion ranged from 58% in Quebec to 68% in the Prairies.[9] For Canada as a whole, it increased with each quintile in 1990, from 26% in the first to 83% in the fifth—and the nearer the fifth quintile, the faster the rate of increase (see Figure 6.10). In 1970, in just over half of husband–wife families, both spouses held paid employment in the fifth income quintile, narrowing the gap between the proportions of dual incomes in the first and fifth quintiles.

Also note that, in 1990, the proportion of children under age 18, both of whose parents were working, varied by income quintile: it went from 42.3% for the first quintile to 59.0% for the second, 70.5% for the third, 81.3% for the fourth, and 87.5% for the fifth, with no substantial variation in the trend from one age group to another (Public Use Microdata File on Family). Section 6.3 will show that family size has a decisive impact on the labour force activity of mothers.

FIGURE **6.10**

PROPORTION OF HUSBAND–WIFE FAMILIES WHERE BOTH SPOUSES ARE GAINFULLY EMPLOYED, BY FAMILY INCOME QUINTILE,[1] 1970, 1980 AND 1990

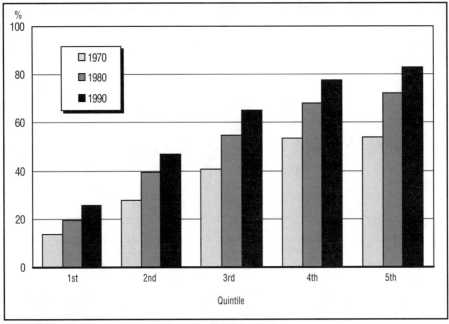

1. Families have been classified by income in ascending order. Thus the first quintile represents the 20% of families with the lowest incomes.

Note: The data for this figure are from Appendix 6, Table 5.

Source: Census of Canada, 1971, 1981 and 1991, special compilation.

6.3 WOMEN'S PAID EMPLOYMENT AND CHILDREN'S AGES

More and more wives hold paid employment, regardless of their children's age (see Figure 6.11). In 1990, even when there were three or more children in the family all under age six, about half of wives worked, whereas in 1970 only about one-fifth did.

In 1990, the proportion of wives who held paid employment was as high when there were two children as when there was just one child (about 80%), provided both were over age five (both aged 6 to 14, or one aged 6 to 14 and the other aged 15 or older). Mothers who leave the labour force when their second child is born probably do so only temporarily. When the family had three or more children at home, the mother was less likely to hold paid employment than when there were just two, age for age. However, once again it shows the deterrent effect of having at least one child under age six. About 75% of mothers with three or more children at home held paid employment when the youngest was aged 6 to 14 (either all children were in this age group or there were older brothers or sisters). However, this percentage drops to about 60% when the youngest was under age six but the family had one or more older children, and, finally, to about

50% when all children were under age six. The smaller proportion in the labour force of wives who had children under age six probably explains to some degree the difference in income noted earlier (see Figure 6.3) between families with children and those without when the wife is aged 15 to 29. However, this absence from the labour market and the resultant lower income are temporary for a good many families where the mother takes maternity leave for only a short time.

FIGURE 6.11

PROPORTION OF WIVES WHO ARE GAINFULLY EMPLOYED, BY NUMBER AND AGE OF CHILDREN UNDER AGE 16, 1970 AND 1990

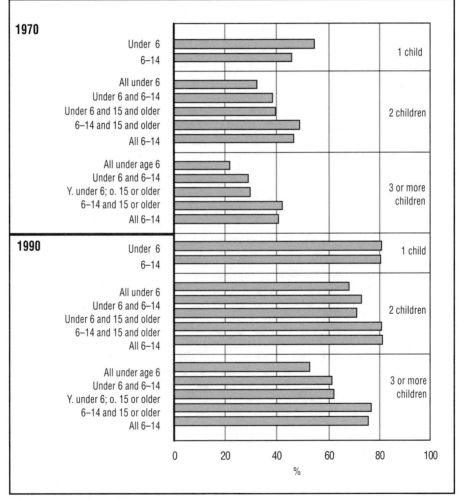

Note: Y. = youngest; o. = oldest.

The data for this figure are from Appendix 6, Table 6.

Source: Census of Canada, 1971, 1981 and 1991, Family Public Use Microdata Files.

In 1970, the difference by number of children and age was similar, except that the deterrent effect of the presence of children under age 6 extended also to the presence of children aged 6 to 14. Thus, while in 1990, as many wives were in the labour market whether their only child was under age 6 or aged 6 to 14, in 1970 fewer were in the market when their child was aged 6 to 14 than when the child was under age 6. Also in 1970, the proportion of mothers of two children aged 6 to 14 who held paid employment was smaller than that of mothers of two children, one of which was aged 6 to 14 and the other age 15 or older, while in 1990 the proportions were the same.

There is a connection between the presence in the family of children aged 15 and older and a higher proportion of mothers in full-time paid employment among all those employed (see Figure 6.12). Thus, in 1990, in families with two children, the proportion of mothers working, especially full time, was higher in families where one of the children was aged 15 or older, regardless of whether the other child was under age 6 or aged 6 to 14, than in families where both children were under age 15, regardless of the ages of the two children (both under age 6, both aged 6 to 14, or one under age 6 and the other aged 6 to 14). The same phenomenon occurs in larger families. In all likelihood, the mother can count on an older child to look after one or more younger ones until she gets home from work.

A slightly higher proportion of wives held full-time paid employment in 1990 than in 1970, particularly when there was at least one child aged 15 or older at home. The proportion who were working part time, however, gained ground among mothers with three or more children, all under age 6 or aged 6 to 14, and, though very slightly, among mothers with at least one child under age 6.

Generally speaking, lone mothers were more inclined to hold paid employment than wives in 1970, while the opposite was true in 1990 (see Figure 6.13). This explains the growing gap between the income of husband–wife families and that of lone-parent families, as suggested in the comments about Figure 6.2. However, the proportion of lone mothers holding paid employment increased from 1970 to 1990. The difference between wives and lone mothers in 1990 was not very great when all children were over age five. It was, however, considerably greater when all children were under age six. For example, lone mothers held paid employment in just slightly more than 60% of cases when they had one child under age 6, and in 75% of cases when their only child was aged 6 to 14, whereas 80% of wives were active in the labour force in both cases. If lone mothers with young children held paid employment less often than wives with young children, it was perhaps because a number of them, particularly those who were single, quit school at an early age because they were pregnant, and their lack of schooling and experience (Crompton 1994) therefore made it difficult for them to get jobs that paid well enough to adequately cover the costs related to employment (such as day-care costs).

FIGURE 6.12

WIVES WORKING MOSTLY FULL TIME AS A PROPORTION OF ALL WIVES WHO ARE GAINFULLY
EMPLOYED, BY NUMBER AND AGE OF CHILDREN, 1970 AND 1990

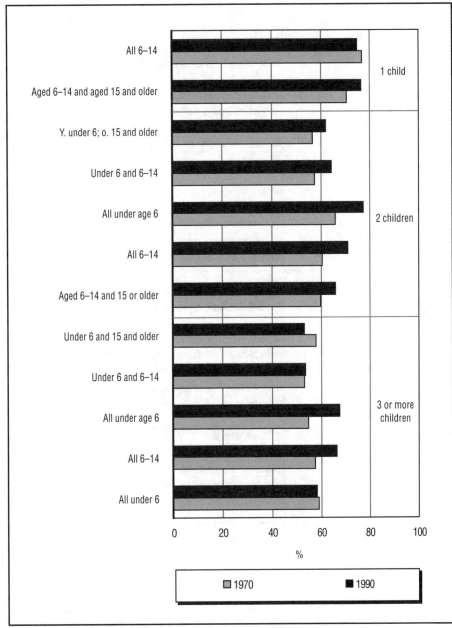

Note: Y. = youngest; o. = oldest.

The data for this figure are from Appendix 6, Table 6.

Source: Census of Canada, 1971, 1991, Family Public Use Microdata Files.

FIGURE 6.13

PROPORTION OF WIVES AND LONE MOTHERS WHO HAVE CHILDREN UNDER AGE 16 AND ARE
GAINFULLY EMPLOYED, BY NUMBER AND AGE OF CHILDREN, 1970 AND 1990

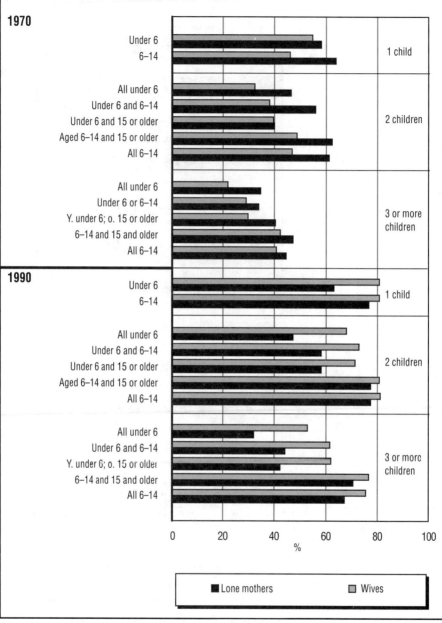

Notes: Y. = youngest; o. = oldest.

Data for this figure are from Appendix 6, Tables 6 and 7.

Source: Census of Canada, 1971, 1981 and 1991, Family Public Use Microdata Files.

The increased employment of mothers is undeniably one of the factors that has most significantly altered the context in which children are raised; while showing the percentage of wives and lone mothers who are gainfully employed, Figure 6.13 reveals the percentage of children affected by their mother's labour force activity by characteristics of their sibling relationships. Studies based on the data of 1990 General Social Survey, cycle 5: Family and Friends (GSS) show that besides having two parents who work, more than 50% of young children of two-parent families have at least one parent who works outside regular hours. Consequently, these children, like their parents, must face "family time" that is often infringed upon by the parents' work. There is no need to draw attention to the many strategies parents must devise to ensure their young children are properly cared for (Lapierre-Adamcyk and Marcil-Gratton 1995).

FIGURE 6.14

GAINFUL EMPLOYMENT OF HUSBANDS, LONE FATHERS AND LONE MOTHERS, BY AGE, 1990

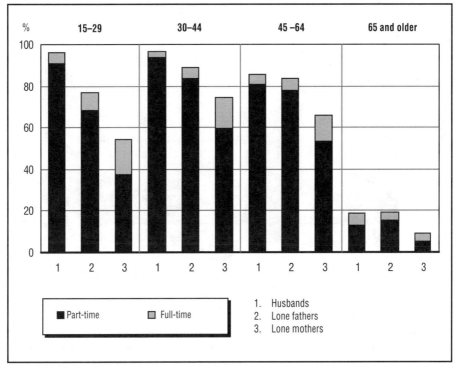

Note: The data for this figure are from Appendix 6, Table 8.

Source: Census of Canada, 1991, Family Public Use Microdata Files.

6.4 LONE FATHERS AND EMPLOYMENT

Chapter 1 reveals that lone fathers are more inclined to live with other persons than are lone mothers. Thus, they are more inclined than lone mothers to be gainfully employed, since they have someone at home to look after the children while they are at work. Furthermore, they are more likely than their female counterparts to be employed full time (see Figure 6.14). However, the proportion of lone fathers who are gainfully employed is smaller than the proportion of husbands who are. But the difference among those aged 45 to 64 when the children are grown is negligible. It is reasonable to think that it is easier for fathers than mothers to have paid employment because the children in their custody are, on average, older, while the care of younger children is more often entrusted to the mother. Of lone parents aged 30 to 44, the proportion of males who hold paid employment does not decline when there are children under age six (see Figure 6.15). Only for females does this proportion drop appreciably when the lone parent has custody of at least one child under age six.

FIGURE 6.15

GAINFUL EMPLOYMENT OF LONE PARENTS AGED 30 TO 44, BY SEX AND PRESENCE OF CHILDREN UNDER AGE 6, 1990

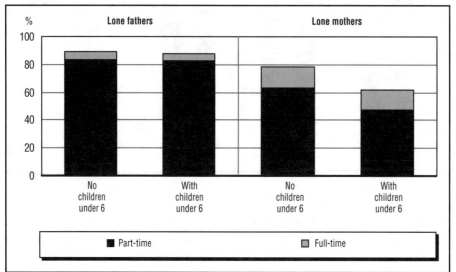

Note: The data for this figure are from Appendix 6, Table 8.

Source: Census of Canada, 1991, Family Public Use Microdata Files.

6.5   CONCLUSION

In recent decades, the proportion of persons living as part of a legally married couple has gradually diminished as three factors converge: the declining popularity of legal marriage, the growing number of divorces, and the increase in male mortality as the population ages. However, husband–wife families where the spouses are legally married, on average, rank at the top of the income ladder. And the income gap between husband–wife families with children and lone-parent families is widening. When lone parents are young, their average income is even lower than that of non-family persons of the same sex and age.

Although, in general, women still earn less than men, whether they are gainfully employed often accounts for the difference in income between family types. Husband–wife families were not as hard hit by the recession in the early 1980s as were male lone-parent families or non-family males, at least partly because women in husband–wife families had paying jobs—that is, because there were two incomes for this family type. The income gap widened from 1970 to 1990 between husband–wife families and lone-parent families because women in husband-wife families were more likely than lone mothers to hold paid employment in 1990, while the opposite was true in 1970. And the more likely it is for a woman to hold paid employment, the greater are the family's chances of being in the highest income quintile.

The different comparisons made in this chapter show the extent to which male–female differences in income and employment determine the material well-being of households and families.

ENDNOTES

1. See the 1991 Census of Canada, *Educational Attainment and School Attendance,* in Statistics Canada Catalogue no. 93-328, Table 1.
2. Estimate based on the 1991 Census of Canada, *Selected Income Statistics,* in Catalogue no.93-331, Table 8.
3. Note that income is always expressed in 1990 dollars for purposes of comparison.
4. See also Rashid (1991).
5. See the 1991 Census Public Use Microdata File on Family.
6. Ibid.
7. See the 1991 Census of Canada, *Educational Attainment and School Attendance,* in Catalogue 93-328, Table 2.
8. Families as yet without children (wife under age 35); families with children present (by wife's age, under age 35, aged 35–54 and 55 and older); families where there are no longer children present (by wife's age, 35–54 and 55 and older); families that have remained childless (by wife's age, 35–54 and 55 and older).
9. Information taken from a special compilation based on the Census of Canada for the years 1971, 1981 and 1991.

APPENDIX 6

TABLE 1

AVERAGE INCOME OF FAMILIES, BY TYPE; OF NON-FAMILY PERSONS, BY SEX; OF MALES, FEMALES AND HOUSEHOLDS, 1960 TO 1990

Type of family	1960	1970	1980	1985	1990
			In 1990 dollars ($)		
Husband-wife families	28,246	38,386	50,123	50,068	54,667
Male lone-parent families	24,692	30,270	41,333	38,902	40,792
Female lone-parent families	17,648	20,820	24,523	23,871	26,550
All families	**27,470**	**37,006**	**47,566**	**47,087**	**51,342**
Non-family males	13,216	16,841	22,931	22,028	23,669
Non-family females	8,839	11,540	16,509	17,035	18,892
Males	20,164	25,203	30,085	28,960	30,205
Females	8,325	11,113	14,963	15,703	17,577
Households	..	36,094	43,497	42,648	46,137

.. figures not available.

Source: Census of Canada, 1961, 1971, 1981, 1986 and 1991; Census of Canada, 1971, Individual Public Use Microdata Files; Census of Canada, 1981 and 1991, Family Public Use Microdata Files.

TABLE 2

AVERAGE INCOME, BY TYPE OF FAMILY, MARITAL STATUS AND AGE OF WIFE, LONE PARENT OR NON-FAMILY PERSON, CANADA, 1990

Type of family	Marital status	15–29	30–44	45–64	65 and older	All ages
			in 1990 dollars ($)			
Husband–wife families with no children	Married couple	48,409	60,376	48,189	36,986	**46,653**
	Common-law couple	40,807	56,820	47,969	35,551	**46,424**
	Total	**45,157**	**59,332**	**48,175**	**36,957**	**46,615**
Husband–wife families with children	Married couple	42,887	59,126	70,127	55,371	**59,750**
	Common-law couple	34,802	52,971	61,573	48,837	**46,788**
	Total	**41,360**	**58,670**	**69,917**	**55,338**	**58,737**
Husband–wife families	Married couple	45,323	59,455	59,223	38,909	**54,936**
	Common-law couple	38,832	54,691	51,544	35,875	**46,625**
	Total	**43,359**	**58,934**	**58,873**	**38,854**	**53,998**
Male lone-parent families	Never married	17,034	28,101	27,254[1]	--	**24,697**
	Separated, divorced or married	23,654	35,809	47,865	40,249	**40,773**
	Widowed	--	36,766	51,212	44,881	**46,623**
	Total	**20,803**	**35,135**	**47,813**	**43,314**	**40,716**
Female lone-parent families	Never married	11,339	18,157	29,958	28,829	**15,525**
	Separated, divorced or married	13,934	24,385	34,725	36,961	**26,304**
	Widowed	19,867[1]	27,463	37,143	38,195	**36,453**
	Total	**12,437**	**23,405**	**35,442**	**37,955**	**26,616**
Non-family males	Never married	18,655	27,471	24,047	20,446	**22,269**
	Separated, divorced or married	20,533	29,112	28,229	21,148	**26,855**
	Widowed	12,276[1]	31,049[1]	27,654	21,199	**22,456**
	Total	**18,802**	**28,100**	**26,687**	**20,993**	**23,669**
Non-family females	Never married	15,173	26,913	25,403	21,468	**20,559**
	Separated, divorced or married	15,745	22,683	19,310	15,268	**19,140**
	Widowed	10,231[1]	19,799	19,086	16,609	**17,058**
	Total	**15,206**	**25,338**	**20,717**	**17,029**	**18,892**

-- Percentage omitted (fewer than 10 cases in the sample).

1. Fewer than 100 cases in the sample.

Note: Husbands, wives, lone parents and non-family persons who are non-permanent residents are excluded.

Source: Census of Canada, 1991, Family Public Use Microdata Files.

TABLE 3

INCOME COMPOSITION OF LONE-PARENT FAMILIES, BY AGE OF LONE FATHER AND AGE AND MARITAL STATUS OF LONE MOTHER, CANADA, 1990

Type of family	Marital status	Source of income	15–29	30–44	45–64	65 and older
					%	
Lone fathers	Total	Parent's employment	77.8	82.9	66.2	11.6
		Children's employment	0.9	4.5	19.8	40.7
		Transfers	17.2	9.6	7.5	26.4
		Other	4.1	3.0	6.6	21.3
		Total	**100.0**	**100.0**	**100.0**	**100.0**
Lone mothers	Never married	Parent's employment	41.1	63.9	61.1	10.1[1]
		Children's employment	0.0	3.1	22.2	40.7[1]
		Transfers	55.2	28.6	12.8	33.1[1]
		Other	3.6	4.5	3.9	16.1[1]
		Total	**100.0**	**100.0**	**100.0**	**100.0**
	Separated, divorced or married	Parent's employment	54.9	66.7	52.0	10.5
		Children's employment	0.0	6.2	28.2	49.4
		Transfers	38.8	17.7	9.7	26.6
		Other	6.3	9.3	10.1	13.5
		Total	**100.0**	**100.0**	**100.0**	**100.0**
	Widowed	Parent's employment	46.8	48.9	26.9	3.3
		Children's employment	0.7	12.0	40.7	47.2
		Transfers	34.6	23.4	18.9	30.4
		Other	17.9	15.7	13.5	19.1
		Total	**100.0**	**100.0**	**100.0**	**100.0**

1. Fewer than 100 cases in the sample.

Note: Percentages may not add to 100 due to rounding.

Parents who are non-permanent residents have been excluded.

Source: Census of Canada, 1991, Family Public Use Microdata Files.

Table 4

Husband–Wife Families, by Gainful Employment of the Spouse, Life Cycle, Wife's Age and Family Income Quintile,[1] 1990

Life cycle	Employment of spouses	Income quintile					
		1st	2nd	3rd	4th	5th	Total
No children	Husband only	14.7	7.6	3.9	1.6	1.3	**5.3**
as yet, wife	Wife only	6.8	2.4	1.3	0.5	0.4	**2.0**
under 35	Both spouses	71.0	89.5	94.6	97.9	98.2	**91.4**
	Neither spouse	7.5	0 5	0 2	0.1	0.1	**1.3**
	Total (%)	**100.0**	**100.0**	**100.0**	**100.0**	**100.0**	**100.0**
	Total (N)	**101,833**	**137,833**	**169,066**	**163,000**	**105,167**	**676,899**
Children	Husband only	37.4	33.6	24.5	14.6	10.2	**24.3**
present, wife	Wife only	5.0	2.1	0.8	0.4	0.2	**1.5**
under 35	Both spouses	44.1	63.1	74.5	84.9	89.4	**71.8**
	Neither spouse	13.5	1.2	0.3	0.1	0.2	**2.4**
	Total (%)	**100.0**	**100.0**	**100.0**	**100.0**	**100.0**	**100.0**
	Total (N)	**194,000**	**307,766**	**353,800**	**309,500**	**171,133**	**1,336,199**
Children	Husband only	29.6	31.6	26.8	17.3	11.6	**19.9**
present,	Wife only	7.7	5.7	3.1	1.6	0.8	**2.6**
wife 34–55	Both spouses	42.9	58.9	68.7	80.4	87.2	**75.0**
	Neither spouse	19.9	3.9	1.3	0.7	0.4	**2.5**
	Total (%)	**100.0**	**100.0**	**100.0**	**100.0**	**100.0**	**100.0**
	Total (N)	**162,400**	**271,566**	**415,466**	**556,099**	**746,166**	**2,151,698**
Children	Husband only	19.8	22.3	27.8	28.6	27.6	**26.1**
present,	Wife only	5.1	7.9	9.0	8.8	6.2	**7.5**
wife 55	Both spouses	12.0	17.2	22.0	32.5	49.4	**30.8**
or older	Neither spouse	63.2	52.7	41.2	30.2	16.8	**35.5**
	Total (%)	**100.0**	**100.0**	**100.0**	**100.0**	**100.0**	**100.0**
	Total (N)	**31,500**	**57,867**	**61,767**	**72,967**	**97,000**	**321,100**
Children	Husband only	22.9	28.3	24.0	13.6	10.5	**19.5**
no longer	Wife only	11.1	10.2	5.3	2.9	1.8	**5.9**
present,	Both spouses	36.4	54.9	67.8	82.5	87.0	**67.3**
wife 35–54	Neither spouse	29.7	6.6	2.9	1.1	0.8	**7.2**
	Total (%)	**100.0**	**100.0**	**100.0**	**100.0**	**100.0**	**100.0**
	Total (N)	**68,767**	**80,100**	**86,300**	**91,767**	**85,767**	**412,700**
Children no	Husband only	9.8	18.2	24.0	25.6	25.8	**18.0**
longer present,	Wife only	3.9	7.4	8.2	7.8	4 6	**6.1**
wife 55	Both spouses	6.5	12.6	24.2	34.0	44.6	**18.3**
or older	Neither spouse	79.8	61.8	43.6	32.6	25.0	**57.7**
	Total (%)	**100.0**	**100.0**	**100.0**	**100.0**	**100.0**	**100.0**
	Total (N)	**361,066**	**304,833**	**176,900**	**121,033**	**114,633**	**1,078,466**

Canadian Families at the Approach of the Year 2000

TABLE 4 (CONCLUDED)

HUSBAND–WIFE FAMILIES, BY GAINFUL EMPLOYMENT OF THE SPOUSE, LIFE CYCLE, WIFE'S AGE AND FAMILY INCOME QUINTILE,[1] 1990

Life cycle	Employment of spouses	Income quintile					
		1st	2nd	3rd	4th	5th	Total
Remained	Husband only	23.7	21.6	14.1	6.1	3.8	**10.7**
childless,	Wife only	9.2	9.7	6.3	3.4	2.2	**5.0**
wife	Both spouses	42.9	63.5	78.8	89.9	93.6	**80.6**
35–54	Neither spouse	24.3	5.1	0.8	0.7	0.4	**3.8**
	Total (%)	**100.0**	**100.0**	**100.0**	**100.0**	**100.0**	**100.0**
	Total (N)	**25,500**	**32,533**	**43,533**	**54,767**	**82,867**	**239,200**
Remained	Husband only	9.5	16.9	23.1	20.6	20.7	**16.7**
childless,	Wife only	2.9	5.8	6.5	8.9	6.5	**5.5**
wife 55	Both spouses	5.6	9.5	13.7	24.6	33.1	**14.0**
or older	Neither spouse	81.9	67.9	56.6	46.0	39.7	**63.9**
	Total (%)	**100.0**	**100.0**	**100.0**	**100.0**	**100.0**	**100.0**
	Total (N)	**45,600**	**38,800**	**25,500**	**20,233**	**18,033**	**148,167**

1. Families have been classified by income in ascending order. Thus, the first quintile represents the 20% of families with the lowest incomes.

Note: Percentages may not add to 100 due to rounding. Parents who are non-permanent residents have been excluded.

Source: Census of Canada, 1991, Family Public Use Microdata Files.

TABLE 5

HUSBAND–WIFE FAMILIES WHERE BOTH SPOUSES ARE GAINFULLY EMPLOYED, BY FAMILY INCOME QUINTILE,[1] 1970, 1980, 1990

		1st	2nd	3rd	4th	5th	Sum	Total[2]
		Number						
Husband	1970	109,545	253,615	384,705	545,535	497,385	1,790,785	..
and	1980	177,110	434,290	651,955	819,180	863,940	2,946,475	**2,946,505**
wife	1990	254,070	581,820	892,345	1,069,740	1,164,420	3,962,395	**3,962,425**
Total	1970	**790,045**	**913,455**	**943,575**	**1,016,065**	**921,900**	**4,585,040**	..
	1980	**900,200**	**1,105,015**	**1,186,800**	**1,205,860**	**1,197,570**	**5,595,445**	**5,611,445**
	1990	**982,250**	**1,240,430**	**1,368,755**	**1,380,235**	**1,406,450**	**6,378,120**	**6,402,095**
Husband and	1970	13.9	27.8	40.8	53.7	54.0	39.1	..
wife as percent-	1980	19.7	39.3	54.9	67.9	72.1	52.7	**52.5**
age of the total	1990	25.9	46.9	65.2	77.5	82.8	62.1	**61.9**

.. figures not available

1. Families have been classified by income in ascending order. Thus, the first quintile represents the 20% of families with the lowest incomes.

2. Including no income.

Source: Census of Canada, 1971, 1981, 1991, special compilation.

THE LIVING CONDITIONS OF FAMILIES: INCOME AND LABOUR FORCE ACTIVITY

TABLE 6
GAINFUL EMPLOYMENT OF THE WIFE, BY NUMBER AND AGE OF CHILDREN, 1970, 1980, 1990

Number of children	Children's age	Wife's employment	1970	1980	1990
No children		Full-time	37.1	42.3	43.7
		Part-time	9.6	11.5	12.3
		Not employed	53.3	46.2	44.0
		Total (%)	**100.0**	**100.0**	**100.0**
		Total (N)	**1,439,500**	**2,012,709**	**2,555,497**
1 child	Under 6	Full-time	42.0	50.8	60.4
		Part-time	12.7	19.2	20.3
		Not employed	45.3	30.0	19.3
		Total (%)	**100.0**	**100.0**	**100.0**
		Total (N)	**390,100**	**459,086**	**461,866**
	6–14	Full-time	32.5	47.8	61.6
		Part-time	13.5	18.8	19.1
		Not employed	54.0	33.4	19.4
		Total (%)	**100.0**	**100.0**	**100.0**
		Total (N)	**174,300**	**220,094**	**253,033**
	15 and older	Full-time	30.5	32.2	45.2
		Part-time	15.2	16.6	17.1
		Not employed	54.3	51.2	37.7
		Total (%)	**100.0**	**100.0**	**100.0**
		Total (N)	**305,600**	**510,635**	**660,366**
2 children	All under 6	Full-time	18.3	27.6	42.2
		Part-time	14.2	23.4	25.8
		Not employed	67.5	49.0	32.0
		Total (%)	**100.0**	**100.0**	**100.0**
		Total (N)	**248,000**	**311,451**	**303,900**
	Under 6; aged 6–14	Full-time	21.8	30.9	46.7
		Part-time	16.4	23.5	26.1
		Not employed	61.8	45.6	27.2
		Total (%)	**100.0**	**100.0**	**100.0**
		Total (N)	**177,300**	**266,103**	**273,666**
	Y. under 6; o. 15 or older	Full-time	26.1	34.6[1]	55.1
		Part-time	13.5	21.4[1]	16.1
		Not employed	60.5	44.1[1]	28.8
		Total (%)	**100.0**	**100.0**	**100.0**
		Total (N)	**11,900**	**7,421**	**10,533**

TABLE 6 (CONTINUED)

GAINFUL EMPLOYMENT OF THE WIFE, BY NUMBER AND AGE OF CHILDREN, 1970, 1980, 1990

Number of children	Children's age	Wife's employment	1970	1980	1990
2 children	All 6–14	Full-time Part-time Not employed	28.1 18.6 53.3	37.3 26.0 36.7	53.5 27.8 18.7
		Total (%)	**100.0**	**100.0**	**100.0**
		Total (N)	**213,200**	**344,044**	**404,533**
	6–14; 15 and older	Full-time Part-time Not employed	29.2 19.7 51.2	37.8 24.0 38.2	57.5 23.2 19.4
		Total (%)	**100.0**	**100.0**	**100.0**
		Total (N)	**161,800**	**208,188**	**242,500**
	All 15 and older	Full-time Part-time Not employed	31.0 18.8 50.2	39.0 20.5 40.5	54.6 19.7 25.7
		Total (%)	**100.0**	**100.0**	**100.0**
		Total (N)	**163,600**	**306,655**	**404,066**
3 or more children	All under 6	Full-time Part-time Not employed	12.6 9.3 78.2	14.8 19.6 65.6	28.0 24.7 47.3
		Total (%)	**100.0**	**100.0**	**100.0**
		Total (N)	**50,800**	**40,376**	**42,433**
	Under 6 and 6–14	Full-time Part-time Not employed	15.4 13.6 71.0	21.8 21.6 56.5	32.7 28.8 38.6
		Total (%)	**100.0**	**100.0**	**100.0**
		Total (N)	**379,300**	**241,076**	**249,666**
	Y. under 6; o. 15 or older	Full-time Part-time Not employed	16.2 13.5 70.3	23.1 19.3 57.6	41.8 20.3 38.0
		Total (%)	**100.0**	**100.0**	**100.0**
		Total (N)	**161,600**	**50,746**	**45,733**
	6–14 and 15 and older	Full-time Part-time Not employed	24.3 18.0 57.7	32.5 23.3 44.2	51.0 25.8 23.3
		Total (%)	**100.0**	**100.0**	**100.0**
		Total (N)	**455,700**	**364,566**	**238,266**

TABLE 6 (CONCLUDED)

GAINFUL EMPLOYMENT OF THE WIFE, BY NUMBER AND AGE OF CHILDREN, 1970, 1980, 1990

Number of children	Children's age	Wife's employment	1970	1980	1990
3 or more children	All	Full-time	24.0	32.3	43.9
	6–14	Part-time	16.7	24.6	31.7
		Not employed	59.4	43.2	24.4
		Total (%)	**100.0**	**100.0**	**100.0**
		Total (N)	**164,900**	**111,917**	**107,400**
	All	Full-time	30.2	33.7	50.4
	15 and	Part-time	15.1	19.8	19.2
	older	Not employed	54.7	46.5	30.5
		Total (%)	**100.0**	**100.0**	**100 .0**
		Total (N)	**58,900**	**156,333**	**111,100**
Total		**Full-time**	**29.7**	**38.0**	**47.5**
		Part-time	**13.7**	**17.8**	**18.5**
		Not employed	**56.7**	**44.3**	**34.0**
		Total (%)	**100.0**	**100.0**	**100.0**
		Total (N)	**4,556,500**	**5,611,401**	**6,364,560**

1. Percentage calculated for fewer than 100 cases in the sample.

Notes: Y. = youngest; o. = oldest. Totals may not equal 100 due to rounding.

For purposes of historical comparability, in 1991, families where the husband or wife was a non-permanent resident have been excluded.

Source: Census of Canada, 1971, 1981, 1991, Family Public Use Microdata Files.

TABLE 7

GAINFUL EMPLOYMENT OF LONE PARENTS, BY SEX OF PARENT AND NUMBER AND AGE OF CHILDREN, 1970, 1980 AND 1990

Number of children	Age of children	Parent's employment	Mother			Father		
			1970	1980	1990	1970	1980	1990
1 child	Under 6	Full-time	47.6	49.0	45.8	92.5[1]	87.1[1]	78.5
		Part-time	10.3	15.0	17.0	3.0[1]	4.7[1]	4.9
		Not employed	42.1	36.1	37.1	4.5[1]	8.2[1]	16.7
		Total (%)	100.0	100.0	100.0	100.0	100.0	100.0
		Total (N)	29,000	67,726	91,633	6,700	6,069	11,000
	6–14	Full-time	52.0	58.6	61.7	81.0[1]	83.0	82.3
		Part-time	11.7	14.4	15.0	6.0[1]	6.0	6.6
		Not employed	36.4	27.0	23.4	13.1[1]	11.1	11.1
		Total (%)	100.0	100.0	100.0	100.0	100.0	100.0
		Total (N)	30,800	70,142	103,867	8,400	13,821	21,600
	15 and older	Full-time	47.1	36.1	40.9	77.7	61.9	62.1
		Part-time	11.5	9.5	9.4	5.9	4.3	4.9
		Not employed	41.3	54.5	49.6	16.3	33.8	33.0
		Total (%)	100.0	100.0	100.0	100.0	100.0	100.0
		Total (N)	64,100	181,928	251,566	20,200	49,145	69,633
2 children	All under 6	Full-time	36.6	31.4	32.0	83.8[1]	100.0[1]	82.4[1]
		Part-time	9.9	21.4	15.3	8.1[1]	0.0[1]	5.5[1]
		Not employed	53.5	47.3	52.8	8.1[1]	0.0[1]	12.1[1]
		Total (%)	100.0	100.0	100.0	100.0	100.0	100.0
		Total (N)	10,100	17,311	24,700	3,700	1,464	3,033
	under 6; 6–14	Full-time	36.4[1]	43.5	42.3	88.5[1]	92.8[1]	82.9
		Part-time	19.3[1]	18.1	15.9	0.0[1]	7.2[1]	4.9
		Not employed	44.3[1]	38.4	41.8	11.5[1]	0.0[1]	12.2
		Total (%)	100.0	100.0	100.0	100.0	100.0	100.0
		Total (N)	8 800	22,150	36,433	2,600	2,903	4,100
	Y. under 6; o. 15 and older	Full-time	30.0[1]	--	44.3	--	80.2[1]	85.0[1]
		Part-time	10.0[1]	--	13.9	--	0.0[1]	5.0[1]
		Not employed	60.0[1]	--	41.8	--	19.8[1]	10.0[1]
		Total (%)	100.0	--	100.0	--	100.0	100.0
		Total (N)	1,000	--	2,633	--	1,377	667

TABLE 7 (CONTINUED)

GAINFUL EMPLOYMENT OF LONE PARENTS, BY SEX OF PARENT AND NUMBER AND AGE OF CHILDREN, 1970, 1980 AND 1990

Number of children	Age of children	Parent's employment	Mother			Father		
			1970	1980	1990	1970	1980	1990
2 children	All 6–14	Full-time	48.4	54.2	60.2	87.5[1]	97.0[1]	79.5
		Part-time	12.9	17.7	17.3	4.7[1]	1.1[1]	7.5
		Not employed	38.7	28.1	22.5	7.8[1]	1.9[1]	13.0
		Total (%)	100.0	100.0	100.0	100.0	100.0	100.0
		Total (N)	18,600	41,261	58,467	6,400	5,496	10,733
	6–14 15 and older	Full-time	47.2	52.9	61.2	92.5[1]	84.2[1]	85.6
		Part-time	15.2	10.9	16.2	3.8[1]	5.1[1]	6.1
		Not employed	37.7	36.2	22.7	3.8[1]	10.7[1]	8.3
		Total (%)	100.0	100.0	100.0	100.0	100.0	100.0
		Total (N)	17,800	27,021	37,333	5,300	7,770	7,633
All	15 and older	Full-time	46.4	41.0	53.4	86.4[1]	74.1	71.6
		Part-time	9.8	10.6	11.4	6.8[1]	3.2	4.0
		Not employed	43.8	48.4	35.3	6.8[1]	22.8	24.4
		Total (%)	100.0	100.0	100.0	100.0	100.0	100.0
		Total (N)	22,400	62,457	75,700	5,900	14,843	20,100
3 or more children	Under 6	Full-time	17.4[1]	23.9[1]	23.0	--	--	72.7[1]
		Part-time	17.34[1]	6.2[1]	9.0	--	--	9.1[1]
		Not employed	65.2[1]	69.9[1]	68.0	--	--	18.2[1]
		Total (%)	100.0	100.0	100.0	--	--	100.0
		Total (N)	2,300	1,669	3,333	--	--	367
	Under 6; 6–14	Full-time	22.0	27.2	30.7	94.9[1]	81.8[1]	74.8[1]
		Part-time	12.1	13.1	13.4	2.6[1]	18.2[1]	5.1[1]
		Not employed	65.9	59.7	55.9	2.6[1]	0.0[1]	20.2[1]
		Total (%)	100.0	100.0	100.0	100.0	100.0	100.0
		Total (N)	17,300	13,971	24,800	3,900	1,877	3,300
	Y. under 6; o. 15 and older	Full-time	32.4	36.9[1]	30.6	64.3[1]	86.0[1]	72.0[1]
		Part-time	7.8	10.3[1]	11.7	10.7[1]	7.0[1]	4.0[1]
		Not employed	59.8	52.8[1]	57.8	25.0[1]	7.0[1]	24.0[1]
		Total (%)	100.0	100.0	100.0	100.0	100.0	100.0
		Total (N)	10,200	5,471	6,867	2,800	1,567	833

TABLE 7 (CONCLUDED)

GAINFUL EMPLOYMENT OF LONE PARENTS, BY SEX OF PARENT AND NUMBER AND AGE OF CHILDREN, 1970, 1980 AND 1990

Number of children	Age of children	Parent's employment	Mother			Father		
			1970	1980	1990	1970	1980	1990
3 enfants et plus	6–14; 15 and older	Full-time	32.4	40.5	51.6	78.9[1]	85.6[1]	79.0
		Part-time	14.8	20.0	18.9	11.3[1]	8.4[1]	8.0
		Not employed	52.8	39.5	29.5	9.9[1]	6.0[1]	13.0
		Total (%)	100.0	100.0	100.0	100.0	100.0	100.0
		Total (N)	39,200	39,872	24,500	7,100	9,696	5,400
	All 6–14	Full-time	31.8	34.4	45.4	93.6[1]	94.7[1]	78.4
		Part-time	12.7	28.4	21.8	0.0[1]	0.0[1]	8.1
		Not employed	55.6	37.2	32.7	6.4[1]	5.4[1]	13.5
		Total (%)	100.0	100.0	100.0	100.0	100.0	100.0
		Total (N)	12,600	11,917	11,300	4,700	1,895	2,467
	All 15 and older	Full-time	32.3[1]	39.1	49.0	80.8[1]	70.6[1]	65.4
		Part-time	11.8[1]	13.0	11.1	15.4[1]	8.1[1]	2.3
		Not employed	55.9[1]	47.9	40.0	3.9[1]	21.3[1]	32.3
		Total (%)	100.0	100.0	100.0	100.0	100.0	100.0
		Total (N)	9,300	25,594	17,433	2,600	6,063	4,333
Total		**Full-time**	**41.6**	**43.1**	**47.8**	**83.7**	**74.6**	**71.4**
		Part-time	**12.2**	**13.4**	**13.4**	**5.8**	**4.9**	**5.3**
		Not employed	**46.1**	**43.5**	**38.8**	**10.5**	**20.4**	**23.3**
		Total (%)	**100.0**	**100.0**	**100.0**	**100.0**	**100.0**	**100.0**
		Total (N)	**293,500**	**589,336**	**770,566**	**81,100**	**124,163**	**165 200**

-- Percentage omitted (fewer than 10 cases in the sample).

1. Percentage calculated for fewer than 100 cases in the sample.

Notes: Totals may not add to 100 due to rounding.

Y. = youngest; o. = oldest.

Lone parents who are non-permanent residents have been excluded.

Source: Census of Canada, 1971, 1981, 1991, Family Public Use Microdata Files.

Table 8

Gainful Employment of the Husband or Lone Parent, by Age and Presence of Children Under 6, 1990

Type of family	Presence of children under 6	Employment of husband or lone parent	15–29	30–44	45–64	65 and older	All ages
Husband– wife families	At least 1	Full-time	91.3	94.3	88.3	63.6[1]	93.3
		Part-time	4.0	2.7	4.5	4.6[1]	3.0
		Not employed	4.8	3.1	7.3	31.8[1]	3.7
		Total (%)	100.0	100.0	100.0	100.0	100.0
		Total (N)	330,566	998,066	57,700	1,467	1,387,799
	None	Full-time	90.7	93.5	80.7	12.9	72.7
		Part-time	5.9	3.0	4.6	5.9	4.5
		Not employed	3.4	3.5	14.7	81.2	22.9
		Total (%)	100.0	100.0	100.0	100.0	100.0
		Total (N)	421,900	1,517,098	2,101,765	935,966	4,976,728
	Total	**Full-time**	**91.0**	**93.8**	**80.9**	**13.0**	77.2
		Part-time	**5.1**	**2.9**	**4.6**	**5.9**	4.1
		Not employed	**4.0**	**3.4**	**14.5**	**81.1**	18.7
		Total (%)	100.0	100.0	100.0	100.0	100.0
		Total (N)	752,466	2,515,164	2,159,465	937,432	6,364,527
Male lone- parent families	At least 1	Full-time	68.5	83.0	85.5[1]	--	79.0
		Part-time	7.5	4.6	1.8[1]	--	5.1
		Not employed	24.0	12.5	12.7[1]	--	15.9
		Total (%)	100.0	100.0	100.0	--	100.0
		Total (N)	6,667	14,667	1,833	--	23,333
	None	Full-time	68.3[1]	83.8	77.9	15.1	70.1
		Part-time	11.7[1]	5.7	5.6	3.8	5.4
		Not employed	20.0[1]	10.6	16.5	81.1	24.5
		Total (%)	100.0	100.0	100.0	100.0	100.0
		Total (N)	2,000	51,367	66,400	22,067	141,833
	Total	**Full-time**	**68.5**	**83.6**	**78.1**	**15.6**	71.4
		Part-time	**8.5**	**5.4**	**5.5**	**3.8**	5.4
		Not employed	**23.1**	**11.0**	**16.4**	**80.7**	23.3
		Total (%)	100.0	100.0	100.0	100.0	100.0
		Total (N)	8,667	66,033	68,233	22,233	165,167

TABLE 8 (CONCLUDED)

GAINFUL EMPLOYMENT OF THE HUSBAND OR LONE PARENT, BY AGE AND PRESENCE OF CHILDREN UNDER 6, 1990

Type of family	Presence of children under 6	Employ- ment of husband or lone parent	15–29	30–44	45–64	65 and older	All ages
Female lone- parent families	At least 1	Full-time	34.6	47.5	41.5[1]	--	**40.4**
		Part-time	16.8	14.5	13.2[1]	--	**15.7**
		Not employed	48.6	38.0	45.3[1]	--	**43.9**
		Total (%)	**100.0**	**100.0**	**100.0**	--	**100.0**
		Total (N)	**103,667**	**84,767**	**1,767**	--	**190,400**
	None	Full-time	50.5	63.5	53.6	5.4	**50.3**
		Part-time	19.7	15.2	12.6	3.6	**12.6**
		Not employed	29.8	21.3	33.8	91.1	**37.1**
		Total (%)	**100.0**	**100.0**	**100.0**	**100.0**	**100.0**
		Total (N)	**21,000**	**261,300**	**205,900**	**91,967**	**580,166**
	Total	**Full-time**	**37.3**	**59.6**	**53.5**	**5.4**	47.8
		Part-time	**17.3**	**15.0**	**12.6**	**3.6**	13.4
		Not employed	**45.5**	**25.4**	**33.9**	**91.0**	38.8
		Total (%)	**100.0**	**100.0**	**100.0**	**100.0**	**100.0**
		Total (N)	**124,667**	**346,066**	**207,666**	**92,167**	**770,566**

-- Percentage omitted (fewer than 10 cases in the sample).

1. Percentage calculated for less than 100 cases in the sample.

Notes: Totals may not equal 100 due to rounding.

Families where the husband, wife or lone parent is a non-permanent resident have been excluded.

Source: Census of Canada, 1991, Family Public Use Microdata Files.

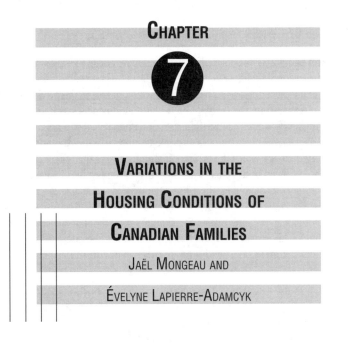

CHAPTER 7

VARIATIONS IN THE HOUSING CONDITIONS OF CANADIAN FAMILIES

JAËL MONGEAU AND

ÉVELYNE LAPIERRE-ADAMCYK

Chapter 6 provides an in-depth examination of the two fundamental factors affecting the living conditions of Canadian families: parents' labour force activity and family income. In that chapter, we first explore the extent of the increase in the labour force activity of women, especially mothers, and reveal the increase in the number of families where both parents are economically active. Then, in analysing the changes in income structure, we conclude that the most affluent families were essentially two-income families.

There is no doubt a connection between the variations in income of different family types and the considerable diversity of lifestyles—lifestyles that are more freely chosen in the case of more affluent families, and certainly more likely to be imposed in the case of lower-income families. Housing is probably one of the most revealing indicators of family lifestyle, reflecting the choices and constraints families face.

The purpose of this chapter is to examine the relationships between the different family types and the housing conditions available to families according to their resources. It first looks at home ownership, examining its various facets, including the relationship between family type and the likelihood of home ownership, the differences related to life-cycle stage, the effect of income and housing selection, as well as the variations in crowding by tenure and family type. It then analyses the weight of housing costs in relation to family income, paying particular attention to the links between family type and financial outlay, and taking into account tenure and whether the family has two incomes.

But, before we present the analysis of family housing conditions, a review of the definitions of "owner family" and "tenant family" based on Census of Canada data is in order. We complete this review with a brief presentation of the evolution of Canadian households and home ownership, which is linked to that of urbanization in the various regions of the country.

7.1 DEFINITIONS OF OWNER FAMILY AND TENANT FAMILY

Tenure can be determined based on census data obtained in response to a question on whether a household member owns or rents his or her dwelling. The data, however, do not indicate which household member is the owner or tenant, only that this person lives in the dwelling. When only the family occupies its dwelling, the resident owner or tenant is necessarily a member of the family unit. When the family shares its dwelling with other persons, it is not known whether the owner or tenant is a family member. But it is possible to know whether the primary household maintainer is a family member. Since the primary maintainer pays the rent or mortgage, taxes, electrical bills, and so on, it can be assumed that when this person is a family member, the family owns or rents the unit. In 97% of families, the primary household maintainer is a family member,[1] whether the dwelling is occupied by an owner or a tenant. We refer, then, to "owner families" and "tenant families," although in very rare instances the family is neither the owner nor the tenant of the dwelling it occupies. This possibility should be kept in mind when interpreting certain tables, particularly those that compare families living on their own with those that live with other persons.

From the census it is also possible to distinguish, among owners, those who pay a mortgage from those who do not. This distinction is used at times because it allows for slight differentiations to be made between the living conditions of owners. It is especially helpful in interpreting home ownership according to income variation.

7.2 THE EVOLUTION OF HOME OWNERSHIP IN CANADA

According to Steele (1994), the advantages of ownership are: greater control over housing, the possibility of accumulating wealth while being housed, and access to types of housing not available for a rent. For many households, these advantages largely offset the disadvantages: higher transaction costs, the risk of selling at a loss, the risk of greater losses if unable to make payments, and the onus of managing and maintaining the dwelling. In general, then, it can be asserted that the quality of life of owners is bound to be higher than that of tenants, and that is probably why many Canadian households have chosen to own their home. According to the 1991 Census, 63% of households are owner households.

However, "ownership is possible only if income is high enough" [translation] (Steele 1994, p. 52). The study presented in Chapter 6 shows that household incomes have risen in recent decades. One might therefore expect to see the proportion of owners increase over time. The proportion of owner households has declined appreciably from 1961 to 1971, and rose only marginally thereafter so that, by 1991, it had not yet regained its 1961 level. Steele (1994) attributes this development to increased urbanization and the rise in the number of non-traditional households. First, home ownership is less common in urban than in rural areas. In traditional rural areas, that is, areas where farmers operate their own small-scale farms, farmers own the house in which they live. Secondly, non-traditional households (young singles living alone or with other singles; persons who are separated or widowed and living alone; and lone-parent families) are smaller, often have no children, and usually are not very affluent. Non-traditional households are less likely to have owner-occupants.

The proportion of owners is higher in the Atlantic provinces (74%) and lower in Quebec (56%) than elsewhere in Canada (see Figure 7.1). According to Steele (1994), a link can be established between the Atlantic region's higher proportion of owners and its low rate of urbanization (51%)[2] compared with the rest of Canada (77%). However, the small proportion of owners in Quebec cannot be explained by its large urban population (78%)—a larger urban population than anywhere else in Canada. As Choko and Harris point out, tenure depends on a combination of factors: "economic, political and cultural factors operating in specific historical, geographical and cultural contexts" [translation] (Choko and Harris 1992, p.1). In trying to compare the degree of home ownership in Montreal with that in Toronto, these same authors note that many have often tried to ascribe the low proportion of owners in Montreal to cultural factors (French Canadians are less inclined to own than English Canadians) or economic factors (the lower income level in Montreal), but both explanations are unsatisfactory. The differences in housing stock between the two cities must also be taken into account, "plexes" being far more common in Montreal than in Toronto. Note, however, that ownership is on the rise in Quebec, and catching up somewhat to levels in other regions of the country.

FIGURE 7.1

PROPORTION OF OWNERS, BY REGION, 1961 TO 1991

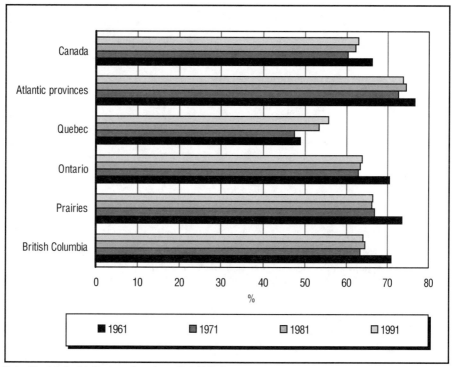

Note: The data for this figure are from Appendix 7, Table 1.
Source: Census of Canada, 1961, 1971, 1981 and 1991.

Family households are more likely than non-family households to own (see Figure 7.2). This is due to a strong link in the housing market between the type of building and tenure. Thus, single-family dwellings, better suited to the needs of families with children (providing such amenities as a yard or basement), are more readily available for ownership, while apartments in apartment blocks, less suited to family needs, are available for rent.

FIGURE 7.2
PROPORTION OF OWNERS, BY TYPE OF HOUSEHOLD, 1961 TO 1991

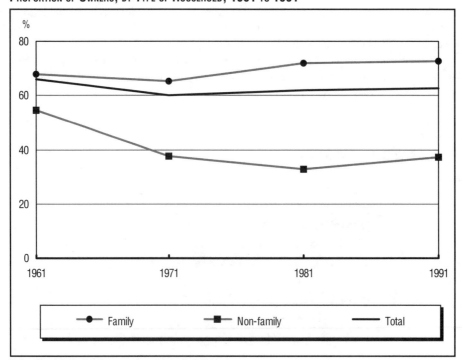

Note: The data for this figure are from Appendix 7, Table 1.
Source: Census of Canada, 1961, 1971, 1981 and 1991.

Also, from 1961 to 1971, the proportion of owners declined less among family households than it did among non-family households (see Figure 7.2), and the proportion of owner-family households was even higher in 1981 and 1991 than in 1961. The impetus here is the effect of the proliferation of non-traditional households on the evolution of ownership, already noted by Steele (1994). The higher proportion of non-family households and their lesser tendency, compared with family households, to own their own home contributed to the decline in the number of owners among all households.

Ownership among non-family households, however, rose from 1981 to 1991. With the surge in joint ownership, it became easier for some of these households to own. A portion of this increase was due to the phenomenon of gentrification,[3] of which many young and middle-aged singles were a part (Ley 1985). Also, a number of elderly people held onto their home following their children's departure or the death of their spouse, during the transition from a family household to a non-family household.

7.3   HOME OWNERSHIP AND FAMILY TYPE

As just explained, ownership rose slightly for family households in the 30 years from 1961 to 1991, the proportion of owner families increasing from 68% to 73%. As one might suspect, given the variations in family income shown in Chapter 6, in 1991 the percentage of owners varied considerably by family type. Among Canadian families, married couples were the most inclined (80%) to own their home (see Figure 7.3). Families of widows and lone fathers follow fairly closely at 72% and 63%, respectively. Next on the list of homeowners are families of common-law couples (47%), families of divorced mothers (40%), and, finally, far behind, families of single mothers (12%). These differences increase according to the differences in age structure of the couples and parents who head these families: widowed mothers are generally older, while common-law couples and single mothers are decidedly younger. The standardized percentages that eliminate this effect narrow the differences, but the order by family type remains the same.

FIGURE 7.3

PROPORTION OF OWNERS, BY TYPE OF FAMILY, **1991**

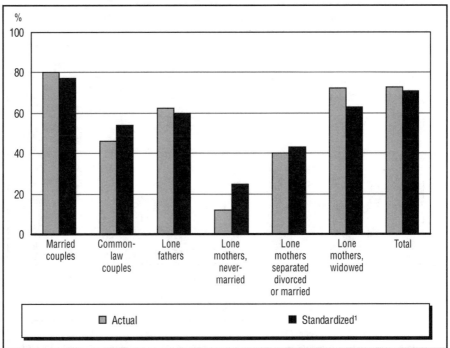

1.   The percentages have been standardized by allocating each age group the same weight.

Note: The data for this figure are from Appendix 7, Table 2.

Source: Census of Canada, 1991, special compilation.

Other factors linked to family living conditions and life cycle (or life courses) are also related to the variations in home ownership, which, of course, depend mainly on the family's available resources. Before examining the links between these resources and ownership, let us look at two of these factors and their connection to ownership: living arrangements and certain life-cycle stages.

Here the term "living arrangements" refers to whether families share their dwelling with other persons not of the family unit. Figure 7.4 shows the link between this factor and ownership. First, as a rule, families living on their own appear less likely to own their home than families living with other persons, with the exception of the families of widows. Keep in mind that the definition of owner-family imposed by the census data causes some uncertainty about the ownership status of families that share their home. The data available in the Public Use Microdata File on Individuals do not dispel this uncertainty, but do provide information that qualifies the results obtained by family type. Using this file's data, it is possible to determine whether the primary household maintainer is the husband, the lone parent, or some other person, but not whether this other person is a family member. In the case of families living on their own, there can be no confusion since, by definition, the owner can only be a family member. When the primary maintainer is reported as being someone other than the husband or the lone parent, that person must be the wife or one of the children (see Figure 7.4).

FIGURE 7.4

PROPORTION OF OWNER FAMILIES, BY IDENTITY OF PRIMARY HOUSEHOLD MAINTAINER, TYPE OF FAMILY AND LIVING ARRANGEMENTS, 1991

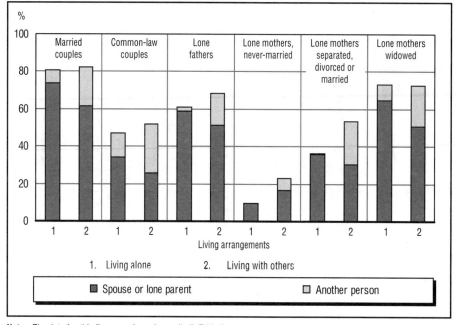

Note: The data for this figure are from Appendix 7, Table 3.

Source: Census of Canada, 1991, Individual Public Use Microdata Files.

For families that share their dwelling, the situation is different. For a certain proportion of those whose primary maintainer is "another person," this other person will be the wife (in a two-parent family) or a child (in a two-parent or lone-parent family). Here, the definition is not inconsistent with the reality. It is impossible to tell what this proportion is, but some assumptions can be made to reduce the uncertainty. We already know that only 3% of all families are financially supported by someone who is not a family member (see Section 7.1). We assume they all fall into the category of families that share their dwelling. Since this category accounts for 11.2% of families, families supported by "another person" constitute 27% (3.0 / 11.2 = 26.7%) of families that share their dwelling. We further assume that this percentage does not vary by type of family, and, finally, that the proportion of owner families they represent is the same as the proportion of owner families among all families. If this proportion (27%) is compared with the percentage of owners who share their dwelling (see Figure 7.4), then, excluding common-law couples and divorced mothers, the proportion for which the primary maintainer is another person is about 27%. This confirms that comparisons based on families who share their dwelling are unsound. It can no longer be maintained that families living on their own are less likely to own than other families, quite the contrary. Again remember that families who share their dwelling account for just 11.2% of all families. The proportion is just 9.7% for married couples and 9.1% for common-law couples, but 19.7% for families of lone mothers and 31.6% for families of lone fathers.

Having shown the extent of the uncertainty created by the definitions of owner family and tenant family, let us examine the significant results of Figure 7.4. Note that when the primary maintainer in an owner family is the husband or lone parent, the family is more likely to live on its own. Also note that fewer husbands are the primary maintainer in common-law couples living on their own than in married couples, since in the former financial responsibility tends to be shared more evenly and the couple is, on average, younger. Also, almost no lone-parent families have a child as the primary maintainer, with the exception of families of widows with older children.

We can also try to assess whether the decision to share housing might be a strategy for acquiring ownership of one's home or retaining ownership during hard times. Although living arrangements cannot be used to verify this assumption directly, they can provide some helpful information. This assumption cannot be dismissed out of hand, since most families who share their dwellings are financially responsible for them. For example, in this group we would expect to find families who, to help meet their financial obligations, often rent out a room to relatives. Finally, it is reasonable to believe that the small minority of families who live with other persons and have been mistakenly classified as owners would generally benefit from taking in another family, probably their family of origin in the case of young common-law couples or young women who are separated or divorced.

In short, the analysis of ownership based on these definitions can be pursued with confidence, and the assumption that some families share their dwelling with persons other than family members to acquire or retain ownership can be accepted as likely.

7.4 HOME OWNERSHIP AND LIFE-CYCLE STAGES

The variations in the proportion of families who own their home by family type do not reveal the full range of family realities. As we have demonstrated, the age structure intensifies the differences between family types. We can therefore assume that the stage reached in the life cycle also affects home ownership. The analysis of this aspect considers only two-parent families.

This classification by life cycle employs the main stages described in Chapter 2. Figure 7.5 shows the proportion of owner families among young couples without children, couples with children, postparental couples, and childless couples by the wife's age. Fewer than half of young couples without children are owners; they are young, less well off financially and probably much more mobile. Within this group, common-law couples are even less eager to buy their home (32%) than are married couples (58%). Young couples appear more interested in being homeowners when they have children: nearly 70% own. There is also a notable difference between married couples (73%) and common-law couples (45%) in this regard. As age increases, so does the percentage of owners, and it is even higher when there are still children living in the home. It is difficult, however, to interpret the slight increase in ownership among older couples and couples where the wife is aged 35 to 54: Is this a life-cycle effect, or an effect of the prevailing economic conditions for the different generations being compared? There are no satisfactory answers to this question. But it is interesting to note the marginal difference between couples who have remained childless and those whose children have left home. The decision to own does not appear to be based solely on the comfort needed to raise small children.

FIGURE 7.5

PROPORTION OF OWNERS AMONG HUSBAND–WIFE FAMILIES, BY LIFE CYCLE AND WIFE'S AGE, 1991

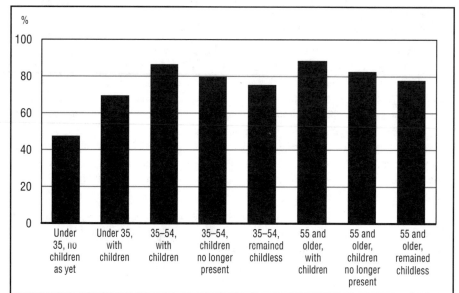

Note: The data for this figure are from Appendix 7, Table 4.

Source: Census of Canada, 1991, Family Public Use Microdata Files.

It is clear, however, that the life-cycle stage is a decisive factor, even when only families with children under age 16 are considered (see Figure 7.6). The age of the children, which is related to that of the parents, becomes an important indicator. A clear relation can be seen between the increase in the percentage of owners and an increase in the children's age. The number of children being equal, this percentage is at least 10% higher among families with only children aged 6 to 15 than among families with only children under age 6. This relationship, not shown here, can also be seen in lone-parent families (see Appendix 7, Table 5).

FIGURE 7.6

PROPORTION OF OWNER HUSBAND–WIFE FAMILIES AMONG PRIMARY HOUSEHOLDS WITH NO UNATTACHED INDIVIDUALS WHERE THE PRIMARY MAINTAINER IS THE HUSBAND OR WIFE, BY NUMBER OF CHILDREN UNDER AGE 16 AND THEIR AGE, 1991

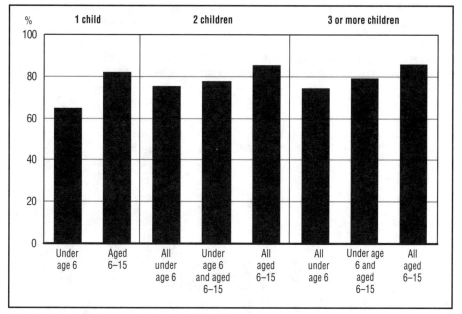

Note: The data for this figure are from Appendix 7, Table 5.
Source: Census of Canada, 1991, Households and Housing Public Use Microdata Files.

The link between home ownership and life-cycle stages, while shedding light on the evolution of family life, is not surprising; indeed Chapter 6 describes a very clear connection between these various stages and the variations in family income.

Income certainly is a factor in family home ownership. Ownership appears to be more within reach of higher-income families. This was the finding for husband–wife families (see Figure 7.7). These families, systematically classified by life-cycle stage, are more likely to own their home if they fall within the fifth income quintile (the highest incomes) than when they are in the first quintile. Figure 7.7 includes an additional factor that effectively illustrates the link between income and ownership: young high-income families come to own their home by obtaining a mortgage. It was found that, among families where the wife is under age 35, the percentage of owners with no mortgage is much the same, regardless of income. Any difference in the percentage of owners is wholly attributable to the fact that those who can borrow are far more likely to be in the fifth income quintile. This effect drops off with age such that, among older families, there are relatively fewer mortgages and the difference in the percentage of owners narrows between income categories. This is probably attributable to two convergent trends. The first trend concerns less-affluent families who require much more time to accumulate the capital needed to purchase their home. They manage to do so only when they are quite far along in their life cycle. Here we note that the desire to purchase a home continues past the age at which couples have small children. Many of these couples consider the purchase of a home to be an investment for retirement. The second trend concerns older families for whom income is a less reliable indicator of the level of wealth. There are doubtless families in the lower income quintiles whose income has dropped, but who had saved enough beforehand to purchase a home.

FIGURE 7.7

PROPORTION OF OWNERS AMONG HUSBAND–WIFE FAMILIES WHERE THE WIFE IS UNDER AGE 65, BY LIFE CYCLE, 1ST AND 5TH FAMILY INCOME QUINTILES[1] IN 1990, 1991

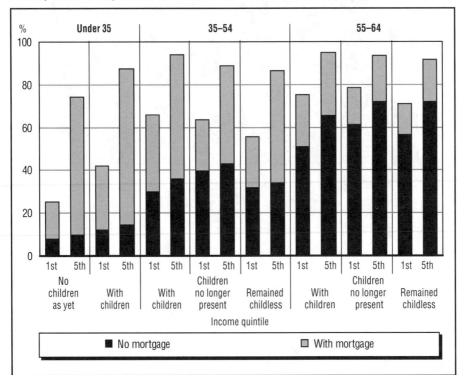

1. Families have been classified by income in ascending order. Thus, the first quintile represents the 20% of families with the lowest incomes.

Note: The data for this figure are from Appendix 7, Table 4.

Source: Census of Canada, 1991, Family Public Use Microdata Files.

Once again, it can be seen that purchasing a home is part of the savings strategy of all couples rather than something done simply out of concern to provide children with a more comfortable living environment. In fact, the proportion of owner couples that have remained childless is nearly as high as that of owner couples that have had children.

In short, these data reveal that families are turning in droves to home ownership. Ownership is not achieved at the same rate by all couples. Couples with a high income reach this stage when still young and just starting their family because it is easy to obtain credit. Low-income families purchase later in life because it is difficult for them to save the capital needed to buy. Although the arrival of children is an incentive to purchase a home, it is not the most decisive factor, as can be seen from the small percentage difference between owner couples who have had children and those who have remained childless.

We now tackle another issue: What type of dwelling do couples and families want?

7.5   CHOICE OF HOUSING, FAMILY STATUS AND HOME OWNERSHIP

In Canada, housing stock is dominated by the single-detached dwelling, often regarded as the ideal type of housing for raising a family: room outside where the children can play within their parents' view and without disturbing the neighbours, a basement that can be converted into a playroom, and so on (see Figure 7.8). However, in this regard, there are significant regional variations. This type of dwelling is most common in the Atlantic provinces (71%), followed by the Prairies (67%). In Quebec, however, fewer than half of households occupied such housing in 1991. There is a very strong link between the type of building and tenure. Recall that the proportion of owners is smallest in Quebec and greatest in the Atlantic region (see Figure 7.1). Ontario has the highest proportion of apartments in buildings of five or more storeys (16% versus 2% in the Atlantic region, and about 5% elsewhere in the country), probably because it has the highest rate of urbanization in the country. Quebec has by far the highest proportion of dwellings in buildings of under five storeys (35%); included in this category are attached duplexes (containing two housing units), triplexes (three units) and quadruplexes (four units), which are quite uncommon elsewhere in Canada. These buildings contain mostly rental units; there is a single owner, which helps reduce the proportion of owners in Quebec in relation to the other regions of the country. Buildings of under five storeys are also very popular in the suburbs of Canadian cities, especially in Quebec.

FIGURE 7.8

TYPE OF BUILDING OF OCCUPIED DWELLINGS, BY REGION, 1991

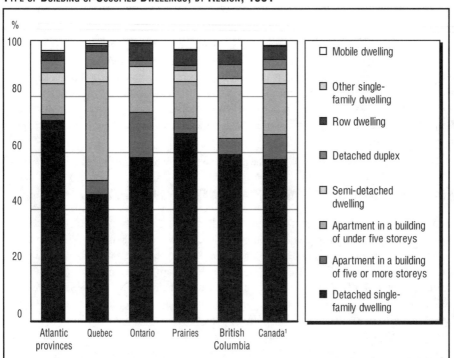

1. Including the Yukon and Northwest Territories.

Note: The data for this figure are from Appendix 7, Table 6.

Source: Census of Canada, 1991, Households and Housing Public Use Microdata Files.

The existence of housing stock with particular characteristics determines to some extent the options available to families when choosing one type of dwelling over another. For example, single-family dwellings are available mainly to those who want to own, whereas those who want to rent such a unit find them more difficult to come by. But housing stock characteristics also reflect the tastes and preferences of consumers. There is, of course, considerable inertia in this respect as the housing renewal rate is quite slow. The choices made early in the century, even late in the last century, are still part of the landscape in the urban areas developed during that time. But again, it is reasonable to think that these choices were based on cultural values still embedded in the preferences of households today. When discussing the housing choices families make, the inherent constraints of the housing market, in terms of both tenure (ownership or rental) and building types, must be kept in mind.

To analyse the links between family type and type of housing, the housing types are grouped into three categories: single-detached dwellings, referred to hereafter as "single-family dwellings"; the types of housing generally found in low-rise buildings, ranging from row housing to semi-detached houses, duplexes, triplexes, and buildings of under five storeys; and housing in buildings of five or more storeys. Also, families were classified into five categories according to family type and life cycle: husband–wife families with children under age 16; husband–wife families without children under age 16, subdivided according to the age of the primary maintainer (under age 35, and over age 35); families of lone mothers with children under age 16; and families of lone fathers with children under age 16. (This less detailed classification was imposed on the analysis by the availability of data in the 1991 Census Public Use Microdata File on Households and Housing, which contains information on types of housing.)

As one might expect, the relative size of each housing category varies appreciably according to family type (see Table 7.1). Nearly three-quarters of husband–wife families with children and older families without children live in single-family dwellings, while this is true of only a minority of lone mothers (33%) and young couples without children (42%). We also found that far fewer families live in highrise apartments than in other types of buildings. Fewer than 3% of two-parent families with children under age 16 live in such housing. The highest percentage— just 12%—is for lone fathers with children under age 16. The intermediate category takes in a variety of situations for which the significance in terms of the living conditions they represent for families is difficult to assess. Remember, however, that more than half of these dwellings are in low-rise buildings of under five storeys (see Figure 7.8) and that therefore the available outside play area for children may be limited. Nearly three in five lone mothers are in this situation compared with only one in five mothers in a two-parent family (see Table 7.1). These results bring to light the appeal of single-family dwellings for couples raising children and for older families, most of whom already have had children. This is probably not because of any constraint regarding the availability of such housing, but rather the reverse: because families want to live in single-family dwellings, the market supplies them.

TABLE 7.1

DISTRIBUTION OF FAMILIES, BY TYPE OF FAMILY AND TYPE OF BUILDING LIVED IN, 1991

Type of family	Single-family dwellings	Other dwellings	Buildings of five or more storeys	Total
Husband–wife families with no children under 6, maintainer under 35	41.9	48.4	9.7	**100.0**
Husband–wife families with children under 16	73.7	23.7	2.6	**100.0**
Lone mothers with children under 16	32.6	59.6	7.8	**100.0**
Lone fathers with children under 16	55.0	33.0	12.0	**100.0**
Husband–wife families with no children under 16, maintainer 35 or older	72.7	21.6	5.7	**100.0**

Source: Census of Canada, 1991, Individual Public Use Microdata Files.

There are indications that tend to support this interpretation. When tenure (that is, owner or tenant status) is included, the analysis reveals that those whose incomes allow them more freedom of choice opt in droves to purchase a single-family dwelling. The results of Figure 7.9 wholly support this. For each family type, Figure 7.9 shows the following two aspects of the housing situation simultaneously: first, the percentage of owner families and of tenant families, and, secondly, the type of housing these families occupy. The percentages shown in the figure correspond with the distribution of owners and tenants by type of housing. As the symbols used are the same, differing only in boldness of type, it is possible to understand a fairly complex reality at a glance. To show how to interpret this figure, we will use the example of husband–wife families with children under age 16. The left side, representing owners, shows that 78% of this group of families own their home. Of this 78%, 86% have opted for a single-family dwelling and 14% for housing in a low-rise building. The right side shows the distribution of the 22% of tenant families by type of housing: 31% occupy single-family dwellings, 59% live in low-rise buildings and 10% live in highrise buildings. Also evident is the overall relative number of single-family dwellings, the proportion occupied by owners being juxtaposed with that occupied by tenants. This is a visual representation of the 73% shown earlier in Table 7.1.

FIGURE 7.9

TENURE AND TYPE OF BUILDING, BY TYPE OF FAMILY, 1991

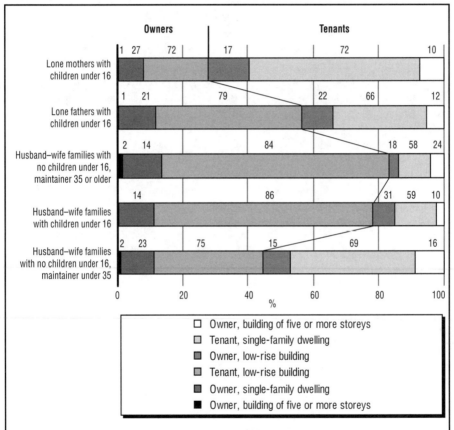

Note: The data for this figure are from Appendix 7, Table 7.

Source: Census of Canada, 1991, Households and Housing Public Use Microdata Files.

Let us continue with our comparison of the different choices made by the various family types. It is immediately apparent that ownership is a decisive factor in the choice of housing, and is primarily a matter of financial resources coupled with life-cycle stage, as shown in Section 7.4. Once this factor is taken into account, the variations in the type of housing are considerably reduced. The percentage of families that choose single-family dwellings varies between 33% and 74%, depending on family type (see Table 7.1). Still more than 70% are owners, ranging from 72% of lone mothers to 86% of two-parent families with children under age 16. Among tenants, single-family dwellings are clearly less common, probably because they are less available for rent. The percentage is about 20% for all categories, except for two-parent families with children under age 16 for which it is nearly one-third.

Another interesting and significant result shows the popularity of single-family dwellings with those who can afford to choose more freely, that is the very large number of owners who purchase single-family dwellings. Almost none buy apartments in highrise buildings, regardless of their family status. Even young couples without children who become owners opt in large numbers to buy single-family dwellings as a savings strategy and to prepare for the arrival of children. Similarly, it seems that after grown children leave home, older couples tend to remain in their single-family dwelling rather than choose a less onerous form of ownership.

The profile of tenants differs from that of owners: a small majority opts for housing in low-rise buildings (58% to 72%). This type of housing offers less room than a single-family dwelling, particularly outside. Leisure activities are therefore restricted for both children (for example, no playground) and adults (for example, no garden). And, obviously, available housing in highrise buildings is more affordable: 10% to 24% of the various family types choose such housing, the highest percentages being for families without children.

The link between family income and ownership has already been mentioned (see Figure 7.7). One might well wonder whether the type of housing chosen varies from one income category to another. It has just been shown that there is a strong connection between tenure and housing type. Are the choices the same for more affluent families as they are for less affluent families? In other words, are the constraints of the housing market the same for the different income categories? To answer this question, let us look at two-parent families with children under age 16 (see Figure 7.10). Figure 7.10 is similar to Figure 7.9, except income categories are replaced by family types. First note the gradual increase, from 52% to 93%, in the percentage of owner families as we move from families with the lowest income (first quintile) to those with the highest income (fifth quintile). Owner behaviour varies little, regardless of income level: most owners purchase single-family dwellings—82% to 89%, depending on income. Highrise apartment buildings are virtually passed by, being the choice of no more than 1% in each income category. In contrast, tenants in the top income bracket, though relatively few, behave quite differently from other tenant families: 45% choose to rent a single-family dwelling compared with slightly less than one-third of the families that are least well off. However, about 10% of tenants occupy an apartment in a highrise, regardless of their income level.

FIGURE 7.10

TENURE AND TYPE OF BUILDING AMONG HUSBAND–WIFE FAMILIES WITH CHILDREN UNDER AGE 16, BY FAMILY INCOME QUINTILE[1] IN 1990, 1991

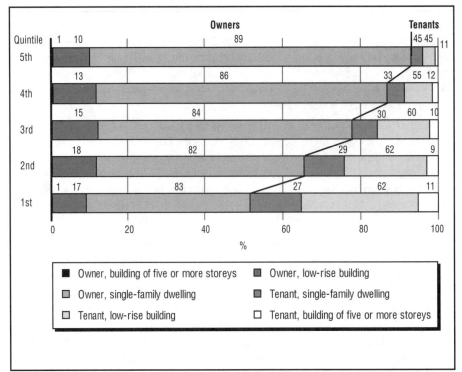

1. Families have been classified by income in ascending order. Thus, the first quintile represents the 20% of families with the lowest incomes.
Note: The data for this figure are from Appendix 7, Table 7.
Source: Census of Canada, 1991, Households and Housing Public Use Microdata Files.

For the other types of family, the relationship between income and the type of housing chosen appears appreciably the same as for two-parent families with children under age 16 (see Table 7.2). Its effect is reflected in ownership. Regardless of family type or income level, most families that can and do decide to become owners purchase a single-family dwelling, as shown by the concentration of the housing market in such housing, undoubtedly in response to consumer demand. On the rental side, their concentration is less, all family categories considered, as families are more evenly dispersed among housing types.

TABLE 7.2

TYPE OF BUILDING, BY TENURE, TYPE OF FAMILY AND FAMILY INCOME QUINTILE,[1] 1991[2]

Family income quintile	Owners				Tenants			
	Single family dwelling	Low-rise buildings	Buildings of five or more storeys	Total	Single family dwellings	Low-rise buildings	Buildings of five or more storeys	Total
	%				%			
Type of family								
Husband–wife families with no children under 16, maintainer under 35								
1st	71.9	25.7	2.5	100.0	14.8	72.6	12.6	100.0
2nd	72.2	26.1	1.7	100.0	14.8	73.2	12.0	100.0
3rd	74.4	23.9	1.7	100.0	14.8	69.0	16.3	100.0
4th	75.8	22.2	2.0	100.0	15.4	63.8	20.8	100.0
5th	77.1	19.9	3.0	100.0	16.7	57.0	26.4	100.0
Total	**75.0**	**22.8**	**2.2**	**100.0**	**15.0**	**15.8**	**69.2**	**100.0**
Type of family								
Husband–wife families with children under 16								
1st	82.5	16.9	0.6	100.0	27.3	62.0	10.7	100.0
2nd	82.0	17.6	0.4	100.0	29.4	61.8	8.8	100.0
3rd	84.4	15.2	0.4	100.0	29.8	59.8	10.4	100.0
4th	86.5	13.1	0.5	100.0	33.1	55.3	11.6	100.0
5th	89.3	10.2	0.5	100.0	44.6	44.8	10.7	100.0
Total	**85.7**	**13.8**	**0.5**	**100.0**	**30.6**	**59.2**	**10.2**	**100.0**
Type of family								
Lone mothers with children under 16								
1st	72.7	25.8	1.5	100.0	17.2	72.9	9.9	100.0
2nd	69.5	29.3	1.1	100.0	16.1	72.4	11.5	100.0
3rd	74.2	24.5	1.3	100.0	19.9	67.1	12.9	100.0
4th	70.5	26.7	2.8	100.0	23.5 [3]	66.3 [3]	10.2 [3]	100.0
5th	75.2	24.0	0.8	100.0	25.6 [3]	64.1 [3]	10.3 [3]	100.0
Total	**71.9**	**26.7**	**1.4**	**100.0**	**17.2**	**72.5**	**10.3**	**100.0**
Type of family								
Lone fathers with children under 16								
1st	77.4	22.2	0.5	100.0	20.4	68.9	10.7	100.0
2nd	75.8	23.4	0.8	100.0	20.3	66.5	13.1	100.0
3rd	79.1	20.2	0.7	100.0	24.4	63.5	12.2	100.0
4th	79.8	20.2	0.0	100.0	38.6 [3]	47.7 [3]	13.6 [3]	100.0
5th	86.2	11.9	1.8	100.0	33.3 [3]	12.5 [3]	54.2 [3]	100.0
Total	**78.8**	**20.5**	**0.7**	**100.0**	**22.4**	**65.8**	**11.9**	**100.0**
Type of family								
Husband–wife families with no children under 16, maintainer 35 or older								
1st	83.2	15.5	1.3	100.0	16.2	61.9	22.0	100.0
2nd	83.2	15.2	1.6	100.0	16.8	59.0	24.3	100.0
3rd	83.2	15.0	1.8	100.0	16.7	58.0	25.3	100.0
4th	83.4	14.8	1.8	100.0	19.6	55.9	24.5	100.0
5th	85.2	12.0	2.8	100.0	22.7	47.2	30.1	100.0
Total	**83.8**	**14.3**	**1.9**	**100.0**	**17.7**	**57.8**	**24.5**	**100.0**

1. Families have been classified by income in ascending order. Thus, the first quintile represents the 20% of families with the lowest incomes.

2. Households with no attached individuals where the primary maintainer is the husband, wife or lone parent.

3. Percentage calculated for fewer than 100 cases.

Note: Totals may not add to 100 due to rounding.

Source: Census of Canada, 1991, Households and Housing Public Use Microdata File.

It is interesting to note that, unlike families with children, whether two-parent or lone-parent families, families without children are more likely to live in a highrise building. This is less true of the most affluent couples, whether owners of all ages (3%) or younger tenants (26%), and of older tenant couples in all income categories (22% to 30%) (see Table 7.2).

In short, most families choose a single-family dwelling once they can afford to own one. While the market doubtless imposes some constraints, it appears to be responding to a very high demand by families for this type of dwelling.

7.6 FAMILY STATUS, OWNERSHIP, TYPE OF HOUSING AND CROWDING

As we have just seen, housing conditions vary considerably, although most families live in a single-family dwelling that they own. Our analysis next attempts to determine these families' quality of life by exploring what is known about their living space.

The number of rooms in a dwelling is related to living conditions to the extent that, when considered along with the size of the household, it gives some idea of whether the dwelling is crowded, and crowding may well affect the inhabitants' quality of life. For example, crowding may limit privacy and can exacerbate the inevitable conflicts between household members. But how is crowding determined? Several means of measurement are proposed.[4] They can be divided into two categories: measurements based on the number of rooms and those based on surface area. It is already apparent that crowding is a subjective concept: Is it preferable to have a number of small rooms, or fewer, but larger, rooms? Be that as it may, the Census of Canada has no information about the surface area of dwellings, and our measurement must therefore be based on the number of rooms. The easiest method of measurement, and the one used in the variables developed by Statistics Canada, is to calculate the average number of people per room. If there is more than one person per room, the dwelling is classified as crowded. The main drawback of this indicator is that it ignores the fact that some rooms, such as the kitchen, are used by everyone, while others, such as bedrooms, are set aside for the personal use of family members. But counting the number of bedrooms per person poses another problem: each family is free to allocate the rooms of their dwelling, with the exception of the kitchen and bathroom, to specific uses.

Aware that the reality of some families may be far removed from these criteria, we developed an indicator for assessing the number of persons per bedroom, since the main purpose of this part of our analysis is to shed light on children's living conditions according to the space they have at home. It is well known that, in Canadian society, the ability to give each child their own bedroom is a commonly held value. This value is certainly not absolute; it has doubtless varied considerably over time and continues to be observed to varying degrees depending on the family (for example, it is easier for young children of the same sex than for adolescents of the opposite sex to share a bedroom) and social status group. But it seems to be a good indicator of the comfort of a dwelling.

The crowding indicator is calculated as follows: the numerator is the number of persons per household less the parents (two in the case of couples, one in the case of lone-parent families). In most cases, this gives the number of children. The denominator is the number of rooms in the dwelling less three basic rooms (kitchen, living room and parents' bedroom). The remainder should correspond with the number of children's bedrooms. This gives an index of the average number of children per bedroom. If the index is greater than one, the dwelling is classified as crowded. This measurement of crowding is certainly not perfect, and is especially flawed in the case of families not living on their own. In these situations, it is reasonable to think that the sense of crowding varies, depending on the relationships between the family and the persons sharing the unit. For example, a grandmother's presence is less intrusive than that of a boarder, although the presence of an intrusive grandmother may be more oppressive than that of a discreet boarder! When the data permit, families living on their own in the dwelling are distinguished from other families.

Figure 7.11 shows the proportion of families in crowded housing by type of family and tenure. Nearly 7% of families live in crowded housing: the percentage is about 6% for husband–wife families, but climbs to more than 19% for families of lone mothers, and to 16% for families of lone fathers. The differences are, however, quite marked between owners and tenants: tenant families (16%) are four times more likely to live in crowded housing than owner families (4%). The relationship is somewhat weaker for female lone-parent families: 36% of them rent housing that is crowded compared with 29% of their male counterparts.

FIGURE 7.11

PROPORTION OF FAMILIES LIVING IN CROWDED HOUSING,[1] BY TENURE AND TYPE OF FAMILY, 1991

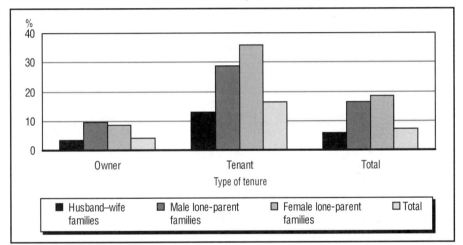

1.   For the definition of "crowding," see Section 7.6.
Note: The data for this figure are from Appendix 7, Table 8.
Source: Census of Canada, 1991, Individual Public Use Microdata Files.

Figure 7.12 shows the impact of living arrangements on the crowding index. Of husband–wife families, those that live on their own are far less likely to live in crowded housing (4.5%) than those that share their housing (17.0%). Also, whether they live on their own or share their housing, families with children are more affected by crowding by an overall ratio of three to one. This is most significant in terms of children's quality of life. Table 7.3 shows, for various family categories, the percentage of children who live in crowded housing by number of children in the family and living arrangements. Keep in mind that the crowding index is intended to measure a family's ability to give each child their own bedroom. Overall, 15.6% of children live in crowded housing. This proportion varies considerably by family type, number of children and living arrangements. For each category of family, whether or not the family lives on its own, crowding increases with the number of children. This is not in itself surprising since, while there may be a desire to provide each child with their own bedroom, not all families, particularly those with three or more children, can do so since larger dwellings are not within everyone's price range. It can also be seen that the percentages are distinctly lower among families of married couples. These families, generally more stable and affluent, can provide their children with more space. In contrast, the percentage of children living in crowded housing is systematically higher when the family shares the dwelling with other persons. Crowding affects one in five children when the child is the only child of a married couple, one in three when the child is the only child of a lone mother sharing housing, and rises to 60% for children in a family of three or more children headed by the mother. Some circumstances therefore do not seem especially favourable to children's quality of life, as a fair percentage of children are deprived of having more space of their own. Any judgment made, however, should not be too categorical: sharing a bedroom with a brother or sister may not always be detrimental, and, in some cases, the decision to sacrifice space in order to share housing may ensure there is someone responsible at home with the children when their parents are not there. This probably has some beneficial effect, considering the problems related to child care.

TABLE 7.3

PERCENTAGE OF CHILDREN LIVING IN CROWDED HOUSING, BY TYPE OF FAMILY, NUMBER OF CHILDREN IN THE FAMILY AND LIVING ARRANGEMENTS, 1991

Type of family	Number of children	Living arrangements		Total
		Family living alone	Family living with other persons	
		%		
Married couples				
	1 child	3.2	19.4	5.0
	2 children	6.0	23.6	7.5
	3 or more children	19.6	32.0	20.7
Common-law couples				
	1 child	6.9	29.9	16.1
	2 children	17.7	34.3	24.2
	3 or more children	35.6	54.3	43.5
Lone fathers				
	1 child	3.8	22.8	5.4
	2 children	13.6	34.1	15.2
	3 or more children	37.3	52.1	38.8
Lone mothers				
	1 child	9.8	31.0	14.5
	2 children	21.0	41.2	24.3
	3 or more children	47.2	60.3	49.4
	Total	12.8	34.3	15.6

Note: The grand total and the total families living with other persons include 2.9% of all children for whom it cannot be determined, from the Individual Public Use Microdata File, whether the family shares its housing with other persons. All these children are in families with three or more children, and 45.9% of them live in crowded housing. For the definition of "crowding," see Section 7.6 of this chapter.

Source: Census of Canada, 1991, Individual Public Use Microdata Files.

To continue our study of the relationship between housing conditions and crowding, we again refer simultaneously to two characteristics that have proven significant in terms of the choices families make, namely, tenure and the type of housing. Figure 7.13 shows the proportion of families living in crowded housing, by tenure and type of family, for husband–wife families and for families of lone fathers and lone mothers. For each type of housing, it was found that tenant families are more likely than owner families to live in crowded housing. Thus, for single-family dwellings the rate of crowding is 10% for tenants and 3% for owners; for dwellings in low-rise buildings the rate is 16% and 7%; and in highrise buildings the rate is 18% and 7%. At different levels, the profile is about the same for each type of family, the rate of crowding ranging from 24% to 29% of lone fathers and lone mothers who rent housing in low- or highrise buildings. These results clearly show the strong link between the space families have and the type of housing. However, lone-parent families, which have, on average, less in the way of financial resources than husband–wife families, are far more likely to live in housing that is crowded, regardless of its type.

FIGURE 7.12

PROPORTION OF HUSBAND–WIFE FAMILIES LIVING IN CROWDED HOUSING,[1] BY LIVING ARRANGEMENTS AND PRESENCE OF CHILDREN, **1991**

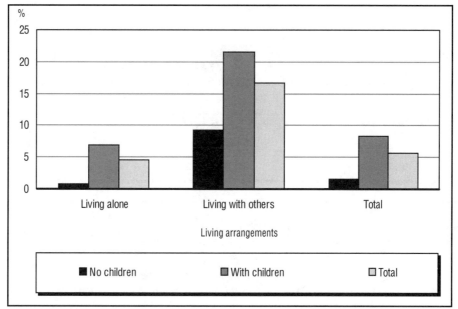

1. For the definition of "crowding," see Section 7.6.
Note: The data for this figure are from Appendix 7, Table 8.
Source: Census of Canada, 1991, Individual Public Use Microdata Files.

Responses to a census question about the need for repairs to the dwelling reveal something about the perceived housing conditions. By combining this information with the crowding index, it is possible to determine the percentage of families living in more difficult conditions—in either crowded or run-down housing. There is a very clear connection between this percentage, which is not very high, and tenure. Owner families fare well in this regard, with fewer than 2% living in crowded housing in need of repairs. Among tenant families, the proportion is nearly three times higher; lone-parent families are therefore particularly affected, as they are much more likely to rent.

FIGURE 7.13

PROPORTION OF FAMILIES LIVING IN CROWDED HOUSING,[1] BY TYPE OF FAMILY, TENURE AND TYPE OF BUILDING, 1991

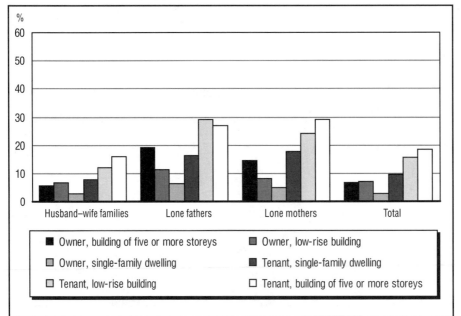

1.   For the definition of "crowding," see section 7.6.
Note: The data for this figure are from Appendix 7, Table 9.
Source: Census of Canada, 1991, Households and Housing Public Use Microdata Files.

Once again, it is appropriate to look to the children and examine the proportion who live in crowded housing. Recall that 15.6% of children are in this situation; this proportion varies greatly not only by family type and living arrangements, but also by type of housing and tenure. Children who live in buildings of five or more storeys are more likely to have to share their bedroom or lack space. More than 30% of children live in this type of housing, and the figure rises to between 44% and 52% in tenant families (see Figure 7.14). Remember too, however, that only 3% of all children live in such housing. In low-rise buildings, the rate of crowding may also be relatively high, particularly among children living with just one parent; but only 7% of children are affected. According to the profile of families, children of two-parent families living in single-family dwellings have more space. Not only do they have more room indoors, but they also have more room outdoors in their immediate environment suitable for playing their favourite games and sports, whether they are tots or teens.

FIGURE 7.14

PROPORTION OF CHILDREN UNDER AGE 16 LIVING IN CROWDED HOUSING,[1] BY TYPE OF FAMILY, TENURE AND TYPE OF BUILDING, 1991

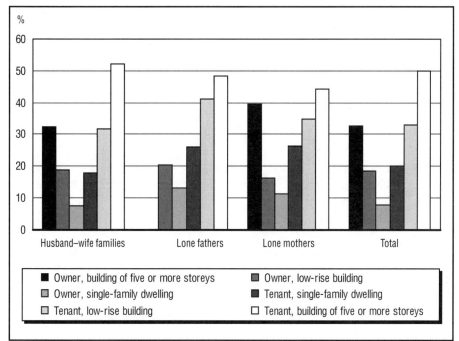

1. For the definition of "crowding," see section 7.6.
Note: The data for this figure are from Appendix 7, Table 9.
Source: Census of Canada, 1991, Households and Housing Public Use Microdata Files.

In short, it cannot be concluded that Canadian families on the whole live in very poor housing conditions. A small nucleus of families, with a definite overrepresentation of lone-parent families, experience hardship (that is, crowded and poorly maintained housing)—a problem that is more readily apparent when children, rather than families, are examined directly.

7.7 FAMILY TYPES AND FINANCIAL OUTLAY

The expression "financial outlay" refers to the owner's major payments (main ownership costs or gross rent) as a percentage of household income. In the 1991 Census, the owner's major payments included electricity, fuel, water, and other municipal services for all households, monthly mortgage payments, property taxes (municipal and school taxes), as well as condominium fees for owners and monthly cash rent for renters. The income used to calculate the financial outlay is the total of all incomes of all household members, whether or not they contribute to the owner's major payments. The financial outlay can be calculated only for non-farm dwellings.

When the Canada Mortgage and Housing Corporation (CMHC) agrees to back a mortgage loan to a household wishing to buy its own home, it estimates that the household's financial outlay, for mortgage payments plus the owner's major payments, should not exceed 30% of its income (sometimes 32%). The Canadian loan industry applies the same standard.[5] Beyond this limit, a household is considered unable to afford the housing (Miron 1993), and households that spend 30% or more of their income on housing costs can be deemed to have insufficient residual income to meet their other basic needs (Bergeron 1994; Morissette and Péron 1992). Financial outlay is therefore an indicator of a household's material well-being, but has its limitations. Obviously, high-income households can afford to pay more than 30% of their income on housing, but rarely need to do so. Also, non-housing expenses vary according to the age and number of persons in the household. In the following paragraphs, the expression "families with a housing affordability problem" refers to families that spend 30% or more of their household income on housing.

First of all, the financial outlay varies substantially according to tenure; tenants spend a higher proportion of their income on the owner's major payments than owners. Consequently, in 1991, the proportion of one-family households with a housing affordability problem was higher among tenants (29%) than among owners (14%) for Canada as a whole.[6] There are two main reasons for this. Firstly, some owners either never or no longer had a mortgage to repay. Second, on average, owners had higher incomes than tenants. Thus, when only owners with an outstanding mortgage are considered, 23% had a housing affordability problem;[7] this proportion is almost as high as that for tenants.

Regardless of whether families have children under age 16, or whether those with children are two-parent or lone-parent families, tenants are always more likely than owners with a mortgage to spend 30% or more of their income on housing (see Figure 7.15). The only exception is young couples who do not yet have children, perhaps because, when tenants, they are less likely to live in a single-family dwelling than couples with children, this housing generally being more costly to rent than other types (see Figure 7.9). It should not be too hastily concluded that all young couples without children who spend 30% or more of their income on housing have a housing affordability problem, since, having no children, they may have fewer variable expenses than families with children.

FIGURE 7.15

PROPORTION OF HOUSEHOLDS[1] WITH A FINANCIAL OUTLAY OF 30% OR MORE IN 1990, BY TENURE AND LIFE CYCLE, 1991

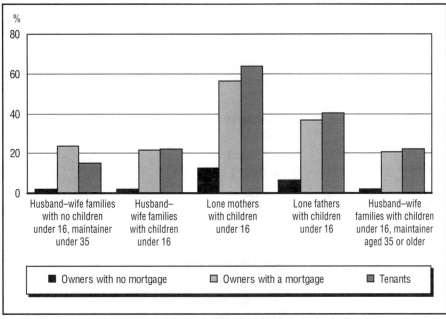

1. Households composed of one economic family where the maintainer is the husband, wife or lone parent.
Note: The data for this figure are from Appendix 7, Table 10.
Source: Census of Canada, 1991, Households and Housing Public Use Microdata Files.

Husband–wife families are less likely than lone-parent families to have a housing affordability problem. Of lone mothers with children under age 16, 60% have this problem when they are tenants and 57% when they are owners with an outstanding mortgage. Of husband–wife families, only about 20% have a housing affordability problem, whether they are tenants or owners with an outstanding mortgage.

The need for space, and therefore quite often the cost of housing, increases as children are born and get older; income, however, does not always increase at the same rate. While employment income also tends to increase with age, this increase is sometimes offset by the mother leaving the labour force. Thus, in 1990, the proportion of families with a housing affordability problem was smaller among two-parent families where both spouses were gainfully employed than among other two-parent families, regardless of the age and number of children (see Figure 7.16). However, the differences were greater by children's age than by number of children. The proportion of families with a housing affordability problem is lower the older the children, and varies little according to the number of children. For example, of husband–wife families where both spouses held paid employment in 1990, the proportion, which is 17% when the family had just one child under age six, barely rises when there were two children in that same age group, and drops slightly when there were three or more children under age six. The proportion is lower when the children were aged 6 to 15, whether there was one child (12%), two children (13%), or three or more (15%). If the proportion of those who spend 30% or more on housing diminishes as the children's age increases, it is partly because the parents' incomes increase as they and their children grow older.

FIGURE 7.16

PROPORTION OF FAMILIES WITH A FINANCIAL OUTLAY OF 30% OR MORE IN 1990, BY TYPE OF FAMILY, NUMBER AND AGE OF CHILDREN UNDER AGE 16, 1991

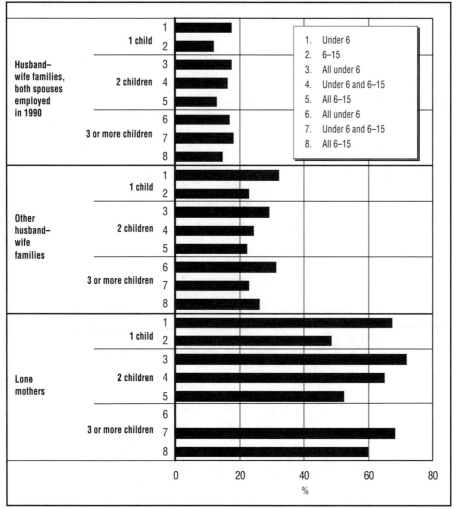

Note: The data for this figure are from Appendix 7, Table 11.

Source: Census of Canada, 1991, Households and Housing Public Use Microdata Files.

For the two-parent families who could not rely on a second income, we determined that the proportion of families with a housing affordability problem drops with the age and number of children. There is probably an effect of choice at work here: it seems that more wives leave the labour force on having their second or third child when the family is already financially comfortable without the wife's employment income. Among lone mothers, the proportion of families with a housing affordability problem increases with the number of children, instead of remaining stable or decreasing as it does for two-parent families. It remains quite high, dipping below 50% only when there is just one child aged 6 to 15 (48%). It ranges from 52% when there are two children aged 6 to 15, to 72% when there are two children under age 6. (There were not enough lone mothers with three or more children under age six to calculate their distribution by financial outlay.)

Other than gainful employment of the wife, another strategy that may alleviate the burden of the owner's major payments is shared housing. For all family types, the proportion of households that spend 30% or more of their income on housing is lower among families that live with other people. But, by far, mostly single lone mothers and separated, divorced or married mothers on their own are less likely to have a housing affordability problem when they live with others (see Figure 7.17). In the case of single lone mothers, this may mean returning home to live with their parents. In other family types, it may mean taking in someone on a low income (such as elderly parents, divorced or widowed brothers or sisters or boarders). Even when they share their housing, 40% of single lone mothers and 26.5% of separated, divorced or married mothers on their own live in housing whose cost represents 30% or more of the household income, whereas this is true of only 14% of husband–wife families who live with others.

In short, tenants are more inclined to have a housing affordability problem than owners, especially owners with no mortgage to repay. Income is a decisive factor here: lone-parent families spend far more of their income on housing than two-parent families, especially when the parent is female; and proportionally more families with younger children spend 30% or more of their income on housing because the parents' incomes are smaller. The burden is somewhat alleviated when both spouses work.

FIGURE 7.17

PROPORTION OF FAMILIES LIVING IN HOUSEHOLDS THAT SPENT 30% OR MORE OF THEIR INCOME ON HOUSING COSTS IN 1990, BY TYPE OF FAMILY AND LIVING ARRANGEMENTS, 1991

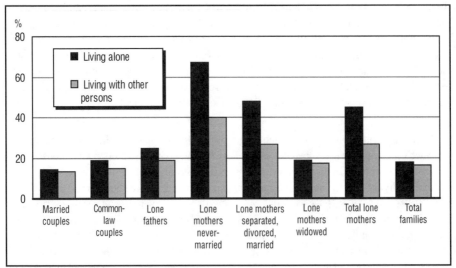

Note: The data for this figure are from Appendix 7, Table 12.
Source: Census of Canada, 1991, special compilation.

7.8   CONCLUSION

The type of tenure has a decisive impact on the other characteristics of housing. First, there is a strong link between tenure and the type of dwelling, making it virtually essential for a family to own its home in order to have housing with a private outdoor area where the children can play, that is, to own a single-family dwelling. Secondly, the owner's major payments represent a smaller percentage of the household income of owners than of tenants. And proportionally fewer owner-occupied dwellings are crowded or in need of repair.

Owners, then, are generally better housed than tenants. However, home ownership is not equally affordable by everyone, owing largely to the income disparities between types of household and between types of family, as well as to the strong link between tenure and the type of building. Home ownership is far more common among families than among non-family households, and among husband–wife families than among lone-parent families. It is slightly more common among married couples than among common-law couples, and among families with older children than among those with younger children.

A double income helps couples reduce the proportion of household income spent on the owner's major payments. This, however, is not an option for lone-parent families, a significantly greater proportion of whom spend 30% or more of their income on housing.

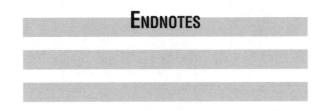

ENDNOTES

1. Based on the 1991 Census of Canada, *Families: Social and Economic Characteristics,* in Statistics Canada Catalogue no. 93-320, Table 2, p. 64.

2. Based on the 1991 Census of Canada, "Population and Dwelling Counts," *Urban Areas,* in Statistics Canada Catalogue no. 93-305, Table 4, p. 68.

3. Phenomenon defined as "the gradual influx of households of high social status into less affluent neighbourhoods [. . . which] raises housing prices [. . . and] causes [. . .] the displacement of lower-income and often elderly households" [translation] (Senécal, Tremblay and Teufel, 1990, p. 14).

4. For a review of the various measurements of crowding, see Morris and Winter (1978).

5. Information provided by CMHC.

6. Based on the 1991 Census of Canada, *Housing Costs and Other Characteristics of Canadian Households,* in Statistics Canada Catalogue no. 93-330, tables 4 (p. 74) and 5 (p. 112).

7. Ibid.

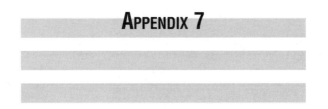

TABLE 1

TENURE, BY TYPE OF HOUSEHOLD AND REGION, 1961 TO 1991[1]

	Family				Non-family				Total			
Year	Owner	Tenant	Total (%)	Total (N)	Owner	Tenant	Total (%)	Total (N)	Owner	Tenant	Total (%)	Total (N)
Atlantic												
1961	76.7	23.3	100.0	373,284	74.5	25.5	100.0	46,652	76.5	23.5	100.0	419,936
1971	74.5	25.5	100.0	431,000	61.9	38.1	100.0	71,130	72.7	27.3	100.0	502,120
1981	80.1	19.9	100.0	545,570	50.1	49.9	100.0	128,620	74.3	25.7	100.0	674,190
1991	80.2	19.8	100.0	616,285	51.9	48.1	100.0	178,995	73.8	26.2	100.0	795,285
Quebec												
1961	51.1	48.9	100.0	1,059,060	32.0	68.0	100.0	132,308	49.0	51.0	100.0	1,191,368
1971	52.8	47.2	100.0	1,325,055	22.0	78.0	100.0	278,625	47.4	52.6	100.0	1,603,685
1981	63.2	36.8	100.0	1,654,740	21.6	78.4	100.0	518,110	53.3	46.7	100.0	2,172,860
1991	67.3	32.7	100.0	1,864,810	27.2	72.8	100.0	767,685	55.6	44.4	100.0	2,632,500
Ontario												
1961	72.3	27.7	100.0	1,422,985	59.2	40.8	100.0	217,765	70.5	29.5	100.0	1,640,750
1971	68.0	32.0	100.0	1,822,800	39.9	60.1	100.0	402,410	63.0	37.0	100.0	2,225,205
1981	72.9	27.1	100.0	2,240,390	33.6	66.4	100.0	729,390	63.3	36.7	100.0	2,969,780
1991	73.1	26.9	100.0	2,664,700	38.0	62.0	100.0	969,680	63.7	36.3	100.0	3,634,380
Prairies												
1961	75.4	24.6	100.0	707,453	62.5	37.5	100.0	127,534	73.4	26.6	100.0	834,987
1971	71.9	28.1	100.0	816,485	46.5	53.5	100.0	203,290	66.8	33.2	100.0	1,019,765
1981	76.0	24.0	100.0	1,061,655	38.6	61.4	100.0	387,275	66.0	34.0	100.0	1,448,945
1991	75.7	24.3	100.0	1,184,045	42.9	57.1	100.0	478,770	66.3	33.7	100.0	1,662,825
British Columbia												
1961	74.3	25.7	100.0	379,348	55.2	44.8	100.0	80,184	71.0	29.0	100.0	459,532
1971	71.0	29.0	100.0	519,905	36.3	63.7	100.0	147,415	63.3	36.7	100.0	667,325
1981	75.6	24.4	100.0	714,910	35.9	64.1	100.0	281,730	64.4	35.6	100.0	996,645
1991	74.0	26.0	100.0	864,225	41.1	58.9	100.0	376,670	64.0	36.0	100.0	1,240,890
Canada												
1961	67.7	32.3	100.0	3,948,753	54.6	45.4	100.0	605,740	66.0	34.0	100.0	4,554,493
1971	65.4	34.6	100.0	4,925,435	37.5	62.5	100.0	1,105,370	60.3	39.7	100.0	6,030,805
1981	71.7	28.3	100.0	6,231,950	32.8	67.2	100.0	2,049,580	62.1	37.9	100.0	8,281,530
1991	72.7	27.3	100.0	7,213,135	37.2	62.8	100.0	2,778,415	62.8	37.2	100.0	9,991,550

1. Before 1986, dwellings on Indian reserves were classified as either "owned" or "rented." In 1991, the latter were classified as "band housing." Also, only in 1991 do the data include temporary residents.

Note: Totals may not add to 100 due to rounding.

Source: Census of Canada, 1961, 1971, 1981, 1991.

TABLE 2

TENURE, BY FAMILY STRUCTURE AND AGE OF WIFE OR LONE PARENT, 1991

Type of family	Tenure			15–29	30–44	45–64	65 and older	All ages
Married couples	Tenant			41	18	13	20	20
	Owner	Total		59	82	88	80	80
		With mortgage		50	59	33	10	43
		No mortgage		9	23	55	70	37
	Total (%)			**100**	**100**	**100**	**100**	**100**
	Total (N)			**754,970**	**2,249,810**	**1,803,050**	**680,170**	**5,488,000**
Common-law couples	Tenant			69	43	34	39	54
	Owner	Total		31	58	66	61	47
		With mortgage		26	46	36	11	35
		No mortgage		5	12	30	50	12
	Total (%)			**100**	**100**	**100**	**100**	**100**
	Total (N)			**326,895**	**279,115**	**86,620**	**11,950**	**704,575**
Lone-parent families	Of lone father	Tenant		63	45	33	22	38
		Owner	Total	37	55	68	78	63
			With mortgage	27	40	36	17	35
			No mortgage	10	15	32	61	28
	Total (%)			**100**	**100**	**100**	**100**	**100**
	Total (N)			**8,255**	**64,345**	**65,205**	**21,740**	**159,545**
	Of lone mother never-married	Tenant		95	84	69	55	88
		Owner	Total	5	17	31	46	12
			With mortgage	4	13	20	19	9
			No morgage	1	4	11	27	3
	Total (%)			**100**	**100**	**100**	**100**	**100**
	Total (N)			**77,220**	**61,795**	**9,735**	**1,110**	**149,860**
	Of lone mother separated, divorced or married	Tenant		79	63	48	40	60
		Owner	Total	21	37	52	60	40
			With mortgage	15	28	31	18	27
			No mortgage	6	9	21	42	13
	Total (%)			**100**	**100**	**100**	**100**	**100**
	Total (N)			**52,090**	**260,475**	**125,165**	**9,435**	**447,165**
	Of lone mother widowed	Tenant		60	35	27	26	28
		Owner	Total	41	65	73	74	72
			With mortgage	18	26	21	14	18
			No mortgage	23	39	52	60	54
	Total (%)			**100**	**100**	**100**	**100**	**100**
	Total (N)			**1,400**	**20,280**	**79,685**	**78,085**	**179,445**
Total	**Tenant**			**54**	**26**	**17**	**21**	**28**
	Owner	**Total**		**46**	**74**	**83**	**79**	**73**
		With mortgage		**39**	**54**	**32**	**11**	**40**
		No mortgage		**7**	**20**	**51**	**68**	**33**
	Total (%)			**100**	**100**	**100**	**100**	**100**
	Total (N)			**1,220,815**	**2,935,805**	**2,169,430**	**802,525**	**7,128,605**

Note: Totals may not add to 100 due to rounding.
Source: Census of Canada, 1991, special compilation.

TABLE 3

PROPORTION OF FAMILIES LIVING IN AN OWNER-OCCUPIED DWELLING, BY IDENTITY OF THE PRIMARY HOUSEHOLD MAINTAINER, TYPE OF FAMILY AND LIVING ARRANGEMENTS, 1991

| Type of family | Living arrangements | % of owners | | Distribution of maintainers who are owners | | |
		Maintainer is spouse or lone parent	Maintainer is another person	Spouse or lone parent	Another person	Total
Married couples	Family living alone	74.0	6.8	91.6	8.4	**100.0**
	Family living with others	61.6	20.6	74.9	25.1	**100.0**
Common-law couples	Family living alone	34.0	12.9	72.5	27.5	**100.0**
	Family living with others	25.5	26.3	49.3	50.7	**100.0**
Lone fathers	Family living alone	58.9	2.0	96.7	3.3	**100.0**
	Family living with others	51.4	17.1	75.1	24.9	**100.0**
Lone mothers, never married	Family living alone	9.7	0.1	99.2	0.8	**100.0**
	Family living with others	16.8	6.5	72.2	27.8	**100.0**
Lone mothers, Separated, divorced or married	Family living alone	35.7	0.7	98.0	2.0	**100.0**
	Family living with others	30.2	23.2	56.6	43.4	**100.0**
Lone mothers, widowed	Family living alone	64.4	8.7	88.1	11.9	**100.0**
	Family living with others	50.8	22.0	69.8	30.2	**100.0**

Source: Census of Canada, 1991, Individual Public Use Microdata Files.

TABLE 4

TENURE OF HOUSEHOLD MAINTAINER IN HUSBAND–WIFE FAMILIES, BY LIFE CYCLE AND FAMILY INCOME QUINTILE[1] IN 1990, 1991

Life cycle	Tenure		1st quintile	2nd quintile	3rd quintile	4th quintile	5th quintile	Total
Under 35, no children as yet	Tenant		74.8	68.1	56.1	40.9	25.6	**52.9**
	Owner	Total	25.2	31.9	43.9	59.1	74.4	**47.2**
		With mortgage	17.3	24.6	36.8	52.5	64.6	**39.6**
		No mortgage	8.0	7.3	7.1	6.7	9.7	**7.6**
	Total		**100.0**	**100.0**	**100.0**	**100.0**	**100.0**	**100.0**
Under 35, with children	Tenant		58.0	42.4	27.8	17.8	12.7	**31.0**
	Owner	Total	42.0	57.6	72.2	82.2	87.3	**69.1**
		With mortgage	29.8	45.3	61.2	70.7	72.9	**57.0**
		No mortgage	12.2	12.3	11.0	11.5	14.4	**12.0**
	Total		**100.0**	**100.0**	**100.0**	**100.0**	**100.0**	**100.0**
35–54, with children	Tenant		33.9	25.0	16.7	10.7	6.0	**13.6**
	Owner	Total	66.1	75.0	83.3	89.3	94.1	**86.4**
		With mortgage	36.0	44.3	52.9	58.3	58.2	**53.9**
		No mortgage	30.1	30.7	30.4	31.0	35.9	**32.5**
	Total		**100.0**	**100.0**	**100.0**	**100.0**	**100.0**	**100.0**
35–54, children no longer present	Tenant		36.5	23.9	20.7	15.4	11.0	**20.6**
	Owner	Total	63.5	76.1	79.9	84.6	89.0	**79.4**
		With mortgage	23.6	31.4	39.0	45.3	45.8	**37.9**
		No mortgage	39.9	44.7	40.9	39.3	43.1	**41.5**
	Total		**100.0**	**100.0**	**100.0**	**100.0**	**100.0**	**100.0**
35–54, remained childless	Tenant		44.4	38.0	30.0	21.0	13.4	**24.7**
	Owner	Total	55.6	62.0	70.0	79.0	86.6	**75.3**
		With mortgage	23.9	32.4	41.1	51.2	52.7	**44.5**
		No mortgage	31.7	29.6	28.9	27.8	33.9	**30.8**
	Total		**100.0**	**100.0**	**100.0**	**100.0**	**100.0**	**100.0**
55–64, with children	Tenant		24.7	16.2	13.2	9.3	5.2	**11.2**
	Owner	Total	75.3	83.8	86.8	90.7	94.8	**88.8**
		With mortgage	24.4	21.4	23.1	28.0	29.2	**26.1**
		No mortgage	50.8	62.4	63.8	62.7	65.6	**62.7**
	Total		**100.0**	**100.0**	**100.0**	**100.0**	**100.0**	**100.0**
55–64, children no longer present	Tenant		21.4	14.3	12.8	10.5	6.7	**14.3**
	Owner	Total	78.6	85.7	87.2	89.6	93.3	**85.7**
		With mortgage	17.2	18.3	21.1	24.4	21.3	**19.8**
		No mortgage	61.4	67.5	66.1	65.2	72.1	**65.9**
	Total		**100.0**	**100.0**	**100.0**	**100.0**	**100.0**	**100.0**

Table 4 (CONCLUDED)

TENURE OF HOUSEHOLD MAINTAINER IN HUSBAND–WIFE FAMILIES, BY LIFE CYCLE AND FAMILY INCOME QUINTILE[1] IN 1990, 1991

Life cycle	Tenure		1st quintile	2nd quintile	3rd quintile	4th quintile	5th quintile	Total
55–64, remained childless	Tenant		29.0	19.4	18.4	12.0	8.6	**18.8**
	Owner	Total	71.0	80.6	81.6	88.0	91.5	**81.2**
		With mortgage	14.2	15.0	17.5	19.2	19.7	**16.6**
		No mortgage	56.8	65.6	64.0	68.8	71.8	**64.5**
	Total		**100.0**	**100.0**	**100.0**	**100.0**	**100.0**	**100.0**
65 and older, with children	Tenant		22.5	20.2	13.2	11.6	5.3	**13.8**
	Owner	Total	77.5	79.8	86.8	88.4	94.7	**86.2**
		With mortgage	15.5	12.8	14.8	17.3	14.9	**15.0**
		No mortgage	62.0	67.0	72.0	71.1	79.8	**71.2**
	Total		**100.0**	**100.0**	**100.0**	**100.0**	**100.0**	**100.0**
65 and older, children no longer present	Tenant		25.9	20.5	15.0	12.3	11.2	**20.5**
	Owner	Total	74.1	79.5	85.0	87.7	88.8	**79.5**
		With mortgage	10.0	9.7	10.1	9.0	7.2	**9.6**
		No mortgage	64.2	69.8	74.9	78.6	81.6	**69.9**
	Total		**100.0**	**100.0**	**100.0**	**100.0**	**100.0**	**100.0**
65 and older, remained childless	Tenant		30.4	26.9	22.6	16.8	18.3	**25.3**
	Owner	Total	69.6	73.1	77.5	83.2	81.7	**74.7**
		With mortgage	7.7	5.9	7.1	7.5	6.1	**6.9**
		No mortgage	61.9	67.3	70.3	75.7	75.6	**67.8**
	Total		**100.0**	**100.0**	**100.0**	**100.0**	**100.0**	**100.0**
55 and older, with children	Tenant		24.2	17.5	13.2	9.8	5.2	**11.8**
	Owner	Total	75.8	82.6	86.8	90.2	94.8	**88.2**
		With mortgage	22.4	18.7	20.9	25.5	27.1	**23.6**
		No mortgage	53.4	63.9	65.9	64.7	67.7	**64.6**
	Total		**100.0**	**100.0**	**100.0**	**100.0**	**100.0**	**100.0**
55 and older, children no present	Tenant		24.2	17.6	13.8	11.2	8.5	**17.5**
	Owner	Total	75.8	82.4	86.2	88.8	91.5	**82.5**
		With mortgage	12.7	13.7	16.3	18.6	15.8	**14.6**
		No mortgage	63.1	68.7	69.9	70.3	75.8	**68.0**
	Total		**100.0**	**100.0**	**100.0**	**100.0**	**100.0**	**100.0**
55 and older, remained childless	Tenant		29.9	23.7	20.7	14.3	13.4	**22.5**
	Owner	Total	70.1	76.3	79.3	85.7	86.6	**77.5**
		With mortgage	10.0	9.7	11.9	13.5	13.0	**11.1**
		No mortgage	60.1	66.6	67.5	72.2	73.6	**66.4**
	Total		**100.0**	**100.0**	**100.0**	**100.0**	**100.0**	**100.0**

1. Families have been classified by income in ascending order. Thus, the first quintile represents the 20% of families with the lowest incomes.

Note: Totals may not add to 100 due to rounding. Dwellings where the primary maintainer is a temporary resident have been excluded.

Source: Census of Canada, 1991, Family Public Use Microdata Files.

Table 5

Tenure of Households with no Unattached Individuals, by Type of Family, Number of Children under Age 16 and their Age, 1991

Number of children	Age of children	Tenure	Husband–wife	Lone father	Lone mother
					%
None		Owner	76.8	69.4	59.6
		Tenant	23.2	30.6	40.4
		Total	**100.0**	**100.0**	**100.0**
1 child	Under 6	Owner	64.8	50.0	14.5
		Tenant	35.2	50.0	85.5
		Total	**100.0**	**100.0**	**100.0**
	6–15	Owner	81.7	55.2	33.6
		Tenant	18.3	44.9	66.4
		Total	**100.0**	**100.0**	**100.0**
2 children	All under 6	Owner	75.2	43.6[1]	12.9
		Tenant	24.8	56.5[1]	87.2
		Total	**100.0**	**100.0**	**100.0**
	Under 6 and 6–15	Owner	77.6	55.4	22.7
		Tenant	22.4	44.6	77.3
		Total	**100.0**	**100.0**	**100.0**
	All 6–15	Owner	85.3	64.0	38.6
		Tenant	14.7	36.0	61.4
		Total	**100.0**	**100.0**	**100.0**
3 or more children	All under 6	Owner	73.9	--	8.4[1]
		Tenant	26.1	--	91.6[1]
		Total	**100.0**	**100.0**	**100.0**
	Under 6 and 6–15	Owner	79.2	57.7[1]	23.8
		Tenant	20.8	42.3[1]	76.2
		Total	**100.0**	**100.0**	**100.0**
	All 6–15	Owner	85.5	62.8[1]	41.0
		Tenant	14.5	37.2[1]	59.0
		Total	**100.0**	**100.0**	**100.0**

-- Percentage omitted (fewer than 10 cases in the sample).

1. Percentage calculated for fewer than 100 cases in the sample.

Note: Totals may not add to 100 due to rounding.

Source: Census of Canada, 1991, Households and Housing Public Use Microdata Files.

TABLE 6

TYPE OF BUILDING OF OCCUPIED DWELLINGS, BY REGION, 1991

	Region					
Type of building	Atlantic	Quebec	Ontario	Prairies	British Columbia	Canada[1]
					%	
Detached single-family dwellling	71.5	45.3	58.5	66.8	59.5	**57.6**
Apartment in a building of five or more storeys	2.0	5.0	16.0	5.4	5.5	**8.9**
Apartment in a building of under five storeys	11.1	34.9	10.1	13.3	19.0	**18.4**
Semi-detached dwelling	4.1	4.6	6.1	3.6	2.6	**4.7**
Detached duplex	4.3	6.1	2.4	1.8	4.7	**3.7**
Row dwelling	2.8	2.3	6.0	5.5	5.0	**4.6**
Other single-family dwelling	0.6	0.8	0.5	0.3	0.2	**0.5**
Mobile dwelling	3.7	1.0	0.6	3.3	3.5	**1.8**
Total	**100.0**	**100.0**	**100.0**	**100.0**	**100.0**	**100.0**

1. Including Yukon and Northwest Territories.

Note: Totals may not add to 100 due to rounding. Dwellings where the primary maintainer is a temporary resident have been excluded.

Source: Census of Canada, 1991, Households and Housing Public Use Microdata Files.

TABLE 7

TENURE AND TYPE OF BUILDING IN HUSBAND–WIFE FAMILIES, BY LIFE CYCLE AND FAMILY INCOME QUINTILE IN 1990, 1991

Life cycle	Tenure and type of building	1st	2nd	3rd	4th	5th	**Total**
				%			
Husband–wife families with children under 16	Owner, building of five or more storeys	0.3	0.3	0.3	0.4	0.5	**0.4**
	Owner, low-rise building	8.7	11.5	11.8	11.4	9.5	**10.8**
	Owner, single-family dwelling	42.7	53.9	65.6	75.1	83.0	**67.1**
	Tenant, single-family dwelling	13.2	10.1	6.6	4.4	3.1	**6.7**
	Tenant, low-rise building	30.0	21.2	13.3	7.3	3.1	**12.9**
	Tenant, building of five or more storeys	5.2	3.0	2.3	1.5	0.8	**2.2**
	Total	**100.0**	**100.0**	**100.0**	**100.0**	**100.0**	**100.0**
	Owners	51.7	65.7	77.7	86.8	93.0	**78.3**
	Tenants	48.3	34.3	22.3	13.2	7.0	**21.8**

TABLE 7 (CONTINUED)

TENURE AND TYPE OF BUILDING IN HUSBAND–WIFE FAMILIES, BY LIFE CYCLE AND FAMILY INCOME QUINTILE IN 1990, 1991

Life cycle	Tenure and type of building	1st	2nd	3rd	4th	5th	Total
				%			
Husband–wife families with no children under 16, maintainer under 35	Owner, building of five or more storeys	0.5	0.5	0.7	1.2	2.3	1.0
	Owner, low-rise building	5.1	7.6	10.2	12.9	14.8	10.2
	Owner, single-family dwelling	14.3	20.9	31.9	44.1	57.4	33.6
	Tenant, single-family dwelling	11.8	10.5	8.4	6.4	4.3	8.3
	Tenant, low-rise building	58.2	52.0	39.4	26.7	14.5	38.2
	Tenant, building of five or more storeys	10.1	8.5	9.3	8.7	6.7	8.7
	Total	**100.0**	**100.0**	**100.0**	**100.0**	**100.0**	**100.0**
	Owners	19.9	28.9	42.9	58.2	74.5	44.8
	Tenants	80.1	71.1	57.1	41.8	25.5	55.2
Husband–wife families with no children under 16, maintainer under 35	Owner, building of five or more storeys	1.0	1.2	1.5	1.6	2.6	1.6
	Owner, low-rise building	11.4	12.1	12.4	12.8	11.0	11.9
	Owner, single-family dwelling	61.2	66.3	68.7	72.4	78.2	69.7
	Tenant, single-family dwelling	4.3	3.4	2.9	2.6	1.9	3.0
	Tenant, low-rise building	16.4	12.0	10.1	7.4	3.9	9.7
	Tenant, building of five or more storeys	5.8	4.9	4.4	3.2	2.5	4.1
	Total	**100.0**	**100.0**	**100.0**	**100.0**	**100.0**	**100.0**
	Owners	73.5	79.7	82.6	86.8	91.7	83.2
	Tenants	26.5	20.4	17.4	13.2	8.3	16.8
Lone-parent families with children under 16, maintainer is male	Owner, building of five or more storeys	0.2	0.4	0.5	0.0	1.5	0.4
	Owner, low-rise building	8.0	12.1	14.3	16.1	9.8	11.6
	Owner, single-family dwelling	28.0	39.1	55.9	63.6	70.7	44.4
	Tenant, single-family dwelling	13.0	9.8	7.1	7.8	6.0	9.8
	Tenant, low-rise building	43.9	32.2	18.6	9.7	9.8	28.7
	Tenant, building of five or more storeys	6.8	6.4	3.6	2.8	2.3	5.2
	Total	**100.0**	**100.0**	**100.0**	**100.0**	**100.0**	**100.0**
	Owners	36.2	51.6	70.7	79.7	82.0	56.4
	Tenants	63.8	48.4	29.3	20.3	18.1	43.6

TABLE 7 (CONCLUDED)

TENURE AND TYPE OF BUILDING IN HUSBAND–WIFE FAMILIES, BY LIFE CYCLE AND FAMILY INCOME QUINTILE IN 1990, 1991

Life cycle	Tenure and type of building	1st	2nd	3rd	4th	5th	Total
				%			
Lone-parent families with children under 16, maintainer is female	Owner, building of five or more storeys	0.3	0.5	0.8	2.0	0.6	**0.4**
	Owner, low-rise building	4.2	12.5	15.7	19.2	18.1	**7.5**
	Owner, single-family dwelling	11.9	29.5	47.5	50.7	56.9	**20.2**
	Tenant, single-family dwelling	14.4	9.3	7.2	6.6	6.3	**12.4**
	Tenant, low-rise building	61.0	41.7	24.2	18.6	15.6	**52.1**
	Tenant, building of five or more storeys	8.3	6.7	4.7	2.9	2.5	**7.4**
	Total	**100.0**	**100.0**	**100.0**	**100.0**	**100.0**	**100.0**
	Owners	16.4	42.4	64.0	71.9	75.6	**28.1**
	Tenants	83.6	57.6	36.0	28.1	24.4	**71.9**

1. Families have been classified by income in ascending order. Thus, the first quintile represents the 20% of families with the lowest incomes.

Note: Totals may not add to 100 due to rounding. Dwellings where the primary maintainer is a temporary resident have been excluded.

Source: Census of Canada, 1991, Households and Housing Public Use Microdata Files.

TABLE 8

PROPORTION OF FAMILIES LIVING IN CROWDED HOUSING,[1] BY TENURE, TYPE OF FAMILY AND LIVING ARRANGEMENTS, 1991

Tenure	Type of family	Living arrangements		Total
		Family living alone	Living with others	
Owner	Husband–wife families with children	4.0	15.4	**5.1**
	Husband–wife families with no children	0.2	6.7	**0.9**
	All husband–wife families	**2.6**	**12.0**	**3.5**
	Male lone-parent families	3.9	20.1	**9.41**
	Female lone-parent families	3.9	23.6	**8.7**
	Total	**2.7**	**14.0**	**4.0**
Renter	Husband–wife families with children	19.3	46.0	**22.0**
	Husband–wife families with no children	2.3	18.4	**3.6**
	All husband–wife families	**10.8**	**34.2**	**12.9**
	Male lone-parent families	20.4	50.5	**28.6**
	Female lone-parent families	21.8	47.4	**25.9**
	Total	**13.4**	**39.8**	**16.4**

TABLE 8 (CONCLUDED)

PROPORTION OF FAMILIES LIVING IN CROWDED HOUSING,[1] BY TENURE, TYPE OF FAMILY AND LIVING ARRANGEMENTS, 1991

Tenure	Type of family	Living arrangements		Total
		Family living alone	Living with others	
Total	Husband–wife families with children	7.0	21.6	8.4
	Husband–wife families with no children	0.8	9.3	1.6
	All husband–wife families	4.5	16.7	5.7
	Male lone-parent families	10.3	29.7	16.4
	Female lone-parent families	14.7	34.8	18.6
	Total	**5.6**	**20.8**	**7.3**

1. For the definition of "crowding," see Section 7.6.

Source: Census of Canada, 1991, Individual Public Use Microdata Files.

TABLE 9

PROPORTION OF FAMILIES AND CHILDREN LIVING IN CROWDED HOUSING,[1] BY TYPE OF FAMILY, TENURE AND TYPE OF BUILDING, 1991

	Tenure and type of building	Type of family			Total
		Husband–wife families	Lone fathers	Lone mothers	
		%			
Families	Owner, building of five or more storeys	5.8	19.2[2]	14.6	**6.7**
	Owner, low-rise building	6.8	11.5	8.3	**7.0**
	Owner, single-family dwelling	2.8	6.3	4.8	**2.9**
	Tenant, single-family dwelling	7.7	16.5	17.7	**9.6**
	Tenant, low-rise building	12.1	29.1	24.2	**15.6**
	Tenant, building of five or more storeys	15.9	26.9	29.1	**18.5**
	Total	**5.3**	**14.2**	**16.4**	**6.6**
Children	Owner, building of five or more storeys	32.3	--	39.4[2]	**32.8**
	Owner, low-rise building	18.8	20.5	16.5	**18.7**
	Owner, single-family dwelling	7.5	13.2	11.2	**7.7**
	Tenant, single-family dwelling	18.0	26.0	26.5	**20.0**
	Tenant, low-rise building	31.6	41.1	35.0	**33.1**
	Tenant, building of five or more storeys	52.3	48.3	44.2	**50.0**
	Total	**13.3**	**24.0**	**27.9**	**15.3**

-- Percentage omitted (fewer than 10 cases in the sample).

1. For the definition of "crowding," see Section 7.6.

2. Percentage calculated for fewer than 100 cases in the sample.

Note: Families where the primary maintainer or their spouse is a temporary resident have been excluded.

Source: Census of Canada, 1991, Households and Housing Public Use Microdata Files.

TABLE 10

FINANCIAL OUTLAY IN 1990, BY TENURE AND LIFE CYCLE, 1991

Life cycle	Financial outlay	Owners with no mortgage	Owners with a mortgage	Tenants
		%		
Husband–wife families with no children under 16, maintainer under 35	0–14%	91.6	17.3	43.8
	15–29%	6.4	59.3	40.9
	30% or more	2.1	23.5	15.3
	Total	**100.0**	**100.0**	**100.0**
Husband–wife families with children under 16	0–14%	93.2	23.2	32.8
	15–29%	4.8	55.3	45.1
	30% or more	1.9	21.5	22.2
	Total	**100.0**	**100.0**	**100.0**
Lone mothers with children under age 16	0–14%	65.2	6.0	5.9
	15–29%	22.1	37.4	30.3
	30% or more	12.7	56.6	63.8
	Total	**100.0**	**100.0**	**100.0**
Lone fathers with children under age 16	0–14%	82.7	15.7	19.8
	15–29%	11.0	47.3	39.9
	30% or more	6.3	37.0	40.3
	Total	**100.0**	**100.0**	**100.0**
Husband–wife families with no children under age 16, maintainer aged 35 or older	0–14%	87.0	35.6	35.3
	15–29%	10.8	43.8	42.6
	30% or more	2.2	20.5	22.1
	Total	**100.0**	**100.0**	**100.0**

Note: Totals may not add to 100 due to rounding. Families where one of the spouses was a temporary resident have been excluded.

Source: Census of Canada, 1991, Households and Housing Public Use Microdata Files.

TABLE 11

FINANCIAL OUTLAY IN 1990, BY TYPE OF FAMILY, NUMBER OF CHILDREN UNDER AGE 16 AND AGE, 1991

Number of children	Age of children	Type of family	Financial outlay 0–14%	15–29%	30% or more	Total
			%			
None		Husband–wife, both employed in 1990	56.7	32.6	10.7	**100.0**
		Other husband–wife families	60.7	25.5	13.7	**100.0**
		Female lone-parent families	43.2	33.7	23.1	**100.0**
1 child	Under 6	Husband–wife, both employed in 1990	32.1	50.5	17.4	**100.0**
		Other husband–wife families	28.8	39.1	32.2	**100.0**
		Female lone-parent families	8.5	24.2	67.4	**100.0**
	6–15	Husband–wife, both employed in 1990	51.6	36.3	12.1	**100.0**
		Other husband–wife families	45.1	32.2	22.8	**100.0**
		Female lone-parent families	16.1	35.5	48.4	**100.0**
2 children	All under 6	Husband–wife, both employed in 1990	31.0	51.5	17.5	**100.0**
		Other husband–wife families	23.5	47.4	29.1	**100.0**
		Female lone-parent families	5.5	22.8	71.8	**100.0**
	Under 6 and 6–15	Husband–wife, both employed in 1990	37.2	46.7	16.1	**100.0**
		Other husband–wife families	31.3	44.2	24.5	**100.0**
		Female lone-parent families	8.0	27.2	64.8	**100.0**
	All 6–15	Husband–wife, both employed in 1990	46.1	41.1	12.9	**100.0**
		Other husband–wife families	38.8	39.1	22.2	**100.0**
		Female lone-parent families	11.8	35.8	52.4	**100.0**
3 or more children	All under 6	Husband–wife, both employed in 1990	34.3	48.7	16.9	**100.0**
		Other husband–wife families	25.6	43.2	31.2	**100.0**
		Female lone-parent families	5.3[1]	23.4[1]	71.3[1]	**100.0**
	Under 6 and 6–15	Husband–wife, both employed in 1990	36.4	45.6	18.0	**100.0**
		Other husband–wife families	30.6	46.4	23.0	**100.0**
		Female lone-parent families	8.1	23.7	68.2	**100.0**
	All aged 6–15	Husband–wife, both employed in 1990	43.1	42.2	14.7	**100.0**
		Other husband–wife families	36.1	37.8	26.2	**100.0**
		Female lone-parent families	11.4	28.7	59.9	**100.0**
Total		**Husband–wife, both employed in 1990**	**48.7**	**38.5**	**12.9**	**100.0**
		Other husband–wife families	**52.3**	**30.3**	**17.5**	**100.0**
		Female lone-parent families	**23.9**	**31.9**	**44.2**	**100.0**

1. Percentage calculated for fewer than 100 cases.

Note: Totals may not add to 100 due to rounding. Families where the husband, wife or lone mother is a temporary resident have been excluded.

Source: Census of Canada, 1991, Households and Housing Public Use Microdata Files.

TABLE 12

FINANCIAL OUTLAY IN 1990, BY TYPE OF FAMILY AND LIVING ARRANGEMENTS, 1991

| Type of family | Financial outlay | Living arrangements | | |
		Family living alone	Family living with other persons	Total
Married couples	0–14%	49.8	55.0	**50.3**
	15–29%	35.7	31.4	**35.3**
	30% or more	14.4	13.5	**14.3**
	Total (%)	**100.0**	**100.0**	**100.0**
	Total (N)	**9,852,810**	**1,080,240**	**10,933,075**
Common-law couples	0–14%	38.5	47.4	**39.3**
	15–29%	42.8	37.6	**42.4**
	30% or more	18.7	15.0	**18.3**
	Total (%)	**100.0**	**100.0**	**100.0**
	Total (N)	**1,277,185**	**126,840**	**1,404,025**
Husband–wife families	0–14%	48.5	54.2	**49.1**
	15–29%	36.6	32.1	**36.1**
	30% o more	14.9	13.7	**14.8**
	Total (%)	**100.0**	**100.0**	**100.0**
	Total (N)	**5,564,990**	**603,540**	**6,168,550**
Lone fathers	0–14%	39.9	47.2	**42.3**
	15–29%	35.4	34.3	**35.0**
	30% or more	24.7	18.6	**22.7**
	Total (%)	**100.0**	**100.0**	**100.0**
	Total (N)	**107,090**	**51,780**	**1,58,870**
Lone mothers never-married	0–14%	6.8	21.9	**9.3**
	15–29%	25.9	38.3	**28.0**
	30% or more	67.4	39.9	**62.7**
	Total (%)	**100.0**	**100.0**	**100.0**
	Total (N)	**1,24,130**	**25,230**	**149,345**
Lone mothers separated, divorced or married	0–14%	16.1	36.5	**20.4**
	15–29%	36.0	36.9	**36.2**
	30% or more	47.9	26.5	**43.4**
	Total (%)	**100.0**	**100.0**	**100.0**
	Total (N)	**351,060**	**94,655**	**445,725**
Lone mothers widowed	0–14 %	53.2	55.6	**53.7**
	15–29%	28.2	27.1	**27.9**
	30% or more	18.7	17.4	**18.4**
	Total (%)	**100.0**	**100.0**	**100.0**
	Total (N)	**143,135**	**35,780**	**178,925**
Total lone mothers	**0–14%**	**22.8**	**38.5**	**26.0**
	15–29%	**32.1**	**34.9**	**32.7**
	30% or more	**45.1**	**26.6**	**41.3**
	Total (%)	**100.0**	**10.0**	**100.0**
	Total (N)	**618,325**	**155,670**	**774,000**

TABLE 12 (CONCLUDED)

FINANCIAL OUTLAY IN 1990, BY TYPE OF FAMILY AND LIVING ARRANGEMENTS, 1991

| Type of family | Financial outlay | Living arrangements | | Total |
		Family living alone	Family living with other persons	
Total families	**0–14%**	45.9	50.8	46.4
	15–29%	36.1	32.8	35.7
	30% or more	18.0	16.5	17.9
	Total (%)	100.0	100.0	100.0
	Total (N)	6,290,415	810,985	7,101,410

Note: Totals may not add to 100 due to rounding.

Source: Census of Canada, 1991, special compilation.

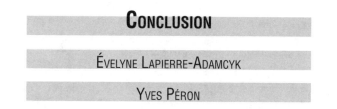

CONCLUSION

ÉVELYNE LAPIERRE-ADAMCYK

YVES PÉRON

To conclude this socio-demographic analysis of the family, we present an overview of the highlights of the study and reflect briefly on the future of the family as revealed by the ample data and statistical analyses. This overview is particularly useful for those who are reading quickly, are less keen on tables and graphs, and are skimming only for the most unique and striking features to get a general idea of the new image of the Canadian family. Therefore, only the most significant elements are reviewed in order to link several socio-economic issues of the evolution of the family, identify new avenues of study and, finally, reflect on concepts needed to improve data collection.

The last 30 years attest to the emergence of new family models that are different from and continually changing in relation to the model of the stable family, which traditionally dissolved only upon the death of one of the spouses. While many modern-day families still follow a relatively predictable path, they are surrounded by an environment where the risk of dissolution is high and the likelihood of eventually having to rebuild one's family structure has increased substantially.

The socio-demographic analysis conducted in this monograph is based primarily on basic demographic trends: the doubling of the population in 40 years, the drop in fertility by more than half, the marked increase in union dissolutions and divorce, and the declining popularity of legal marriage. A careful study of the evolution of households and families from 1951 to 1991 reveals a profound transformation in how Canadian men and women live together. As the number of households is increasing far more rapidly than the population, the size of households is shrinking considerably: the average number of family members decreased from 4.0 to 2.7 in 40 years. Small households of one or two persons now predominate; however, they account for just one-third of the population. There has also been a notable reduction in the relative importance of family households as a proportion of all households: in 1951, they made up 89% of the total while in 1991 they represented just 72%. This decline is almost entirely attributable to the greater propensity of people to live alone: one-person households rose from 7.4% of the total in 1951 to 23% in 1991. The behaviour of families themselves is changing. Almost all family households are one-family households that consist only of the members of a given family unit. This is consistent with the marginalization of three-generation households and of families that share their housing with persons outside the family unit.

From these facts emerges a profile where uniformity predominates. In 1991, 9 in 10 households consisted of just one person or family unit; in 1956 this proportion was 8 in 10. Where does the perception of the diversification of lifestyles originate? The answer lies within the transformation of the family unit itself. Due to a re-evaluation of the importance of the institution of marriage, proven mainly by a substantial increase in separations and divorces, the relative importance of lone-parent families has grown from 12.7% to 20.0% in 20 years among families with children. Soon after, the popularity of marriage declined. In 1991, 11% of couples were living common law; this proportion rose to 23% among couples where the woman was under age 35. Therefore, the traditional family unit, consisting of a married couple and their children, no longer accounted for as large a part of the family landscape. Blended families are another aspect of this landscape related to the new complexity of the paths of each member of a couple and their ties with their children. A blended family is formed when a lone-parent family once again becomes a "two-parent" family and the non-custodial parent is replaced by a stepparent. Therefore, by definition, a blended family consists of at least one child who is not the natural or adopted child of the two members of the couple. These families are not easily observed and, even after extensive analyses of the available data, their number and characteristics remain uncertain. We identify blended families and establish estimates of these families through the observation of the paths of individuals. In 1991, these families represented slightly more than 10% of couples with children. Increasingly more common, blended families are also characterized by the fact that in one-third of cases children of the current union are added to the children of a previous union of one of the parents. A small minority include children born of previous unions of both spouses, and only 1% of blended families blend children of three different sibling relationships (that is, children of the wife, of the husband, and of both spouses).

One of the most important contributions to this study has been the use of a dual perspective in analysing family units at given points in time to yield the profile described above and to analyse individual paths marked by family events. This second perspective shows the extent of the increase in common-law unions as a prelude to marriage and remarriage. For example, nearly half of young Canadian men and women who were married for the first time had lived common law with their spouse before marrying them, and about two in three remarried women aged 25 to 54 in 1990 had lived common law before legalizing their union with their partner. Common-law unions are often unstable, even when they have produced children. Therefore, their dissolution is the cause of half of all lone-parent episodes among single mothers. In contrast, 65% of blended families are formed by this type of union; this formation of a new couple is often the choice that ends a period of lone parenthood (for 55% of women and only 40% of men).

Often a transitional state, common-law unions occur at various stages in the lives of men and women, and they occur far more often than suggested by the proportion of common-law families observed in 1991.

The same is true of lone parenthood. More and more men and women will experience at least one episode of lone parenthood, and these episodes will not last as long as those experienced by previous generations. We observe, moreover, that lone parenthood affects men and women in different ways. Twice as many lone mothers as lone fathers will remain in this status for at least 10 years. Conversely, brief episodes are proportionally twice as common among men as among women. These trends are largely explained by the fact that men enter new unions more quickly than women.

In contrast with the past, when blended families were formed following a period of lone parenthood resulting from widowhood, more than half of recent blended family episodes arose following a separation or divorce. In these cases, the non-custodial natural parent remained, to some extent, accessible to the children. We know that most children live with their mother following the breakdown of a union, and this may distance them from their father. Thus the blended family takes on special significance in the lives of men. When they form a blended family, men who do not live with their children risk growing even further apart from them as their new family becomes the centre of their attention and obligation, demanding an emotional and material commitment that likely makes them even less available to their children from previous unions.

In short, we found that the diversification of family behaviours multiplied family experiences in the lives of individuals. If the trends observed in 1990 continue, about four in five men and four in five women will form an "intact" two-parent family at least once in their lifetime, one in three women (and one in four men) will experience lone parenthood, and one in six women (and nearly one in five men) will live in a blended family. These trends could become much more prominent since the younger the generation, the more developed the paths-tree and the greater the number of paths taken, even though these generations are not as far along their marital and parental life courses.

The complex paths that now mark the lives of adults have inevitable repercussions on the lives of the children whose family environment has been transformed. First, because of the decline in fertility, most children now find themselves in small families and rarely have more than two siblings. Children also are more and more likely to have parents who live common law. However, the most significant change is most likely produced by the greater marital instability of the parents, meaning that children are more likely to experience periods in lone-parent families, and at an increasingly early age. Consequently, more and more children are experiencing the physical and often emotional remoteness of one of their parents, usually the father, as our analysis of male family paths shows (see Chapter 4). The blended family calls for further adjustments when a stepparent, sometimes accompanied by children, enter the child's family.

The expression "two-parent family" and the very large percentage of children who live in such a family therefore mask a far greater diversity. For example, in 1991, of 100 children about age seven, 86 were in a two-parent family: 72 of those were in an intact family, and 14 were in a blended family. The other 14 children were in a lone-parent family, some for the second time.

Therefore, the diversification of adult family paths is sure to cause profound changes in the life courses of children. This complexity is not reduced for either the adults or children by the evolution of more standard living conditions, namely the remarkable increase in the number of dual-income families. The increase in the economic activity of mothers seems to respond to two convergent trends: the desire of women to participate in the labour force and the need for a second income to maintain a desired standard of living. In general, we found that two-parent families where both spouses are working fall into the high-income categories. There is, however, a link between the type of family and income. For example, common-law couples have lower incomes than married couples. With regard to the tendency of mothers to work outside the home, a growing discrepancy is found between the income of two-parent families and that of lone-parent families. This new reality is of concern because it underscores the fact that so many lone-parent families fall into the low-income categories. Obviously, these families have only one income, and the problem is made worse by the fact that young mothers living on their own find it harder to reconcile economic activity with caring for their children.

Economic constraints are also evident in various housing conditions, such as home ownership; access to dwellings large enough for adults and children; the money required to obtain adequate housing; and the need to share one's housing with people outside the family unit. All these factors are linked to the various types of family: double-income, two-parent families enjoy more favourable housing conditions, regardless of the criteria applied, and young lone mothers face the greatest hardship. These variations in housing conditions affect children's quality of life according to the type of family to which they belong.

The analyses in this monograph show that family structures have changed. The number of families formed around common-law unions, young lone-parent families and blended families has increased, while two-parent families based on marriage have declined. They also show that these changes, measured across the range of families, do not reveal their full import until observed through individual paths. These paths have grown more diverse and consist of varied sequences that are virtually impossible to predict. The decline in the popularity of legal marriage as a necessary condition for living together as husband and wife, and the parallel increase in cohabitation, are undeniably decisive factors in the variety of family behaviour sequences. Moreover, the diversification of individual paths is expressed differently for men and women, and is rapidly altering the family environment of children.

EVOLUTION OF THE FAMILY: A REFLECTION ON THE SIGNIFICANCE OF THE PRINCIPAL CHANGES

In this study, we thoroughly observe, measure and illustrate contemporary family life in its various forms. Our primary goal is to shed light on new behaviours and clarify the relative magnitude of these behaviours. To this end we scrutinize the data; clarify the meanings of definitions; demonstrate the data's limitations, and sometimes their inability to express the new realities; and combine sources to extract the most significant information. We also effectively profile new types of families and the role they play today. The scope of the changes and their impact on the lives of men, women and children leave no doubt about the marked contrast between families of the 1950s and those of the 1990s. These changes affect basic aspects of the lives of individuals and of society. They invite further consideration to discover their meaning, which is slowly emerging in the context of the socio-demographic analysis that has guided us.

What, then, do these changes mean? First, the evolution of the composition of households confirms that the desire for autonomy is a very important value in Canadian society. The inclination of people who do not belong to a family unit to live alone has grown over decades marked by the greater wealth of society and individuals. Also, the family unit greatly values its privacy, rarely sharing its housing with relatives and almost never sharing it with strangers. People grow apart from their families, and families become estranged from their relatives. This desire for independence probably corresponds in part with the disappearance of the traditional sense of responsibility between parents and children and among relatives, which the community now assumes but does not fully replace. While the bonds between individuals and their relations are more tenuous, it is reasonable to assume that the bonds between parents and children remain strong, despite the living arrangements that protect the privacy of each.

A second aspect of change in the family, which is of considerable interest, is the transformation of male–female relationships. There is no denying that men and women today are seeking personal fulfillment and greater autonomy. Although one could argue that traditional life already allowed men considerable autonomy within the couple, family and society, it is equally true that women's status was one of more or less total dependence. Broader access to education and eventually to the labour market accompanied and produced changes in women's attitudes.

While the impact of these changes is only gradually affecting women's standard of living, they are profound and no doubt irreversible. Modern concepts of women's role in society, which they themselves are first to accept, are penetrating the lives of couples more and more deeply. As a result, relationships between men and women in the workplace and in conjugal life are becoming more equal. While the battle is far from over, some optimists maintain it has already been won! Women are attending university and having as much if not more success than men. They have already started establishing themselves in many occupations previously dominated by men, so that few male preserves remain. And the best-protected preserve is probably in a "couple" where the very definitions of virility and femininity are at stake. Here, however, women have made especially significant gains by controlling their fertility, due to the development of effective methods of birth control and access to abortion. In this new context of sexual freedom outside of marriage and the social acceptance of cohabitation, first as a prelude to marriage and now as a substitute, marriage is being challenged. Common-law union seems a more favourable state than marriage for more egalitarian couple relationships. Women are almost as economically active as their spouses, and housework tends to be more equitably shared, even though complete equity has not yet been achieved!

A third aspect of change, linked to the previous one, concerns the very nature of marital commitment. Even in societies where divorce is more common than in Canada, traditional marriage is based on a presumption of stability. For the past two decades, fragility—witness the high incidence of divorce and the precariousness of common-law relationships—seems to be the hallmark of unions. Of course, many marriages last and a number of couples living common-law will remain together for their entire lives. But the permanent nature of marriage is gone: society has accepted that union dissolution is part of the landscape, somewhat in the way it accepts death as a part of life. Of course, some couples evade voluntary dissolution, but the foundation on which the family was built has become fragile.

The fragility of marital unions is no doubt in response to the endless search for happiness and self-fulfillment, which drives modern people. Once love cools, passion wanes, and family life imposes perceived constraints such as intolerable limitations on achieving personal goals, men and women seek to rediscover their freedom, often by renewing their search for a partner who will help them blossom. And the birth of children no longer warrants continuing a relationship the couple deems unsatisfactory. This weakening of marital bonds therefore affects the bonds between parents and their children. First, the parents' separation leads to a readjustment of their responsibilities toward their children. This is of course unavoidable when all members of the family no longer live under the same roof. Secondly, this new sharing of responsibility does not usually go smoothly. Experience shows that most children live with their mother, and that all too often the fathers grow apart from their children, seldom see them and even fail to provide for their needs.

The breakdown of the family alone affects the relationships between parents and children and the splitting of responsibilities between the natural parents. The blending of families, resulting in a new type of family, further complicates matters. While blended families have always existed, they traditionally followed the death of a parent and his or her subsequent replacement by a stepparent who came into the family. Today's blended family comes about primarily following a separation or divorce. The non-custodial parent is still in the picture and continues, or should continue, to assume their emotional and material responsibilities vis-à-vis their children. The stepparent's role is still poorly defined; it doubtless varies according to the many situations these families face. There is no model. And the role becomes even more ambiguous when the non-custodial parent re-creates a new family to which other children are born. As discussed, it is primarily men who face these situations: the role of father is undergoing a profound crisis that we have scarcely begun to reflect upon.

It is children, however, who risk being the first casualties of the decisions of their parents—decisions over which they have very little control. In more fortunate cases, when the parents separate peacefully, the children still must give up having both parents present together and divide their time between two homes. In less fortunate cases, they are the victims of fierce negotiations between exasperated parents and are often neglected by the absent parent. The arrival of new partners in their parents' lives does not simplify their environment and requires adjustments, and the children risk being torn between divergent loyalties.

Finally, the instability of conjugal unions tends to lead to periods of economic uncertainty. Maintaining a comfortable standard of living clearly depends largely on two incomes in two-parent families. Union dissolution creates family units living on one income, and thus is associated with fairly long periods when families have access to fewer financial resources; all too often, poverty sets in. This is especially true of young mothers who have children and live on their own. Too often when they do work, they earn a low income and cannot afford child care. Often, they must leave the work force and begin the cycle of dependency on government assistance, which is difficult to break. Moreover, the state is questioning its role, and there are many indications that it is preparing to withdraw, at least in part, from the responsibilities it assumed before the financial crisis became intolerable. There is reason to be concerned that the most vulnerable families will suffer from this withdrawal of state assistance.

FAMILY CHANGES AND SOME OF THE SOCIAL ISSUES THAT HAVE ARISEN

New family realities are emerging, driven by the forces of contemporary society that encourage individuals to seek greater autonomy. This, in turn, is reducing the dominance of traditional institutions that once provided the framework for and sustained families. Families gave people the support they needed throughout the various stages of the life cycle. Families were always there, ready to protect, too often to overprotect, from the ups and downs of life. Also, institutions, such as family law, religion, community associations, and so on, supported families by imposing constraints on the behaviour of individuals: the well-being of society took precedence over personal fulfilment. Today's families have become autonomous in relation to their relatives, as have family members in relation to their family. They have also overcome institutional constraints and so have become more vulnerable to hardship.

The changes in the family therefore require major adjustments on the part of the society in which they occur. First, male–female relationships, which began their transformation some time ago, must continue to strive for the equality so greatly sought after—in social and economic life as well as in marital and family life. Some negative consequences of union dissolutions, including the impoverishment of lone-parent families, would be greatly mitigated if men and women had equal access to paid employment and if mothers and fathers equally shared responsibility for their children.

Secondly, the dissolution of the couple must not signify the breakdown of the family; the relationships between parents and children must survive. While formally acknowledging that irrevocable legal marriage is no longer the basis of the family, society must attempt to support and strengthen the filial bond to ensure the well-being of children and parents. In this regard, a more equal division of parental responsibilities between fathers and mothers, as already mentioned, is necessary, as is adequate support for the parent who must, when unavoidable, assume sole custody of the children. There is also a definite need to redefine the role of fathers in relation to their children, particularly when they do not live with them or when they take on new family responsibilities. The role and obligations of stepparents should also be considered at a time when families are forming, dissolving and reforming every day.

Thirdly, in order to enjoy a comfortable standard of living, most parents in today's families are active in the labour force. This means that the time spent on economic activity directly conflicts with family time, particularly time spent caring for the children. The presence of both parents in the labour force reflects not only the economic needs of families, but also the strong desire of women, expressed in a thousand ways, to participate fully in the labour force. This established trend will not change, particularly as the labour market can no longer operate without the presence and skills of women. Women's desire to participate in the labour force, along with a new concept of how we live our lives, is creating a child-care vacuum. To fill it, society has thus far relied on the initiative of parents, who usually have to manage without the support of their employer, community or government services. Parents, especially mothers, must ensure that their small children are cared for 24 hours a day and not let their jobs suffer for it. Society as a whole, the labour market, and the state in particular have not yet decided to tackle this issue head on. Given the necessary economic activity of parents, a social structure must be established to address, above all, the needs of young children, and target all families that have children with special needs who require care, in particular the children of low-income parents who are quite often lone-parents. Fourthly, this study shows that most Canadian families want housing with enough space, both inside and out, to allow for personal privacy and the leisure activities of children and adolescents. This is how we interpret the clear predominance of single-family dwellings. Clearly, this type of housing is available only to those who can afford to own their own home. This is a constraint that affects many families forced to live in less satisfactory conditions. When performing residential planning, the state and other relevant institutions must be aware that all families, regardless of their income, need adequate space in which to raise healthy children. Furthermore, special provisions are also needed for families in difficulty, taking into account specifically the needs of their children.

A fifth concern, although not specifically addressed in this monograph, is the effect of family changes on the living conditions of the elderly. The decline in fertility has considerably reduced the number of children who can help their elderly parents financially or when they can no longer take care of themselves. The dissolution of unions forces couples to prematurely divide up their accumulated wealth, thereby reducing the resources each will have on retirement, particularly if they, and especially the women, do not form a new couple. Pooling resources, often eagerly anticipated by young couples starting a family, can seem far less desirable to older men and women who are less confident of the stability of their new conjugal relationship and are often determined to pass their wealth on to their children rather than to their new spouse. The issue of the needs of elderly parents, whom families are called upon to provide for, also raises the problem of the increased responsibilities of older couples; families must simultaneously continue to support their children—often still economically dependent on them even when they no longer live at home—and at the same time support elderly parents whose physical or financial autonomy is waning. This problem appears to be especially prevalent among women, who we still depend upon to look after the children and the sick, even when they have job responsibilities. Obviously, not everyone faces these difficult situations, but they do exist and call for a reorganization of certain institutional structures and major changes in attitude.

Finally, we know that the state intervenes in many ways, assuming the responsibility for functions the traditional family once performed as a matter of course: children's education and health care for the sick and elderly. The state also intervenes to redistribute wealth among the various socio-economic groups, taking family obligations somewhat into account. But this form of intervention seems to be losing ground in favour of measures aimed at state support according to family income and the family's ability to provide for its basic needs. This is the subject of social debate between two philosophies—one justifying state intervention and the other opposed—and of two policies that are in theoretical conflict. According to the first, the desire to view family obligations as a criterion for the redistribution of wealth recognizes the social role of the family and its contribution to the maintenance and development of society. According to the second, family obligations are considered primarily a private matter in which the state should not interfere, family income being the criterion forming the basis for the distribution of wealth. There is, then, a conflict between those who support horizontal intervention, aimed at all families, and those who support vertical intervention, aimed at needy families.

The changes in the family argue for the development of policies that combine these two strategies. The state, to which today's citizens quickly turn in difficult times, must consider the ramifications of the redefinition of family ties in its reflection on program and policy development. The diversification of individual paths, the transitional periods marked by uncertainty, and the new family environment of children constitute the framework for government action to ensure the well-being of the greatest number of citizens.

SOME AVENUES OF STUDY

While past studies have shed light on the scope of the changes that have taken place, thus far they have not shown the impact of these changes on the nature of the bonds between spouses, between parents and children, and between siblings, particularly in blended families. One might well wonder how the trade-offs between traditionally married spouses compare with those of unmarried spouses, or even with those of the spouses in a blended family. Do these couples share their assets in the same way as married couples? Do they share similar attitudes and values about starting their family or having children? Do they share housework on the same basis? Do they do so more or less equitably?

Without doubt, the most important question concerns child care, that is, the means of providing the care necessary for children's well-being. Are there differences between the various types of family with respect to child care? While one can assume that this care depends on different conditions according to family type, one can also assume that it has been profoundly altered by the entry of mothers into the labour force. In the past, families were characterized by the sharing of tasks: the father worked outside the home to ensure the economic welfare of his family and the mother worked in the home to ensure the children's education and the comfort of the home. Over the decades observed, a major transformation has occurred. In most families both parents now work outside the home and the standard of living appears to be maintained by the economic contribution of both spouses. Single-income families appear to be somewhat disadvantaged. The 1995 General Social Survey on Family, cycle 10 and current longitudinal surveys (in particular, the National Longitudinal Survey of Children and Youth and the Survey of Labour Income Dynamics) should yield new data that will provide partial answers to the questions raised by the links between the evolution of individual families making the transition from one form to another, and the evolution of the resources available to them.

The diversification of individual family paths is not taking place in a vacuum; it joins other aspects of personal life that have their own dynamics. Consider, for example, the family paths of the husband and the children and, specifically, the stages of occupational life and their repercussions on residential history. This is another area that should be studied. The significance of our results showing the special nature of male life courses should be recalled; a closer study of these life courses raises the issue of the emotional bonds men have with their children and the financial, material and moral responsibilities they must assume for them, often when they no longer live with them. Conversely, the life courses of women, which remain closely entwined with those of their children—the vast majority of custodial parents being women—are doubtless deeply altered by their labour force activity. As yet, little is known about how these various aspects are interrelated. Under what circumstances and in which direction does the occupational path alter the family path? Conversely, does the family path reorient the occupational path?

Contemporary life is characterized by the independence of individuals and families. As we have noted, the propensity to share housing with persons who are not family members has decreased considerably; multiple- and one-family households that share their housing have become almost the exception, and are usually lone-parent family households. The search for independence seems to correspond with the deep desire of individuals to be in full control of their lives and seek the satisfaction of self-fulfilment. But there is another side to this situation. The independence sought can, in certain instances, turn to isolation that is difficult to bear and from which one cannot escape without major compromise, leading to precarious circumstances marked by poverty. Periods of transition, particularly lone parenthood, appear to be characterized by greater economic hardship. In these situations, incomes are lower, the quality of housing is often inferior and the dwelling is commonly shared with non-family persons. These periods are becoming shorter and shorter and necessarily fall between two episodes of increasing uncertainty: problems related to the dissolution of the previous family and apprehension about the possibility of forming a new family. While adults, who control the decisions that lead to transitions, are less affected by these changes, it is reasonable to think that children, who see their parents separate and form a new family with a new spouse, have to adjust emotionally to demanding, if not traumatic, situations. Are the networks surrounding individuals or families linked in a way that supports them effectively while respecting their decisions? What is their role, and how do they enable individuals and families to meet their basic needs? How do they intervene in the unfolding of family paths? Do they provide support during transitional periods when solidarity within the family must be rethought and rebuilt?

Finally, without having exhausted the avenues suggested by the results, we point out the need for an analysis that explores the variations in behaviour between social or cultural categories in order to gain a better understanding of the dynamics underlying personal choices. In this regard, qualitative study brings interesting hypotheses to the forefront, which nevertheless require verification using larger samples.

REPERCUSSIONS OF FAMILY CHANGES ON THE COLLECTION AND TREATMENT OF DATA

The changes in family reality challenge a number of concepts frequently used in data collection operations, whether they are censuses or surveys. Three points are particularly noteworthy: clarification of the bonds between family members at the time of observation; the marital and family histories of parents; and non-resident family members. Each is discussed in turn.

First, there is the problem of imprecision caused by the nature of the bonds between family members when they were observed. We must find out more about the nature of marital bonds. It must be possible to distinguish, first of all, common-law couples from married and remarried couples, and secondly, natural, step- and adopted children. The identification of blended families continues to pose problems in virtually all available sources.

To understand clearly the dynamics of families, particularly those of blended families, it is necessary to know the previous status of each spouse, that is, both their marital and reproductive histories. The dynamics of two single people with no children who are entering their first union differ from the dynamics of a blended family where the wife has already had two children, experienced a fairly lengthy period of lone-parenthood, and whose husband is also the father of a child who usually lives with the mother, but visits the father two weekends a month. Besides clarifying the family dynamics observed, this retrospective information will make it possible to measure the diversity of individual paths and analyse the mechanisms that underlie the transitions between various family types.

Another concept worthy of noting is the co-residence of the members of a family unit. Several data sources, including the census, limit membership in a family to just the family members who live in the same dwelling. Though this has caused few major problems in the past, new questions should be added to the census to take into account the specific situation of parents and children who no longer live together—an increasingly common scenario. This would reflect children of lone-parent families and some children living in a blended family, as well as non-custodial parents who care for their children at least part time and assume part of the financial responsibility for their needs. Current definitions completely overlook this information. The drawbacks of this limitation of family data are just as significant with respect to the family status of the elderly.

Finally, the improvement of the definitions used should not overshadow one last, very important, aspect of the collection of longitudinal data now underway. Such data make it possible to observe several facets of the lives of individuals and families simultaneously. This, together with the possibility of reconstructing the family and occupational paths of individuals, breathes new life into the study of the family by offering the benefits of the most advanced analytical methods.

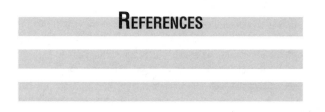

REFERENCES

Ambert, Ann-Marie. 1986. "Being a stepparent: Live-in and visiting stepchildren." *Journal of Marriage and the Family*. 48, 4: 795–804.

Balakrishnan, T.R., G. Edward Ebanks and Carl F. Grindstaff. 1979. *Patterns of Fertility in Canada, 1971*. Census Analytical Study series (Statistics Canada Catalogue no. 99-759E). Ottawa: Minister responsible for Statistics Canada.

Balakrishnan, T.R., Vaninadha K. Rao, Évelyne Lapierre-Adamcyk and Karol J. Krotki. 1987. "A hazard model analysis of the covariates of marriage dissolution in Canada." *Demography*. 24, 3(August): 395–406.

Balakrishnan, T.R., Évelyne Lapierre-Adamcyk and Karol J. Krotki. 1993. *Family and Childbearing in Canada: A Demographic Analysis*. Toronto: University of Toronto Press.

Beaujot, Roderic P., Ellen M. Gee, Fernando Rajulton and Zenaida R. Ravanera. 1995. *Family Over the Life Course*. Current Demographic Analysis series (Statistics Canada Catalogue no. 91-543E). Ottawa: Minister responsible for Statistics Canada.

Beaujot, Roderic P. and J.S. Bland. 1978. "Components of change analysis with applications to households in Canada." *Genus*. 34(1-2): 145-154.

Bergeron, Richard. 1994. *Formation et partage de la valeur en immobilier résidentiel: éléments d'une économie coopérative du logement*. Research paper made possible through a grant from the Conseil pour la recherche en sciences humaines. Montréal: Université de Montréal, Faculté de l'aménagement, Institut d'urbanisme.

Björnberg, Ulla. 1991. "Parenting in transition: an introduction and summary." In *European Parents in the 1990s: Contradictions and comparisons*. Edited by Ulla Bjornberg for the European Coordination Centre for Research and Documentation in Social Sciences. New Brunswick (U.S.A.) and London (U.K.): Transaction Publishers, 1–44.

Boulet, Jac-André and Laval Lavallée. 1984. *The Changing Economic Status of Women*. A study prepared for the Economic Council of Canada. Ottawa: Minister of Supply and Services Canada.

Bozett, Frederick W. and Shirley M. H. Hanson. 1991. *Fatherhood and Families in Cultural Context*. Focus on Men series, vol. 6. New York: Springer Publishing Company.

Bumpass, Larry L., T. Castro-Martin and J. A. Sweet. 1991. "The impact of family background and early marital factors on marital disruption." *Journal of Family Issues*.12, 1: 22–42.

Burch, Thomas K. 1990. *Families in Canada*. Focus on Canada series (Statistics Canada Catalogue no. 98-127). Ottawa: Minister responsible for Statistics Canada.

Burch, Thomas K. and Ashok K. Madan. 1986. *Union Formation and Dissolution: Results from the 1984 Family History Survey.* (Statistics Canada Catalogue no. 89-560-XPB). Ottawa: Minister responsible for Statistics Canada.

Che-Alford, Janet, Catherine Allan and George Butlin. 1994. *Families in Canada*. Focus on Canada series (Statistics Canada Catalogue no. 96-307E). Ottawa: Minister responsible for Statistics Canada.

Choko, Marc H. and Richard Harris. 1992. *La propriété résidentielle à Montréal et à Toronto de 1921 à 1951 : deux villes, deux mondes*. Études et documents series no. 65. Montreal: INRS-Urbanisation.

Cloutier, R. 1990. *La garde de l'enfant après la séparation des parents*. Report submitted to the Conseil québécois de recherche sociale. Québec: Le Conseil.

Crompton, Susan. 1994. "Left behind: Lone mothers in the labour market." *Perspectives on Labour and Income*. (Statistics Canada Catalogue no. 75-001E). 6, 2(Summer): 23–28.

Dandurand, Renée B. 1994. "Divorce et nouvelle monoparentalité." In *Traité des problèmes sociaux*. Edited by Fernand Dumont, Simon Langlois and Yves Martin. Québec: Institut québécois de recherche sur la culture, 519–544.

Dandurand, Renée B. and Lise Saint-Jean. 1988. *Des mères sans alliance: monoparentalité et désunions conjugales*. Québec: Institut québécois de recherche sur la culture.

Dandurand, Renée B., Roch Hurtubise and Céline Le Bourdais, eds. 1996. *Enfances. Perspectives sociales et pluriculturelles*. Proceedings of the International Colloquy, Montréal, August 1995. Sainte-Foy: Institut québécois de recherche sur la culture.

Demers, Marius. 1991. *La rentabilité du diplôme*. Québec: Government of Quebec, Ministry of Education, Research and Development division.

Desrosiers, Hélène and Céline Le Bourdais. 1992. "Les familles composées au féminin: évolution, ampleur, et caractéristiques du phénomène au Canada." In *Comprendre la famille*, Proceedings of the first Québec symposium on research on the family. Edited by G. Pronovost. Québec: Presses de l'Université du Québec, 71–95.

—. 1993. "Les unions libres chez les femmes canadiennes : étude des processus de formation et de dissolution." In *Population, reproduction, sociétés : perspectives et enjeux de démographie sociale : mélanges en l'honneur de Joel W. Gregory*. Edited by Dennis D. Cordell, Danielle Gauvreau, Raymond R. Gervais and Céline Le Bourdais. Montréal: Les Presses de l'Université de Montréal, 197–214.

—. 1995. "New forms of male family life in Canada." In *Changing Fatherhood: A Multidisciplinary Perspective*. Edited by Mirjam van Dongen, Gerard Frinking and Menno Jacobs. Amsterdam: Thesis Publishers, 29–59.

—. 1996. "Progression des unions libres et avenir des familles biparentales." *Recherches féministes*. 9, 2: 65–83.

Desrosiers, Hélène, Céline Le Bourdais and Benoît Laplante. 1995. "Les dissolutions d'union dans les familles recomposées: l'expérience des femmes canadiennes." *Recherches sociographiques*. 36, 1: 47–64.

Desrosiers, Hélène, Céline Le Bourdais and Karen Lehrhaupt. 1994. *Vivre en famille monoparentale et en famille recomposée: portrait des Canadiennes d'hier et d'aujourd'hui*. Études et documents series no. 67. Montreal: INRS-Urbanisation.

Desrosiers, Hélène, Céline Le Bourdais and Yves Péron. 1993. "Dynamic of Single Parent Status in Canada." *European Journal of Population / Revue européen de démographie*. 9, 2: 197–224. [Abstract in English.]

Dominion Bureau of Statistics. 1953a. *Housing and Families,* Vol. III. (Statistics Canada Catalogue no. 98-1951E). Ottawa: Minister of Trade and Commerce.

—. 1953b. *Population: General Characteristics*, Vol. I. (Statistics Canada Catalogue no. 98-1951E). Ottawa: Minister of Trade and Commerce.

—. 1956. *General Review and Summary Tables,* Vol. X. (Statistics Canada Catalogue no. 98-1951E). Ottawa: Minister of Trade and Commerce.

—. 1957. *Population: Households by Characteristics of Head*. (Statistics Canada Catalogue no. 93-503). Ottawa: Minister of Trade and Commerce.

—. 1962. *Households and Families: Families by Size,* Vol. II (Part 1). Bulletin 2.1–5 (Statistics Canada Catalogue no. 93-514). Ottawa: Minister of Trade and Commerce.

—. 1963a. *Households and Families: Families by Marital Status and Age of Head.* Vol. II (Part 1). Bulletin 2.1–7 (Statistics Canada Catalogue no. 93-516). Ottawa: Minister of Trade and Commerce.

—. 1963b. *Households and Families: Households by Type.* Vol. II (Part 1). Bulletin 2.1–2 (Statistics Canada Catalogue no. 93-511). Ottawa: Minister of Trade and Commerce.

—. 1964. *Housing: Dwelling Characteristics by Type of Household.* Vol. II (Part 2). Bulletin 2.2–9 (Statistics Canada Catalogue no. 93-531). Ottawa: Minister of Trade and Commerce.

—. 1965. *Population Sample: Incomes of Individuals (Classifications by Occupation, Class of Worker, etc.).* Vol. IV. Bulletin 4.1–2 (Statistics Canada Catalogue no. 98-502). Ottawa: Minister of Trade and Commerce.

—. 1966. *Population Sample: Family Incomes (by Family Size, Counties and Census Divisions).* Bulletin SX–7 (Statistics Canada Catalogue no. 98-521). Ottawa: Minister of Trade and Commerce.

—. 1967. *General Review: Household Size and Composition.* Vol. 7 (Part 1, 2). Bulletin 7.2–3 (Statistics Canada Catalogue no. 99-528). Ottawa: Minister of Trade and Commerce.

—. 1968. *Households and Families: Households by Type.* Vol. II. (Statistics Canada Catalogue no. 93-605). Ottawa: Minister of Trade and Commerce.

—. 1970. *Housing: Introductory Report to Volume II.* Part 2. Bulletin 2.2–13 (Statistics Canada Catalogue no. 93-535). Ottawa: Minister of Industry, Trade and Commerce.

—. 1971. *Households and Families: Introduction to Volume II.* Part 2-1. 1966 Census of Canada (Statistics Canada Catalogue no. 93-601). Ottawa: Minister of Industry, Trade and Commerce.

Dooley, Martin D. 1988. *An Analysis of Changes in Family Income and Family Structure in Canada Between 1973 and 1986 with an Emphasis on Poverty Among Children.* Research Paper No. 238. Hamilton: Program for Quantitative Studies in Economics and Population (QSEP), McMaster University.

Duchesne, Louis. 1993. *La situation démographique au Québec, édition 1993.* Québec: Bureau de la statistique du Québec, Government of Quebec.

Dulac, G. 1993. *La paternité: les transformations sociales récentes,* Québec: Conseil de la famille.

Dumas, Jean and Alain Bélanger. 1994. *Report on the Demographic Situation in Canada 1994: The Sandwich Generation: Myths and Realities.* Current Demographic Analysis series (Statistics Canada Catalogue no. 91-209E). Ottawa: Minister responsible for Statistics Canada.

—. 1996. *Report on the Demographic Situation in Canada 1995: Demographic Similarities and Differences between Ontario and Quebec.* Current Demographic Analysis series (Statistics Canada Catalogue no. 91-209E). Ottawa: Minister responsible for Statistics Canada.

Dumas, Jean and Yves Péron. 1992. *Marriage and Conjugal Life in Canada.* Current Demographic Analysis series (Statistics Canada Catalogue no 91-534E). Ottawa: Minister responsible for Statistics Canada.

Ermisch, J.F. and E. Overton. 1985. "Minimal household units: A new approach to the analysis of household formation." *Population Studies: A Journal of Demography.* 39, 1(March): 33–54.

Ferri, E. 1995. "La recherche sur les familles recomposées en Grande-Bretagne." In *Les recompositions familiales aujourd'hui.* Edited by M.-T. Meulders-Klein and I. Théry. Paris: Éditions Nathan, 77–85.

Festy, P. 1994. "L'enfant dans la famille, vingt ans de changements." Special issue of *Population.* Paris: Institut national d'études démographiques 49e année. 49, 6: 1245–1296.

Furstenberg, F.F. Jr. 1988. "Good Dads—Bad Dads: Two Faces of Fatherhood." In *The Changing American Family and Public Policy.* Edited by A. Cherlin. Washington: Urban Institute Press, 193–218.

—. 1994. "Reflections on the Sociology of Childhood." In *Childhood as a Social Phenomenon: Lessons from an International Project.* Edited by J. Qvortrup. Vienna: European Center, 29–43.

Gauthier, H. 1971. *The Census Definition of Family: 1871–1971.* Population and Housing Research Memorandum. Ottawa: Minister responsible for Statistics Canada.

Gauthier, Pierre. 1987. "Les "nouveaux pères." La paternité en émergence." In *Couples et parents des années quatre-vingt.* Edited by Renée B. Dandurand. Québec: Institut québécois de recherche sur la culture, 69–80.

Gee, Ellen Margaret Thomas. 1980. "Female marriage patterns in Canada: Changes and differentials." *Journal of Comparative Family Studies.* II, 4: 457–473.

Gera, Surenda and K. McMullen. 1991. "Unemployment in Canada: issues, findings, and implications." In *Canadian Employment: Lessons from the 80s and Challenges for the 90s.* Edited by Surendra Gera. Ottawa: Minister of Supply and Services, 1–19.

Hardey, Michael and Graham Crow, eds. 1991. *Lone Parenthood: Coping with Constraints and Making Opportunities in Single-Parent Families.* Toronto: University of Toronto Press.

Harrison, Brian R. 1979. *A User's Guide to 1976 Data on Households and Families.* Working Paper No. 1, Housing and Family series (Statistics Canada Catalogue no. STC3448). Ottawa: Minister responsible for Statistics Canada.

Henripin, Jacques. 1972. *Trends and Factors of Fertility in Canada.* One of a series of 1961 Census monographs prepared for the Census Division (Statistics Canada Catalogue no. 99-541E). Ottawa: Dominion Bureau of Statistics. [Originally published in French in 1968].

Hudson, Joe and Burt Galaway, eds. 1993. *Single Parent Families: Perspectives on Research and Policy.* Toronto: Thompson Educational Publishing Inc.

Jacobsen, Linda and Brad Edmondson. 1993. "Father figures." *American Demographics.* 15, 8: 22–62.

Juby, Heather. 1992. *De la reconstitution à la projection des ménages: une application au Canada.* Doctoral thesis. Université de Montréal: Département de démographie

Juby, Heather and Céline Le Bourdais. 1995. "Les parcours familiaux des Canadiennes." *Sociologie et Sociétés.* 7, 2: 143–161.

—. 1997. *The Growing Complexity of the Paternal Life Course.* Paper presented to the annual symposium of the Population Association of America, Washington D.C., March 1997.

Kuijsten, Anton. 1995. "Comment on Hélène Desrosiers & Céline Le Bourdais 'New Forms of Male Family Life in Canada'." In *Changing Fatherhood. A Multidisciplinary Perspective.* Edited by Mirjam van Dongen, Gerard Frinking and Menno Jacobs. Amsterdam: Thesis Publishers, 61–66.

La Novara, Pina. 1993. *A Portrait of Families in Canada.* Target Groups Project (Statistics Canada Catalogue no. 89-523E). Ottawa: Minister responsible for Statistics Canada.

Lapierre-Adamcyk, Évelyne and Nicole Marcil-Gratton. 1995. "Prise en charge des enfants: stratégies individuelles et organisation sociale." *Sociologie et Sociétés.* 27, 2: 121–142.

Lapierre-Adamcyk, Évelyne, Céline Le Bourdais and Karen Lehrhaupt. 1995. "Leaving home: Young Canadians born between 1921 and 1960." *Population.* 50, 4-5: 1111–1136. [Abstracts in English, French, Spanish.]

Le Bourdais, Céline and Hélène Desrosiers. 1988. *Trajectoires démographiques et professionnelles: une analyse longitudinale des processus et des déterminants.* Research paper submitted to the Minister of Health and Welfare within the scope of the study, "Étude sur l'évolution démographique et son incidence sur la politique économique et sociale." Montreal: INRS-Urbanisation.

Le Bourdais, Céline and Nicole Marcil-Gratton, eds. 1994. "L'enfance." Special two-volume issue of *Cahiers québécois de démographie.* 23, 1: 150 and 23, 2: 370.

—. 1996. "Family transformations across the Canadian/American border: when the laggard becomes the leader." *Journal of Comparative Family Studies.* 27, 3: 415–436.

Le Bourdais, Céline and D. Rose 1986. "Les familles monoparentales et la pauvreté." *International Review of Community Action.* 16, 56: 181–189.

Le Bourdais, Céline and A. Sauriol. 1995. "Transformations familiales et partage des tâches domestiques." In *Réconciliation travail-famille: les enjeux de la recherche*. Edited by F. Descaries and C. Corbeil. Montreal: Université du Québec. *Cahiers du réseau de recherches féministes*. 3: 143–162.

Le Bourdais, Céline, Hélène Desrosiers and Benoît Laplante. 1995. "Factors related to union formation among single mothers in Canada." *Journal of Marriage and the Family*. 57, 2: 410–420.

Le Gall, D. 1992. *Parâtres d'aujourd'hui: formes du rôle beau-parental dans les familles héritières d'une union antérieure avec enfants*. Paper presented to the symposium "La construction de la parenté." Université de Genève, 11–12 December.

Le Gall, D. and C. Martin. 1987. *Les familles monoparentales : évolution et traitement social*. Paris: Les Éditions ESF.

Léridon, Henri. 1993. "Recomposer les familles dans les sources statistiques." In *Les recompositions familiales aujourd'hui*. Edited by M.-T. Meulders-Klein and I. Théry. Paris: Éditions Nathan, 51–66.

Léridon, H. and C. Villeneuve-Gokalp, with Laurent Toulemon. 1994. *Constance et inconstances de la famille*: *biographies familiales des couples et des enfants*. Paper No. 134, Paris: Institut national d'études démographiques. Presses Universitaires de France.

Ley, David. 1985. *Gentrification in Canadian Inner Cities: Patterns, Analysis, Impacts and Policy*. Ottawa: Canada Mortgage and Housing Corporation.

Lindsay, Colin. 1992. *Lone-parent Families in Canada*. Target Group Project (Statistics Canada Catalogue no. 89-522E). Ottawa: Minister responsible for Statistics Canada.

Loken, D. R. 1973. *Household in the Canadian Census: Definitions and Data*. Working Paper No. 16. Demographic and Socio-economic series. Ottawa: Minister responsible for Statistics Canada.

Lund, Mary. 1987. "The non-custodial father: Common challenges in parenting after divorce." In *Reassessing Fatherhood: New Observations on Fathers and the Modern Family*. Edited by C. Lewis and M. O'Brien. Beverly Hills: Sage, 212–224.

Marcil-Gratton, Nicole. 1988. *Les modes de vie nouveaux des adultes et leur impact sur les enfants au Canada*. Research paper submitted to the Secrétariat de l'étude sur l'évolution démographique et de son incidence sur la politique économique et sociale. Montréal: Université de Montréal, Département de démographie, Groupe de recherche sur la démographie québécoise.

—. 1993. "Growing up with a single parent, a transitional experience?: Some demographic measurements." In *Single Parent Families: Perspectives on Research and Policy*. Edited by B. Galaway and J. Hudson. Toronto: Thompson Educational Publishing, 73–90.

Marcil-Gratton, Nicole and Évelyne Lapierre-Adamcyk. 1989. "North America and the third contraceptive revolution: the spectacular rise of sterilization as the most used method." *Espace, Populations, Sociétés*. 2: 239–248.

McDaniel, Susan A. and Carol Strike. 1994. *Family and Friends*. General Social Survey, Analysis series, Cycle 5 (Statistics Canada Catalogue no. 11-612E). Ottawa: Minister responsible for Statistics Canada.

McKie, Craig. 1994. "Temporary Residents of Canada." *Canadian Social Trends*. (Statistics Canada Catalogue no. 11-008E). 32(Spring): 12–15.

Miron, John R. 1993. "Demographic and economic factors in housing demand." In *House, Home and Community: Progress in housing Canadians, 1945 to 1986*. Edited by J. Miron. Montréal and Ottawa: McGill-Queen's University Press and Canada Mortgage and Housing Corporation, 22–40.

Moore, Maureen. 1988. "Female lone parenthood: the duration of episodes." *Canadian Social Trends*. (Statistics Canada Catalogue no. 11-008E). 10: 40–42.

—. 1989. "How long alone? The duration of female lone parenthood in Canada." *Transition*. 19, 1(March): 4–5.

Morissette, Denis and Yves Péron. 1992. "Les familles en difficulté de logement." In *Comprendre la famille*. Proceedings of the first Québec symposium on research on the family, 1991; paper presented at the Université du Québec à Trois-Rivières. Edited by G. Pronovost. Sillery: Presses de l'Université du Québec, 307–314.

Morris, Earl W. and Mary Winter. 1978. *Housing, Family, and Society*. New York: John Wiley & Sons.

Moxnes, K. 1991. "Changes in family patterns—Changes in parenting? A change toward a more or less equal sharing between parents." In *European Parents in the 1990s. Contradictions and Comparisons*. Edited by Ulla Björnberg. New Brunswick (U.S.A.) and London (U.K.): Transaction Publishers, 211–228.

Norris, D. A. and T. Knighton. 1995. *The Collection of Family Data: Limitations of Traditional Approaches and New Initiatives*. Paper presented to the annual symposium of the Population Association of America. San Francisco, April.

Oderkirk, Jillian and Clarence Lochhead. 1992. "Lone parenthood: Gender differences." *Canadian Social Trends*. (Statistics Canada Catalogue no. 11-008E). 27(Winter): 16–19.

Pool, Ian and Maureen Moore. 1986. *Lone Parenthood: Characteristics and Determinants—Results from the 1984 Family History Survey*. (Statistics Canada Catalogue no. 89-564-XPB). Ottawa: Minister responsible for Statistics Canada.

Priest, G.E. 1982. "Operationalizing the family life-cycle concept within the context of United Nations recommendations for the 1980 censuses." *Health and the Family Life Cycle*. Wiesbaden and Genève: Federal Institute for Population Research and World Health Organization, 65–88.

Rajulton, Fernando. 1992. *Life History Analysis: Guidelines for Using the Program LIFEHIST (PC version)*. Discussion paper no. 92-5. London, Ont.: The University of Western Ontario, Population Studies Centre.

Rajulton, Fernando and T.R. Balakrishnan. 1990. "Interdependence of transitions among marital and parity states in Canada." *Canadian Studies in Population*. 17, 1: 107–132.

Ram, Bali. 1990. *New Trends in the Family: Demographic facts and figures*. Current Demographic Analysis series (Statistics Canada Catalogue no. 91-535E). Ottawa: Minister responsible for Statistics Canada.

Rao, Vaninadha K. 1989a. "Analysis of first marriage patterns in Canada." In *The Family in Crisis: A Population Crisis?* Proceeding of a colloquium organized by the Federation of Canadian Demographers and sponsored by the Royal Society of Canada, University of Ottawa: 1986. Edited by J. Légaré, T.R. Balakrishnan and R.P. Beaujot. Ottawa: Royal Society of Canada, 287–302.

—. 1989b. "What is happening to cohabitation in Canada?" International Population Conference New Delhi 1989. New Delhi: B.R. Publishing Corp. 3: 269–286.

—. 1990. "Marriage risks, cohabitation and premarital births in Canada." *European Journal of Population/ Revue européenne de démographie*. 6, 1(May): 27–49.

Rashid, Abdul. 1991. "Women's earnings and family incomes." *Perspectives on Labour and Income* (Statistics Canada Catalogue no. 75-001E). 3, 2: 27–37.

Romaniuc, Anatole. 1984. *Fertility in Canada: From Baby-boom to Baby-bust*. Current Demographic Analysis series (Statistics Canada Catalogue no. 91-524E). Ottawa: Minister responsible for Statistics Canada.

Roussel, Louis. 1980. "Mariages et divorces. Contribution à une analyse systématique des modèles matrimoniaux." *Population*. 35, 6 (November/December): 1025–1040. [Abstract in English, 1040.]

Seltzer, Judith. A. 1991. "Relationships between fathers and children who live apart: The father's role after separation." *Journal of Marriage and the Family*. 53, 1:79–101.

Senécal, Paul, Carole Tremblay and Dominique Teufel. 1990. *Gentrification ou étalement urbain? Le cas du centre de Montréal et de sa périphérie*. Montreal: Société d'habitation du Québec, Direction génerale de la planification de la recherche, Direction de l'analyse et de la recherche.

Shelton, Beth. A. and Daphne John. 1993. "Does marital status make a difference? Housework among married and cohabiting men and women." *Journal of Family Issues.* 14, 3: 401–420.

Statistics Canada. 1973a. *Children in Families, Vol. II (Part 2).* Bulletin 2.2-3 (Statistics Canada Catalogue no. 93-715). Ottawa: Minister responsible for Statistics Canada.

—. 1973b. *Households by Type, Vol II (Part 1).* Bulletin 2.1-3 (Statistics Canada Catalogue no. 93-703). Ottawa: Minister responsible for Statistics Canada.

—. 1974. *Households by Type showing Selected Characteristics of Head, Vol. II (Part 1).* Bulletin 2.1-7. 1971 Census of Canada (Statistics Canada Catalogue no. 93-707). Ottawa: Minister responsible for Statistics Canada.

—. 1975a. *Family Characteristics by Marital Status, Age and Sex of Head, Vol. II (Part 2).* Bulletin 2.2-6. 1971 Census of Canada (Statistics Canada Catalogue no. 93-718). Ottawa: Minister responsible for Statistics Canada.

—. 1975b. *Families by Labour Force Activity of Family Members, Vol. II (Part 2).* Bulletin 2.2-11. 1971 Census of Canada (Statistics Canada Catalogue no. 93-723). Ottawa: Minister responsible for Statistics Canada.

—. 1975c. *Incomes of Families, Family Heads and Non-family Persons, Vol. II (Part 2).* Bulletin 2.2-12. 1971 Census of Canada (Statistics Canada Catalogue no. 93-724). Ottawa: Minister responsible for Statistics Canada.

—. 1975d. *Income of Individuals by Schooling, Age and Sex, for Canada and Provinces, Vol. III (Part 6).* Bulletin 3.6-5. 1971 Census of Canada (Statistics Canada Catalogue no. 94-763). Ottawa: Minister responsible for Statistics Canada.

—. 1977. *Housing: Introduction to Volume II (Part 3).* 1971 Census of Canada (Statistics Canada Catalogue no. 93-726). Ottawa: Minister responsible for Statistics Canada.

—. 1978a. *Dwellings and Households: Private households by type.* 1976 Census of Canada (Statistics Canada Catalogue no. 93-806). Ottawa: Minister responsible for Statistics Canada.

—. 1978b. *Dwellings, Private Households and Families.* 1976 Census of Canada (Statistics Canada Catalogue no. 93-801). Ottawa: Minister responsible for Statistics Canada.

—. 1982a. *Census Families in Private Households: Persons, children at home, structure and type, living arrangements.* 1981 Census of Canada, National series, Vol. 1 (Statistics Canada Catalogue, no. 92-905). Ottawa: Minister responsible for Statistics Canada.

—. 1982b. *Occupied Private Dwellings: Type and tenure (also showing collective dwellings).* 1981 Census of Canada, National series, Vol. 1 (Statistics Canada Catalogue no. 92-903). Ottawa: Minister responsible for Statistics Canada.

—. 1982c. *Private Households: Type, number of persons, composition.* 1981 Census of Canada, National series, Vol. 1 (Statistics Canada Catalogue no. 92-904). Ottawa: Minister responsible for Statistics Canada.

—. 1984a. *Census Families in Private Households, Income.* 1981 Census of Canada, National series, Vol. 1 (Statistics Canada Catalogue no. 92-936). Ottawa: Minister responsible for Statistics Canada.

—. 1984b. *Private Households, Income.* 1981 Census of Canada, National series, Vol. 1 (Statistics Canada Catalogue no. 92-934). Ottawa: Minister responsible for Statistics Canada.

—. 1984c. *Population, Total Income.* 1981 Census of Canada, National series (Statistics Canada Catalogue no. 92-928). Ottawa: Minister responsible for Statistics Canada.

—. 1987. *Dwellings and Households: Part I.* 1986 Census of Canada, The Nation series (Statistics Canada Catalogue no. 93-104). Ottawa: Minister responsible for Statistics Canada.

—. 1989a. *Family Income: Census families.* 1986 Census of Canada, The Nation series (Statistics Canada Catalogue no. 93-117). Ottawa: Minister responsible for Statistics Canada.

—. 1989b. *Household Income: Private households*. 1986 Census of Canada, The Nation series (Statistics Canada Catalogue no. 93-119). Ottawa: Minister responsible for Statistics Canada.

—. 1989c. *Total Income: Individuals*. 1986 Census of Canada, The Nation series (Statistics Canada Catalogue no. 93-114). Ottawa: Minister responsible for Statistics Canada.

—. 1991. *The 1990 General Social Survey—Cycle 5: Family and Friends. Public Use Microdata File and User's Guide*. (Statistics Canada Catalogue no. 12M0005GPE). Ottawa: Minister responsible for Statistics Canada.

—. 1992a. *Age, Sex and Marital Status*. 1991 Census of Canada, The Nation series (Statistics Canada Catalogue no. 93-310). Ottawa: Minister responsible for Statistics Canada.

—. 1992b. *1991 Census Dictionary*. (Statistics Canada Catalogue no. 92-301E). Ottawa: Minister responsible for Statistics Canada.

—. 1992c. *Families: Number, type and structure*. 1991 Census of Canada, The Nation series (Statistics Canada Catalogue no. 93-312). Ottawa: Minister responsible for Statistics Canada.

—. 1992d. *Dwellings and Households*. 1991 Census of Canada, The Nation series (Statistics Canada Catalogue no. 93-311). Ottawa: Minister responsible for Statistics Canada.

—. 1993a. *The Canada Year Book 1994*. (Statistics Canada Catalogue no. 11-402E). Ottawa: Minister responsible for Statistics Canada.

—. 1993b. *Selected Income Statistics*. 1991 Census of Canada, The Nation series (Statistics Canada Catalogue no. 93-331). Ottawa: Minister responsible for Statistics Canada.

—. 1993c. *Families: Social and Economic Characteristics*. 1991 Census of Canada, The Nation series (Statistics Canada Catalogue no. 93-320). Ottawa: Minister responsible for Statistics Canada.

—. 1993d. *Fertility*. 1991 Census of Canada, The Nation series (Statistics Canada Catalogue no. 93-321). Ottawa: Minister responsible for Statistics Canada.

—. 1994a. *Coverage, 1991 Census Technical Reports: Coverage*. Reference Products series (Statistics Canada Catalogue no. 92-341E). Ottawa: Minister responsible for Statistics Canada.

—. 1994b. *1991 Census Public Use Microdata File on Families: data documentation*. 1991 Census of Canada (Service no. 48-041E). Ottawa: Minister responsible for Statistics Canada.

—. 1994c. *1991 Census Public Use Microdata File Housing and Households: data documentation*. 1991 Census of Canada (Service no. 48-040E). Ottawa: Minister responsible for Statistics Canada.

—. 1994d. *1991 Census Public Use Microdata File on Individuals: data documentation*. 1991 Census of Canada (Service no. 48-039E). Ottawa: Minister responsible for Statistics Canada.

—. 1994e. *Revised Intercensal Population and Family Estimates, July 1, 1971–1991*. (Statistics Canada Catalogue no. 91-537). Ottawa: Minister responsible for Statistics Canada.

—. 1994f. *Women in the Labour Force, 1994 Edition. Target Groups Project*. (Statistics Canada Catalogue no. 75-507E). Ottawa: Minister responsible for Statistics Canada.

—. 1995. *Canadian Economic Observer: Historical Statistical Supplement 1994/95*. (Statistics Canada Catalogue no. 11-210). Ottawa: Minister responsible for Statistics Canada.

Steele, Marion. 1994. "Les revenus, les prix et le choix du mode d'occupation." In *House, Home and Community: Progress in housing Canadians, 1945 to 1986*. Edited by J. Miron. Montreal and Kingston: McGill–Queen's University Press and Canada Mortgage and Housing Corporation, 45–70.

Stone, Leroy O. and Andrew J. Siggner. 1974. *The Population of Canada: A Review of the Recent Patterns and Trends*. C.I.C.R.E.D. series. New York: United Nations Committee for International Coordination of National Research in Demography for World Population Year, 1974.

Théry, I. 1986. "Divorce, enfants, stabilité: 'le nouveau désordre familial'." *Actions et recherches sociales*. 22, 1: 53–60.

—. 1993. "Introduction générale: Le temps des recompositions familiales." *Les recompositions familiales aujourd'hui*. Edited by M.-T. Meulders-Klein and I. Théry. Paris: Éditions Nathan, 5–21.

Villeneuve-Gokalp, Catherine. 1991. "Du premier au deuxième couple: les différences de comportement conjugal entre hommes et femmes." *La nuptialité: Évolution récente en France et dans les pays développés*. Proceedings of the IXᵉ Colloque national de démographie. Edited by T. Hilbert and L. Roussel. Paris: Institut National d'Études Démographiques–PUF, 179–192.

Wargon, Sylvia T. 1979a. *Canadian Households and Families: Recent demographic trends*. (Statistics Canada Catalogue no. 99-753E). Ottawa: Minister responsible for Statistics Canada.

—. 1979b. *Children in Canadian Families*. (Statistics Canada Catalogue no. 98-810). Ottawa: Minister responsible for Statistics Canada.

Wu, Zheng. and Balakrishnan, T.R. 1994. *Dissolution of Premarital Cohabitation in Canada*. Discussion paper no. 94-5. London (Ont.): Population Studies Centre.

Zhao, John Z., Fernando Rajulton and Zenaida R. Ravanera. 1993. *Family Structure and Parental Characteristics: Analysis of Home-Leaving of Children as Reported by Parents—General Social Survey, Canada*. Discussion paper no. 93-2. London (Ont.): Population Studies Centre.

Page numbers in italic indicate a figure or table. Figures or tables on the same page as a textual discussion of the topic are not differentiated. The letter "n" following a page number indicates a note; for example, "11n.2" indicates note 2 on page 11.

See also Prairie provinces
Atlantic provinces
    children, by age and family environment,
        227, *228*
    children, by parents' marital status and
        region, *229*
    children in lone-parent families, 230, 232
    home ownership, 275
    housing types, 283, *284, 309*
    tenure, by type of household, *303*
    See also specific province
Autonomy, 320, 325

Baby boom (post-war), 5, 6, 37
Baby boomers
    aging, 5, 7–8, 37
    marriage market, 48
    number of households, 13
Birth control, 57, 59
Birth outside union
    increasing, 55, 226
    means of entry to lone fatherhood, 170–71,
        181, 199n.27
    means of entry to lone motherhood, 115,
        124–25, 142n.24
Birth rate *See* Fertility
British Columbia
    children, by age and family environment,
        227, *228*
    children, by parents' marital status and
        region, *229*
    children in lone-parent families, 230, 232
    home ownership, 275
    housing types, 283, *284, 309*
    population over time, *2, 3*
    tenure, by type of household, *303*

Canada Mortgage and Housing Corporation,
    296
Census
    and General Social Survey, cycle 5: Family
        and Friends, 103, 141n.3
    data drawbacks, 101
    effects of family changes, 326
    enumeration method, 10–11
    reporting of family relationships, 22–23, 37
Census families *See* Families, census
Children
    adult men as, 158–60, 196, 200
    adult women as, 104, 105–7, 139, 141nn.8,
        14, 143, *144*
    by age and family environment, 212, *213*
    by age, family environment and region, *228*
    by age and family income, 246, *247*
    by age and number of siblings and family
        environment, 219, *220*
    by age and parents' marital status, 213
    by age and parent's sex and marital status, 214
    by age and sibling relationship, 216, *217*
    by family environment, 221
    by family environment in blended family,
        222–23
    by family environment and income, 247, *248*
    by family type and father's age, 164–65,
        167, 168
    by family type and woman's age, 110–11
    by marital status of parent or parents, 211–12
    by number of siblings and family
        environment, 217–19
    by parents' marital status, region and family
        type, 229–30
    Canadian diversity, 226–27, *228*
    crowding, by family type, number of children
        and living arrangements, 291–92
    crowding, by family type, tenure and type
        of housing, 294–95, *312*
    custody, 67, 69, 155, 157, 241, 318–19
    defined, 103, 210
    effect of family trends, 321–22, 323, 324–25
    effect on family income, 239–41, *264–66,*
        267–69, 270–71
    effect on home ownership of husband–wife
        families, 281
    effect on women's employment, 250–55
    family paths, 224–26
    historical evolution of family environment,
        211–12
    in lone-parent family, 212, 214–16, 230,
        231, 232
    in lone-parent family, by region, 227, *228*,
        230, *231*, 232
    in two-parent family, *211*, 212, *213*
    in two-parent family, by number, 78, *79*,
        80–81, *82*
    in two-parent family, by region, 227, *228*
    non-family persons as, 25
    proportion in population, 6–7, 210
    relevance as basis of measurement, 208,
        232–33
    siblings in blended family, 224
    See also Siblings
Children's departure, by means of exit
    for men in blended family, 189, 198n.17, *206*
    for men in two-parent family, 177–78,
        199n.23, *203–4*
    for women in blended family, 132, *152*
    for women in two-parent family, 121, *122*,
        142nn.20,30, *149–50*

Crowding
  by tenure and family type, 291
  by tenure, family type and living
    arrangements, *311–12*
  by tenure, family type and type of housing,
    293–94
  method of measurement, 290–91
  of children, by family type, number of
    children and living arrangements, 291–92

Deaths, 1951 to 1991, *4, 5*
See also Widowhood
Divorce
  effect on number of children, 219
  increasing rate, 51–53, 98
  legislation, 51–52
  length of marriage, 53
  lone parents, 74
  means of entry to blended family, 318–19
  means of entry to lone-father status, 170–71,
    181
  means of entry to lone-mother status, 115,
    124–26
  means of exit for men in blended family,
    189, *206*
  means of exit for men in two-parent family,
    178, 199n.23, *203–4*
  means of exit for women in blended family,
    132, *152*
  means of exit for women in two-parent family,
    121, *122*, 142nn.20,30, *149–50*
  remarriage, 53–54
  societal attitude toward, 48
Dwelling
  collective, 10–11
  private, 10–11
  rural, 50, 274
  urban, 50, 274

Economic families *See* Families, economic
Education
  and age at marriage, 50
  democratization of, 235
  and fertility, 60
  and income, 240
  of women, 235
Elderly persons
  effect of family trends, 323–24
  home ownership, 276–77
  in private households, 14
  non-family, 25, 37
  proportion in population, 9, 37
Emigration, 1986, 6

Employment, conflict with family time, 323
Ethnicity and fertility, 60

Families
  analysis methods of formation and
    dissolution, 118, 174–75
  average income compared to household
    income, 236–37
  changing trends of state support, 324
  defined, 1
  diversification of lifestyles, 317–20
  effect of marital dissolution, 321
  increasingly seek autonomy, 320, 325
  relationships and census methods, 22–23
  transformation of male–female relationships,
    320–21
  trends and effect on children, 321, 322, 324
  trends and effect on data collection, 326
  trends and effect on economy, 321
Families, blended
  children by region, 229–30
  defined, 128, 141n.12, 185
  dissolution of, 131–32, 189–90
  formation of, 128–30, 185–88
  identifying, 144–45, 153nn.4,5
  increasing in number, 210, 318
  men in, 164–66, *167*
  men's probability of entering, 185–88
  men's probability of exiting, 189–90, *206*
  not identified in census data, 101
  number of children, *218*, 219, 221–23
  sibling relationships, 224
  types, 222
  women in, 109–13
  women's probability of entering, 128, *129*,
    130, *131*
  women's probability of exiting, by age,
    131, *132, 133*, 142n.27, *152*
Families, census
  declining in size, 61, 78–83, 99, 208, *209*
  defined, 1, 24–25, 47, 72
  distribution, by type, 72–76, 99
  diverse, 99
  households, 26, *27*, 37
  identification of living arrangements, 143,
    153nn.1–3
Families, common-law *See* Families,
    husband–wife
  Families, economic
  defined, 1, 23
  households, 23–24
Families, husband–wife
  by age, 64, *65, 66*

common-law, 23, 48, 73, 84–86, 99
crowding, by living arrangements and
    presence of children, 292, *293*
crowding, by tenure, 291
crowding, by tenure and living arrangements,
    311–12
crowding, by tenure and type of housing,
    293–95
defined, 47
financial outlay for housing, by living
    arrangements, 299, *300, 315*
financial outlay for housing, by number and
    age of children, 298–99, *314*
financial outlay for housing, by tenure and
    life cycle, 297
home ownership, 277
home ownership, by various factors, 277–83
housing, by life cycle, 285
housing, by tenure and income, *289*
housing, by tenure and life cycle, 285–87
income, 237–39
income, by age, 239, *240*
income, by employment of spouse, life cycle
    and wife's age, *262–63*
income, by husband's age and type of
    employment and by presence of children
    under 6, *270–71*
income, by life cycle and employment, 245–49,
    250
income, by marital status and wife's age, *260*
income, by wife's age, family type and
    presence of children, 240–41
income over time, *259*
income quintiles where both are employed,
    263
irregular growth, 76–78
number of children, *218*, 219, *220*
percentage of children, *211, 213*
presence or absence of children, 83–86, *87*
proportion in population, 73–74
siblings relationships, *220*, 224
size (number of children in home), 78, *79*,
    80–81, *82*
tenure, by housing, life cycle and family
    income, *309–10*
tenure, by life cycle and family income, *306–7*
wife's age, by various factors, 76, *77*
women's life-cycle stage, 78, *79*, 80–81,
    82, 84
    See also Families, blended
Families, lone-parent
    age, 35, *36*
    causes, 67, 74
    defined, 47

dissolution of, 126–28, 182–85
diverse, 93–97
effect of various factors, 88
formation of, 124–26, 180–82
income, 237–39
income, by marital status and age, *260*
income, by parent's age and marital status,
    242–43
income, by parent's age and type of
    employment and by presence of children
    under 6, *270–71*
income, by parent's sex and children's
    number and age, *267–69*
income over time, *259*
increasing numbers, 87–89, 318
longitudinal studies, 123–24, 141n.17
marital status, 74
number of children, *218*, 219, *220*
percentage of children in, *211*, 212, 214–16
proportion in population, 73
size (number of children), 89–93
source of income, by father's age or by
    mother's age and marital status, 243,
    244, 261
tenure, by age of parent, *304*
tenure, by housing, life cycle and family
    income, *310–11*
Families, re-created
    defined, 109
    men in, 164, *167*, 199n.21
    women in, 109–11, 142nn.18,29
Family environment
    conclusions, 232
    defined, 209
    effect on income, 247, *248*
    historical evolution, 211–12
Family path trees
    children, 224–26
    men, 193–95, 197, 198n.18,34–36
    women, 134–39, *140*, 142nn.30–35
Fertility
    decline affects sibling relationships, 216
    declining rate, 16, 57, *58, 59, 60*
    defined, 100n.3
    and education, 60
    and ethnicity, 60
    and family dissolution, 224
    historical trends, *4, 5*
    and language, 60
    male reporting, 199n.26
    narrowing sociocultural differences, 60
    and religion, 60
    and women in labour market, 236
    See also Births

Financial outlay for housing
   by family type and living arrangements,
      299, *300, 315–16*
   by family type and number and age of
      children, 297–99, *314*
   by family type, tenure, life cycle and presence
      or absence of mortgage, 296–97
   by tenure and life cycle, *313*
   what it comprises, 296
Foreign residents, defined, 11

Gender *See* Sex
General Social Survey, cycle 5: Family and
   Friends, 103, 141n.3, 156–57
Gentrification
   defined, 301n.3
   effect on home ownership, 276
Government transfers
   increase, 238
   theoretical conflicts, 324

Head of household *See* Household maintainers
High-rise multiple-family dwellings
   by family income, 287, *288*
   by family type, 285
   by region, 283, *284, 309*
   crowding, by tenure and family type, 293–94
   crowding of children, by tenure and family
      type, 294–95
   tenure, by family type, 285–86
   tenure, by family type and family income,
      288, *289*, 290
   tenure, by family type, life cycle and family
      income, *309–11*
Home ownership
   advantages and disadvantages, 274
   by family type, 277–80, 300
   by household maintainer, family type and
      living arrangements, *305*
   by life-cycle stages, 280–83
   choice of housing, 283–90, 300
   crowding, 290–95
   financial outlay, 296–300
   historical evolution, 274–77
Household maintainers
   home ownership, by family type and living
      arrangements, *305*
   nearly always a family member, 274
   non-family persons, *32*
Household maintainers, female
   number and sex of persons in household,
      by maintainer's age, *41*

size of household, by maintainer's age, *21*
Household maintainers, male
   number and sex of persons in household,
      by maintainer's age, *24, 41*
   size of household, by maintainer's age, *22*
Households
   average income compared to family income,
      236–37
   and census families, 24–26, *27–29*, 30
   defined, 1, 11–12
   and economic families, 23–24
   enumeration method, 10–11
   family relationships, 22–23
   income over time, *259*
   minimal units, 31–32, *33–34*, 35, *36*, 37
   multiple-family, 26, 30, 37, 278–79
   non-family persons, 26, *27*
   one-family, 26, 30, 37, 317
   and population count, 12–15
   size, 16, *17*, 18–19, *20*, 21, 317
Households, collective
   defined, 11
   enumeration problems, 13
   number of persons, 12–13
   quantity, 12
Households, private
   by age of maintainer, 21, *22*, 24
   by family type, 26, *27*
   by size, 16, *17*, 18–19, *20*
   defined, 11
   enumeration problems, 15
   number of persons, *12*, 13–14
   quantity, *12*, 13, 37
Housing
   by family type and income, 288, *289*, 290
   by family type and life cycle, 284–85
   by family type and tenure, 285–86
   by region, 283, *284, 309*
   effect of consumer preferences, 284
   of husband–wife families, by tenure, income
      and presence of children under 16, 287, *288*
Husband–wife families *See* Families,
   husband–wife
Husbands
   by age, 64, *65, 66*
   by age and family type, *34*
   common-law, *75*
   defined, 63
   family income, by age, type of employment
      and presence of children under 6, *270–71*
   labour market participation, by age, *255, 256*
   See also Men

predominantly female, 89
Lone-parent families *See* Families, lone-parent
Low-rise multiple-family dwellings
    by family income, 287, *288*
    by family type, 285
    by region, 283, *284, 309*
    crowding, by tenure and family type, 293–95
    tenure, by family type, 285–86
    tenure, by family type and family income,
        288, *289*
    tenure, by family type, life cycle and family
        income, *309–11*

Manitoba
    population over time, *2*
    See also Prairie provinces
Marriage
    age at, 50–51
    as means of exiting lone fatherhood, *205*
    children, by region and age, 226–27, *228*
    decline in popularity, 63, 64, 98, 100n.1
    family income, by wife's age and presence of
        children, 241–42
    financial outlay for housing, by living
        arrangements, 299, *300, 315*
    home ownership, 277
    home ownership, by household maintainer,
        family type and living arrangements, *305*
    home ownership, by household maintainer
        and living arrangements, 278–79
    income, by wife's age, *260*
    increasing dissolution, 321
    interval to first birth, 57
    marital history of men in, 161–62, 170–72
    marital history of women in, *107*, 108, 114–17
    means of exiting lone fatherhood, 183–84
    means of exiting lone motherhood, 127–28,
        151
    means of forming blended family, 128, *129*,
        130, 185–86
    men in two-parent families, *201–2*
    men who have returned home to parents,
        159, 160
    number of children, *218*, 219, *220*
    number of children in blended family, 222–23
    parental history of men in, 162–63, 166–68,
        170–71
    parental history of women in, 110–11
    percentage of children in, *211, 213*
    percentage of crowded children, by family
        type, number of children and living
        arrangements, 291–92

tenure, by age of wife, *304*
total rates for divorced persons, 53–55
total rates for singles, 48, *49, 50*
women exiting two-parent families, 119–20,
    121, 142n.20, *149–50*
women in two-parent families, 119–20, *121*,
    142n.19, *147–48*
See also Common-law union
Men
    age at marriage, 50–51
    age, by family status, 158
    comparison of survey and census data, by
        family status and age, 200
    decreasing labour market participation, 235
    family path trees, 193–95, 197, 198nn.18,
        34–36
    having "child" status, 196, 200
    income, *237*
    income, by marital status and age, *260*
    income of non-family men, *238, 239*
    income over time, 235, *237, 259*
    living with parents, 67
    marital history, by age, 161–62
    marital and parental history of lone fathers,
        170–71
    marital and parental history of non-family
        persons, 171–72
    non-family, *45*, 69–70, *71, 72*
    parental history, by age, 162–63
    parental history of those in couple with
        children, 164–68
    parental history of those in couple without
        children, 168–69
    probability and method of exiting two-parent
        family, 177–80, *203–4*
    probability of exiting blended family, 189–90,
        206
    probability of forming blended family,
        185–88
    probability of living in two-parent family,
        175–77, *201–2*
    probability of lone-parent episode, by age
        and reason for entry, 180–82
    reliability of fertility data, 156
    remarriage rates, 54
    total marriage rates of singles, 48, *49*
    See also Husbands; Lone fathers; Sex
Migration, historical trends, 3, *4*, 5–6
Mortgages
    appropriate percentage of income, 296
    home ownership, by life cycle, 281–82
Multiple-family households, 26, 30, 37

Data in many forms

Statistics Canada disseminates data in a variety of forms. In addition to publications, both standard and special tabulations are offered. Data are available on the Internet, compact disc, diskette, computer printouts, microfiche and microfilm, and magnetic tape. Maps and other geographic reference materials are available for some types of data. Direct online access to aggregated information is possible through CANSIM, Statistics Canada's machine-readable database and retrieval system.

How to obtain more information

Inquiries about this publication and related statistics or services should be directed to the Office of the Director General, Census and Demographic Statistics Branch, Statistics Canada, Ottawa, Ontario, K1A 0T6 (telephone: 613 951-9589) or to the Statistics Canada Regional Reference Centre in:

Halifax	(902) 426-5331	Regina	(306) 780-5405
Montréal	(514) 283-5725	Edmonton	(403) 495-3027
Ottawa	(613) 951-8116	Calgary	(403) 292-6717
Toronto	(416) 973-6586	Vancouver	(604) 666-3691
Winnipeg	(204) 983-4020		

You can also visit our World Wide Web site: http://www.statcan.ca

Toll-free access is provided **for all users who reside outside the local dialling area** of any of the Regional Reference Centres.

National enquiries line	**1 800 263-1136**
National telecommunications device for the hearing impaired	1 800 363-7629
Order-only line (Canada and United States)	**1 800 267-6677**

How to order publications

Statistics Canada publications may be purchased from local authorized agents and other community bookstores, the Statistics Canada Regional Reference Centres, or from:

Statistics Canada,
Operations and Integration Division
Circulation Management
120 Parkdale Avenue
Ottawa, Ontario
K1A 0T6

Telephone: (613) 951-7277 or 1 800 700-1033
Fax: (613) 951-1584
Toronto (credit card only): (416) 973-8018
Internet: order@statcan.ca.

Standards of service to the public

Statistics Canada is committed to serving its clients in a prompt, reliable and courteous manner and in the official language of their choice. To this end, the agency has developed standards of service which its employees observe in serving its clients. To obtain a copy of these service standards, please contact your nearest Statistics Canada Regional Reference Centre.